French Intellectuals Against the Left

BERGHAHN MONOGRAPHS IN FRENCH STUDIES

The Populist Challenge: Political Protest and Ethno-nationalist
Mobilization in France
Jens Rydgren

French Intellectuals against the Left: The Antitotalitarian Moment
of the 1970s
Michael Scott Christofferson

Sartre against Stalinism
Ian H. Birchall

FRENCH INTELLECTUALS AGAINST THE LEFT

The Antitotalitarian Moment of the 1970s

Michael Scott Christofferson

Berghahn Books
New York • Oxford

First published in hardback in 2004 by

Berghahn Books

www.berghahnbooks.com

First paperback edition published in 2004

Library of Congress Cataloging-in-Publication Data

Christofferson, Michael Scott.
French intellectuals against the left : the antitotalitarian moment of the 1970's / Michael
Scott Christofferson..
p. cm. (Berghahn monographs in French studies)
Includes bibliographical references and index.
ISBN 1-57181-428-0 (cl : alk. paper) -- ISBN 1-57181-427-2 (pbk : alk. paper)
1. Liberalism--France--History--20th century. 2. Intellectuals--France--Political
activity--History--20th century. I. Title II. Series.

JC574.2.F8C47 2004
320.53'0944'09047—dc21

2003043795

British Library Cataloguing in Publication Data

A catalogue record for this book is available from
the British Library.

Printed in the United States on acid-free paper

CONTENTS

To My Parents

ACKNOWLEDGEMENTS

Like many scholarly monographs, this book has been a project long in the making that has benefited from assistance from many different individuals and institutions. I am grateful to be able to thank at least some of them here.

French Intellectuals Against the Left began as a Columbia University Ph.D. dissertation. At Columbia I enjoyed close, critical readings of my work by dissertation committee members Victoria De Grazia, Mark Kesselman, Robert Paxton, and Anders Stephanson. Chapter 6, a previous version of which was published in *French Historical Studies* 22, 4 (fall 1999), was also improved by the criticism of Isser Woloch at Columbia, New School Professors James Miller and Margaret Jacob, and the anonymous readers of *French Historical Studies*. My fellow graduate students, notably Greg Brown, Nira Kaplan, and Paul Edison, gave me crucial intellectual and moral support. Most of all, I would like to thank my dissertation advisor Robert Paxton for his continuing guidance and support. Without his willingness to direct a thesis by an unremarkable graduate student on a controversial topic of all-too-recent history, this book would have never been written. His advice steered me away from many pitfalls and has made this book much better than it otherwise would have been.

Outside of Columbia University, I benefited greatly from comments on papers given at conferences including the Interdisciplinary Conference on Cold War Culture: Film, Fact, and Fiction, the Eleventh International Conference of Europeanists, and the annual meetings of Western Society for French History, the American Historical Association, and the Society for French Historical Studies. Finally, I owe a great debt to my father and fellow historian Tom Christofferson, with whom I have discussed this project at length over the years.

In France, I enjoyed gratuitous assistance from many different individuals. I am most grateful to Benoit Falaize and Professor Jean-François Sirinelli for discussions of my research with them. Professor Sirinelli and Professor Emmanuel Le Roy Ladurie were kind enough to introduce me to people whom I interviewed. Cornelius Castoriadis and Jean-Marie Domenach granted me access to sources at their disposal. The staff at Reid Hall, the Bibliothèque nationale, the Institut mémoires de l'édition contemporaine, the Bibliothèque de documentation internationale contemporaine, the library of the Fondation nationale des sciences politiques, and the Institut national de l'audiovisuel were all especially helpful. Finally, I would like to thank Eric Berthon for both putting me up during various trips Paris and making my stays in Paris a joy.

Although the research and writing of this book was not funded by big research grants, I received substantial financial assistance from diverse sources for which I am extremely grateful. The initial research in Paris was made possible by federal government student loans and a grant from my parents, Tom and Ramona Christofferson. Further research and writing after my return to New York City was financed by money saved while I worked in generously compensated jobs at Chase Manhattan Bank and Trinity College. Unemployment benefits from the state of Connecticut, following my one-year position at Trinity College, were also helpful. After the dissertation was completed, I received support for further research in Paris from a Penn State Institute for the Arts and Humanistic Studies Faculty Research Grant.

The most important acknowledgements are the least specific. I would like to thank my wife, Claudia Sabino, for both enduring this project in good humor and giving me her support when I needed it most. Lastly, I would like to thank my parents for all that they have done to make this book and many other wonderful things in my life possible. I dedicate *French Intellectuals Against the Left* to them.

ABBREVIATIONS

APL	Agence de presse Libération
BRD	German Federal Republic
CAP	Comité d'action des prisonniers
CDU	German Christian Democratic Party
CERES	Centre d'études, de recherches et d'éducation socialiste
CFDT	Confédération française démocratique du travail
CGT	Confédération générale du travail
CIEL	Comité des intellectuels pour l'Europe des libertés
CNE	Comité national des écrivains
CVB	Comités Vietnam de base
EHESS	École des hautes études en sciences sociales
ENS	École normale supérieure
FLN	Front de libération nationale
GIP	Groupe d'information sur les prisons
GP	Gauche prolétarienne
IMEC	Institut mémoires de l'édition contemporaine
INA	Institut national de l'audiovisuel
JCR	Jeunesse communiste révolutionnaire
MFA	Portuguese Armed Forces Movement
NRP	Nouvelle résistance populaire
OAS	Organisation de l'armée secrète
OPS	Organisation partisane secrète
PCF	Parti communiste français
PCI	Italian Communist Party
PCMLF	Parti communiste marxiste-léniniste de France
PCP	Portuguese Communist Party

PS	Parti socialiste
PSI	Italian Socialist Party
PSP	Portuguese Socialist Party
PSU	Parti socialiste unifié
RDR	Rassemblement démocratique révolutionnaire
RPF	Rassemblement du peuple français
SFIO	Section française de l'Internationale ouvrière
SNESup	Syndicat national de l'enseignement supérieur
SPD	German Social Democratic Party
UEC	Union des étudiants communistes
UJCML	Union des jeunesses communistes marxistes-léninistes
UNEF	Union nationale des étudiants de France

INTRODUCTION

French Antitotalitarianism in Comparative Perspective

In the latter half of the 1970s a critique of left-wing totalitarianism took French intellectual life by storm. In books and pamphlets, in the press and on television, antitotalitarian intellectuals loudly and dramatically denounced Marxist and revolutionary politics as fatally affiliated with totalitarianism. Originating within the intellectual Left and facing minimal opposition from it, antitotalitarianism rapidly marginalized Marxist thought and undermined the legitimacy of the French revolutionary tradition, paving the way for the postmodern, liberal, and moderate republican political alternatives of the 1980s and 1990s. Antitotalitarianism also radically altered the political judgments and *engagements* of intellectuals of the noncommunist Left, inaugurating a crusade against communism abroad and worsening the already difficult relations at home between them and the parties of the French Left. In the eyes of the British Marxist Perry Anderson, Paris, the capital of the European (and, in many regards, the world) Left after World War II, had become "the capital of European reaction."[1]

Antitotalitarian intellectuals have represented their own critique of totalitarianism as an abrupt rupture in French intellectual politics induced by revelations about the nature of communism. Intellectuals, the antitotalitarians argue, had moved uncritically from one revolutionary enthusiasm to another during the thirty years preceding the critique of totalitarianism. According to antitotalitarian historians such as François Furet, Pierre Rosanvallon, and Jacques Julliard, the remarkably long-lasting blindness of French intellectuals to the repressiveness of communist régimes and the shortcomings of revolutionary politics was due to the longstanding hegemony of the Jacobin revolutionary tradition within French political culture.[2] Intellectuals would only be awakened from the long slumber of their critical faculties by the publication of Aleksandr Solzhenitsyn's *Gulag Archipelago* in 1974. *The Gulag Archipelago*'s revelations regarding commu-

---

nism, combined with the failure of post-1968 revolutionary politics and the collapse of third-world revolutionary utopias, led French intellectuals to critique communism and revolutionary politics as totalitarian, according to this interpretation.

Rather than test this thesis and explore alternatives to it, historians and other commentators on French intellectual politics have generally accepted it at face value, using it to structure narratives of blindness and awakening that find expression in titles of French works on intellectual politics such as Pierre Rigoulot's *Les Paupières lourdes* (heavy eyelids) and Jeannine Verdès-Leroux's *Le Réveil des somnambules* (the awakening of the sleepwalkers).[3] Scholarly works on the critique of totalitarianism have done little more than recast into academic prose the consciousness of the antitotalitarian moment itself. In this regard they are hardly exceptional. Histories of French intellectual politics and culture since World War II have—no doubt due to the importance of French thought to contemporary historical consciousness in general—too often been constructed around an identification with a privileged intellectual or moment of consciousness that grounds the interpretation.[4] Problematic in the best of cases, this approach has been particularly damaging to historical understanding of the antitotalitarian moment. Because of the broad claims of the critique of totalitarianism, any uncritical identification with it cannot fail to have a significant and potentially distorting impact on the historiography. This is clearly demonstrated by the Anglo-American academic incarnations of this antitotalitarian recasting of French intellectual politics: Sunil Khilnani's *Arguing Revolution* and Tony Judt's *Past Imperfect*.

Sunil Khilnani's *Arguing Revolution* contends that intellectuals after the Liberation "adopted and persisted with the language of revolutionary politics" for reasons that "do not lie in the details of a particular social and economic conjecture."[5] Rather, Khilnani, drawing on Furet, argues that intellectuals used the language of the Jacobin revolutionary tradition because it was *the* tradition of the Left. Further, they were attracted to the French Communist Party (PCF) and the USSR because the former had appropriated this tradition for its political project.[6] For Khilnani, this Jacobin tradition was hegemonic in the French Left and possessed a number of "fundamental traits" that were "fully shared": a culture at the core of which is "the image of the revolution" and "a belief in centralized political power." This Left "focused on questions of political legitimacy rather than forms of rule" and made claims to legitimacy in such universal terms that at critical moments "any divergence or dissent consequently came to be described as betrayal or treason."[7] Because "French liberalism was disabled by the absence of a well-founded tradition of rights discourse and by a feeble conception of the relations between civil society and the modern state," "the arguments of the liberal and non-Communist Left lacked conviction" and French intellectuals, unable to conceive of an alternative, persisted in politics inspired by the Jacobin revolutionary tradition.[8] After the challenge of 1968 to Jacobin statism threw this political culture into crisis, François Furet offered a way out of the impasse by critiquing the Jacobin tradition as protototalitarian and thereby clearing the path to liberal political thought and moderate, pluralist republicanism.

The interpretive thrust of Tony Judt's *Past Imperfect* is remarkably similar to that of Khilnani's work. Judt also argues against explanations of the postwar politics of French intellectuals by the immediate context.[9] Although he hardly ignores the heritage of the 1930s and the war years, Judt contends that the singularity of French intellectual discourse after the Liberation can ultimately be explained by an "empty space" at the heart of French political thought: the absence of a liberal political tradition.[10] Lacking a tradition that values "negative liberties," liberties of individuals affirmed against the collectivity, French intellectuals could not conceive of grounding their political judgment in Kantian ethics, which Judt holds to be the only viable protection against murderous historicism and nihilistic radicalism.[11] Judt doubts that much changed after 1956. To be sure, he admits that intellectuals abandoned communism after 1956, but for him this resulted in little more than a transfer of allegiances to third-world revolutionary movements. According to Judt, the move away from communism was not accompanied by any serious reflection on it or any distancing from Marxist or utopian perspectives.[12] Even the critique of totalitarianism of the 1970s brought about less change in intellectual politics than is commonly believed because it did not effect the triumph of liberalism in France. Moreover, "it is a rare French thinker who has faced and engaged the real problem with totalitarianism, which is that it is a logical and historical derivative of precisely that universalist vision of republican democracy that still bedazzles so many French thinkers."[13]

Interpretations like those of Judt and Khilnani have placed serious obstacles in the way of our understanding of the critique of totalitarianism. By privileging Furet's analysis as both the key to interpreting the broad sweep of French intellectual politics and the way out of totalitarian politics for the French Left, Judt and Khilnani have rewritten the history of postwar French intellectual politics in an antitotalitarian key and adopted an uncritical perspective on Furet's important role in that history. They have reduced the thirty years between the Liberation and the critique of totalitarianism to the history of an absence—that of liberalism—in French political culture. Unappreciative of political alternatives to liberalism, they have minimized the extra-liberal evolution of French intellectual politics after 1956. Thus, the antitotalitarian moment of the 1970s appears to them, as it does to most other commentators and the antitotalitarian intellectuals themselves, as a sharp—although in Judt's opinion insufficient—break from the essential sameness of more than a quarter century of radical intellectual politics informed by the Jacobin revolutionary tradition.

A critical history of postwar intellectual politics and of the critique of totalitarianism in particular needs to depart from the identificatory approach, of which Judt and Khilnani offer only the most illustrative examples. It must denaturalize the history and at least temporarily suspend political judgment. It must also recognize that historical processes work in ways that are incoherent or at best ironic from the perspective of political philosophies and treat concepts like totalitarianism and liberalism as historically determined efforts to confront particular problems, not eternally valid concepts that offer ready-made solutions to the problem of historical understanding. Consequently, as a history of the French critique of totalitarianism of the 1970s, this book begins with a denaturalization of the concept of totalitarianism.

*   *   *

Coined by opponents of Italian fascism in 1923 to designate its authoritarianism, the term "totalitarian" (*totalitario*) was embraced by Mussolini and the Italian fascists themselves shortly thereafter to indicate the voluntarism of their movement. (Mussolini spoke in 1925 of the fascists' "fierce totalitarian will.")[14] As the fascist party declined in importance within the régime, the term increasingly referred in fascist usage to the fascist state's domination of society and the individual. Ironically, although the term "totalitarian" has generally been seen to be a more apt description of Nazi Germany than fascist Italy, the Nazis, after toying with the term "total state" advanced by the philosopher Carl Schmitt, rejected its application to their régime. The primacy that the Nazis gave to their movement and the German racial community made the emphasis on the state in the Italian usage of the term "totalitarian" and by the German advocates of the "total state" seem misplaced.[15]

Although the Nazis avoided the appellation "totalitarian" for their régime, its opponents did not; and in the wake of the Nazi seizure of power and the exile of anti-Nazi German intellectuals the term gained general currency throughout Western Europe and the United States. Yet, despite its increasing application to fascist Italy, Nazi Germany, and the Soviet Union beginning in the mid 1930s, the use of the term "totalitarian" was more tentative and suggestive than systematic and analytical before the Cold War.[16] In all its variants—Liberal, Marxist, and Christian—the concept of totalitarianism lacked theoretical elaboration. Further, those who used the concept of totalitarianism did not agree on key issues like the origins of totalitarianism and its fundamental characteristics. Some liberals like Friedrich Hayek believed that totalitarianism was a product of socialist economic planning; others like Hans Kohn viewed totalitarianism as an extreme form of nationalism. Whereas liberals generally saw totalitarianism as a negation of liberalism, some Marxists like Herbert Marcuse held that totalitarianism developed out of liberalism. Christian thinkers like Luigi Sturzo and Jacques Maritain generally interpreted totalitarianism as an anti-Christian "political religion." Finally, little agreement existed on whether or not the Soviet Union should be labeled totalitarian.

Hans Kohn hesitated to do so because he saw communism as rational, universalistic, and non-aggressive in its foreign relations—a development out of the Enlightenment liberal tradition. Communist dictatorship was, Kohn emphasized, transitory in theory. Similar reasoning led Raymond Aron to object to Élie Halévy's assimilation of the Soviet Union to fascism in 1936. On the other hand, anti-Stalinist Marxists such as Victor Serge and Leon Trotsky described the Soviet Union as totalitarian when discussing its authoritarian repression of internal dissent (Serge) or its failure to bring the proletariat to power (Trotsky).[17]

A variety of understandings and usages of the term "totalitarianism" survived into the Cold War. Marcuse's *One Dimensional Man* continued the Marxist tradition of applying the term to liberal capitalism; Waldemar Gurian and others continued to voice the interpretation of totalitarianism as a political religion; and some liberals maintained objections to the term's application to the Soviet Union for reasons similar to those advanced by Kohn as early as 1935. And, there was little agreement on the origins of totalitarianism. Yet, despite the survival of multiple usages and continued debate on important questions, the Cold War saw the distillation of a dominant definition of the concept generally shared by its advocates throughout Western Europe and the United States.[18]

The elaboration of the Cold War understanding of the concept of totalitarianism was largely the product of German speaking émigrés to the United States, whose formulations quickly conquered public and academic discourse in the United States, Great Britain, and the German Federal Republic. Divorced from the antifascist politics that had played a key role in the concept's initial elaboration in the 1920s and 1930s, they developed the concept largely within a liberal political framework. Unlike advocates of the concept in the 1930s who were divided over whether it applied to the Soviet Union, the Cold War theorists focused on communism. Although Nazi Germany remained important to discussions of totalitarianism, fascist Italy did not. Most of the scholarly and polemical literature either ignored it or denied that it was totalitarian. The emphasis on communism shifted the focus of the concept by asserting the central importance of ideology. This contributed to the instrumentalization of the concept in relation to the Cold War.

Two books were key to the making of the Cold War concept of totalitarianism: Hannah Arendt's *The Origins of Totalitarianism* and Carl Friedrich and Zbigniew Brzezinski's *Totalitarian Dictatorship and Autocracy*.[19] On the surface *The Origins of Totalitarianism* and *Totalitarian Dictatorship and Autocracy* offer very different approaches to the issue of totalitarianism. Arendt's analysis is a wide-ranging, philosophically informed search for the origins of totalitarianism, which comes up with an essentialist definition of totalitarianism. For Arendt, totalitarianism's essence is terror that seeks to destroy the autonomous individual in order to establish the reign of an ideology. Friedrich and Brzezinski's book, by contrast, is unconcerned with totalitarianism's origins and offers a phenomenological definition of totalitarian dictatorships as régimes that share six traits: "an official [totalitarian] ideology," "a single mass party led typically by one man," "a system of terroristic police control," "a technologically conditioned near-complete monopoly of control" of mass communication, "a similarly technologically conditioned near-complete monopoly of control" of armed combat, and "central control and direction of the entire economy."[20] Perhaps most importantly, Arendt differs from Friedrich and Brzezinski in her understanding of power in totalitarian régimes. For Friedrich and Brzezinski totalitarian régimes are monolithic. Within them decisions are made at the top and blindly executed by those below the leader in the state and party. For Arendt, totalitarian régimes are essentially shapeless, with constantly shifting lines of authority and centers of power acting in service of totalitarian ideology.

Despite these differences, the two books' analyses of totalitarianism are significantly convergent, especially when compared to the diversity of pre-Cold War analyses. Both consider totalitarian régimes sui generis, focus on Nazi Germany and the Soviet Union under Stalin, and give little attention to fascist Italy. [21] Differences between the Nazi and Stalinist régimes are given short shrift in analyses that focus on their apparent similarities. Both give pride of place to ideology in interpretations that consider totalitarianism to be most fundamentally the result of an effort to make history conform to a utopian ideology. Remaking the world in the image of ideology requires massive, essentially arbitrary terror that does not solely strike real opponents of the régime and only increases over time. Rather than appeal to the interests of the people, totalitarian régimes rule through ubiquitous terror and propaganda, which destroy all opposition, atomize the population, make resistance and reform virtually impossible, and eventually forge mass support for their policies. Externally, totalitarian régimes are naturally expansionist; their ideology requires nothing less than world domination. The practical policy conclusions are sobering. Arendt, who compares the consequences for humanity of an eventual victory of totalitarian rule to those of the hydrogen bomb, calls war against totalitarianism "necessary war" and argues that "the politically most important yardstick for judging events in our time" is "whether they serve totalitarian domination or not." Friedrich and Brzezinski consider that "the possibility of peaceful coexistence of the nations peopling the world presupposes the disappearance of totalitarian dictatorships"; "those who reject the system have no alternative but to strive for its destruction."[22]

Ironically, precisely when these books brought the concept of totalitarianism into its Cold War heyday in the United States, West Germany, and Great Britain, conditions were emerging in the Soviet Union that would cast doubt on the concept's validity. The end of mass terror, the relative liberalization of Soviet cultural life under Khrushchev, the emergence of dissidence after his ouster in 1964, and then the transformation of Bolshevik ideology into a justification of the staid power and privilege of the Nomen-klatura under Brezhnev all dramatically contradicted the Cold War concept of totalitarianism's understanding of terror, ideology, and the space available to dissent in the Soviet Union. At the same time, the emergence of détente in U.S.-Soviet relations belied predictions of the Soviet Union's expansionist drive. Criticisms of the moralizing tone of the totalitarianism literature in the early 1960s culminated in a forceful attack on the literature's justificatory function for U.S. foreign policy during the Vietnam War. All of these factors led scholars in those countries where the Cold War concept of totalitarianism had reigned supreme to question, modify, and in many cases repudiate the concept.[23]

Perhaps the most dramatic revisions were among the original formulators and advocates of the concept. In her introduction to the 1966 edition of *The Origins of Totalitarianism* Arendt, pointing to the important changes enumerated above, argued that Stalin's death had been "decisive" and that "the Soviet Union can no longer be called totalitarian in the strict sense of the term." Concerned about the Cold War misuse of the concept, she also argued against its application to all communist régimes.[24] While Arendt felt no need to revise her theory in light of recent events—despite her theory's absolute inability to account for the Soviet Union's post-Stalinist evolution—Friedrich and Brzezinski did rethink the concept. In the 1965 edition of *Totalitarian Dictatorship and Democracy*, revised by Friedrich alone, Friedrich significantly diluted their interpretation, writing notably that it is "not tenable" to argue "that totalitarian régimes will become more and more total." Friedrich de-emphasized secret police terror, added psychic and party-controlled terror to his definition of totalitarianism, and argued that the emergence of a substantial, coerced consensus behind the régime made overt terror less necessary. In a 1967 conference paper, Friedrich took this revision even further, substantially normalizing totalitarian régimes by arguing that they "will probably resemble other governments so far as their ends or objectives are concerned" and "that totalitarian dictatorship, like other political phenomena, is a relative rather than an absolute category."[25] As his nonparticipation in the revision of *Totalitarian Dictatorship and Autocracy* indicates, Brzezinski drifted away from using the concept to describe contemporary Soviet reality in the 1960s and 1970s, arguing that the syndrome of traits that he and Friedrich had enumerated in 1956 was insufficient to identify totalitarian régimes. "Institutionalized revolutionary zeal" aimed at transforming society was, he now argued, the "essence" of totalitarianism. Although Brzezinski continued to hold that the Soviet Union under Stalin had been totalitarian, he argued that totalitarianism had come to an end after Stalin's death when the party ceased efforts to revolutionize society, leaving the surviving totalitarian elements of the political system dysfunctional to the new Soviet system.[26]

Within American, West German, and British academia, Friedrich's efforts to modify the concept of totalitarianism so that it could still apply to the contemporary Soviet Union were not successful. His successive revisions deprived the concept of coherency and raised the suspicion that Friedrich was motivated by a desire to be able, as Frederick Fleron wrote in 1967, to "continue to pin a 'boo' label on a 'boo' system of government."[27] Sovietologists moving away from the concept of totalitarianism embraced comparative political frameworks and increasingly analyzed the contemporary Soviet Union with the same concepts as they used with other régimes. Robert Tucker argued as early as 1960 for the comparison of the Soviet Union with other "revolutionary mass-movement régimes under single-party auspices," a challenge taken up by Richard Lowenthal, who analyzed the Soviet Union as a form of "dictatorship of development." H. Gordon Skilling studied contemporary Soviet politics in terms of the interaction of interest groups, an approach Jerry Hough developed further into what he called "institutional pluralism," which explicitly compared the Soviet and Western democratic political systems and minimized differences in political participation between the two.[28]

While most political scientists limited their revisionist interpretations to the post-Stalinist period, histories of Stalinism implicitly and explicitly challenged the applicability of the concept of totalitarianism to it by showing the complexities of relations between the party-state and society and the confused and improvised nature of party-state action. Moshe Lewin argued as early as 1965 that the collectivization of agriculture, which totalitarian theory considered to be dictated by ideology, was largely improvised. Later, in the 1980s, J. Arch Getty would similarly contend that the indecision and chaos of the Great Purge indicate that it was probably not the product of a master plan dictated by Stalin. In fact, Getty argued that it was a largely improvised affair in which party officials on different levels played an important role. Sheila Fitzpatrick's studies of social and cultural life made the case that Soviet society was not passive in Stalin's revolution from above. Because, for example, Stalin's policies offered real prospects of social mobility to workers, many could support them out of interest rather than propaganda or terror, Fitzpatrick argued.[29]

Although the concept of totalitarianism enjoyed a revival in the 1980s and after the collapse of communism, it remains a profoundly problematic and ultimately unhelpful concept for understanding the Nazi and Soviet dictatorships for two fundamental reasons. First, it misinterprets relations between the party-state and society in supposedly totalitarian régimes. Second, the concept of totalitarianism's explicit comparison between the Soviet and Nazi régimes insists on their essential sameness, when in fact the differences between the régimes outweigh their similarities.

Recent research on Nazi Germany has made a total hash of the totalitarianism theory's understanding of its internal dynamics. Nazi Terror has been shown to be neither total, nor ubiquitous, nor indiscriminate. Most ordinary Germans had little to fear from it. Terror targeted the political, racial, and social enemies of the régime and posed little threat to the population at large, even when their transgressions were brought to the attention of the authorities. Further, ordinary Germans generally supported terror because they saw it as in their interests. Indeed, terror against the régime's enemies relied on citizen denunciations to such an extent that some historians have argued that German society under the Nazis was largely self-policing and the Gestapo "reactive."[30] Similarly, the participation of police battalion members in the Holocaust has been shown to be uncoerced. Whether one accepts the explanation of this behavior by Goldhagen as a consequence of a tradition of German eliminationist anti-Semitism that predates the Nazis or by Browning as a result of a combination of conformity, deference to authority, and wartime brutalization, in neither case is "totalitarianism" a factor.[31] Many historians now believe that the Nazi régime enjoyed a substantial active consensus that was neither coerced by terror nor imposed by brainwashing propaganda. Propaganda worked to the extent that it matched "everyday German understandings." The régime won converts for its successes, notably increasing employment, reversing the Versailles settlement in the 1930s, and then conquering much of Europe between 1938 and 1941.[32] Indeed, it is hard not to conclude that many Germans supported the Nazi effort to build a racial empire precisely because they saw it as in their interests. The persecution and then genocide of the Jews gave Germans the opportunity to profit from "Aryanization"; war brought both plundered goods and plundered labor, which gave "even the most incompetent dullard" a chance to "lord … over Poles and Russians"; and racial policy gave welfare benefits to Germans deemed to be racially worthy.[33]

Although scholarship on the history of Stalinist Russia is not as advanced as that on Nazi Germany, the first works that have appeared after the archives began to open following the collapse of the Soviet Union tend—without supporting all of the earlier claims of the revisionists—to confirm criticisms of the concept of totalitarianism. Research has shown that there was no master plan for the terror that by fits and starts followed the assassination of Kirov in 1934 and that the terror was not aimed at atomizing the population or frightening it into passivity. Rather, the terror, far from being random, targeted specific sectors of the population perceived, by the régime and also by much of the population, to include real enemies of the régime. Although the amount of terror was greater in the Stalinist Soviet Union than Nazi Germany, it seems likely that most of the population did not feel threatened by it, if only because it largely focused on the Soviet elite and the everyday presence of the party-state on the ground was relatively weak. Further, the terror offered the population opportunities to criticize local conditions and leaders and obtain redress of grievances as long as criticism did not turn against the national leadership or the régime. Only during the Great Purges of 1937-38, when a hysterical proliferation of accusations, arrests, and executions resulted in a situation of complete chaos, does it appear likely that the ordinary Soviet citizen feared arrest. Yet, when the Great Purges ended in the fall of 1938 the régime publicly criticized their excesses—something a régime bent on terrorizing the entire population would not have done. Studies of peasants and workers under Stalin reveal that neither was cowed by terror or brainwashed by propaganda. In the relatively fluid situation in the countryside during and after collectivization, peasants stubbornly fought for their interests and obtained concessions from the régime in some instances. Justifiably bitter over the violence of collectivization and their second-class status in its aftermath, peasants would only be reconciled with the régime after the reforms of the Khrushchev and Brezhnev eras substantially increased the collective farmers' standard of living. Workers, benefiting from the high demand for labor in the 1930s, foiled government efforts to control them through harsh legislation and were able to obtain improvements in living and working conditions by criticizing local officials. Although—unlike Nazi Germany—the Soviet Union did not have a popular consensus behind it in the 1930s, it clearly enjoyed support or at least acquiescence from significant sectors of the urban population in spite of (or perhaps even because they believed in the correctness of) the régime's coercion.[34]

Incapable of accounting for the internal dynamics of Nazi Germany and Stalinist Russia, the concept of totalitarianism is no less a failure as a basis for a comparison between these two régimes that asserts their essential similarity. Indeed, comparison has increasingly revealed fundamental differences between the two régimes. The Nazis came to power with the acquiescence of the existing elites in an advanced industrial country with a democratic political system. Once in power, they worked with old régime elites while attempting to construct a racial utopia, notably by systematically exterminating the Jewish people and waging a war of racial conquest. Justified by an exclusionary anti-Enlightenment biological and racial ideology and Hitler's charismatic authority, racial domination became the primary focus of the régime during World War II. The Bolsheviks, by contrast, came to power in a backward country through a coup d'état and civil war following the collapse of the autocratic old régime. Adhering to a universalistic and humanistic Enlightenment philosophy of emancipation, the Bolsheviks swept aside the old régime's elite and attempted to build socialism through a state-controlled modernization of the country. Although the carnage wrought by Stalinism was enormous, the Stalinist Soviet Union—unlike Nazi Germany—sought neither the extermination of entire biologically-defined categories of people ("the liquidation of the Kulaks as a class" being rather different from the genocide of the Jews) nor a war of conquest. Its goals were more limited and rational. Further, neither terror nor Stalin's charismatic rule were—again unlike terror and Hitler's charisma in Nazi Germany—immanent to the Soviet régime. Whereas terror directed against those deemed racially inferior was arguably intrinsic to the Nazi régime, terror largely came to an end in the Soviet Union following the death of Stalin. And, while Hitler embodied

Nazism, Stalin was more a product of the system and the Stalin cult unessential to it. The Soviet Union would, of course, survive Stalin. Its emancipatory, Enlightenment ideology would arguably contribute to the relative liberalization of the régime after Stalin's death and helps explain why the Soviet Union and Central European communist régimes came to a relatively peaceful end in contrast to the Nazi *Götterdämmerung*.[35]

Given that the concept of totalitarianism was at a low point in its Cold War homelands in the mid 1970s and that there were then and still remain important cognitive reasons to reject it, the French critique of totalitarianism of the 1970s is puzzling. Why would French intellectuals turn to the concept of totalitarianism to describe not only the Stalinist, but also the contemporary Soviet Union (as well as Marxist and revolutionary politics in general) when their homologues in other Western countries were abandoning it? A comparison of the Cold War uses of the concept of totalitarianism in Western Europe and the United States helps us begin to answer this question. As we shall see, throughout the Cold War the concept of totalitarianism was highly instrumentalized, and its instrumentalization varied considerably from country to country. Although developments within communist countries have impacted receptivity to the concept of totalitarianism, in no case has there been a one-to-one correspondence between the two. Everywhere, the international situation and the domestic political resonance of the concept have been important to determining its success.

In the United States the fortunes of the concept of totalitarianism have been very closely related to developments in the international situation. Usage of the term to describe both Nazi Germany and the Soviet Union, although increasingly common in the late 1930s, became the norm after the Nazi-Soviet Pact of August 1939. The invasion of the Soviet Union by the Nazis in June 1941 partially reversed this trend until the growth of tensions between the Soviet Union and the United States after the war renewed the attractiveness of the concept. President Truman adopted the term when he announced the Truman Doctrine in March 1947, making the fight against "totalitarianism" the focus of U.S. foreign policy. "Totalitarianism" would enter American law in 1950 with the McCarran Internal Security Act, which barred "totalitarians" from entering the country. Détente and then criticism of U.S. foreign policy in Vietnam—which was justified by the concept of totalitarianism—were at least as important as change within the Soviet Union to the move away from the concept in the 1960s and 1970s. Likewise, the renewal of Cold War tensions in the early 1980s contributed to a revival of the concept despite the fact that, by any objective measure, the communist world was becoming less totalitarian and not more so.[36]

The concept of totalitarianism was invaluable to American foreign policy after World War II. In the insightful analysis of Herbert Spiro and Benjamin Barber, "it explained and it rationalized American policy in terms which both preserved America's pragmatic self-image *and* carried a moral conviction which pragmatism itself lacked." Crucial to legitimizing the United States's abandonment of isolationism, the theory of totalitarianism also helped America explain communist behavior and American difficulties in the developing world as well as justify the reversal of the wartime alliance, the use of force in foreign relations, and support for friendly noncommunist dictators.[37] The close connection between the concept of totalitarianism and American foreign policy needs is reflected in the profile of Soviet Studies during the Cold War. The field was dominated by people who came to it out of an interest in national security and not "an intellectual passion for Russian-Soviet civilization." Indeed, according to Stephen Cohen, many hated their subject. Connections between Soviet Studies programs and the government were close. The federal government and private foundations heavily subsidized Soviet Studies, and many Soviet Studies graduates worked for the federal government. The loyalty-security crusade of the early Cold War kept the profession relatively free of, or intimidated those with, unorthodox views.[38]

Although the fortunes of the concept of totalitarianism rose and fell with the fever chart of the Cold War, this does not mean that it was unimportant in American domestic politics. Antitotalitarianism, which had become synonymous with anticommunism by the 1950s, was used to justify the marginalization and repression of dissident and progressive movements of all varieties, to promote religion and morality against godless, immoral communism, and—in its Hayekian version—to defeat social-democratic policy options. There can be no doubt that the retreat from the concept of totalitarianism in the 1960s and its revival in the early 1980s had domestic political causes as first the New Left fought against and then the neoconservatives fought for a concept that restricted political possibilities.[39]

Much more than any other postwar European state, the German Federal Republic (BRD) was a product of the Cold War and an anticommunism that blended into antitotalitarianism. The June 1948 currency reform and the May 1949 promulgation of the Basic Law that founded the BRD followed directly out of American Cold War decisions, and anticommunism played a central role in the 1949 *Bundestag* elections, in which socialist economic options were roundly defeated. Anticommunism also dominated the rearmament debate of the early 1950s, which resulted in the second founding of the BRD in 1955 when the Treaty of Paris granted it near-complete sovereignty in return for Cold War rearmament within the framework of NATO. Although the German Social Democratic Party (SPD) initially opposed rearmament and German integration into NATO and often suffered politically from the Right's assimilation of it to communism, it, like the ruling Christian Democratic Party (CDU), was anticommunist. Anticommunism was shared by all the major political forces in Germany. According to Andrei S. Markovits, until the late 1960s "virtually all public discourse in the Federal Republic was engulfed by an anticommunism bordering on an article of faith if not outright hysteria."[40] The German Communist Party suffered the consequences; it was banned for twelve years beginning in 1956.

The theory of totalitarianism not only justified the anticommunist identity of the BRD, but it also worked on the Nazi past. The equivalency that the theory of totalitarianism established between Nazism and communism downplayed the significance of the former and served, like contemporaneous explanations of Nazism by Hitler's evil genius, to exculpate the West German elite and institutions by minimizing their role in and personal responsibility for the Nazi régime.[41] By giving priority to the mobilization of the BRD against the new totalitarian enemy to the East, the theory of totalitarianism helped halt denazification and shift the emphasis of reeducation from uprooting Nazism to combating communism. As in the United States, during the 1950s the theory of totalitarianism not only was hegemonic in scholarly circles, but also penetrated deeply into society, occupying a central place in the secondary school curricula, for example. Further, the concept of totalitarianism contributed to the formation of a postwar West German identity as a victim nation by making Germans the victims of the totalitarian designs of a handful of Nazis and by turning the suffering of German POWs and women in the hands of the Soviet Union into the equivalent of "the suffering of 'victims of the Germans'" during World War II. Consequently, in Germany, as in the United States, Cold War theorizing about totalitarianism helped marginalize the Holocaust in historical consciousness. [42]

Given its role in the very constitution of the BRD, the concept of totalitarianism would find itself severely challenged by the general crisis of the postwar order in the late 1960s. The New Left's questioning of postwar domestic and international political structures, of the dominant memory of World War II, and of the consumer culture that thrived during the great economic expansion of the 1950s and 1960s all undermined the legitimacy of the concept of totalitarianism, which some German scholars like Christian Ludz had begun to question as early as 1961. Anticommunism and the theory of totalitarianism seemed to the New Left to play a system-legitimizing and exculpatory role for both American foreign policy in Vietnam and the BRD's social and political order. Looking back on the Nazi past and seeing the older generation more as "perpetrators of fascism" than "survivors of totalitarianism,"[43] the New Left indignantly protested that the BRD was—as the presence of former Nazis in positions of power indicated—based on the abandonment of denazification and the cement of anticommunism. Even consumer society, the culture of the *Wirtschaftswunder*, was accused of serving to divert Germany from a reckoning with the Nazi period. For the writer Heinrich Böll the currency reform of June 1948 marked the end of hopes placed in *Stunde Null* and the beginning of German amnesia as it embraced prosperity.[44] In Reiner Werner Fassbinder's masterful and enormously popular 1978 film *The Marriage of Maria Braun*, the revival of an unreformed Germany through the *Wirtschaftswunder* has consequences that are nothing short of apocalyptic.[45] Encouraged by a normalization of relations with Eastern Europe and a new acceptance of German responsibility for World War II brought about by Willy Brandt's *Ostpolitik*, anti-anticommunism and *Faschismustheorien*—which emphasized the responsibility of the German elite and the continuity between the Third Reich and the BRD—became *de rigueur* within the West German New Left.[46] Although the theory of totalitarianism and narratives of German victimhood were revived in the *Historikerstreit* of the mid 1980s, the West German intellectual Left remained steadfastly opposed to both right up to the collapse of communism in Eastern Europe.[47]

In Italy, like France, the fate of the concept of totalitarianism was determined much more by domestic politics, notably that surrounding the Italian Communist Party (PCI). Italy had a strong communist party after World War II, and although its Cold War political opponents attacked it as totalitarian, the concept of totalitarianism failed to gain wider legitimacy. Friedrich and Brzezinski's *Totalitarian Democracy and Autocracy* never appeared in Italian, and Arendt's *The Origins of Totalitarianism* was published in an Italian edition only in 1967. The historian of Italian fascism and critic of the PCI Renzo De Felice claimed in 1975 that no serious discussion of the concept of totalitarianism had occurred in Italy. The concept, he noted, "remained an analysis for a handful of specialists who for the most part rejected it." This failure of the concept of totalitarianism was largely attributable, De Felice argued, to the "cultural hegemony of the Communist party." [48]

If Italy, unlike France, did not experience a critique of totalitarianism in the 1970s, it can largely be explained by the PCI's moderation. After 1956 the PCI distinguished itself from the French Communist Party (PCF) by its greater independence from the Soviet Union, commitment to democratic politics, and respect for intellectuals. The PCI moved toward polycentrism in international communism after 1956 and developed "a strategy based on acceptance of the republican constitution and parliamentary democracy," leading it to sharply criticize the 1968 Soviet intervention in and subsequent normalization of Czechoslovakia, the 1979 invasion of Afghanistan, and the 1981 declaration of martial law in Poland. When student protest erupted in the late 1960s the PCI was relatively open to it, and in the 1970s it "opened up to the representatives of Marxist dissent" and abandoned "any attempt to dictate to intellectuals." Seeing in the PCI a means to increase their influence in society, many Italian intellectuals aligned themselves, if only superficially, with the party in the mid 1970s. The PCI's approach reflected a commitment since the end of World War II to a broad penetration of Italian national life, which received even greater emphasis with the party's "historic compromise" of 1973-79, an attempt—in accordance with the lessons that PCI leader Enrico Berlinguer drew from Italian politics after World War I, the contemporary extreme right's strategy of tension, and the overthrow of the Allende government in Chile—to fend off the threat of fascism and establish the respectability of the PCI. The PCI's "historic compromise" led it to moderate its politics and support first tacitly and then actively the Christian Democratic led governments of the years 1976-79. Although the PCI enjoyed some initially spectacular electoral successes, the end result was a disaster for the party. Implicated in unpopular and repressive government policies and falling short of obtaining political power, the PCI quickly lost credibility and was increasingly criticized from the Left for taking a social-democratic turn.[49]

Because of the choices made by the PCI, when it came under attack in the late 1970s, 1980s, and beyond the emphasis was on antifascism and the party's role in the wartime Resistance—which had initially established its credibility as a mass, national, and democratic party and had been the foundation of much of the rhetoric of the historic compromise. The extreme Left attacked the PCI for having repeated its supposed 1940s betrayal of revolution in the 1970s. The Right, on the other hand, contested the PCI's attempt to claim legitimacy by appealing to Resistance antifascism. De Felice began the assault in late 1987 when he charged that antifascism blocked political reform and "was used by the communists to assume a patina of democracy." De Felice elaborated on these charge in his *Rosso e Nero* (1996), in which he contended that politically motivated communist violence during the Resistance and the hand of Moscow in PCI Resistance decisions undermined the PCI claim to be a national and democratic party. Although this reevaluation of the Resistance quickly led to the charge that the PCI was totalitarian, the focus was always on the history of Resistance and the foundation of the postwar Italian Republic, not totalitarianism.[50]

The relative failure of the concept of totalitarianism in Italy may also be a consequence of its limited utility for the Italian Right. Whereas in West Germany it served to exculpate the elite and—in the recent work of Ernst Nolte—even the Nazis to some extent, in Italy the comparative dimension of the concept of totalitarianism—like that of the concept of fascism—threatened to implicate Italian fascism and the Italian elite in the crimes of Nazism. Thus, Renzo De Felice was very careful in his revisionist interpretation of fascist Italy to highlight the differences between Italian fascism and German Nazism, holding notably that "Italian Fascism is sheltered from the accusation of genocide, and quite outside the shadow [of guilt] for the Holocaust."[51] Throughout his career he rejected the classic theory of totalitarianism because it "concludes by reducing fascism, Nazism, and communism ... to a common denominator that I do not accept."[52] When De Felice finally described Italian fascism of the late 1930s as totalitarian in the fifth volume of his monumental biography of Mussolini published in 1981, he rejected all existing theories of totalitarianism because they gave insufficient attention to the differences between fascist Italy and Nazi Germany or the Stalinist Soviet Union. Mussolini's totalitarianism, he insisted in terms that made it seem almost benign, was more "moral" than "repressive."[53] Perhaps because of the contortions required to separate fascist Italy from other régimes considered to be totalitarian, De Felice's "analysis of totalitarianism," his student Emilio Gentile would later say, "remained rudimentary and was not always clearly or coherently defined."[54]

France was similar to Italy in that domestic politics was the primary determinant of the concept of totalitarianism's reception. The Cold War—although important—was much less constitutive of the postwar domestic order in France than in West Germany or even Italy. And, unlike the United States, where the Cold War was a crusade at the center of foreign policy, the French "experienced the Cold War simultaneously as a neces-sity, a bother and an opportunity."[55] It was a necessity insofar as the French government saw no alternative to supporting the Western Alliance; it was a bother in that it complicated efforts to pursue national goals such as dealing with the German menace; and it was an opportunity because in instances like the French war in Indochina it occasionally allowed France to harness American power in support of French interests. In any case, French national leaders were generally not comfortable with the bipolar nature of the Cold War and often sought to escape its logic in order to find room to maneuver internationally. The theory of totalitarianism, which emphasized this bipolar logic, could not serve as a foundation for their foreign policy. Thus, not surprisingly, French studies of the Soviet Union after World War II did not emerge out of an interest in national security (as was the case in the United States); rather, communism as a model with possible political relevance for France was more often the stake of research. Many, if not most, French students of the Soviet Union had been either fellow travelers of communism or communist party members at one point or another.[56]

It was the possibility of communism at home, notably because of the strength of the French Communist Party (PCF), that gave the concept of totalitarianism some resonance in France. All major political parties accused the PCF of being totalitarian after it was excluded from the gov-ernment in 1947, yet the concept failed to conquer the academy or wider intellectual circles and did not gain a central place in the secondary school curriculum. Raymond Aron, the primary French exponent of the concept, failed to convert other intellectuals to it. Friedrich and Brzezinski's *Totali-tarian Dictatorship and Autocracy*, although introduced to a French audience by Aron's 1957-58 lectures at the Sorbonne, was never published in French.[57] Despite Arendt's efforts to find a French publisher, her *Origins of Totalitarianism* did not appear in a complete French translation until 1984.[58] If the concept of totalitarianism was far less successful in France than in West Germany or the United States in the early Cold War, this had much to do with the strength and legitimacy of the PCF as well as with the French intellectual Left's hopes for radical change. The PCF deployed its considerable postwar influence against the concept of totalitarianism; and

French intellectuals, who saw the PCF as a necessary partner in—if not always a preferred agent of—a revolutionary transition to socialism, could hardly countenance the ostracization of the PCF that accepting the concept of totalitarianism would entail.

The fate of the concept of totalitarianism in France turned largely on the relationship between left-wing intellectuals and the PCF. Unlike the PCI, the PCF failed to establish distance between itself and the Soviet Union or pursue a moderate politics that might have sheltered it from the charge of totalitarianism. And whereas in West Germany and the United States "New Left"[59] politics undermined the legitimacy of the concept of totalitarianism, in France it prepared the ground for antitotalitarianism by turning left-wing intellectuals against the PCF after 1956. The PCF did much to encourage the growth of intellectual hostility toward it. Its support of the repression of the Hungarian Revolution, its *ouvriérisme*—which gave intellectuals little power or independence—its failure to lead the opposition to the Algerian War, and its hostility to the student movement in 1968 all fed "New Left" critiques of communism. Furthermore, when received ideas about the French experience during World War II were questioned, the PCF was deemed guilty of manipulating antifascism to its benefit and cooperating with de Gaulle in the erection of a "resistancialist" myth that minimized the significance of Vichy in French history and exaggerated the importance of the Resistance.[60] Yet, unlike in West Germany, French debates about World War II were not central to those on the concept of totalitarianism. The concept was hardly used in the important discussion of Vichy in the 1970s and 1980s.[61] The French discussion of totalitarianism focused almost exclusively on communism and made little reference to the existing international scholarship on the topic. The narrow focus and provincial character of the French critique of totalitarianism can be explained by its emergence in the heated debate about contemporary French communism in those years. In the 1970s the PCF allied with the Socialist Party (PS) in a Union of the Left, which promised to institute socialism when it came to power. The electoral success of this coalition led French intellectuals of the Left to fear that the PCF, which in their mind had changed little since the Stalinist era, would impose a repressive form of socialism in France similar to that then existing in Eastern Europe. The critique of totalitarianism was developed to combat this perceived threat.

This comparison between developments in the United States, West Germany, Italy, and France has suggested that the concept of totalitarianism's implantation has a variable geography that is largely determined by the concept's instrumentalization. The concept's instrumentalization and consequent implantation varied in relation to the politics of the Cold War and domestic communism in each country. Especially given that the concept of totalitarianism seems to be more the product of local political agendas than cool reflection, its history is more political than intellectual history. Further, because the concept's history is inseparable from its instrumentalization, it cannot be written as an intellectual morality tale of objectively justified adhesions to and politically motivated deviations from an apparently evident truth about régimes deemed to be totalitarian.[62] Nor is it possible, following Judt and Khilnani, to write its history in terms of intellectuals' failure to embrace a particular political philosophy or culture. Rather than focus on absences (either of objectivity or of a favored political tradition), this book seeks to explain the history of French intellectuals' critique of totalitarianism of the 1970s by focusing on the concrete political problems faced by intellectuals and the resources that they used to confront them.

To fully situate the critique of totalitarianism, establish its significance, and rectify antitotalitarian misreadings of recent history, the story begins in chapter 1 with an examination of the evolution of French intellectuals' political projects, notably their initial attachment to and then evolution away from communism, between the Liberation and the mid 1970s. Left-wing intellectuals' support for the French Communist Party (PCF), the Soviet Union, and revolutionary violence was moderated by a serious commitment to the preservation of liberty within socialism and the revolutionary project that informed the evolution of intellectual politics during and after the first heady postwar decade. In the latter half of the 1950s events in communist Eastern Europe, the Algerian War, and the coming of the Fifth Republic had a profound impact on intellectual politics. Khrushchev's secret speech and the crushing of the Hungarian Revolution in 1956 decisively compromised the image of the Soviet Union, while the failure of the PCF to de-Stalinize and adequately resist either the Algerian War or the coming of the Fifth Republic distanced left-wing intellectuals from it. More profoundly, the PCF's failures were often understood to be those of the working class, which appeared increasingly less revolutionary; and the conduct of the Algerian War brought the entire political class and the state into question. In reaction to these events intellectuals gave the revolutionary project a direct-democratic orientation and recast the revolutionary subject so as to ensure that revolution secured and extended liberty and democracy. The direct-democratic alternative resonated with French political traditions going back to the French Revolution of 1789. Long attractive to French intellectuals who saw in it a means to restore, however briefly, both the autonomy of the individual and the collective will and thereby purify and regenerate politics,[63] direct democracy was additionally appealing in this period because it offered intellectuals a politics appropriate to their growing power in the mass media that allowed them to bypass the political elite and directly address the people.

The year 1968 renewed hopes for revolution and gave the intellectual Left's politics a profoundly anti-authoritarian, anti-institutional, and direct-democratic orientation that—although indebted to the efforts to rethink revolution after 1956—was substantially new in the depth of its democratic and libertarian exigencies. Given expression in redefinitions of the intellectual by Jean-Marie Domenach, Michel Foucault, and Jean-Paul Sartre, as well as in projects such as the Groupe d'information sur les prisons and the newspaper *Libération*, these exigencies outlasted the revolutionary tide and ensured that the revolutionary movement would not be sustained once the élan of 1968 had dissipated. At the extreme, post-1968 intellectual politics developed into a late *gauchisme* marked by its refusal to countenance the exercise of political power. This new intellectual politics and the deepening of long-standing critiques of communism and revolution after 1968 put intellectuals on a collision course with the Socialist and Communist parties, which formed a Union of the Left in 1972 on the basis of a Common Program of Government advocating a state-centered socialism. The critique of totalitarianism reflected in both its radicalism and themes not an absolute reversal of intellectual politics attributable to the shock of Aleksandr Solzhenitsyn's *Gulag Archipelago* or the collapse of third-world revolutionary utopias but rather the profundity of the chasm separating intellectual politics marked by a diffuse post-1968 *gauchisme* in disarray from that of the parties of the Left rapidly advancing toward political power.

Indeed, the close look at the reception of Solzhenitsyn's *Gulag Archipelago* in chapter 2 reveals that it did not have a decisive impact on French intellectuals' evaluations of communism, if only because it was not received as a revelation. It was not *The Gulag Archipelago*'s content, but the PCF's attack on the book and its defenders and, more broadly, concern that the communists were trying to control the Union of the Left that worried French intellectuals and constituted the Solzhenitsyn affair of 1974. To the extent that intellectuals like Claude Lefort and André Glucksmann found inspiration in Solzhenitsyn's tomes, their reading of him was heavily filtered through their own late *gauchiste* politics. To be sure, references to Solzhenitsyn and the metaphor of the gulag were ubiquitous in the antitotalitarian politics of the late 1970s, but that reflected their usefulness in political battles within the Left, not *The Gulag Archipelago*'s revelatory impact.

Chapter 3 traces relations between intellectuals and the Union of the Left from 1972 to the emergence of the critique of totalitarianism in 1975. Incompatible with the direct-democratic tendencies of French intellectual politics, this alliance and its program were received coldly by noncommunist intellectuals from their inception. Intellectuals feared that the PCF's "Stalinist" politics made it a threat to democracy, and they rejected the Common Program's state-centered approach to building socialism. In 1975 these reservations led them to elaborate a critique of totalitarianism in reaction to two developments within the French Left: the PCF's ideological offensive against the PS beginning in October 1974 and the PCF's response to developments in the Portuguese Revolution in the summer of 1975. The PCF's actions and the PS's measured response to them led many French intellectuals to fear that the communists were, although losing the battle for electoral influence within the Left, becoming ideologically hegemonic within it. The communists would, they argued in an analysis that rejected the Mitterrandist understanding of the dynamic within the Left in terms of power, call the shots in a future coalition government of the Left even if the socialists were the larger party. First emerging in the autumn of 1975 among the intellectuals associated with the journal *Esprit*, the critique of totalitarianism soon spread throughout the intellectual Left.

One of the ways in which intellectuals waged their antitotalitarian campaign against the PCF was, we see in chapter 4, by protesting against repression by Eastern European communist régimes. Protest against this repression was not entirely new. Beginning with the crushing of the Hungarian Revolution in 1956, left-wing intellectuals had raised their voices in order to highlight the difference between their vision of a socialism that respects liberty and the socialism practiced beyond the iron curtain and advocated by the PCF. Analyzing the campaigns against Czechoslovakian "normalization" and in favor of the release of the Soviet dissidents Leonid Plyushch and Vladimir Bukovski, this chapter shows that protest intensified in the 1970s because of intellectuals' fears that the Union of the Left threatened liberty in France and reached new heights in 1977, when it appeared likely that the Left would win the 1978 legislative elections. The confrontation with the Union of the Left also forced an evolution of the politics of protest as intellectuals sought more vigorously to ensure the future of liberty in France. In 1976 protest previously motivated by the ambition of reconciling socialism and liberty was replaced by protest divorced from the socialist project that turned increasingly in an anticommunist and antitotalitarian direction. In 1977 fear of the threat posed by the PCF to liberty and the new emphasis on Eastern European dissidence made possible the emergence of the French "dissident" intellectual who presented himself or herself as dissident vis-à-vis the possible future French government of the Left.

Chapter 5 examines the significance of 1977, the year of the new philosophers, dissidence, and the crisis of Marxism in French intellectual politics. Although new philosophers such as André Glucksmann and Bernard-Henri Lévy were skillful in their use of the mass media, they and their pessimistic political philosophies were able to occupy the center stage of French politics, intellectual or otherwise, in 1977-78 above all because they played on fears of a Left victory in the 1978 legislative elections and were either supported or at least tolerated by prominent figures on the French intellectual scene who shared their fears of the parties of the Left. This chapter's in-depth study of the debate about the new philosophers reveals that by 1977 a large number of intellectuals of the noncommunist Left—such as Jean-Marie Domenach, Michel Foucault, and Philippe Sollers, for example—either embraced or tolerated the conclusion that communism, Marxism, and revolution were totalitarian. Further, those who rejected this conclusion—such as Claude Mauriac, Jean Elleinstein, and Nicos Poulantzas, for example—had lost all ability to define the agenda in intellectual politics. This chapter also shows the extent to which the content of intellectuals' analyses of totalitarianism was derivative of the contemporary debate over the Union of the Left. Antitotalitarian intellectuals argued that totalitarianism was not the product of social or historical conditions, a thesis that minimized the danger posed by the Union of the Left. Rather, they found the origins of totalitarianism in revolution, revolutionary projects and ideology, and the oligarchic tendencies of political parties. Finally, they began to uncover its origins in French history, notably the French Revolution. These understandings of totalitarianism all served to highlight the danger of a totalitarian adventure in contemporary France. They also underscore the depth of the critique of totalitarianism in French intellectual life.

Given the domestic political origins and focus of the critique of totalitarianism, its most important intellectual product was appropriately François Furet's revisionist history of the French Revolution, studied in chapter 6. In his *Penser la Révolution française* of 1978 Furet, relying on a mode of argumentation that was perhaps more political than scholarly, applied to the French Revolution the contemporary understanding that revolutionary politics necessarily ends in totalitarianism as a result of its inevitably Manichean ideological dynamics. Furet's interpretation cast the French Revolution as the founding moment of a proto-totalitarian political culture, thereby justifying fears of totalitarianism in France that might otherwise seem inappropriate given the country's long democratic tradition. Furet's French Revolution became for both his contemporaries and later scholars the origin, foundation, and explanation of intellectuals' postwar political adventures with communism and revolutionary politics. For intellectuals like Furet who had been communists in their youth, this interpretation may have been attractive because it was comforting, but it, like the use of the concept of totalitarianism, arguably came at the cost of a serious distortion of the historical record.

The legacies of antitotalitarianism, considered in the epilogue, are considerable. Most obviously, it made intellectuals suspicious of—and at times overtly hostile toward—the socialist-led government of the early 1980s. Until the communists left the government in June 1984 intellectuals feared that France would take a totalitarian turn with the Left in power. At the same time, the collapse of the intellectual Left resulted in a reconfiguration of intellectual politics. The immediate beneficiaries were postmodernism and liberalism, both of which thrived on the loss of direction experienced by intellectuals in the early 1980s. Yet, as antitotalitarianism receded from the forefront of intellectual politics in the later 1980s and 1990s it was republicanism that came to dominate intellectual politics. French intellectuals found in republicanism both answers to the new political problems of the 1980s and 1990s, such as immigration and globalization, and a way to revive—on a more modest level—the universalism to which they remained attracted and which the antitotalitarian critique of the revolutionary project had brought into question.

Notes

1. Perry Anderson, *In the Tracks of Historical Materialism* (London, 1983), 32.
2. François Furet, *Penser la Révolution française* (Paris, 1978); Pierre Rosanvallon and Patrick Viveret, *Pour une nouvelle culture politique* (Paris, 1977); Jacques Julliard, *Contre la politique professionnelle* (Paris, 1977).
3. Jeannine Verdès-Leroux, *Le Réveil des somnambules: le parti communiste, les intellectuels et la culture (1956-1985)* (Paris, 1987) and Pierre Rigoulot, *Les Paupières lourdes: les français face au goulag: aveuglements et indignations* (Paris, 1991). Other evaluations along these lines include: Pierre Grémion, *Paris-Prague: la gauche face au renouveau et à la régression tchécoslovaques (1968-1978)* (Paris, 1985); Pierre Grémion, *Intelligence de l'anticommunisme: le Congrès pour la liberté de la culture à Paris* (Paris, 1995); Gil Delannoi, *Les Années utopiques (1968-1978)* (Paris, 1990); Tony Judt, *Past Imperfect: French Intellectuals, 1944-1956* (Berkeley, 1992); and Sunil Khilnani, *Arguing Revolution: The Intellectual Left in Post-war France* (New Haven, 1993). For essays offering some dissent from this dominant perspective see Jean-Claude Guillebaud, *Les Années orphelines: 1968-1978* (Paris, 1978) and Louis Janover, *Les Dissidents du monde occidental: critique de l'idéologie anti-totalitaire* (Paris, 1991).
4. For example, for Mark Poster, *Existential Marxism in Postwar France: From Sartre to Althusser* (Princeton, 1975) the privileged perspective is that of Sartre; for Kristin Ross, *Fast Cars, Clean Bodies: Decolonization and the Reordering of French Culture* (Cambridge, Mass., 1995) it is that of Henri Lefebvre; for H. Stuart Hughes, *The Obstructed Path* (New York, 1968) it is that of Max Weber; and, as I argue below, for Judt, *Past Imperfect*, and Khilnani, *Arguing Revolution*, it is that of François Furet.
5. Khilnani, *Arguing Revolution*, 17.
6. Ibid., 32.
7. Ibid., 7-9.
8. Ibid., 135.
9. Judt, *Past Imperfect*, 6-7.
10. Ibid., 226.
11. Ibid., chap. 12.
12. Ibid., 282-90.
13. Ibid., 313.
14. Enzo Traverso, "Introduction: le totalitarisme. Jalons pour l'historie d'un débat," in *Le Totalitarisme: le XXe siècle en débat*, ed. Enzo Traverso (Paris, 2001), 20.
15. Traverso, "Introduction," 19-28; Abbott Gleason, *Totalitarianism: The Inner History of the Cold War* (New York, 1995), 13-28.
16. Such is the conclusion of both Traverso's sweeping survey and Jones's monograph: Enzo Traverso, "Introduction," 45, and William David Jones, *The Lost Debate: German Socialist Intellectuals and Totalitarianism* (Chicago, 1999), 17.
17. Friedrich A. Hayek, *The Road to Serfdom* (Chicago, 1944); Hans Kohn, "La Dictature communiste et la dictature fasciste: une étude comparative," in Traverso, *Le Totalitarisme*, 155-70 (first published in a 1935 and a revised 1941 edition); Herbert Marcuse, "The Struggle Against Liberalism in the Totalitarian View of the State," in his *Negations: Essays in Critical Theory*, trans. Jeremy J. Shapiro (Boston, 1968), 3-42 (first published in 1934); Luigi Sturzo, "L'État totalitaire," in Traverso, *Le Totalitarisme*, 216-34 (first published in 1935); Jacques Maritain, "Totalitarismes fascistes et totalitarisme communiste," in Traverso, *Le Totalitarisme*, 234-43 (first published in 1936); Élie Halévy, "L'Ère des tyrannies," in his *L'Ère des tyrannies: Études sur le socialisme et la guerre*, 6th ed. (Paris, 1938), 213-27 (a 1936 text); Raymond Aron, "Contribution d'Aron à l'Ère des tyrannies," in *Machiavel et les tyrannies modernes*, ed. Rémy Freymond (Paris, 1993), 307-8 (a 1936 text) and Aron, "Le Socialisme et la guerre," in Freymond, *Machiavel*, 308-31 (first published in 1939); Victor Serge, "Lettre sur le totalitarisme stalinien," in Traverso, *Le Totalitarisme*,

278-81 (a 1933 text); and Léon Trotsky, "L'URSS dans la guerre," in Traverso, *Le Totalitarisme*, 315-23 (a 1939 text).

18. Herbert Marcuse, *One Dimensional Man: Studies in the Ideology of Advanced Industrial Society* (Boston, 1964); Waldemar Gurian, "Totalitarianism as a Political Religion," in *Totalitarianism*, ed. Carl J. Friedrich (New York, 1954), 119-29. A developed analysis of the varieties of definition and usage of the concept in the Cold War is offered by Benjamin R. Barber, "Conceptual Foundations of Totalitarianism," in Carl J. Friedrich, Michael Curtis, and Benjamin R. Barber, *Totalitarianism in Perspective: Three Views* (New York, 1969), 3-52.

19. Hannah Arendt, *The Origins of Totalitarianism*, new edition (New York, 1966; first edition 1951); Carl J. Friedrich and Zbigniew K. Brzezinski, *Totalitarian Dictatorship and Autocracy* (New York, 1961; first published in 1956).

20. Friedrich and Brzezinski, *Totalitarian Dictatorship and Autocracy*, 9-10.

21. Arendt argues that fascist Italy was not totalitarian. Friedrich and Brzezinski question, without making a final determination, whether fascist Italy was totalitarian. Arendt, *The Origins of Totalitarianism*, 258-59 and fn. 11, p. 308; Friedrich and Brzezinski, *Totalitarian Dictatorship and Autocracy*, 277.

22. Arendt, *The Origins of Totalitarianism*, 442, 443. Friedrich and Brzezinski, *Totalitarian Dictatorship and Autocracy*, 68. The following useful comparisons of the two books are drawn on here: Robert Burrowes, "'Totalitarianism' The Revised Standard Version," *World Politics* 21, 2 (Jan. 1969): 272-94 and Simon Tormey, *Making Sense of Tyranny: Interpretations of Totalitarianism* (New York, 1995), chapters 2 and 3.

23. On these issues see Gleason, *Totalitarianism*, 127-42; Stephen F. Cohen, *Rethinking the Soviet Experience: Politics and History Since 1917* (New York, 1985), chap. 1.

24. Arendt, *The Origins of Totalitarianism*, ix, xi-xii, xix.

25. Carl J. Friedrich and Zbigniew Brzezinski, *Totalitarian Dictatorship and Autocracy*, second edition, revised by Carl J. Friedrich (Cambridge, Mass., 1965), 376 and passim. Carl J. Friedrich, "The Evolving Theory and Practice of Totalitarian Regimes," in Friedrich, Curtis, and Barber, *Totalitarianism in Perspective*, 127 and 144. See Burrowes, "'Totalitarianism' The Revised Standard Version," 281-94, for a further discussion of the dilution of the concept by Friedrich.

26. Guiseppe Boffa, *The Stalin Phenomenon*, trans. Nicholas Fersen (Ithaca, 1992), 64. Zbigniew Brzezinski, "Dysfunctional Totalitarianism," in *Theory and Politics/Theorie und Politik: Festschrift zum 70. Geburtstag für Carl Joachim Friedrich*, ed. Klaus von Beyme (Haag, 1971), 375-89.

27. Fleron cited in Achim Siegel, "Carl Joachim Friedrich's Concept of Totalitarian Dictatorship: A Reinterpretation," in *The Totalitarian Paradigm After the End of Communism: Towards a Theoretical Reassessment*, ed. Achim Siegel, Poznan Studies in the Philosophy of the Sciences and the Humanities, vol. 65 (Atlanta, 1998), 278.

28. Gleason, *Totalitarianism*, 127-37. See also Pierre Hassner, "Le Totalitarisme vu de l'ouest," in *Totalitarismes*, ed. Guy Hermet (Paris, 1984), 15-41.

29. Moshe Lewin, "The Immediate Background of Soviet Collectivization," in his *The Making of the Soviet System: Essays in the Social History of Interwar Russia* (New York, 1985), 91-120, first published in *Soviet Studies* 17, 2 (1965); J. Arch Getty, *The Origin of the Great Purges* (New York, 1985); Sheila Fitzpatrick, *Education and Social Mobility in the Soviet Union* (New York, 1979), discussed in Gleason, *Totalitarianism*, 140-41.

30. Robert Gellately, *Backing Hitler: Consent and Coercion in Nazi Germany* (New York, 2001) and Eric A. Johnson, *Nazi Terror: The Gestapo, Jews, and Ordinary Germans* (New York, 1999). Johnson contests Gellately's assertion that German society was self-policing and the Gestapo reactive, but otherwise their interpretations are in agreement.

31. Christopher R. Browning, *Ordinary Men: Reserve Police Battalion 101 and the Final Solution in Poland*, new edition (New York, 1998) and Daniel Jonah Goldhagen, *Hitler's Willing Executioners: Ordinary Germans and the Holocaust* (New York, 1996).

32. Gellately, *Backing Hitler*, 257-60, 259 for the quote.

33. Gellately, *Backing Hitler*, 130 and passim; Michael Burleigh and Wolfgang Wippermann, *The Racial State: Germany 1933-1945* (New York, 1991), 303 for the quote and passim.

34. J. Arch Getty and Oleg Naumov, *The Road to Terror: Stalin and the Self-Destruction of the Bolsheviks, 1932-1939* (New Haven, 1999); Robert W. Thurston, *Life and Terror in Stalin's Russia, 1934-1941* (New Haven, 1996); Sheila Fitzpatrick, *Stalin's Peasants: Resistance and Survival in the Russian Village After Collectivization* (New York, 1994). Useful surveys of recent scholarship include Steven Kotkin, "1991 and the Russian Revolution: Sources, Conceptual Categories, Analytical Frameworks," *The Journal of Modern History* 70 (June 1998): 383-425 and Nicolas Werth, "Le Stalinisme au pouvoir: Mise en perspective historiographique," *Vingtième Siècle* 69 (Feb.-Mar. 2001): 125-35.

35. Ian Kershaw, "Totalitarianism Revisited: Nazism and Stalinism in Comparative Perspective," *Tel Aviver Jahrbuch für deutsche Geschichte* 23 (1994): 23-40; Traverso, "Introduction," 92-99. A useful, if somewhat dated, effort to compare the two régimes is Charles S. Maier, *The Unmasterable Past: History, Holocaust, and German National Identity* (Cambridge, Mass., 1988), chap. 3.

36. Gleason, *Totalitarianism*, 39-50, 72-88, 190-205 and passim.

37. Herbert J. Spiro and Benjamin R. Barber, "Counter-Ideological Uses of 'Totalitarianism,'" *Politics and Society* 1, 1 (Nov. 1970): 7-8 and passim.

38. Gleason, *Totalitarianism*, 121; Cohen, *Rethinking the Soviet Experience*, 10-19, page 11 for the quote.

39. Stephen J. Whitfield, *The Culture of the Cold War*, 2nd ed. (Baltimore, 1996); Gleason, *Totalitarianism*, 64-67.

40. Andrei S. Markovits, "The West German Left in a Changing Europe: Between Intellectual Stagnation and Redefining Identity," in *The Crisis of Socialism in Europe*, ed. Christiane Lemke and Gary Marks (Durham, N.C., 1992), 176. These issues are discussed in detail in Eric D. Weitz, "The Ever-Present Other: Communism in the Making of West Germany," in *The Miracle Years: A Cultural History of West Germany, 1949-1968*, ed. Hanna Schissler (Princeton, 2001), 219-32. In Jeffrey Herf's more appreciative analysis the "anti-totalitarian consensus" was that of a political culture of "militant democracy." Jeffrey Herf, *War by Other Means: Soviet Power, West German Resistance, and the Battle of Euromissiles* (New York, 1991), 5.

41. Note that Kurt Schumacher, the SPD's first postwar leader, rejected this exculpatory use of the concept of totalitarianism. Although he was anticommunist and often used the concept of totalitarianism, he blamed Nazism on the German elite and believed that it, or at least individuals within it, should be held responsible. Significantly though, Konrad Adenauer and the CDU, and not Kurt Schumacher and the SPD, governed the BRD in the 1950s. On Schumacher see Jeffrey Herf, *Divided Memory: The Nazi Past in the Two Germanys* (Cambridge, Mass., 1997), 239-61.

42. On the theory of totalitarianism in Germany see Gleason, *Totalitarianism*, 157-66. The failures of denazification are discussed with reference to this question in Wolfgang Krieger, "Germany," in *The Origins of the Cold War in Europe: International Perspectives*, ed. David Reynolds (New Haven, 1994), 159-61. On the recasting of Germany as a victim nation see: Elizabeth Heineman, "The Hour of the Woman: Memories of Germany's 'Crisis Years' and West German National Identity," in Schissler, *The Miracle Years*, 21-56; Frank Biess, "Survivors of Totalitarianism: Returning POWs and the Reconstruction of Masculine Citizenship in West Germany, 1945-1955," in Schissler, *The Miracle Years*, 57-82, especially p. 58 from which I quote and paraphrase; and Robert G. Moeller, "Remembering the War in a Nation of Victims: West German Pasts in the 1950s," in Schissler, *The Miracle Years*, 83-109. The marginalization of the Holocaust in the United States by the concept of totalitarianism is discussed in Peter Novick, *The Holocaust in American Life* (New York, 1999), 85-87.

43. Biess, "Survivors of Totalitarianism," 72.

44. Ian Buruma, *The Wages of Guilt: Memories of War in Germany and Japan* (New York, 1994), 55-56.

45. Compare with the very different preoccupations of Jacques Tati's *Mon oncle* (1958), the French cinematic masterpiece on the *Trente glorieuses*. On the reception of "The Marriage of Maria Braun" see Joyce Rheuban, ed., *The Marriage of Maria Braun: Rainer Werner Fassbinder, Director*, vol. 4 of *Rutgers Films in Print* (New Brunswick, N.J., 1986).

46. The broad impact of *Ostpolitik* on the West German Left is emphasized by Herf, *War by Other Means*, chapters 3 and 5.

47. Robert G. Moeller, "War Stories: The Search for a Usable Past in the Federal Republic of Germany," *American Historical Review* 101, 4 (1996): 1040-43.

48. Renzo De Felice, interviewed by Michael A. Ledeen, *Fascism: An Informal Introduction to Its Theory and Practice* (New Brunswick, N.J., 1976), 109, 111. On Italian uses of the concept of totalitarianism see also Gleason, *Totalitarianism*, 144-46 and 156-57.

49. Bruno Groppo and Gianni Riccamboni, "Le Parti communiste italien face aux crises du 'socialisme réel,'" *Communisme* 3 (1983): 65-83; Stephen Gundle, *Between Hollywood and Moscow: The Italian Communists and the Challenge of Mass Culture, 1943-1991* (Durham, N.C., 2000), 91 and 143 for the quotes and passim; Paul Ginsborg, *A History of Contemporary Italy: Society and Politics, 1943-1988* (New York, 1990), chap. 10; Marc Lazar, *Maisons rouges: les Partis communistes français et italien de la Libération à nos jours* (Paris, 1992).

50. Borden W. Painter, Jr., "Renzo De Felice and the Historiography of Italian Fascism," *American Historical Review* 95, 2 (April 1990): 391-405 and 403 for the quote. Simone Neri Serneri, "A Past to be Thrown Away? Politics and History in the Italian Resistance," *Contemporary European History* 4, 3 (1995): 367-81; James Edward Miller, "Who Chopped Down that Cherry Tree? The Italian Resistance in History and Politics, 1945-1998," *Journal of Modern Italian Studies* 4, 1 (1999): 37-54.

51. De Felice cited in R. J. B. Bosworth, *The Italian Dictatorship: Problems and Perspectives in the Interpretation of Mussolini and Fascism* (New York, 1998), 101. For a discussion and critique of De Felice's comparison between Italian fascism and German Nazism see Alexander De Grand, "Renzo De Felice, Fascism and Nazism: Non-Converging Parallels?" *Italian Quarterly* 141-42 (summer-fall 1999): 71-76.

52. Renzo De Felice, *Fascism*, 109.

53. Renzo De Felice, *Le Fascisme: Un totalitarisme à l'italienne?* trans. Catherine Brice, Sophie Gherardi-Pouthier, and Francesca Mosca (Paris, 1988), 24-33, 42, 71-73 (a French version of De Felice's *Lo Stato totalitario (1936-1940)* [1981]).

54. Emilio Gentile, "Renzo De Felice: A Tribute," *Journal of Contemporary History* 32, 2 (1997): 149.

55. Georges-Henri Soutou, "France," in Reynolds, *The Origins of the Cold War in Europe*, 96.

56. Sabine Dullin, "Les Interprétations françaises du système soviétique," in *Le Siècle des communismes*, eds. Michel Dreyfus, Bruno Groppo, Claudio Sergio Ingerflom, Roland Lew, Claude Pennetier, Bernard Pudal, and Serge Wolikow (Paris, 2000), 47-49.

57. These lectures were published as Raymond Aron, *Démocratie et totalitarisme* (Paris, 1965).

58. Elisabeth Young-Bruehl, *Hannah Arendt: For Love of the World* (New Haven, 1982), 281. Note though that the third part of *The Origins of Totalitarianism*, "Totalitarianism," was published in French translation in Jacques Julliard's "Politique" collection at Seuil in 1972. Julliard says that internal reviewers at Seuil—considering the book too obscure and the concept of totalitarianism itself problematic—were opposed to its publication, but that when the book came out the reactions to it were less hostile than expected. Jacques Julliard, interview with the author, Paris, France, 21 June 1994.

59. To facilitate comparison, the term "New Left" is used here to describe the new, radical currents of the 1960s and early 1970s. It should not be taken to be a translation of the French "nouvelle gauche."

60. The term "resistancialist" is that of Henry Rousso. See Henry Rousso, *The Vichy Syndrome: History and Memory in France Since 1944*, trans. Arthur Goldhammer (Cambridge, Mass., 1991).

61. Traverso, "Introduction," 86.

62. This mode of historical exposition is not unique to French intellectual history. A common trope of recent denunciations of the West German antifascist intellectual politics of the 1970s and 1980s is superficial and invidious comparison between the supposed salutary shock that *The Gulag Archipelago* gave French intellectuals and the refusal of West German intellectuals to heed Solzhenitsyn's message. See, for example, Christian Joppke, *East German Dissidents and the Revolution of 1989: Social Movement in a Leninist Regime* (New York, 1995), 198 and Peter Schneider, *The German Comedy: Scenes of Life After the Wall*, trans. Philip Boehm and Leigh Hafrey (New York, 1991), 72.
63. Paul M. Cohen, *Freedom's Moment: An Essay on the French Idea of Liberty from Rousseau to Foucault* (Chicago, 1997).

Chapter 1

FROM FELLOW-TRAVELING TO REVISIONISM

The Fate of the Revolutionary Project, 1944-1974

The Limits of Revolutionary Politics and Fellow-Traveling in the Cold War

The experience of war and occupation profoundly shaped the politics of French intellectuals in the years after the Liberation. The sacrifices and suffering of the war years created a popular "expectation of justice"[1] and a desire for radical social and political change among intellectuals. The wartime division of friend and enemy, resistor and Nazi, between whom no middle ground was possible, brought intellectuals into a Manichean world in which refusal to choose sides became a choice for an intolerable status quo. Political violence and historicist ideas of political justice gained legitimacy following the violence of the Occupation and the vindication of de Gaulle, the Resistance, and their violence by history and the Liberation purges.[2] Yet, while it became an imperative for intellectuals to establish social justice, if necessary by means of violent revolution, the experience of fascism also restored the validity of liberal and humanist values, under attack since the late 1920s. The defense and extension of liberty and individual freedoms lay at the core of the Resistance ideal of the good society and found clear expression in the charter of the Conseil national de la Résistance and the ethical code of the Comité national des écrivains (CNE), for example. Although this should not be surprising, even the political project of the left-wing existentialist journal *Les Temps modernes* was, wrote Jean-Paul Sartre, "to militate in our writings in favor of freedom of the person *and* the socialist revolution."[3]

Notes for this section begin on page 75.

Any interpretation of the politics of the postwar French intellectual Left must take seriously its aspirations to liberty and democracy or risk failing to comprehend its evolution in the 1950s and beyond. After the war these aspirations were treated as the goal of a Manichean and potentially violent revolutionary politics, often associated although seldom identified with communism, that was willing to accept great individual and collective sacrifices for a better future. When the messianic urges of the Liberation dissipated and the failures of communism became clearer in the late 1940s and 1950s, intellectuals of the noncommunist Left demanded that liberty and democracy be better secured within political projects, revolutionary or otherwise. Their persistent belief that liberty and democracy could be reconciled with revolution may seem naïve in retrospect, but this is beside the point because it was the left-wing intellectuals' demand that the next revolution be different that guided the evolution of their politics. Furthermore, their politics found sustenance in aspects of French republican and revolutionary political culture that, far from being an obstacle to the critique of totalitarianism of the 1970s, actually prepared the ground for it.

This delicate postwar balance between revolution and liberty can be seen in the critique of Kantian ethics, a key phenomenon in the intellectual politics of the immediate postwar period. Kantian ethics had dominated republican thought and education during the Third Republic, serving as a foundation for a republican secular ethics founded on the individual's use of reason that, while individualistic, refused to allow a person's particular interest to become the basis for conduct and emphasized the individual's duty towards others.[4] First challenged in the 1930s as the social question gained new prominence, the Third Republic entered into a general political crisis, and the older generation and its battles were eclipsed, Kantian ethics collapsed within the intellectual Left following the experience of war, occupation, and resistance.[5]

In the influential writings of Simone de Beauvoir, Maurice Merleau-Ponty, and Jean-Paul Sartre, the postwar critique of Kantian ethics was not a total rejection of all that it represented.[6] Rather, these intellectuals had come to conclude from the wartime experience that, while the realization of Kant's "kingdom of ends" remained the goal of politics, it was naïve to believe that action true to Kant's categorical imperative could achieve it. The existence of men of evil will (that is, collaborators and Nazis) acting contrary to the Kantian project rendered deeply problematic recourse to the categorical imperative as a guide to action.[7] It was not possible to act toward these men in such a way that one's conduct could be considered universally valid. They had to be combated. Liberty, as the history of the Resistance indicated, could not be realized without at least the threat of recourse to violence. Good intentions were not enough; the years of war had offered ample illustration of their impotence compared to the actions of those who understood what was efficacious in a given historical situation. Nor did it seem possible after the war to be "free on one's own"; liberty did not exist independent of the community of the liberty of others. Yet, Merleau-Ponty stressed, it was "not a matter of renouncing our values of 1939, but of fulfilling them."[8] Similarly, Sartre's discussion of the short-comings of Kantian ethics concluded with a rousing call for a liberating Revolution to realize Kant's kingdom of ends: "Thus, we must at the same time teach one group that the kingdom of ends cannot be realized without revolution and the other group that revolution is conceivable only if it prepares the kingdom of ends.... In short, we must militate, in our writings, in favor of the freedom of the person *and* the socialist revolution. It has often been claimed that they are not reconcilable. It is our job to show tirelessly that they imply each other."[9]

Intellectuals' privileged vehicle for revolutionary change was the PCF. Because of the party's important role in the Resistance after the German invasion of the USSR, the PCF could plausibly present itself as a nationalist *"parti des 75,000 fusillés"* (party of the 75,000 Resistance martyrs). Communist martyrdom made the PCF appear to be virtuous, a quality that resonated with the republican tradition and was especially attractive after the discrediting of the Third Republic by its corruption.[10] Further, the concrete place of communism in postwar French politics forced it to the center of left-wing intellectuals' political calculations. With about one-quarter of the vote, control over the labor movement, and an important media presence after the Liberation purge and reorganization of the press, the PCF was an enormous force in French politics. Programs of progressive reform or revolutionary change could not be accomplished without its cooperation. Those with reservations about Soviet socialism could be encouraged by the PCF's proposed French path to socialism, its appeal to national traditions, and its suggestion that there would be continuity between the bourgeois democratic revolution and socialism. The PCF's politics in the immediate postwar years indicated that these were more than empty words. Its support of national reconstruction and the competence and pragmatic reformism that it displayed when exercising responsibility in the government helped allay fears and offered reasons to hope that national renewal could develop through the agency of the PCF.[11]

Yet, for many intellectuals the PCF's close relations with the Soviet Union were an asset, not a liability. The USSR enjoyed a favorable reputation at the conclusion of World War II because of its central role in defeating the Nazis and the hope that it offered for the future.[12] The Soviet victory vindicated the rapid industrialization of the Soviet Union in the 1930s, and for intellectuals who, like Edgar Morin, were knowledgeable of Stalinist repression it "washed away all the past crimes when it did not justify them."[13] In the wake of a war of sacrifices, intellectuals applauded sacrifice for the collective good, like that which they presumed had occurred in the Soviet Union. When in 1949 the left-wing newspaper *Combat* asked "if the future of socialism implies individual and collective sacrifices, is the result worth it?" and "must one sacrifice a generation to others?" the overwhelming majority of respondents said yes to both questions.[14] Read in this climate, Arthur Koestler's *Darkness at Noon* (which appeared in French under the more ambiguous title *Zéro et l'infini*) led many intellectuals closer to communism. Instead of being repelled by Rubashov's fate, the future historian Emmanuel Le Roy Ladurie believed, for example, that "Rubashov was right to sacrifice his life and especially his revolutionary honor so that the best of all possible regimes could be established one day."[15] Following Alexandre Kojève's enormously influential reading of Hegel that emphasized the realization of truth through violence in the master-slave dialectic, Merleau-Ponty argued in *Humanism and Terror* that communism's legitimacy could not be denied by citing liberal principles or the pure morality that it violates. If revolutionary violence leads to a humanist future it might be justified.[16]

Intellectuals' attraction to communism had its limits. *Humanism and Terror* left open the possibility that communism would not be legitimate if not ultimately humanistic. Many leading intellectuals were fellow travelers, but few actually joined the PCF, if only because they wanted to maintain their freedom from party discipline.[17] Although a number of intellectuals prominent in the 1970s and 1980s—such as the historians François Furet and Le Roy Ladurie, the sociologist Edgar Morin, and the philosopher Michel Foucault—had been party members while students in elite educational institutions in the years 1944 to 1956, the younger generation did not join the party *en masse* in these years. Even in the late 1940s at the height of the PCF's influence only about 15 percent of the students at the École normale supérieure were card-carrying communists.[18] For most left-wing intellectuals, the PCF was an indispensable if difficult ally in the revolutionary project. The hardening of communist positions during the Cold War would severely test that alliance, ultimately pushing intellectuals away from French communism and inaugurating their disenchantment with the Soviet utopia.

Beginning in France with the expulsion of the PCF from the Ramadier government in May 1947, the Cold War quickly polarized French politics. In the October 1947 municipal elections the Socialist Party (SFIO) dropped its alliance with the PCF, and De Gaulle's anticommunist Rassemblement du peuple français (RPF) won 38 percent of the vote. Cold War Third Force governments quickly moved to confront striking workers by repressing the strike waves of November to December 1947 and October to December 1948 and sought to systematically dismantle communist positions in society, administration, and government. In December 1947 the labor union Force ouvrière was formed with the aid of the AFL-CIO to challenge the communist-controlled CGT. The government and governing parties engaged in a propaganda war against the PCF aimed at delegitimizing it by its association with the USSR. Guy Mollet contended that the PCF was to the East and not on the Left, and his SFIO used a map locating concentration camps in the USSR as a poster in the 1951 election.[19] The pseudo-movement Paix et liberté, created in 1949 with American encouragement and the French government's financial support and grant of air time on state-controlled radio, poured enormous resources into a nonstop, no holds barred propaganda campaign against communism over the next half-decade.[20] Pressure on the PCF reached its height during the Pinay government when in 1952 after the Ridgeway riot the communist leader Jacques Duclos was arrested and absurdly accused of planning an insurrection. The PCF responded to the onset of the Cold War by adopting class against class rhetoric and accusing the SFIO of opening the door to fascism. Yet, until the miners' strike of late 1948 it maintained hopes of escaping isolation and perhaps even reentering the government. After 1948, French communism, totally ostracized and without immediate political prospects in France, fell back upon a strategy of defending the USSR and a cultural politics based on Zhdanov's distinction between the two camps.[21]

War psychology gripped the nation and the political class in the late 1940s and early 1950s. According to polls, in July 1947 35 percent and in October 1948 41 percent of the French believed that a confrontation between the superpowers was probable, and in August 1950 39 percent believed that a third world war would break out within the next five years.[22] Peasants in the town of Roussillon (Vaucluse), fearful of a new war and occupation, planted wheat as disaster insurance and refused to make long-term investments—considered naïve given the situation.[23] De Gaulle's RPF, a potent electoral force from the October 1947 municipal elections through the 1951 legislative elections, made its case to the electorate by arguing that a global catastrophe was pending, in which case it would be the salvation of France.

With the onset of the Cold War in 1947 many left-wing intellectuals took up the defense of the PCF and the USSR out of fear of fascism, in reaction to the repression of communism in French society, and to keep the hope invested in these forces for radical politics alive. As the PCF and the USSR retreated from their relative postwar openness into dogmatism—evident in the Eastern European show trials of Kostov and Rajk, the anti-Titoist campaign of 1949, and the PCF's handling of these events—intellectuals of the noncommunist Left tried to create a space for a distinctive left-wing politics outside of the two blocs. These efforts were all unsuccessful. The Rassemblement démocratique révolutionnaire, founded in February 1948 by intellectuals including Sartre, David Rousset, and Paul Fraisse who sought to create a foundation for a new political party that would reconcile liberty and revolution, political democracy and economic democracy, national independence and world peace, collapsed before the end of 1949 after dividing over Rousset's rapprochement with the Americans. Likewise, the Combattants de la paix, an organization founded in February 1948 by former resisters seeking to defend the ideals of the Resistance in the face of Cold War politics, only functioned independently of the two blocs for a little more than a year before the PCF gained control of it in

April 1949 and oriented its politics around the theme of the battle for peace as defined by the Comintern. Following the communist takeover, leading noncommunist intellectuals either were expelled (in the case of Jean Cassou) or resigned (in the case of Jean-Marie Domenach) from the organization. Although it escaped institutional takeover because it was a movement of opinion and not an organization, French neutralism of 1949 to 1951 fared no better. Its critique of the French integration into the Atlantic alliance and subordination to the U.S. and its call for armed neutrality had little immediate impact on French policy and were opposed by all major political forces. When the left-wing weekly *L'Observateur*, founded in 1950 by Claude Bourdet, Gilles Martinet, and Roger Stéphane with a neutralist and anticolonial vocation, linked neutralism to a strategy for building a popular front and reconstructing the French Left in 1951, it failed miserably.[24]

There was, the failure of these efforts to forge a third way shows, little room for a political alternative for intellectuals between the American and Soviet camps internationally and De Gaulle's RPF (considered fascist by intellectuals on the Left) and the PCF (considered totalitarian by intellectuals on the Right) domestically. Because the center would not hold, intellectual politics became increasingly binary and Manichean in its logic. Intellectual sociability revolved around the question of communism. The search for truth was often obscured by the desire not to aid the enemy as critiques of communism and the Soviet Union became specifically directed at delegitimizing and ostracizing the PCF. On the Right, intellectuals associated with the RPF and its review *Liberté de l'esprit*—such as Claude Mauriac, Max-Pol Fouchet, André Malraux, Raymond Aron, and Jules Monnerot—were united only by their anticommunism and antitotalitarianism.[25] *Liberté de l'esprit*, like the Congress for Cultural Freedom, rejected all dialogue with communism and regarded anyone who would countenance a political alliance with the PCF as a political untouchable.[26] On the Left, an open articulation of a sustained critique of communism proved to be very difficult. Still, many intellectuals of the noncommunist Left began to take note of communism's failures and develop critical perspectives that would emerge more clearly in the latter half of the 1950s and in the 1960s.

The Kravchenko and Rousset affairs of 1949 to 1951 offer an excellent illustration of both the character of Cold War ideological debate and the drift of left-wing intellectuals away from communism. The French debate on Victor Kravchenko's *I Chose Freedom* ostensibly centered on the question of whether Kravchenko's claim that concentration camps existed in the Soviet Union was correct.[27] The failure of French intellectuals of the Left to take Kravchenko's side or directly and rigorously address the questions he raised has been interpreted as an indication of their political and moral bankruptcy. The Kravchenko affair might be seen more profitably as one of the best examples of the general failure of public debate about communism to advance along anything like a truth-seeking agenda during the Cold War.

Published at the onset of the Cold War in 1947 by Éditions S.E.L.F., a publisher known to be reactionary, *I Chose Freedom* quickly came under attack in a tendentious article, "Comment fut fabriqué Kravchenko," in the communist-controlled journal *Les Lettres françaises*.[28] Responding to the article's accusation that Kravchenko and his book were frauds, Kravchenko brought *Les Lettres françaises* to court for defamation, relishing the opportunity to take on the PCF and undermine the image of the USSR in France. His lawyer Georges Izard and the French and American governments, which gave Kravchenko logistical support, had the same hopes for the case. The PCF also welcomed the trial, believing that it offered the party an opportunity to score political points.

Although the general context of the trial did not help him, Kravchenko did much to damage his own cause. A former Soviet official who had sought political asylum in the U.S. in 1944 and had testified in the U.S. House Un-American Activities Committee, Kravchenko was rightly suspected of being linked to the CIA and American propaganda efforts in France. The participation of Eugene Lyons in the writing of Kravchenko's book gave some credibility to the PCF's claim that *I Chose Freedom* was a Cold War fabrication. Further, his abrasive personality—which echoed the times in its stridency—violent conduct, contradictory statements, and occasional lying undermined his efforts, especially in a France afraid of war. Not only intellectuals on the Left, but also those on the Right distanced themselves from Kravchenko. Not a single significant French personality testified on his behalf. Arthur Koestler, although solicited, did not testify. David Rousset kept his distance from Kravchenko. For Albert Camus Kravchenko had gone "from the profession of profiteer of the Soviet regime to that of profiteer of the bourgeois regime." Even the survivors of the Soviet camps who testified for Kravchenko were troubled by him. Kravchenko quarreled with the Ukrainians over the question of Ukrainian independence. His star witness Margarete Buber-Neumann found Kravchenko to be "a policeman, a hard, harsh, and violent man who treats people like pawns."[29]

Once underway, the trial entered immediately into the logic of internal French politics and conflicts over broader political beliefs. *Les Lettres françaises*, for example, charged that Kravchenko was a traitor to the USSR and, because the USSR had defeated the Nazis, a traitor to France. Izard counterattacked by contending that Maurice Thorez, the general secretary of the PCF, should be considered a traitor by virtue of his desertion from the French army in 1939. There is nothing exceptional about the French turn that the trial took. French internal political concerns had been at the center of the debates over Gide's *Retour de l'URRS* and the Moscow trials in the 1930s.[30] The renewal of debate on the USSR in the 1970s would not be any different in this regard.

Although the orientation of the proceedings around French politics did not help the truth emerge, it would be wrong to conclude that the communists won a moral victory or that French intellectuals were wholly unaffected by what this trial or the concurrent massive influx of other information about the Soviet camps revealed about Soviet repression.[31] The court ruled in favor of Kravchenko, and at least the general public, well informed by the large echo the trial received on the radio and in the press, sided with him. Even within its own constituency, the PCF was unable to control opinion.[32] During the trial the PCF, which had first denied that there were any camps in the USSR, was forced to acknowledge their existence. It fell back to the argument that they were reeducational work camps, not concentration camps.

The evolution of the attitudes of intellectuals of the noncommunist Left is visible in the differences between the *Les Lettres françaises*/Rousset defamation trial of 1950 to 1951 (which also revolved around the question of the camps) and the Kravchenko affair of 1949. To be sure, on one point there is a great similarity: left-wing intellectuals refused to back Rousset's commission to investigate concentration camps in the USSR because they considered him to have placed it within the Western bloc. Yet, whereas both the left-wing Christian personalist journal *Esprit* and *Les Temps Modernes* had been nearly silent during the *Les Lettres françaises*/Kravchenko trial, at the end of 1949 *Esprit* began to take the issue of the camps more seriously and demand that more light be shed on them; and in January 1950 Merleau-Ponty and Sartre, while continuing to hold that the USSR was largely a progressive force, recognized the extent of the Soviet camps, their discrediting of the USSR's claim to have achieved socialism, and the need to analyze their significance.[33]

During the *Les Lettres françaises*/Rousset trial, the PCF, aware of the damage inflicted by the Kravchenko trial, tried to silence debate. From the beginning of the trial it recognized the existence of the camps and argued that they were reeducational, but it sought to avoid discussing the issue and concentrated on attacking the government's politics. Most significantly, of the innumerable fellow travelers the PCF had been able to line up to testify for it during the Kravchenko trial—including Jean Cassou, Louis Martin-Chauffier, Vercors, Emmanuel d'Astier de la Vigerie, and Pierre Cot—only two (Fernand Grenier and J. M. Hermann) returned to testify for it in the new trial. Except for Louis de Villefosse, all other witnesses called in defense of *Les Lettres françaises* during the later trial were PCF members. Further, Martin-Chauffier joined Rousset's commission of inquiry into the camps. Left-wing intellectuals did not generally support Rousset, but neither did the PCF win the debate on the camps.[34]

Although there was no extensive examination of the gulag by the intellectual Left in the 1950s, the progressive, revolutionary quality of the USSR was increasingly questioned following the debates on the camps and the anti-Titoist show trials in Eastern Europe. Likewise, the PCF, facing counterpropaganda challenging its assertions and the decline of its press empire saw—as the Kravchenko affair demonstrated—its hold on both general and intellectual opinion decline.[35] While Sartre captured the headlines (and continues to preoccupy historians) by laying aside his earlier criticism of the PCF and the USSR to adopt a defense of both of them that quickly became an apology for Bolshevism, many, if not most, other left-wing intellectuals began to reconsider and retreat from their *engagement*—notably their fellow-traveling—of the 1940s.[36] Three examples illustrate this shift: Merleau-Ponty and Hegelian political thought, the journal *Esprit*, and the Comité national des écrivains.

As new doubts about the progressiveness of the USSR emerged and the Cold War froze political possibilities, the Hegelian belief that history has a meaning and direction was undermined. In the case of Merleau-Ponty the Korean War precipitated the end of his Marxist *attentisme* and the hope he had placed in the USSR in *Humanism and Terror*. He believed in this new situation that his earlier position had been a "disguised adherence" to communism. Afraid that anticommunism would lead to war, he defined his politics as acommunist rather than anticommunist.[37] Critical of what he would later call the "ultra-Bolshevik" politics expounded by Sartre in *The Communists and Peace*, Merleau-Ponty cut his ties with *Les Temps modernes* in 1953 when it became clear to him that Sartre would not allow dissenting views to be expressed or dialogue undertaken in the journal's pages. Merleau-Ponty retreated to a revised, more modest conception of intellectual *engagement*, a critique of revolutionary theory, and reflection on liberalism.[38] The other major postwar exponents of a Hegelian approach to politics joined Merleau-Ponty in moving away from Hegelianism. Jean Hyppolite retreated from Hegel through Heidegger, effectively dropping the question of political action in the process. Less willing to abandon politics, Eric Weil returned to Kant in an effort to find universal standards by which to judge historical change. Alexandre Kojève moved from a militant to an ironic Hegelianism, concluding that the end of History had arrived and it is an iron cage. In these and other cases, the retreat from Hegel and History was a retreat from political certainty.[39]

Hegelians were not the only ones attracted to revolution and the PCF. The second most influential journal on the intellectual Left next to *Les Temps modernes*, *Esprit* under the leadership of its founder Emmanuel Mounier, committed itself after the war to *engagement* and the achievement of a synthesis between Christian personalism and the French tradition of humanist socialism.[40] *Esprit* became a fellow traveler of the PCF, which, as the representative of the proletariat (often seen at *Esprit* in Christian terms as the poor), was an ally that *Esprit* found necessary for its revolutionary project. *Esprit* also found the PCF to be a useful partner in its more concrete political campaigns, such as those against de Gaulle's RPF, American domination and the Marshall Plan, "bacteriological warfare" in Korea, the European Defense Community, and the Indochinese War. Although Mounier and *Esprit* began to question the great hopes that they had placed in the communist mystique as early as 1947, only in late 1949 and early

1950 would *Esprit* clearly break from its efforts to accommodate communism when it demanded more information about concentration camps in the USSR, criticized the official communist explanation of Titoism, denounced the Kostov and Rajk show trials, and thereby brought the wrath of the PCF down upon it.[41] By the time of his sudden death in April 1950, Mounier was disillusioned about the prospect of revolution, moving away from Marxism, and coming to the conclusion that one could act neither with the communists nor without them.[42] While survivals of philo-communism can be found in *Esprit*'s pages after 1950, the journal under the direction of Albert Béguin (1950-57) continued to drift away from communism. Beginning in the winter of 1953-54, *Esprit*, increasingly conscious of France's economic weakness, started to develop pragmatic and reformist ideas that placed the *redressement* of France before the politics of liberation and would become increasingly important in its politics in the late 1950s and early 1960s.[43]

Finally, the important history of fellow-traveling and its disillusionment in the Comité national des écrivains (CNE) illustrates trends in the late 1940s and early 1950s. Founded in 1941, the CNE emerged from the war as the premier Resistance writers' organization. Immediately after the Liberation it took the lead in the purge of the literary world, creating a blacklist of authors whom it sought to exclude from publishing because they had collaborated during the war. Although differences over the blacklist led to some high profile resignations such as that of Jean Paulhan, the CNE only grew in stature in the immediate aftermath of the war. Membership rose from some 50 writers at the Liberation to 230 in May 1947.[44] The CNE annual book sale became a major literary and *mondain* event. At the February 1946 CNE General Assembly the communists took control of the organization. The communist writer Louis Aragon became the CNE's general secretary and the fellow traveler Jean Cassou replaced the Gaullist Jacques Debû-Bridel as CNE president. While it was careful not to engage the CNE in the most politically controversial issues, the PCF maneuvered the organization to support its peace movement and other communist causes. It defended the Chilean communist writer Néruda and the Greek communist writer Kédros, raised its voice against the imprisonment of the American writer Howard Fast for refusing to cooperate with the House Un-American Activities Committee, and protested the attacks on the PCF at the time of the Ridgeway riots. The CNE's one-sided defense of liberty during the Cold War led to the slow erosion of its membership, which had declined to 176 by March 1952. Discontent came to a head in early 1953 when Serge Groussard called upon the *Comité directeur* of the CNE to denounce the anti-Semitism of the Slansky trial in Czechoslovakia. When it declined to do so, some nineteen CNE members resigned, including the past CNE presidents Jean Cassou and Louis Martin-Chauffier, after which hardly any noncommunist members of the CNE's first clandestine committee remained in the association. To save the CNE from collapse, Elsa

Triolet, who along with Aragon ensured PCF control over the CNE, found it necessary to amend its charter so as to prohibit it from addressing questions that were purely political or did not directly concern writers. The PCF retained control of the CNE, but at the price of losing its claim to be a national organization and restricting its purchase on events.[45]

The Revision of the Revolutionary Project and the Political Demobilization of Intellectuals in the Wake of the Hungarian Revolution and the Algerian War

Events in communist Europe in 1956 opened a new era in French intellectuals' evaluations of the USSR and decisively alienated most intellectuals from the PCF. Khrushchev's "secret" report on the crimes of Stalin at the Twentieth Congress of the Communist Party of the USSR in February 1956 dealt that year's first blow to the image of the USSR. Although most of the report's contents were not new, the identity of its author made it impossible to ignore the failures of Soviet socialism enumerated in the report. Of course, the Soviet leadership's self-criticism initially fueled hope for progress in the USSR,[46] but the brutal repression of the Hungarian Revolution in November 1956 quickly led left-wing intellectuals to other conclusions. Intellectuals throughout the noncommunist Left—in the pages of *Esprit, France observateur, L'Express,* and *Socialisme ou barbarie,* for example—unequivocally condemned the repression and the failures of the Soviet system that lay behind it.[47] By the end of 1956 the Soviet Union had lost much of the mystique surrounding it since the Liberation, and as a consequence, the double standards that had been evoked in its defense were decisively undermined. Indicative of this change in perspective was the replacement of Isaac Deutscher by François Fejtö as the dominant interpreter of current events in Eastern Europe for the noncommunist Left. Most intellectuals of the noncommunist Left would not tolerate Deutscher's contention that the Hungarians had taken de-Stalinization too far. They preferred Fejtö's celebration of the Hungarian workers' councils and his politics of a third way between communism and capitalism to Deutscher's Trotskyism.[48] Significantly, *Les Temps modernes,* while welcoming Fejtö's analysis, did not abandon Deutscher. Although Sartre condemned the invasion and distanced himself from the PCF and the USSR as a result of it, his explanation of the event partially excused the repression by invoking the danger of reaction in Hungary. Sartre argued that the dynamic that led to the repression had been created by a hasty de-Stalinization for which Eastern Europe was not ready. The positions of Sartre and *Les Temps modernes* went against the main current of reaction to the Hungarian Revolution and its repression.[49] More representative of the noncommunist intellectual Left was Maurice Merleau-Ponty, who brought final closure to the line of questioning opened by *Humanism and Terror* by arguing that "the only correct attitude is to see communism relatively as a fact without any special privilege."[50]

The critique of the USSR by left-wing intellectuals after 1956 was not absolute. Although the USSR would no longer be beyond criticism or function as a political model, left-wing intellectuals generally continued to believe that its socialization of the means of production was an important advance over capitalist regimes. They maintained hope that the USSR would eventually reconcile liberty and democracy with socialism. Not until 1968, when state-centered politics fell into disrepute and the invasion of Czechoslovakia forced further reevaluations of the USSR, did the Soviet system lose its last vestiges of legitimacy in the eyes of French intellectuals.[51] The attitudes of intellectuals were, as chapter 4 demonstrates, reflected in the language of their protests of human rights abuses in the USSR, which, between 1956 and 1968, invariably appealed to the good will of the Soviet leaders and the socialist principles of the regime.

Left-wing intellectuals did not adopt the concept of totalitarianism in their analyses of the USSR after 1956. It would have been most surprising if they had done so, given that the partisan political use of the word during the Cold War was fresh in their memory. The word "totalitarian" had functioned and continued to function as a sort of political atomic bomb, used by the Right to discredit the PCF and the USSR and occasionally used by the Left to attack the United States or advanced capitalism.[52] Furthermore, as we have seen in the introduction, intellectuals throughout Western Europe and the United States who had used the concept began to retreat from it after 1956. In France, even the Congress for Cultural Freedom replaced the problematic of totalitarianism with that of the end of ideologies in the late 1950s.[53] Raymond Aron, the foremost French exponent of the concept, moved in the same direction in his writings after 1956. In his lectures at the Sorbonne in the 1957-58 academic year, he argued that the USSR had been fully totalitarian only from 1934 to 1938 and from 1948 to 1952. In a 1957 essay he found Arendt's interpretation of the USSR in *The Origins of Totalitarianism* dangerous because it failed to allow for the possibility of a future evolution of the Soviet régime outside of totalitarianism. In his 1965 preface to his 1957-58 lectures he held that the USSR had liberalized in the interim; there had been a "return to daily life [that] dispels at the same time the illusions of the idealists and the nightmares of the prophets of doom."[54]

The PCF's reaction to the events of 1956 in Eastern Europe decisively alienated intellectuals outside the party and inaugurated a wave of discontent among communist intellectuals. Rather than take Khrushchev's criticisms of Stalinism to heart, the PCF denied the existence of his report and did everything it could to absorb the shock and resist de-Stalinization.[55] It crudely justified the Soviet invasion of Hungary as a reaction against the threat of fascism in Hungary. Although immediate defections from the PCF were limited by a defensive reaction following violent verbal and physical assaults on the party in November 1956, communist intellectuals gave unprecedented vent to their outrage, formed opposition groups within the party that thrived between 1956 and 1958, and left the party in large numbers in these same years.[56]

The blow to the PCF's influence among intellectuals outside the party was more immediate and dramatic. Significant *progressiste* fellow-traveling with the PCF came to an end in 1956. Communist front organizations like the Mouvement de la paix, L'Association France-URSS, and the CNE suffered large-scale resignations, after which they had little importance in French intellectual life. The CNE was challenged by a rival, the Union des écrivains pour la vérité, and was in danger of folding for financial reasons because the violent reaction to events in Hungary forced it to cancel its 1956 book sale. It would not survive the death of its principal organizer, Elsa Triolet, in 1970.[57] Further, many intellectuals concluded that the PCF was not an acceptable political partner as long as it had not de-Stalinized.[58] Left-wing intellectuals who had seen in the Republican Front elections of January 1956 the first step towards a new popular front decided that the PCF's response to the events of 1956 in the communist bloc discredited the party and ruled out any alliance with it. One immediate casualty of the tougher stance toward French communism was the leading association of intellectuals opposed to the Algerian War, the Comité d'action des intellectuels contre la poursuite de la guerre en Afrique du Nord, which fell apart over the question of its communist members' failure to protest repression in Hungary as vigorously as they protested the French war in Algeria.[59]

The founding of de Gaulle's Fifth Republic in 1958 was another important moment in the distancing of the French intellectual Left from the PCF. The PCF was unable to field effective resistance to de Gaulle's rise to power or the September 1958 referendum on the Constitution of the Fifth Republic (approved by just under 80 percent of those voting). After the November 1958 legislative elections, in which the PCF suffered a severe electoral hemorrhage, the PCF appeared to be a paralyzed and declining political force. Furthermore, de Gaulle's victories were widely interpreted as a failure of the working class. The landslide victory of the referendum confirmed emerging suspicions that the modernization of France, of which intellectuals were only now becoming conscious, was integrating the working class into society, decreasing its numbers, and diluting its revolutionary identity.[60] Not only had the USSR and the PCF been discredited by the end of the 1950s, but the proletariat was losing its centrality in the political projects of the French intellectual Left.

The radical political credentials of the PCF and the proletariat were further brought into question by the Algerian War. The PCF had dominated the opposition to the Indochinese War—which helps explain the persistence of Sartre's fellow-traveling—but failed to lend comparable support to the Algerian insurrection. Focusing its energies during the early years of

the Algerian War on defeating German rearmament and building a popular front alliance that would allow it to escape its Cold War political ghetto,
the PCF voted in March 1956 in favor of granting Guy Mollet's government "special powers" to prosecute the war and intervened to moderate
antiwar mobilizations like that of the *"rappelés"* in the autumn of 1955 and
the spring of 1956. Beyond considerations of political strategy, the PCF
had trouble identifying with a nationalist insurrection that was not led by
a Marxist party and was acutely aware of the reluctance of its working-
class base to support the anticolonial struggle in Algeria. Consequently, it
emphasized the need to develop a genuine popular movement against the
war and opposed illegal antiwar activity to the extent of expelling from the
party individuals who lent support to the FLN. It was the struggle against
the fascist Organisation de l'armée secrète (OAS) in the last year of the
war, and not Algerian independence, that finally mobilized the energies of
the PCF and the working class.[61]

The PCF's position and the *"national-mollettiste"* SFIO's prosecution of
the war forced the intellectuals critical of or opposed to the Algerian War
to organize outside of and against the established political parties of the
Left. Communists rallied to dissident communist groups like Tribune du
communisme, L'Étincelle, and La Voie communiste. Mendésistes and SFIO
defectors formed the Parti socialiste autonome (PSA) in 1958; and in 1960
the PSA, some of the dissident communists, and others dissatisfied with
the established Left formed the Parti socialiste unifié (PSU). In the vacuum
created by the failure of the traditional left-wing parties and the larger
labor movement to mount substantial resistance to the war, the Union
national des étudiants de France (UNEF) took a leading role in the antiwar
movement. In short, opposition to the Algerian War divorced intellectual
politics from the French political system. This autonomization of intellectual politics was only furthered by the failure of the parties of the Left to
mount a credible challenge to de Gaulle and the authoritarianism of his
Fifth Republic.[62]

Opposition to the war fueled a critique of the French state and the universalism of the French Left. Population displacements, internments, censorship, and torture above all else showed the French republican state to be
capable of the worst. The opposition made use of analogies between the
deeds of the French state and those of the Nazis and often cast itself as a
revival of the anti-Nazi resistance. In the course of the conflict the Left's
nationalism and paternalism, in short, its assimilationist civilizing mission,
was discredited by its concrete failure in Algeria and the use made of it to
justify the continuation of a brutal war. The moral bankruptcy of the "official Left" during the Algerian War would weigh heavily in the later antitotalitarian conduct of intellectuals who had played important roles in the
opposition to the Algerian War. Some of these intellectuals include: Jean
Daniel, a journalist at *L'Express* during the war and editor of *Le Nouvel
Observateur* in the 1970s; Paul Thibaud, director of the antiwar publication

Vérité-Liberté during the war and editor of *Esprit* beginning in 1977; Laurent Schwartz, a founding member of the Comité Audin against torture during the war and leader of the Comité international des mathématiciens, which intervened in favor of Soviet dissidents in the 1970s; and Jacques Julliard, a leading figure in the wartime UNEF and an important antitotalitarian political analyst in the 1970s. Their Algerian War experiences made these and other intellectuals wary of the French state, critical of universalistic or totalizing political programs, and suspicious of the parties of the Left. For some, like Jacques Julliard, the Algerian War was a decisive moment in their evolution. Julliard's disgust with the conduct of the parties of the Left during the war led him to abandon the idea of pursuing a political career, draw close to the labor movement, and study the history of the revolutionary syndicalist tradition. In retrospect, Julliard considered the Algerian War to be "the first foundation of antitotalitarianism."[63]

Although decolonization brought French universalism into question, one cannot argue that very many French intellectuals responded to the crises of communism and of the proletariat as a revolutionary actor by escaping to *tiers-mondisme*, that is, transferring their allegiances to third-world revolutionary movements in the expectation that these were the agents of history that would bring about a socialist transformation abroad and perhaps even in the metropole.[64] One should not exaggerate the critique of French universalism's depth or pace of development. For one, few intellectuals would ever consider a former colony or any other third-world country to be the agent of France's history. Intellectuals' critiques of the Algerian War were predominantly ethical—as in the protests against torture in which the universality of French civilization went largely unquestioned—or were expressions of concern about what the war was doing to France: corrupting it by the brutal, dirty, and immoral pacification required to win and creating a political dynamic favorable to the triumph of fascism in France.[65] Only a tiny minority of French intellectuals directly supported the Algerian FLN and only some individuals within that tiny minority conceived of their actions within the framework of instituting socialism in either Algeria or France.[66] In unequivocally supporting illegal and indeed revolutionary action, Sartre and *Les Temps modernes* were isolated, and they knew it. Intellectuals at *Esprit*, for example, spurned *Les Temps modernes*'s linkage of the movement against the war with revolution. Jean-Marie Domenach, its director, sharply criticized the manifesto of *tiers-mondisme* that was Sartre's preface to Franz Fanon's *The Wretched of the Earth*, and Jean Daniel, then *L'Express*'s primary correspondent on the Algerian War, accused *Les Temps modernes* in an *Esprit* article of May 1960 of consecrating the FLN in the same manner that Stalinist intellectuals had consecrated the PCF. Within the pages of *France observateur* François Furet's journalism echoed this criticism of *Les Temps modernes*'s revolutionary internationalism. In 1967 Cornelius Castoriadis explained *Socialisme ou barbarie*'s long-standing rejection of *tiers-mondisme* in the following terms: "if the modern part of the world is irredeemably rotten, it would be absurd to think that the revolutionary destiny of humanity could be accomplished in the other part [i.e., the third world]."[67]

At the conclusion of the Algerian War, intellectuals returned to metropolitan concerns, notably the entry of French society into modernity.[68] Even *Les Temps modernes* returned to Europe after the war. André Gorz, who as the journal's political editor led its efforts to study capitalism and the working class in contemporary Europe, argued in 1963 that socialist revolutions in the third world were not possible and that industrialized states were the principal political arena.[69] As for Sartre, he believed that although the Cuban Revolution was a valid model for Latin America, it was not for Europe.[70] There was never enormous interest in *tiers-mondiste* publications. *Partisans*, the leading *tiers-mondiste* journal, had no more than 450 subscribers and its print runs were between 3,500 and 4,000 copies.[71]

Most intellectuals were cautious in their evaluations of revolution and communism in Cuba, Latin America, Vietnam, and China and issued early warnings of the dangers of revolutionary violence in them.[72] To again take the example of *Esprit*, its special issue of 1961 on the Cuban Revolution suspended judgment, but not without raising the possibility that it might become terroristic or totalitarian.[73] *Esprit* also steered clear of Maoism, viewing it critically and seeing it as irrelevant to France.[74] Despite his enthusiasm for the Cuban Revolution and for Chinese communism when he visited China in 1955, Sartre, often portrayed as the *tiers-mondiste par excellence*, systematically refused, for lack of information, to pass judgment on the Chinese Cultural Revolution. Simone de Beauvoir likewise refused, she wrote, to "grant China that blind confidence that the USSR formerly aroused in so many hearts." [75]

The enthusiasm that some—especially from the younger generation—showed for third-world revolutions was not in opposition to, but in accordance with a revision of ideas about revolutionary politics. The Cuban Revolution was attractive in its early years precisely because it did not appear to be like the popular democracies and seemed to have neither bureaucratized nor crushed liberty.[76] As hopes placed in the Cuban Revolution faded, Che Guevara emerged in relief, through his criticisms of the Soviet Union and his revolutionary dynamism, as the symbol of the "refusal to become established, the refusal of bureaucracy."[77] Interest in the Chinese Cultural Revolution followed similar assumptions about its alterity vis-à-vis existing models of revolution.[78] Insofar as intellectuals attracted to third-world revolutions were projecting onto them French utopias, disillusionment with the failure of these revolutions would be at most secondary in turning intellectuals away from revolutionary politics and towards a critique of totalitarianism.

In sum, the Algerian War probably did more to undermine and destroy than to construct in the field of intellectual politics. The republican state, the parties of the Left, and their universalistic politics were all discredited by the Algerian War, and the working class showed itself to be a conservative force in the battle over decolonization. While many left-wing intellectuals rallied to the PSU, it proved to be incapable of attaining a central place in the political system; consequently, the long-term trend was towards a divorce of French intellectuals of the noncommunist Left from electoral politics. And, while some dabbled in third-world revolutionary utopias, actors in the third world would not be able to fill the place previously occupied in the revolutionary imagination by the working class. The revolutionary subject fragmented. After the Algerian War, intellectuals and especially students could appear to be revolutionary because of the leading role they had played in the antiwar movement. Furthermore, as French intellectuals turned inward and away from political parties, Frantz Fanon's emphasis on the revolutionary potential of the third-world peasantry and the lumpenproletariat of the colonies was converted into a focus on the most exploited and marginal groups within French society. In the form of the immigrant worker, *ouvrier spécialisé*, and prison inmate, for example, they would occupy the center stage of intellectual politics in the early 1970s.[79]

The estrangement between intellectuals and the traditional parties of the Left was further encouraged by shifts in the relationship between intellectuals and institutions such as the political system, the mass media, and the republican university. In the Fifth Republic intellectuals played increasingly marginal roles in political parties and government. The École normale supérieure, which had functioned in the Third Republic as the training ground of both the intellectual elite and leading left-wing politicians such as Jean Jaurès, Léon Blum, and Edouard Herriot, no longer produced political leaders after World War II. Its role in the formation of the political elite was increasingly usurped by the École nationale d'administration (ENA), created in 1945. Graduates from the ENA took over the Grands Corps de l'État in the 1950s and 1960s, came to dominate ministerial positions beginning in the early 1970s, and played an increasingly important role within all political parties with the partial exception of the PCF in the 1970s and 1980s.[80]

Intellectuals found compensation for their loss of formal political power in the possibilities opened up by the emerging new mass media. The rapid multiplication of the educated population during the great economic boom of the 1950s and 1960s fed the expansion of cultural journalism and gave intellectuals new opportunities to market their ideas that bypassed both political parties and the republican university. Indeed, intellectuals marginal to the university, like those at the sixth section of the École pratique des hautes études (which later became the École des hautes études en sciences sociales), found that they could use exposure in the cultural press to gain general renown and commercial success, which could then be converted into consecration in the intellectual field itself. The key institution in this transformation of intellectual politics by the mass media was the weekly *Le Nouvel Observateur,* born in 1964 out of the fusion of the failing *France observateur* and journalists disgruntled with *L'Express*'s depoliticization. Defined at its origin as both a commercial and a left-wing enterprise, its commercial imperative of capturing the growing educated audience ruled out extremist discourses and valorized a competing discourse of openness and "intelligence." A major force in politics as a result of its circulation (308,000 and climbing in 1974), *Le Nouvel Observateur* offered the intellectuals who wrote in its columns a significant power base independent of the political parties. Not surprisingly, *Le Nouvel Observateur* was at the center of the political debates of the 1970s and would become one of the principal vehicles of antitotalitarianism.[81]

Ironically, the same expansion of the university population that made *Le Nouvel Observateur* phenomenon possible resulted in a decline in the frequency and weight of political interventions by university academics, who were increasingly occupied by the reform and management of increasingly complex universities in crisis. Further, the increased specialization and numeric growth of the university professoriat led to a decline in the solidarity among academics that had been crucial to their political mobilization in the past as well as a reduction in the symbolic weight of individual academics, who lacked the distinction born of scarcity of either their Third Republic predecessors or the new mass media mandarins.[82] The decline of the academic in intellectual politics dealt a serious blow to what remained of the unitary republican politics of Third Republic vintage, which was intimately associated with the educational system and simultaneously coming under criticism as a result of the Algerian War. The rise of the mass media mandarins, on the other hand, encouraged a direct-democratic intellectual politics that soon became known as *autogestion* (self-management). Excluded from power in the political parties and functioning with growing independence from the republican university, intellectuals writing in *Le Nouvel Observateur* and other large-circulation periodicals found in the politics of *autogestion* a way of bypassing the political elite in favor of their direct connection with the people via the mass media.[83]

Encouraged by institutional change, direct democracy moved to the center of intellectual politics as the failure of Soviet communism and the stagnation of the revolutionary project in France led intellectuals of the noncommunist Left to rethink their politics around two concerns. First, they asked how they could assure, contrary to the course of events in the Soviet Union, that liberty and democracy would be the end product of a socialist revolution. As the twin goals of socialism and liberty to which intellectuals had subscribed at the Liberation began to shift in their relative weight toward liberty, intellectuals became increasingly sensitive to the relationship between means and ends in politics, arguing that the revolutionary movement had to be imbued with democracy and liberty in its earliest phases. In this way, direct democracy became both the goal of revolution and a barricade against an authoritarian outcome to the process of revolutionary transformation.

Intellectuals also asked who is revolutionary, who is the Marxist subject. Reflections on the nature of the revolutionary project and on the Marxist subject were closely related. The crisis of the revolutionary subject was not only a product of the increasing integration of the traditional working class as displayed in its conduct in 1958 and throughout the Algerian War. The form that reflection on this crisis took expressed intellectuals' desire for a different revolution. The course of Soviet history demonstrated that a change in the ownership of the means of production was no longer sufficient. As the central concern of revolution shifted from a change in the nature of property to a change in authority relations, the proximate condition for the realization of liberty and true democracy, it became less evident that the traditional working class could be the agent of *this* revolution. Intellectuals of the noncommunist Left had rejected Stalinism and were intensifying their criticisms of Leninism, and the working class, whether considered to be reformist, beholden to the PCF, or both, showed few signs of following their lead. The new revolution would have to be made by new revolutionaries.

The most important effort to rethink the revolutionary project in accordance with the new emphasis on liberty is Sartre's *Critique of Dialectical Reason*, first published in 1960.[84] This monumental work is Sartre's attempt to de-Stalinize Marxism and, in implicit response to communist criticisms of the 1940s and Merleau-Ponty's critique in *The Adventures of the Dialectic*, reconcile his existentialism with Marxism by accounting for the realization of individual freedom within society and the revolutionary project. Most interesting is the form that Sartre's idea of revolutionary action takes. Sartre argued that the proper revolutionary organization was not the Leninist party, but the democratic group-in-fusion, a union of individuals united without hierarchy or division of labor for a common purpose (like the crowd that stormed the Bastille on 14 July 1789). Sartre's conceptualization of the group-in-fusion and, notably, his inability to give it any permanent or institutional identity in his work expressed his attachment to the liberty of the individual, which, while long-standing, only grew in its dimensions after 1956. Sartre concluded that if the group were given a permanent status it would betray liberty either by becoming terroristic or by becoming a bureaucracy that reproduced the condition of seriality in opposition to which the group had been created. Beyond these unattractive alternatives, Sartre could offer no way by which a group could gain permanency without betraying the freedom of the individual. In the words of the historian Mark Poster, "he [Sartre] would not grant any separate existence to the group beyond the action of individuals. The unity of the group never transcended the common praxis of its members. If it did, if it had an ontological status of its own, it would severely diminish the freedom of the individuals."[85] This Sartre could not accept. As a consequence, Sartre could do no more than outline a politics that alternated between periods of anarchic revolt and others of alienation. Sartre was forced to admit by abandoning his second volume of the *Critique of Dialectical Reason*, published posthumously in 1985, that he could not elaborate a theory of revolutionary transformation that did not betray his attachment to the autonomy of the individual.[86] As a consequence of this choice of liberty over the collective project, by the early 1970s Sartre spoke of liberty as either the essence of socialism or as more important than socialism.[87]

Sartre's failed effort was both influential and representative of wider trends in the revision of revolutionary politics. Workers' councils emerged for other intellectuals as the functional equivalent of Sartre's group-infusion. Their role in the Hungarian Revolution and the Polish movement of 1956 encouraged intellectuals to look to them for the answer to the failure of democracy under communism or, in other words, an alternative to Leninist politics. The theme of workers' councils brought attention to Cornelius Castoriadis, Claude Lefort, and their journal *Socialisme ou barbarie*, important although hitherto largely ignored dissident *gauchiste* voices in French intellectual life, and brought them together with intellectuals associated with the journals *Les Lettres nouvelles*, *Le Surréalisme même*, and *Arguments* in a short lived Cercle international des intellectuels révolutionnaires. This theme of council socialism or *autogestion* became a major component of the socialism of these and other intellectuals who drew increasingly on the *gauchiste* tradition.[88]

Among those calling for a new Left based on workers' councils, the journal *Arguments*, founded in 1956 by Edgar Morin, Colette Audry, Roland Barthes, and Jean Duvignaud, was one of the most influential. *Arguments* undertook an open-ended, integral revision of Marxism by confronting it with modern society.[89] The openness of its critique of Marxism reflected the openness of *Arguments* as a place of intellectual sociability. While its core group consisted of intellectuals who had recently broken with the PCF, *Arguments* had no manifesto or platform, distanced itself from partisan political activism, and welcomed contributions from intellectuals with diverse perspectives.[90] The intellectuals associated with *Arguments* rejected Marxism as a system and Marx's pretensions to the transcendence of philosophy. Instead, they tried to develop Marx's method and free Marx from Lenin by going back to the early Marx and Hegel and working within the "Western Marxist" tradition.[91] Believing that the center of society had shifted from the economic structure to the political and cultural superstructure, they developed a revised version of Marx's concept of alienation to account for the new situation.

The concept of alienation offered Left intellectuals a solution to the multiple dilemmas of their politics. It allowed them to locate a new revolutionary subject whose goals coincided with those of their emerging new revolutionary project. Alienation in production, that is, lack of control over the process and the ends of production, took the place of exploitation as the root of working-class militancy. Rising income need not necessarily lead to reformism, and a new working class that felt its alienation more keenly might become the center of the revolutionary struggle. The theo- rists of the new working class, notably Pierre Belleville, Serge Mallet, Alain Touraine, and André Gorz, having noted that the traditional working class was shrinking and losing its radicalism, argued that as science and tech- nology become more central to capitalism, a new class of technical work- ers emerges that requires and demands a degree of autonomy and creativity that capitalism cannot allow. Their struggle could form the basis of the emergence of an anti-Leninist socialism born out of their rejection of both bureaucracy and capitalism. These new revolutionary actors with new goals would realize socialism through new methods. Gorz, like the other theorists of the new working class, resolved the problem of the tran- sition to socialism by calling for a revolutionary reformism that empowers the base while revealing the contradictions of capitalism. Following the ideas of Gorz and Sartre, *Les Temps modernes* turned its attention increas- ingly to radical union activity and models of worker control.[92]

Taken in a broad sense, alienation, understood as alienation by capitalist social structures, could apply to nearly everyone. Gorz, for example, saw the conflict between autonomy and creativity on the one hand and capital- ism on the other as occurring throughout society. As a consequence, key sectors outside of the working class, like the student population, could also be agents of revolution. Henri Lefebvre, whose work was the most devel- oped effort by a French Marxist to study capitalism outside of production, argued that the emerging "bureaucratic society of controlled consumption" was beginning to submit all sectors of society to its logic and thereby shift the battleground for revolution to the terrain of everyday life.[93]

While concern for liberty made the nature of the revolutionary struggle increasingly difficult to define with precision, the recourse to the concept of alienation wreaked havoc on reflection on the revolutionary subject. On the one hand, the Situationists, influenced by Lefebvre's argument that alienation had entered everyday life, offered an expansive definition of the proletariat as "he who does not have any power over the use of his life and who knows it." In this perspective, the revolutionary project was nothing less than "the conscious domination of history by the men who make it."[94] On the other hand, Lefebvre, who had done so much to extend the scope of the revolutionary subject, concluded in 1967 that the working class was no longer revolutionary.[95] Marxism's identity, especially as a distinct rev- olutionary project, was beginning to dissolve. This was a strange Marxism indeed in which nearly everyone, *except* the working class, was considered to be revolutionary!

Because of this use of the concept of alienation to include innumerable and diverse struggles within the revolutionary project, what would become the new social movements in the 1970s could find a home within Marxism in the 1960s, and their a-Marxist politics could be expressed in a vague Marxist language. The practical experience of the different social movements that emerged after 1968 would progressively prove the difficulty of subsuming the different "alienations" within a Marxist language and party no matter how flexible they might be. For example, the anti-hierarchical Maoist group Vive la Révolution! undertook upon its formation in 1969 a critique of bourgeois society using Lefebvre's concept of everyday life. When it added the issues of sexual repression, women's liberation, and gay rights to its agenda, the organization fell apart as conflicts developed between these new movements and that of the working class. Vive la Révolution! dissolved itself in 1971. The Mouvement de libération des femmes and the Front des homosexuels révolutionnaires emerged out of the experience.[96] The difference, emphasized in many retrospective analyses, between countercultural and political projects after 1968 was not immediately obvious and is somewhat problematic as a categorization of the movements that emerged out of 1968. This difference became visible only after it proved to be impossible for political groups to subsume the different revolts in a single project and became self-evident only after post-1968 revolutionary political projects ended in failure and a renunciation of unitary political projects. In fact, the countercultural coexisted with the political in organizations with nominally Marxist political projects, only to gain an increasingly prominent place within them over time.[97]

Theories of the new working class and of the revolutionary consequences of capitalism's colonization of everyday life offered hope for the democratic, antibureaucratic socialist revolution that had emerged as the political project of many left-wing intellectuals, but before 1968 offered apparent proof of the radicalization of society, prospects for revolution seemed dim and the reality of these new agents of revolution appeared doubtful. Reformism and disengagement consequently became important trends in intellectual politics between the end of the Algerian War in 1962 and the explosion of 1968.

Consciousness of the decline of the traditional working class as a historical actor, the postwar economic boom, and a new, more concrete understanding of society based on empirical sociology led some intellectuals to place their hopes in democratic planning and participation. Former communist and fellow-traveling intellectuals, notably at *Esprit* but also at *Arguments* and elsewhere, found in the fourth (1962-65) plan—which moved beyond economic questions to issues of social development—common reformist ground with liberals and Left Gaullists. Yet democratic planning lost its allure after 1965, when the modernist and reformist presidential candidacy of Gaston Defferre failed and the slowdown of the economy reduced the resources available to it. While helping to move an important fraction of intellectuals away from revolutionary politics, democratic planning could not provide a permanent alternative to it.[98]

Given the shortcomings of democratic planning, the end of the Algerian War and domestic political stagnation—notably the absence of new initiatives on the Left and the Gaullist lock on political power—resulted in depoliticization, a trend evident throughout French intellectual life between 1962 and 1968. After it became disabused of planning, *Esprit*, having no use for the parties of the Left, which it considered bankrupt, emphasized that its project was one of a civilization and not a political one as such. It fell back to a 1930s theme of the journal: the evils of productivism.[99] The visibly disengaged "new novel" was consecrated after the Algerian War, clearly dethroning Sartrian engaged literature, which had already come under severe criticism in the 1950s. The considerable interest in structuralism in the mid 1960s undoubtedly reflected the fact that it offered an ahistorical account of the world at a time when the possibilities for historical change had apparently closed down. Likewise, the emphasis on structure and repetition at the expense of the event in the historiography of the *Annales* school turned it increasingly in an explicitly conservative direction in the hands of third-generation *Annales* historians disillusioned with revolutionary politics, like Emmanuel Le Roy Ladurie and François Furet. The declining interest in politics threw the Left weeklies into crisis, precipitating Jean-Jacques Servan-Schreiber's decision to depoliticize *L'Express* in imitation of foreign magazines like *Time* (in order to attract a readership of *cadres* and the advertising that followed them) and the subsequent founding of *Le Nouvel Observateur* to replace the failing *France observateur*.[100] The success of Althusser's Marxism might also be understood in contrast as a side effect of the widespread political disarray of the intellectual Left in this period. His "scientific" Marxism and his defense of a "theoretical practice" offered refuge, Benny Lévy argues in retrospect, from the internal disintegration of Marxism by *gauchiste* revisionism and the absence of any concrete political project. The militants at Nanterre, where the student revolt of 1968 would begin, found themselves, Daniel Cohn-Bendit tells us, in a "revolutionary ghetto" on the eve of 1968.[101]

Many of those who were to take part in the wave of revolutionary politics after 1968 or in the critique of totalitarianism in the late 1970s were politically demobilized before the May events. Numerous intellectuals who would later be attracted by the revolutionary politics of the Gauche prolétarienne, like Michel Foucault and the Left Gaullists Claude Mauriac and Maurice Clavel, showed few signs of embracing a politics of this sort before May '68. Many intellectuals who had been within the Marxist tradition moved out of politics before 1968. Intellectuals at *Arguments* brought *engagement* into question at the end of the 1950s. At *Socialisme ou barbarie*, first Claude Lefort and then Cornelius Castoriadis retreated from active engagement in revolutionary politics. The review published its last issue in 1965; it had, Castoriadis explained in 1967, lost its raison d'être because "in modern capitalist societies political activity properly speaking tends to disappear." Former student activists, notably the "Italians" of the Union des étudiants communistes (UEC), abandoned militancy after being kicked out of the organization. Even Sartre found himself in a "provisional ivory tower" come May '68, "having broken with the communists, not wanting to engage in politics against them, and especially very interested by what I was writing on Flaubert."[102]

There was, of course, one important exception to the political lassitude of the French intellectual Left before 1968: their mobilization against the American war in Vietnam beginning with its escalation in early 1965. This time, unlike during the French Indochinese War or the Algerian War, French intellectuals rallied unambiguously and in large numbers against the war and in doing so were largely in tune with the French press, political elites, and public opinion. The political parties and the press, like President De Gaulle, were almost unanimously opposed to the American war—although they had different opinions of how it should be resolved. In polls of public opinion in September 1966 and September 1967, 68 percent and 72 percent respectively of those questioned said that the U.S. should withdraw from Vietnam.[103] Given this evidence of overwhelming popular and elite hostility to the war, one must be careful not to hastily identify all French intellectuals' opposition to the war with a commitment to radical politics or revolutionary *tiers-mondisme*. Indeed, the Comité Vietnam national (CVN), which was the focal point of anti-Vietnam War activism for most established intellectuals, presented the war as one of independence and emphasized Vietnamese victimhood. One did not have to be a *tiers-mondiste* to join it in opposition to the war.[104]

Still the 1965-68 campaign against the Vietnam War contributed, especially in the younger generation, to a radicalization of intellectual politics leading up to 1968 by inflating rhetoric (no doubt for good reason given the nature of the war); by mobilizing individuals and groups in demonstrations, petition campaigns, and reflection on politics; by innovating in political tactics and methods; and by accentuating the division between the PCF and the extreme Left. Jean-Paul Sartre, like many others, took a decidedly Manichean view of the war by holding that "the Vietnamese fight for all men and the American forces against everyone" and that the American war was genocidal. For many intellectuals prominent in post-1968 intellectual politics, like Philippe Sollers and Michel Foucault, who signed their first political petitions against the war, the Vietnam War marked the beginning of a political radicalization. For André Glucksmann the years of the Vietnam War were nothing less than "ten years of meditation and of questioning." Finally, for the Trotskyists of the Jeunesse communiste révolutionnaire (JCR) who were behind the CVN and for the Maoists of the Union des jeunesses communistes marxistes-léninistes (UJCML) behind the Comités Vietnam de base (CVB), the war was an occasion to assert an identity more radical than that of the PCF. Against the PCF slogan "Peace in Vietnam," both offered "the FLN will triumph." The UJCML Maoists hoped that their mobilization against the war would provide the spark that would ignite a revolution in the Europe.[105]

Although the Maoists can take little credit, the mobilization against the war contributed to the explosion of May '68. The *lycéen* (high school students') movement began with Comités Vietnam lycéens and spread to a broader anti-authoritarian agenda when antiwar students took on regulations that forbade student political activity in schools. Likewise, the loose structure of the antiwar movement and antiwar meetings—beginning with the "Six Heures pour le Vietnam" meeting of 26 May 1966 that echoed American teach-ins—prefigured the creative anarchy of 1968 and its aftermath. Finally, the intensification of antiwar activities during the Tet offensive increased political tensions in the Latin Quarter in early 1968, and the arrest of JCR militants in connection with attacks on American businesses in Paris by antiwar activists sparked the occupation of the Nanterre campus of the University of Paris that marked the beginning of the upheaval leading to May '68.[106]

Ironically, although the Vietnam War set the stage for May '68, intellectual mobilization against the war declined dramatically after the spring of 1968. The CVBs did not survive 1968, and the CVN slowly withered away. The beginning of negotiations between the United States and the Vietnamese in 1968 had diffused the situation somewhat, and May '68 had finally given intellectuals and militants a political cause at home. The war's conclusion in 1975 would contribute to the unfolding of the critique of totalitarianism, not so much because of disillusionment with the results of the war—which was of decisive importance for only a few individuals like the journalists Olivier Todd and Jean Lacouture and the CVB organizer Jacques Broyelle—but because the end of the war reduced the importance of American imperialism in intellectual politics and allowed other questions to come to the forefront.

May '68 and the Cautious Revival of Revolutionary Politics

The events of May '68 reversed the trend towards intellectual depoliticization by confirming the possibility of revolution in France. Structuralism, which seemed to deny the possibility of the event, was pronounced (somewhat prematurely) dead by its pre-May opponents, and revisionist Marxists bragged of the apparent correctness of their analyses.[107] Students proved, as many of them had predicted, to be a decisive agent of a social upheaval that took *gauchiste* forms. Their demands for autonomy and control at the base, their forming of assemblies governed by direct democracy, and their speaking out (*"prise de parole"*—which was nothing if not a critique of representation) in favor of a transformation of everyday life were echoed throughout society by industrial workers, technicians, artists, doctors, architects, priests, and even football players.[108] The new working class had, it seemed to many, emerged.[109] Social protest in May '68 had a revolutionary flavor. As during the revolutions of the nineteenth century, barricades were erected in Paris. A massive strike movement paralyzed the country, and workers seemed to reject reformism for qualitative demands when they turned down the Grenelle Accords negotiated by their unions.[110] During the last days of May, the government appeared powerless, and revolution seemed to be at hand.

The leaders of the May student uprising put into practice the reconceptualizations of revolutionary politics developed over the preceeding decade. Mostly somewhat older than the students themselves, they had been educated in politics in the course of their militant activity against the Algerian War and during the political battles that they had waged within and increasingly against the PCF.[111] Daniel Cohn-Bendit, the symbol and single most important leader of the student movement, was well acquainted with the efforts to rethink the revolutionary project in the 1960s, having studied sociology with Alain Touraine and Henri Lefebvre at Nanterre and closely read the writings of Cornelius Castoriadis and the journal *Socialisme ou barbarie*.[112] Although an eclectic bunch, those in the anarchistic Movement of 22 March, which was at the epicenter of the revolt at Nanterre and later in the Latin Quarter, seem to have been influenced by Sartre more than anyone else.[113]

Although the *groupuscules* that participated in the student revolt held divergent views of the ultimate course of the Revolution, Cohn-Bendit succeeded in uniting them during May behind a rejection of vanguardism and the organization of the movement in *comités de base*, that is, assemblies practicing direct democracy.[114] When the question of political power was raised, student leaders resisted the temptation to unify the movement behind a revolutionary vanguard posed to seize power. Student leaders briefly considered taking the Paris City Hall and the Presidential Palace (the classic moves in a seizure of power), but they shrunk back from such actions upon considering their consequences. They were not sufficiently convinced of their revolutionary legitimacy to lead their troops into battles in which lives would almost certainly be lost. Although the confrontations between police and students were violent, both the Prefect of Police Maurice Grimaud and the leadership of the UNEF and the Syndicat national de l'enseignement supérieur (SNESup) worked hard to keep violence under control in Paris. As a consequence, there were only five deaths in France directly attributable to the upheaval of May and June 1968. Especially on the "night of the barricades," the violence of the events was probably most important for the symbolic weight that it carried, evoking without actually repeating the drama of the bloody barricades of nineteenth-century revolutions.[115]

The Movement of 22 March explicitly rejected the politics of the seizure of power and, more radically, any subordination of the direct democracy of the action committees to a larger organization. As the most prominent and legitimate voice of the student revolt, it set the tone for the movement. It rebuffed efforts to unite the student movement behind a single program or individual like Pierre Mendès-France.[116] Cohn-Bendit stressed that the movement should not try to seize power, but rather function as an experiment and a critique of institutions that offers a glimpse of a possible alternative society.[117] He believed that "profound aspirations are only expressed in periods of crisis and total break," and he did not want to bring closure to May's creative rupture by institutionalizing the movement.[118] Cohn-Bendit's choices for the movement expressed his idea of the content of socialism: a kind of radical democracy or form of self-organization in which everyone can participate. If the movement were to respect its radical democratic aspirations, it had to foster the "disorder that lets men speak freely" and shun representation, both political representation and, more radically, any representation of the future society.[119] The other two leading figures of the student movement, Jacques Sauvageot, president of the UNEF, and Alain Geismar, head of the SNESup, agreed with Cohn-Bendit that the spontaneity and direct democracy of the movement should not be restricted in favor of a revolutionary vanguard and organization.[120]

1968 was open to many interpretations, but on the noncommunist intellectual Left there was a broad consensus behind two conclusions. For one, the major institutions of French society—above all, the educational and political systems—were bankrupt. The democratic critique of authority, often expressed as a critique of the derivation of a social division of labor from a technical division of labor, fueled a critique of the student-teacher relationship and of the constitution of knowledge for particular, oppressive ends. As for politicians and political institutions, neither those on the Right nor those on the Left were seen as having anything to offer. The state had revealed its repressiveness, and the PCF as well as the CGT had shown themselves to be reactionary by their complicity with the government, demobilization of radical workers, and hostility to the student movement. After 1968 noncommunist intellectuals' critical distance from the PCF turned into open hostility toward it. *Gauchistes* active after 1968 did not hesitate to attack the PCF, which they considered to be as great an enemy as the state or capitalism. May '68's second lesson was that the Revolution was possible, if not imminent. This revolutionary optimism translated into an upsurge in activism throughout the Left. When read through the lens of the revisionist inflation of the revolutionary subject, evaluations of the revolutionary situation could take on a populist orientation.

For theorists of revolution after 1968 the most immediate question was that of revolutionary organization. May '68 may have been revolutionary, but it did not overthrow the regime, and as many saw it, the lack of a revolutionary organization was responsible for this failure. Some, like the Jeunesse communiste révolutionnaire (JCR)—reconstituted as the Ligue communiste after being banned by the government in 1968—argued that May '68 had failed because there had been no revolutionary vanguard and called for a return to Leninist principles of political organization. It assigned itself the task of constructing a vanguard that would be ready to seize power at the next, impending revolutionary crisis. Among revolutionary political organizations that appealed directly to students after 1968, it was the most successful in gaining militants and consequently had the greatest presence on the streets of the Latin Quarter. From a few hundred members in 1968 the JCR/Ligue communiste grew to approximately five thousand in 1972, its peak.[121]

Despite the success of their recruitment efforts, the leaders of the Ligue communiste considered themselves isolated in their Leninism.[122] More commonly, intellectuals of the noncommunist Left, although usually recognizing the need for some form of revolutionary organization, were unwilling to take the route of vanguardist politics. Although, like the Trotskyists of the Ligue communiste, their goal was self-managed socialism, they differed from the Ligue communiste in their belief that true self-managed socialism could emerge only if self-management were practiced throughout all phases of the revolutionary process. Liberty and direct democracy had to be inscribed within the revolutionary organization itself or else revolution would have an authoritarian outcome. This choice should not be surprising; it reflected a major theme of the noncommunist intellectual Left's political thought since the mid 1950s. The qualifications that intellectuals placed on revolutionary politics can be clearly seen in the reactions to May '68 by André Gorz and *Les Temps modernes*; Edgar Morin, Claude Lefort, and Cornelius Castoriadis in their book *Mai 68: la brèche*; and Jean-Marie Domenach and *Esprit*.

At *Les Temps modernes* André Gorz interpreted May '68 as demonstrating the possibility of revolution in Western Europe, blamed its failure on the PCF and CGT, and believed that a new revolutionary organization was needed. Yet, Gorz and *Les Temps modernes* had distanced themselves from Leninism in the 1960s and were not going to return to it after 1968. The new revolutionary organization would, as Gorz conceived it, coordinate and propose "the kind of action, plan, and self-organization that can defeat the machinery of both the state and the traditional working-class organizations." It "would not want to direct and to rule the masses, but would help them towards self-organization, self-rule and the exercise of power from below." If the new organizations did not follow this line, they would "either fail, or resemble the old ones, or both." Under Gorz's leadership, *Les Temps modernes* undertook an explicit critique of Leninism from 1969 to 1971. Like others on the noncommunist intellectual Left, after 1968 *Les Temps modernes* attacked social institutions from a radical democratic perspective. In 1970, for example, it exhorted its readers to "destroy the university" as part of the struggle against the division of labor.[123]

The reflections of Edgar Morin, Claude Lefort, and Cornelius Castoriadis in *Mai 68: la brèche* reveal continuities across May '68 and highlight post-May political themes broadly congruous with *Les Temps modernes*'s posture. All three authors agreed on the importance of the upheaval: it had challenged the rationality and legitimacy of the system, shown revolution to be possible, and opened a new historical era. Further, they all warned against a possible negative development of the movement if it displayed too great a fidelity to older models of revolutionary politics. Morin, who of the three maintained the greatest distance from the movement, refrained from prescribing a course for it and criticized it for being insufficiently liberal and excessively attached to Marxist political rhetoric. He feared that whatever good may come from it in the long term, its immediate consequences would be negative. Stalinist communism and the party of order would probably be reinforced, and "the impatient chimeras of the avant-garde will give new life to the old ghosts and drown out the voices of lucid criticism."[124]

Lefort and Castoriadis, founders of *Socialisme ou barbarie* recognized as major *gauchiste* voices after 1968, displayed more enthusiasm for the movement (both briefly returned to militancy after the events of 1968), but their readings were, like Morin's more cautious one, in continuity with their critiques and redefinitions of the revolutionary project during the preceding decade. Both praised May as a revolution against bureaucracy and hierarchy that rightly refused to offer an illusory undemocratic prefiguration of the good society to come. Both argued that the sectors of education and culture had become the breeding grounds of revolution and that the proletariat was no longer a revolutionary class.[125] Both welcomed the upsurge in revolutionary politics while remaining skeptical of its possibilities.

But Lefort and Castoriadis disagreed on the question of revolutionary organization—the same question that had divided them while they were in *Socialisme ou barbarie* and had resulted in Lefort's departure from it in 1958. Lefort considered the Movement of 22 March to be an acceptable model of revolutionary activism. Its refusal of all hierarchy and discipline undermined through its example the bureaucratic structure of society. In Lefort's mind, the Movement of 22 March's use of exemplary action and refusal to seize power brought the revolutionary struggle to maturity.[126] Castoriadis agreed that the revolutionary movement should concentrate on the fight against bureaucracy and for the auto-organization of society, but he rejected the antinomies proposed by the student revolutionaries between action and reflection, spontaneity and organization, imagination and the project. He wrote, "to accept this antinomy as valid, as unavoidable, is to accept the very essence of the bureaucratic capitalist ideology, it is to accept the philosophy of the reality that exists, it is to refuse the real transformation of the world, it is to integrate revolution into the established historical order."[127] While refusing Lefort's refusal of organization, Castoriadis called for the creation of an antihierarchical, direct-democratic revolutionary organization that would not be set in stone, but would simply *"begin* that which must remain a permanent self-definition and self-organization."[128]

Esprit placed even greater qualifications than *Les Temps modernes* and the authors of *Mai 68: la brèche* on its acceptance of a revival of revolutionary politics in the wake of May '68. *Esprit* was completely surprised by the upheaval of that year and initially considerably reserved towards and even critical of the student movement. In his first response to the events Jean-Marie Domenach criticized the confrontational politics at Nanterre as working "to the detriment of goodwill and emerging dialogues," and on 14 May, on the eve of the strike wave, Paul Thibaud joined Jean-Marie Domenach to warn against "the totalitarian dialectic in which certain *enragés* take pride."[129] Yet, *Esprit* also found in May '68 reasons to criticize its recent attachment to technocratic reformism, proof that technocratic society and Gaullism were failures, and some hope for a renewal of radical reform and the revolutionary project.[130] Believing that May '68 was the type of revolt for which its founder Mounier had called, *Esprit* hoped that the revolutionary climate would not die out, but would rather develop into a movement that would extend criticism, break down social barriers, attack consumer society, and fight for a decentralization of power. The new politics was welcomed because it was "founded no longer on party cards but on the initiative of militants" and broke with "bureaucratic ties." It offered "a revolutionary possibility outside of the communist world" that *Esprit* could support.[131] But *Esprit* placed clear limits on the welcome that it gave to the liberation of revolutionary energy. Domenach and Thibaud, casting an eye back on *Esprit*'s past adventures with communism, stressed that "we do not have … the intention of returning to the illusions of which we rid ourselves."[132] For the cautious revolutionaries at *Esprit* "the new militancy must not be a militancy of propagandists … but a militancy of midwives, an engagement of free men."[133] A cultural revolution in which "the greatest possible number of people take their destiny in their hands" was in the making, but it would succeed only "if it does not withdraw into slogans and intimidation."[134] Domenach, in particular, was worried by the movement's renewal of Marxism and what he considered to be its Marcusian critique of liberalism that "takes up the lines of attack of Marxism without making the necessary distinctions and without proposing any safeguards for essential liberties."[135] Afraid that the importance of liberty escaped the students, Domenach held that "it is urgent that the students of France take into account the experience of the students of Czechoslovakia and of Poland. A political revolution is desirable or even conceivable only if it does not bring Europe back to totalitarian fantasies. Society … is not ready to exchange its fundamental liberties, as degraded as they may be, for dictatorships of minorities."[136] Jacques Julliard, although a major advocate of the direct-democratic politics of *autogestion*, agreed with Domenach that one of the central political questions after May '68 was: "How does one translate into truly liberal institutions, that is to say respectful of the rights of minorities, today's dangerously vague aspirations to a mass direct democracy?"[137]

Post-68 Gauchisme: The Gauche prolétarienne from Direct Democracy to Dissolution.

Less reserved in its revolutionary politics was the Gauche prolétarienne (GP), the history of which is central to the evolution of *gauchisme* and *gauchiste*-oriented intellectual politics after 1968. Although it never had more than a couple thousand members, the GP was the most visible of the *gauchiste* organizations.[138] Its spectacular and, it hoped, exemplary illegal and often violent action attracted considerable attention to it and led the head of the Renseignements généraux to believe that the GP was a greater threat to state security than any other left-wing group.[139] Intellectuals were drawn to the GP more than any other *gauchiste* organization out of solidarity with it in the face of the state's repression and, in many cases, because they appreciated its political philosophy—which was largely in tune with the direct-democratic tendencies of the time—and exemplary action. Intellectuals also found that they could easily relate to the GP's leadership, which had attended the most prestigious French educational institutions.[140] Because common educational, intellectual, and political experiences maintained the cohesion of the GP leadership and its solidarity with other intellectuals into the late 1970s, the GP's importance extends beyond the five years of its formal existence from 1968 to 1973. In general agreement in their evaluations of the significance of the GP's failed militant experiment, anxious to convey to others the lessons that they had learned, highly articulate, and media savvy after years of pondering the symbolic efficacy of their actions, the former members of the GP network proved to be an important force in the political and intellectual debates of the late 1970s and played a major role in the elaboration of the critique of totalitarianism.

The GP emerged in the autumn of 1968 out of a crisis sparked by May '68 in its predecessor, the Union des jeunesses communistes marxistes-léninistes (UJCML), itself founded in 1966.[141] The UJCML was largely the work of students at the École normale supérieure (ENS) (notably the triumvirate of Benny Lévy, Robert Linhart, and Jacques Broyelle), who had been exposed to two influences that set them apart from others in the student movement: Chinese communism and the communist philosopher Louis Althusser. Attracted to the scientific pretensions of Althusser's Marxism, they took his advice in student politics in the mid 1960s. Following Althusser's analysis, they planned to ally with the PCF to defeat other oppositional tendencies in the PCF's student organization, the Union des étudiants communistes (UEC). Believing that the real struggle was for the proper line in the PCF and expecting little out of students as revolutionary actors, they intended to use their base in the UEC to challenge the "revisionist" politics of the PCF.[142]

The UJCML began to turn away from Althusser and towards *gauchisme* in 1966 and 1967 through a reading of the Chinese Cultural Revolution.[143]

They were, it should be noted, already familiar with *gauchiste* critiques of Leninism, including that of *Socialisme ou barbarie*, and had not been prevented by Althusser's antihumanism from reading Sartre with sympathy. Indeed, prominent figures in the UJCML such as Lévy, Broyelle, and Jean-Pierre Le Dantec had gone through a *gauchiste* period before encountering Althusser.[144] For them the Cultural Revolution was anti-Stalinist, antibureaucratic, and anti-authoritarian: in the words of Jean-Pierre Le Dantec, a "return to one of the forgotten origins of Marxism, that of the texts on the Paris Commune taken up by Lenin during the époque of the Soviets: the libertarian source."[145] At the heart of their reading of the Cultural Revolution was the mass line, a mass critique of bureaucracy and of the division of labor in revolutionary society based on the conviction that "the eye of the peasant sees justly" (*"l'œil du paysan voit juste"*). Convinced that truth lay in the masses and that revolutionary practice flowed from this truth, the intellectuals of the UJCML sought to establish unmediated contact with the working class by developing *l'établissement*, the practice of sending students and intellectuals (called *établis*) to the factories. *Établis* took shop-floor jobs where they were to learn from the masses, synthesize their ideas into a critique of the revisionist communists, and ultimately take over Confédération générale du travail (CGT) from the PCF and turn it in a more militant direction.[146]

In May '68, the UJCML, faithful to its *ouvriérisme*, initially dismissed the student movement and argued that the students should not try to act on their own, but rather go to the workers, the true revolutionary actors. The UJCML's controversial position during May led to the organization's collapse later that year. A majority of UJCML militants, believing that May had failed for lack of a revolutionary party, left the UJCML to join the Leninist Maoist party, the Parti communiste marxiste-léniniste de France (PCMLF),[147] and a smaller group of fifty or fewer UJCML members—including most of the leadership as well as the UJCML circle centered in the *khâgne* at the elite *lycée* Louis-le-Grand (that is, the elite intellectuals-in-training of the UJCML)—formed the GP.[148] The GP was led by the UJCML's failure and the spontaneous note struck by May '68 to explicitly critique Leninist concepts of proletarian consciousness and revolutionary organization. Workers did not need a party to bring them revolutionary consciousness. They already possessed the truth and, as the violence during the June 1968 strikes at Flins and Sochaux seemed to indicate, were on the verge of an insurrection that the GP hoped to spark.[149] The PCF and the CGT, which had played a moderating role in the May-June crisis, were now seen as absolute obstacles to revolution, and the GP abandoned the UJCML's effort to infiltrate the CGT in order to transform it from the inside. In making this turn towards a spontaneist view of the revolutionary struggle, the GP linked up Alain Geismar, who had played an important role in May '68 as the representative of the SNESup, and a handful of former members of the Movement of 22 March such as Serge July. Alain

Geismar, Serge July, Herta Alvarez, and Evelyne July developed in their book *Vers la guerre civile* what would become some of the principal themes of the GP, notably the use of exemplary illegal action, the revolutionary potential of the marginal, and the centrality of the division of labor in establishing hierarchy.[150] The addition of Geismar and the Movement of 22 March members gave the GP legitimacy as the heir to 1968 and marked its conversion to direct-democratic revolutionary politics.

The GP took a populist view of the revolutionary actor and a moralist view of politics that celebrated all popular revolt, whatever its character. For Benny Lévy the "philosophical foundation" of the GP was simply the notion that "the principal current of the mass movement is always reasonable."[151] While maintaining that the most revolutionary actors were from the working class, the GP tended to view revolutionary legitimacy as a function of oppression, not exploitation. Thus, the GP's model revolutionaries were *ouvriers spécialisés* (OS), unskilled or semiskilled industrial workers who were often immigrants and were poorly organized by unions. And, following the maxim "one is right to rebel," (*"on a raison de se révolter"*), the GP considered any social group that showed signs of revolt to be part of the forces of revolution. Consequently, the GP supported the struggles of immigrants for housing better than that of the *bidonvilles* (shantytowns), of shopkeepers against the invasion of supermarkets and department stores, and of peasants against the agricultural policy of the Common Market. The rooting of the GP's idea of the revolutionary actor in a moralistic approach to politics would later allow the GP to support truly marginal struggles like those of prisoners and to adopt countercultural themes—despite the resistance of some GP leaders who feared that this politics would alienate the working class.

This combination of populism, voluntarism, and spontaneism rendered the GP's Marxism incoherent. This can be seen in Guy Lardreau's *Le Singe d'or* (1973), recognized by Jean-Pierre Le Dantec and Olivier Rolin to be a synthesis of the GP leaderships' thought at the time.[152] Focusing his criticism on Althusser, Lardreau argues that any effort to construct a scientific Marxism is authoritarian, serving—following Michel Foucault—to "rarify the rebellious discourse" and to remove that which is essential to Marx, the "fundamental intuition" that "one is right to rebel." Revolution must retrieve its dimension of desire and faith. The desire for revolution is a "Pascalian wager" that rests on a "choice to side with the oppressed against repression." Against science that is always "against the people" one must adopt the Kantian injunction "dare to think." The desire of the masses, who "are never wrong," is the basis for revolution. Contrary to Lenin, whose idea of the sovereignty of the masses is bourgeois because it does not question the principle of representation, the masses can make a revolution with their own resources. Lardreau concludes that "one should perhaps return to Rousseau who tried to really conceptualize the sovereign people and not the sovereignty of the people".[153]

Rejecting representation, the GP sought to facilitate the speech (*"prise de parole"*) and violence of the masses through exemplary, illegal, and violent action that would presumably reveal the injustice and repressiveness of the state, incite the people to take matters into their own hands, and prefigure the impending civil war. The GP engaged in violent workplace confrontations organized by *établis* that aimed at undermining the authority of both management and labor unions, as well as more visible, symbolic actions by which it sought to attract attention and sympathy to its cause. The latter included, for example, a raid on the luxury market Fauchon followed by the redistribution of the booty of fois gras, caviar, and the like to the inhabitants of the *bidonvilles* and the theft and redistribution to workers of metro tickets—first-class ones of course—in protest of a fare increase.

The organizational structure of the GP reflected its refusal of representation. The GP was a vague conglomeration of militants committed to a common idea of revolution. The GP leadership did not know and did not care to know the number of militants associated with the GP. There was nothing like a GP card and no regular membership fees.[154] The organization was considered important only insofar as it acted to help the masses act for themselves. Refusing to create a revolutionary vanguard or party, the GP believed that a party would be legitimate only if it emerged out of a mass uprising and was based on the principle that "just ideas come from the practice of the masses."[155] Although the GP initially had something of an organization—a structure of committees at the national, regional, and local levels and a periodic general assembly that was supposed to make all important decisions—most of this would vanish after the government outlawed the GP in May 1970.

Notwithstanding the GP leaders' direct-democratic intentions and the informality of the GP as an organization, the GP was in some respects profoundly hierarchical and undemocratic. Its *Comité exécutif*, the only body that can be said to have represented the organization and made decisions in its name, consisted of a handful of informally co-opted, unaccountable individuals who were mostly young intellectuals with elite educational backgrounds.[156] Although he lacked a formal position, Benny Lévy was first among equals in the *Comité exécutif* and the uncontested leader of the GP. In the GP, as elsewhere in this period, the ideology of direct democracy gave effective power to an intellectual elite.

The intensification of government repression in the spring of 1970 had an important impact on the GP. The *anticasseurs* law of April 1970 criminalized participation in illegal demonstrations and made organizations calling for such demonstrations responsible for violence and destruction of property at them.[157] Jean-Pierre Le Dantec and Michel Le Bris, two successive directors of the GP newspaper *La Cause du Peuple*, were arrested in March and April 1970. A violent demonstration on the occasion of their 27 May 1970 trial offered the government a pretext for outlawing the GP and arresting its titular head, Alain Geismar—despite his absence from the demonstration. To minimize the impact of repression, the GP dissolved its organizational structure with the exception of the *Comité exécutif*. Now known as the "ex-GP,"[158] it rallied to the slogan *"Élargir la Résistance"* (broaden the Resistance). Against what it considered the "new fascism" of the state, the GP tried to rally the forces of mass democracy. Militants were to act on different "fronts" in local, decentralized, and largely unconnected groups embedded in the masses and extending the battle to all areas of life. Seeking to turn justice, human rights, and the principles of 1789 against the bourgeoisie, the GP organized intellectuals in a democratic movement to protect the GP against repression. At the same time, the GP, following its logic of seeking to spark a mass uprising through exemplary actions, organized a clandestine wing, the Organisation partisane secrète (OPS) of the Nouvelle résistance populaire (NRP), which flirted with terrorism.

The *"élargissement"* of the Resistance brought the GP new notoriety as its activities extended into new sectors and alliances with intellectuals were created, but it also undermined the GP's coherency. The *élargissement* soon brought about *éclatement* (breakup) as the different sectors of the GP resisted the *Comité exécutif*'s (especially Benny Lévy's) efforts to subordinate the struggles of particular groups to a revolutionary totalization. A good example of this conflict is the struggle between Lévy and the editors of *J'accuse* and later *La Cause du peuple – J'accuse* for control of these newspapers in the GP network. When Robert Linhart and André Glucksmann launched *J'accuse* (the newspaper of the GP's democratic front) in January 1971, and then when *J'accuse* fused with the ailing GP newspaper *La Cause du peuple* in May 1971, they had gained from the GP leadership recognition of the newspapers' independence sufficient to attract non-Maoist intellectuals to the project. But, in July 1971 Lévy, who feared that Linhart, Glucksmann, and Le Dantec were using the newspaper to establish an independent power base that might challenge his authority, attacked them for emphasizing the struggles of the petty bourgeoisie at the expense of those of the workers and demanded their self-criticism. By the autumn of 1971 the editorial staff of the paper was divided into two warring factions. Although Lévy's *ouvriérisme* prevailed in the winter of 1971 to 1972 when *La Cause du peuple – J'accuse* concentrated almost exclusively on the GP's struggle at the Renault-Billancourt factory, the disappointment of Linhart, Glucksmann, and others would contribute to a direct-democratic critique of the GP that led to its dissolution.[159]

The GP's direct-democratic vision of revolution would also play an important role in its refusal to embrace terrorism and its ultimate abandonment of violent exemplary action when the dialectic of government repression and GP violence threatened to engulf the organization.[160] The leaders of the GP were acutely aware of the danger of terrorism and consciously fought against it. The founding text of the NRP, "Illégalisme et guerre," was very explicit on this account. The essence of the GP's struggle, it emphasized, was not violence, but illegality. The NRP was to prefigure the mass insurrection with symbolic action, but "not to substitute itself in any manner for mass operations." The clandestine OPS was neither to develop into the military wing of a pacific organization nor to operate autonomously of the open movement. To restrain the OPS it was required that its members be only seasoned militants, take part in the open movement, and maintain frequent contacts with workers. Their action was to be guided "by the will of the majority of the people." The foundational text concluded by emphasizing that *"there is no 'military solution' to any of our political problems."*[161] Despite carrying out two kidnappings and planning others, the OPS carefully and successfully avoided situations in which it would find itself using lethal violence. It never carried loaded guns or trained its members in their use—not even when it kidnapped Robert Nogrette, the assistant head of personnel at the Renault factory at Renault-Billancourt, as a reprisal for the killing of the Maoist militant Pierre Overney by a Renault security guard.[162] Further, although it made demands when Nogrette was kidnapped, it was careful never to attach any conditions to them. After forty-eight hours, when the GP judged that it had defied authority long enough and had gotten sufficient publicity out of the kidnapping, it simply released Nogrette without receiving anything in return. The final communiqué of the NRP regarding Nogrette emphasized that "it is not for us to decide the moment that one must begin the extermination of the class enemy, but the people, the people alone."[163]

Rather than feed a cycle of government repression and terrorist violence, the Overney murder and Nogrette kidnapping ultimately resulted in the GP's abandonment of exemplary action as its failure was recognized. The GP had targeted Renault-Billancourt because the great factory complex, the first to refuse the Grenelle Accords in May '68, symbolized working-class militancy. Exemplary action there would, they believed, spark revolution in France. The GP placed in the factory a few *établis* who recruited a handful of workers. Yet, once the GP militant presence became known, both the *établis* and the recruited workers were fired, and the GP was reduced to protests outside of the factory gates and a hunger strike by fired workers demanding to be reinstated. It was during one of these protests in February 1972 that a Billancourt security guard shot and killed Overney. Shortly after the Overney-Nogrette affair, a former member of the Renault *Comité de lutte*, Nicolas Boulte, launched a bitter and damning critique of the GP's failure at Billancourt. He blamed the GP leadership for the death of Overney. In the absence of anything more than superficial political work and of any true legitimacy in the working class, the GP had, he argued, systematically sought violent confrontation. Nogrette's kidnapping likewise showed the complete absence of a GP political project, and "lacking such a project, the commando operations' only goal is to divert the attention of the workers by offering them if need be a show to which they are completely exterior."[164] Although Boulte's critique was initially rejected,[165] by the end of 1972 the GP repudiated all forms of the politics of exemplary action for reasons that echoed Boulte's critiques. Because exemplary action could turn into spectacular action and lead workers to passivity it "risked," Lévy contended, "therefore to end in a new variation of authoritarian Marxism." In their efforts to liberate the masses' "practical thought," militants were henceforth to limit their activity to helping the masses obtain the means that they need to act on their own.[166]

These internal critiques of the GP's politics culminated in 1973 when the GP leadership decided under the influence of the Lip strike to dissolve the GP. Lip was a watchmaking factory in the city of Besançon whose high-quality steel and ruby watches were the pride of French watchmaking. In 1973 Lip was struggling, and its Swiss majority shareholder decided to close down the larger part of its operations there. When the workers at Lip discovered the extent of the planned layoffs, they sequestered the administrators, searched their files, and discovered further, even more ominous plans for their factory. The workers decided to occupy the factory and seize the stock of some 25,000 watches as insurance. They established a system of factory governance and restarted production, selling watches and paying themselves for their work.

The GP viewed Lip as the manifestation of their revolutionary dreams. Workers, with broad support from the population, had engaged in illegal action and taken matters into their own hands by setting up a direct-democratic factory government. In contrast to the GP's failure to mobilize workers at Billancourt, the silent majority at Lip had become *enragés*.[167] Lévy believed that the symbolic power of Lip was having an effect on the entire working class, bringing "the perpetuation of social relations ... into question."[168] Interpreted as an ideological revolution, Lip raised troubling questions for the GP. The GP had played no role in the emergence of the Lip struggle. Rather, the strike had been led by the Confédération française démocratique du travail (CFDT) and Catholic militants like Jean Raguenès, the Dominican monk and Lip *ouvrier spécialisé* who had organized *comités d'action* in the factory. The GP's leadership conceded that the militants at Lip had succeeded where they had failed. Having proven that workers could act on their own, Lip forced the GP to radicalize its self-criticism. Lévy concluded from Lip that they had failed to truly question the concept of organization that had been "handed down by the would-be heirs of Leninism."[169] No matter how close they might be to the base, professional revolutionaries could no longer be a progressive force after Lip. The age of direct democracy had arrived and the entire question of power had to be rethought. If the example of Lip were to spread, the strategy of the *prise du pouvoir* (seizure of power) would have to be abandoned in favor of increasing worker autonomy through partial seizures of power and a concept of antipower.[170] By the end of the summer of 1973, the GP leadership had arrived at the conclusion that their organization, having lost its purpose, had to be disbanded.[171] As had been the case in 1968 when the UJCML fell apart, many militants rejected the aversion of the leadership, dominated by intellectuals, to organization. The GP leaders, notably Lévy, Geismar, and Rolin, had to work hard from the autumn of 1973 through the spring of 1974 to ensure that dissolution was complete and that the worst outcome, a slide into terrorism, did not occur.[172]

The evolution of the GP from 1968 to 1973 was guided by the imperative that direct democracy had to be the end of its politics. This imperative led the GP leaders to question the legitimacy of professional revolutionaries and the notion of the seizure of power as it became evident to them to what extent their political action violated their ideals. They increasingly emphasized that the masses had to be in charge of politics from the beginning of any revolutionary struggle. The only legitimate task for themselves was to help the masses express their desires and act upon them. A politics of antipower or one of partial seizures of power was the only acceptable one. And this politics had to be based on firm moral principles, which constituted, they believed, the foundation of the Catholic militants' success at Lip.[173] The GP's direct-democratic and populist ideals led to one other important final conclusion: all revolts are equal. The struggle of the workers could not be given priority over those of other marginal groups. The legitimacy and equality of all revolts, a radical democratic political philosophy that rejected all representation and political organization, a deep suspicion of all positions of power, and a moralism in politics that draws its intransigence from a brush with the ultimate moral transgression: these were the legacies of the GP for the 1970s.

And China? What role did it play in this history of "Maoist" militancy? Very little. Especially after May '68, the "Maoism" of the UJCML-GP was overwhelmingly determined by domestic obsessions and developments. As it became more securely rooted in the French political landscape, the GP progressively abandoned references to China and Mao. The effigy of Mao on the front page of *La Cause du peuple – J'accuse*, the GP newspaper from May 1971, gradually decreased in size until it vanished with the issue of 14 September 1972, and the number and size of articles on China in the GP press steadily declined from 1968 to 1972, giving way in 1972 to coverage of diverse topics such as prison revolts, the environment, consumerism, abortion, racism, and sexual repression. In retrospect, Olivier Rolin, the head of the GP's Nouvelle résistance populaire, believed that China was basically unimportant to the GP. Precisely because China was not at the center of the GP Maoists' concerns, contrary perspectives on Chinese reality, like Simon Leys's *Les Habits neufs du Président Mao* (1971), which interpreted the Cultural Revolution as a power struggle within the Chinese Communist Party, had little impact on them. They simply dismissed and ignored Leys's book and concentrated on to the domestic issues that concerned them the most. Only after the GP's political project collapsed would these Maoists begin to reflect on China and discover a more troublesome history there.[174]

Intellectuals and the Gauche prolétarienne: Laying the Foundation of the Late-Gauchiste Critique of Political Power

The relationship between left-wing intellectuals and the GP began with an initial gesture of solidarity in the face of state repression, but soon extended far beyond that. The GP's affirmation of the multiplicity of revolts, critique of representation and political organization, and suspicion of power were themes that appealed to many left-wing intellectuals and led them to work with the GP on common political projects. This close relationship between intellectuals and the GP was important to the intellectual Left's further elaboration of direct-democratic politics and its reconceptualization of intellectual engagement. It also proved to be key to the GP's leaders, preventing them from becoming isolated, reinforcing their anti-organizational and direct-democratic tendencies, moving them away from *ouvriérisme*, and possibly discouraging them from becoming terrorists. After the dissolution of the GP, intellectuals affiliated with it helped young former GP leaders reintegrate themselves in French society and, in some cases, promoted them to the pinnacle of the intellectual scene as advocates of political disillusionment. A window on the relationship between the GP and intellectuals offers a view of some key developments leading to the critique of totalitarianism.

Although the GP leadership, having renounced their intellectual identities to serve the people, was initially suspicious of intellectuals, beginning in the spring of 1970 it realized that intellectuals could help the GP escape mounting state repression. First, it called upon Sartre to take over formal responsibility for *La Cause du peuple* (which he did on 1 May 1970), correctly judging that the state would not dare arrest him. When the state shifted its repressive tactics and began to arrest the vendors of *La Cause du peuple*, the GP called upon intellectuals once again. An Association des amis de "la Cause du peuple," headed up by Simone de Beauvoir and Michel Leiris and involving many other intellectual and cultural luminaries, was formed.[175] While supporting the newspaper in general, it organized its sale on the streets of Paris by prominent intellectuals, thereby putting the government in an impossible situation: either arrest the celebrity hawkers and risk an international scandal or ignore them and again reveal its hypocrisy. A second association rallying intellectuals alongside the GP, Secours rouge, was founded in June 1970 and charged with the mission of the "political and juridical defense of the victims of repression."[176] Its activities were diverse, including, for example, lending support to the efforts of imprisoned GP militants to gain the status of political prisoners; demonstrations of solidarity with the Jews accused in the Leningrad trial in the USSR; and the provision of services to *bidonvilles*.

Toward the end of 1970 and in 1971 some intellectuals began to work closely with the GP on projects that had their origin in the defense of victims of repression, but soon went much further in their ambitions. Two of these projects that emerged out of the convergence of intellectuals and the GP, the Groupe d'information sur les prisons (GIP) and the newspaper *Libération*, were among the most important in intellectual politics of the early 1970s. Both projects involved Jean-Paul Sartre and Michel Foucault, two of the most prominent intellectuals of postwar France, and were central to their political evolution in these years. The histories of the GIP, *Libération*, and the encounters of Sartre and Foucault with the GP reveal some of the key features of the politics of the noncommunist intellectual Left in the early 1970s.

For Sartre, 1968 was an important date. Although he played only a minor role in the events and would, by his own account, understand the significance of them only at the end of 1969, they marked a turning point in his politics.[177] For one, after 1968 Sartre had nothing good to say about the PCF or Soviet socialism. Although his hopes for liberalization in the Soviet Union faded after the arrest of the Soviet writers Iuli Daniel and Andrei Siniavski in 1965, Sartre continued to maintain as late as 1967 that the USSR, in contrast to Western democracies, only needed to be reformed, not revolutionized.[178] But in the wake of the Warsaw Pact invasion of Czechoslovakia, which Sartre and de Beauvoir considered to be a "war crime,"[179] Sartre called for a new attitude toward the Soviet Union. It was, he argued, no longer sufficient "that the Left *protest*, become indignant, rebuke, or 'regret.'" Protest had to go beyond the terrain of deontology and take on the regime, because it was the system and not the leaders—prevented by it from acting otherwise—that was to blame for its failures. In sum, "after the month of August 1968, one must abandon with regard to it the refuge of moralism and the reformist illusion."[180]

Sartre's critique of the PCF echoed that of the USSR. The failure of the PCF to be either revolutionary or reformist in 1968 was, he argued, a structural failure. The party's thought and action reflected its organization.[181] The emergence of a significant *gauchiste* movement after 1968 removed the last obstacle to Sartre's abandonment of the PCF: the lack of a credible alternative to it on its Left.[182] Sartre, *gauchiste* after 1968, had nothing but contempt for the PCF. He echoed the GP's invective against it. The PCF acted like the police, was in league with the government against the GP, and had "thought like a fascist" in the Overney affair.[183]

The events of 1968 in France confirmed old themes in Sartre's revolutionary politics and introduced new ones. Sartre maintained that his analysis in his *Critique of Dialectical Reason* remained valid, the question after 1968 being how to develop a party that does not become an institution. Despite his renewed revolutionary enthusiasm after 1968, Sartre was never very optimistic that this could be done.[184] Sartre welcomed May for its innovations: its recentering of revolutionary action on liberty; its radical democratic thrust, which he conceived of as a demand for sovereignty, "that is to say to be able to decide, not alone, each person in his corner, but together, what will be done"; and its critique of the disciplines or of the production and use of knowledge.[185] Sartre's reflection on the themes that he saw in May '68 (liberty, direct democracy, and the critique of knowledge) would become increasingly more pronounced and radical in the course of his work with the GP.

After agreeing to direct *La Cause du peuple* out of a reflex of solidarity, Sartre found himself progressively drawn to the GP and its politics. He found in his relations with the Maoists a certain conviviality that was related to their common education. He was also attracted by their acceptance of the necessity of illegal, even violent action; their rejection of Leninism for spontaneity; their moral approach to politics and society; and their emphasis on direct democracy.[186] These areas of convergence were sufficient to keep Sartre working with the GP Maoists from 1970 to beyond the demise of the GP. Despite the importance of the GP in his own political evolution, Sartre maintained a critical distance from it. He never became a Maoist, was dismissive of Mao's thought, and never adopted the GP's views on China. He demanded that the *gauchiste* press have a greater respect for the truth, and resigned from the directing committee of Secours rouge when he concluded that the Maoists had become too powerful in the organization. He criticized the Maoists when they called for the lynching of a notary whom they accused without evidence of brutally murdering a young working-class woman and when they advocated the guillotine for Touvier. Yet, his voice was not always a moderating one; he also thought that the release of Nogrette was a mistake and defended the killing of Israeli athletes by Palestinian terrorists at the 1972 Munich Olympic games.[187]

The clearest manifestation of the direction taken by Sartre's politics in his years with the GP is his conceptualization of the "new intellectual." The new intellectual emerged in the autumn of 1970, a product of Sartre's contacts with the GP and, perhaps more profoundly, his reflection on 1968. Sartre contrasted the new intellectual with the "classic intellectual." The politics of the latter emerges out of his realization of the contradiction between the universality of his work and its service of the particular. To relieve his unhappy consciousness, the classic intellectual denounces the particular uses of the universal and elaborates the principles of a universal politics. Sartre found this insufficient in the early 1970s. The new intellectual had to prefigure the universalistic society toward which he strives, where there is no room for intellectuals as a separate social category, and contest his particular possession of knowledge, his very status as an intellectual. The new intellectual was a product of the *soixante-huitard* critique of knowledge and of the radical democratic values of May; it had, Sartre argued, first emerged in the attack on the *cours magistral* (lecture course) in May '68. The new intellectual was to follow the masses and put himself and his knowledge in the service of them. After 1968, it was necessary to find "a new way of being with the masses in refusing a distinctive power, in having the same sovereignty as any member of the masses, but no more." Ideally, the intellectual should become an *établi*.[188] Although Sartre was too old to work in the factory and refused to abandon his book on Flaubert, he tried throughout his experience with the Maoists to be a new intellectual.

Sartre's post-1968 politics converged with that of Michel Foucault. Foucault recognized as much in a 1972 interview, noting that both of them had changed since their polemic on the occasion of the publication of Foucault's *Les Mots et les choses*, when Foucault had belittled Sartre's *Critique de la raison dialectique* as "the magnificent and pathetic effort of a man of the nineteenth century to think about the twentieth century."[189] To be sure, irreconcilable differences between them remained. Sartre was a humanist and discussed the origins and finality of political action in terms of the language of alienation.[190] Foucault, on the other hand, maintained without exception in the early 1970s a Nietzschean antihumanist perspective on politics. A politics based on the concept of human nature was unacceptable for Foucault because he believed, as he told Noam Chomsky in a debate of November 1971, that "these notions of human nature, of justice, of the realization of the human essence are notions and concepts that were formed within our civilization, in our type of knowledge, in our philosophical form, and that, as a consequence, they are part of our class system, and that one cannot, as regrettable as it may be, make use of these notions to describe or justify a battle that should—that must in principle—shatter the very foundations of our society."[191] For Foucault, class struggle is based not on a notion of justice, but on the will to power. Only experience, not transcendent values or a new utopia, can guide action. Chomsky, the radical humanist, was shocked by this man, who in his evaluation "didn't inhabit the same moral universe."[192]

Foucault was in Tunisia teaching philosophy in 1968, and it was in his work there with Tunisian students that he rediscovered political activism after a long hiatus subsequent to his departure from the PCF in 1953. Although Foucault was not in France in May '68, May, as Foucault later explained, brought politics to him by politicizing issues that had long interested him, like "psychiatry, internment, the medicalization of a population."[193] Foucault did not become a Marxist after 1968, but after seeing Marxism's power as a Sorelian myth while in Tunisia, he became less dismissive of it. He read or reread the classics of Marxism and began in 1969 to adopt the rhetoric of class struggle in his discussion of politics. Although he engaged in a number of militant actions before 1971—notably at the newly created University of Paris campus at Vincennes—it was with the birth of the Groupe d'information sur les prisons (GIP) early that year that Foucault found his cause. Foucault was one of the founders of the GIP and its prime moving force. From 1971 to 1973 the GIP dominated the life of Foucault; in these years, Foucault was as much a militant as a philosopher.

The idea for the GIP emerged in late 1970 in the minds of Foucault and his companion, Daniel Defert. Defert had joined the GP shortly after it was outlawed in 1970 and at the end of 1970 participated in a group that was to prepare politically the trial of GP militants. The GP had made imprisonment and prison conditions an issue in the autumn of 1970, when GP militants went on a hunger strike to be given the status of political prisoners. Although there was some opposition from *ouvriériste* Maoists, the GP welcomed efforts by the democratic front to investigate prisons. Defert proposed that Foucault head a "commission of inquiry" on the prisons like that of the popular tribunal of Lens, over which Sartre presided in December 1970 to investigate the death of miners in an underground explosion there. Foucault preferred the term *"groupe d'information"* (informational group) over "commission of inquiry" because the former avoided the judicial terminology of the latter and allowed a greater emphasis on collective thought and the *"prise de parole"* of the prisoners.[194]

Written by Foucault, the manifesto of the GIP was signed and presented to the press by himself, Jean-Marie Domenach, and Pierre Vidal-Naquet on 8 February 1971. Noting that due to the repressive measures of the state "none of us can be sure to escape prison," it modestly proposed to "make known what prison is" by requesting information from those with an experience of it. Its only initial goals were to "make known reality" and to offer advice on how to defend oneself when arrested.[195] The GIP's first activities consisted mainly of distributing and collecting questionnaires about prison conditions filled out by prisoners and their families. After the collected information was published at the end of May 1971, the GIP organized campaigns against the conditions of detention and the judicial system, concentrating on the *casier judiciaire*, the abolition of which was one of the principal demands of prisoners and their families.[196] In the autumn of 1971 when prison revolts broke out in France, the GIP's campaigns of solidarity with the prisoners and denunciations of the system were at the center of events.

Behind the GIP project lay a political philosophy that Foucault articulated on numerous occasions. The GIP refused to claim for itself any intellectual or institutional authority. As a *"groupe d'information"* its only goals were that it "search, provoke, and spread information" and "pick out the targets of possible future action."[197] It was to "leave the talking to those who have an experience of prison" and to give them the means to express their consciousness of their experience. Ideally, the work of the GIP would democratize knowledge and de-ghettoize prisoners by breaking down the barriers to communication among prisoners, between prisoners and their families, and between prisoners and society.[198]

Foucault did not see the GIP's action as being based on an idea of what is possible or of what is "good or evil"; his goal was "to make apparent and to transform into a discourse readable by all that which can be unbearable for the most disadvantaged classes in the current justice system."[199] Ultimately, a complete overhaul of the Napoleonic penal code would be necessary, but Foucault would not say what form it should take. Who should do it, according to Foucault? "Precisely those people on whom this undoubtedly unjust justice weighs the heaviest. It is for them to take the reform and refashioning of justice in hand."[200] True to its motto, "let the prisoners talk!" (*"la parole aux détenus!"*), the GIP faded at the end of 1972 after the founding of the Comité d'action des prisonniers (CAP), an organization run by and for prisoners.[201]

Foucault's radical democratic and Nietzschean politics also came through clearly in his February 1972 debate with Benny Lévy and André Glucksmann on popular justice.[202] The debate centered on the question of whether tribunals are appropriate forms of popular justice. Lévy argued that tribunals are necessary to resolve the internal contradictions of the masses and normalize popular justice so that it is executed in the "common interest" and does not become a "settling of scores."[203] While recognizing the legitimacy of Lévy's concerns, Foucault considered tribunals to be a manipulation of popular justice. Popular justice had to be executed by the masses themselves and be based not on "a universal and abstract idea of justice," but on the masses' own experience. Tribunals are a bureaucratization of justice and a reconstitution of the division of labor. Further, the whole penal justice system had to be contested. Used by the bourgeoisie to separate the proletariat from the "non-proletarianized pleb," it constituted an important prophylactic against revolution. The historical model of popular justice for Foucault was the September 1792 prison massacres before they were taken over by the official tribunals set up by the Commune of Paris.[204]

Sartre, who was closer to Lévy than Foucault on this matter, found Foucault more radical than he in his rejection of all judicial institutions.[205] But Foucault's more radical perspective should not conceal his fundamental agreement with Sartre on one issue: the legitimacy of the masses and of their justice. For Sartre, the courts first created by the government during the French Revolution were initially legitimate because they were "conceived of as making the people the judges." Like Foucault, Sartre believed that all justice comes from the people. It is their right of insurrection enshrined in the *Déclaration des droits de l'homme et du citoyen* that is "true justice in the final analysis." Popular tribunals, like that at Lens over which Sartre presided, are, if open to popular participation, "a partial but true manifestation of popular sovereignty." But, Sartre hastened to add, any sanctions against those found guilty by a popular tribunal would have to be decided upon and executed directly by the people.[206]

Convergence between Sartre and Foucault can also be seen in Foucault's reformulation of intellectual politics through his experience with the GIP—a reformulation that echoes Sartre's idea of the "new intellectual." But it is Gilles Deleuze, with whom Foucault elaborates his idea of the "specific intellectual" in a 1972 interview, who puts his finger on the fundamental transformation in intellectual politics that underlies Foucault's (and, for that matter, Sartre's) reconceptualization of the intellectual: the refusal of representation. Deleuze says: "For us the theorizing intellectual has ceased to be a subject, a representing or representative consciousness. Those who act and who struggle have ceased to be represented, be it by a party or a union that unrightfully claims in turn the right to be their consciousness. Who speaks and who acts? It is always a multiplicity, even in the person who speaks and acts. We are all small groups. [*"Nous sommes tous des groupuscules."*] There is no more representation. There is only action, the action of theory and the action of practice in relay relations or in networks."[207]

Recognizing this collapse of representation, Foucault rejected the traditional intellectual, whom he defines as someone who "proclaimed the truth to those who did not yet see it and in the name of those who could not say it." The masses do not need intellectuals to think; indeed, "they knew clearly and perfectly well, much better than the intellectuals [what the intellectuals have recently discovered] and they say it exceedingly well." The traditional intellectual is part of a system of power that forbids the "discourse" and "knowledge" of the masses. The "specific intellectual" should not place himself outside of the masses to "say the mute truth for all," but fight with the masses and specifically "against forms of power there where he is the object and the instrument of them at the same time: in the order of 'knowledge,' of 'truth,' of 'consciousness,' and of 'discourse.'"[208] What counts is the "counter-discourse" of the prisoners or delinquents and not a discourse or theory on delinquency.[209] Or, as Foucault would later put it, "the knowledge of an intellectual is always partial in relation to the knowledge of workers." Intellectuals should not try to "develop the consciousness of workers because it already exists," but, because they are "plugged … into the informational machinery," their role can be to "allow this consciousness, this knowledge of workers to enter into the informational system."[210]

Despite the self-effacement of the intellectual within it, the GIP's refusal of representation, critique of knowledge, and trust placed in the masses were highly appealing to many French intellectuals. *Esprit* made the GIP its political model and focused on helping the marginal and oppressed solve their own problems.[211] Developed while he was working on the GIP, Domenach's new idea of the role of the intellectual as a "socio-cultural facilitator" echoed those of Sartre and Foucault in its emphasis on the self-abnegation of intellectuals and direct democracy.[212] GIP committees were created throughout France and included as many as two to three thousand people.[213] Innumerable other *groupes d'information* were modeled after it, including a Groupe d'information santé, a Groupe d'information sur les asiles, a Groupe d'information et de soutien des travailleurs immigrés, and a Groupe d'information sur l'armée. Although none of these were as successful as the GIP, they all attracted large numbers of militants, practiced the GIP's "militancy of the intolerable," and broke with established models of intellectual politics. According to a contemporary analysis by Philippe Meyer, they refused to become an "enlightened and representative avant-garde" and rather sought to "create alliances with the 'most oppressed' that would allow them to once again give expression to their own problems."[214]

The origins and ambitions of *Libération*, the last and the most successful of the GP press initiatives, were similar to those of the GIP. It grew out of the GP press network's effort to facilitate the *"prise de parole"* of the people, a journalistic project shared by much of the rest of the *gauchiste* press of the day.[215] *La Cause du peuple* treasured direct expression by workers. Its editorial board took working-class voices sent to it by militants and integrated them into a more traditional lyrical, militant journalism.[216] *J'accuse* and *La Cause du peuple – J'accuse* sought to do much the same thing, with the exception that with these newspapers the GP journalistic project became that of many philosophers, writers, painters, filmmakers, and professional journalists.[217] This journalistic project became more mainstream with the birth of L'Agence de presse Libération (APL) on 18 June 1971.[218] The APL emerged as a response to the brutal police beating of Alain Jaubert, a scientific journalist working for *Le Nouvel Observateur*, at a 29 May 1971 demonstration. An "informational commission" was formed by concerned journalists and intellectuals. Its report, written by Michel Foucault, concluded that the press and opinion were being intimidated by the police.[219] The APL, the brainchild of Jean-Claude Vernier, was founded to fight this intimidation, combat false news, and give *"la parole au peuple."* It called upon the people to send it information—*Comités de l'APL* were formed for this purpose—that it would diffuse after verification. After initially issuing inaccurate and triumphalist dispatches, the APL, under the leadership of its *directeur-gérant* Maurice Clavel, was reorganized in the autumn of 1971 and became a legitimate and respected press agency by the end of that year.[220]

In gestation in GP and APL circles from the summer of 1972, the first issue of *Libération* came out on 22 May 1973. The manifesto of *Libération*, written by Philippe Gavi and Benny Lévy, revised by Sartre, and discussed at length by Foucault, offered an entire political philosophy in the guise of a press project. It gave *Libération* the task to "take on secrecy" and "help the people *prendre la parole.*" While noting the diversity of opinions within the team, it declared that it was united on the essential, that "news comes from the people and returns to the people." According to the manifesto, "the doctrine of *Libération* is 'People *prends la parole* and keep it!'" *Libération* journalists were to be informed in their work by the maxim that "the further one climbs the social ladder, the more one finds corruption." The manifesto explicitly rejected conventional electoral politics "in favor of a new politics that is born of the popular forces' direct refusal of a society founded on injustice." Because "that which is essential is that the people impose their direct control," *Libération* would, it said, "echo popular demands" during the electoral campaign of 1973.[221]

Libération sought in its functioning and organization to implement its radical democratic political principles. It was to rely on the people for its financing and basic organization. It launched a popular subscription in December 1972 and was to use the network of committees established by the APL to gather news. The newspaper was to be run according to the principles of direct democracy; the division of labor was to be challenged within it. Not surprisingly, initial operations were a bit chaotic as general assemblies wrote and rewrote articles and the *fabricants* sought to exercise their right, enshrined in *Libération*'s founding manifesto, to some degree of control over the newspaper's content.

Libération enjoyed the enthusiastic participation of intellectuals. Sartre and Foucault in particular put a large amount of their time and resources into it. Both were involved in the meetings leading up to the launching of the newspaper, both participated in the writing of *Libération*'s manifesto, and both, along with Maurice Clavel, contributed substantial sums of money to the effort. Sartre and Foucault also had high hopes for *Libération*. Unlike in the case of *La Cause du peuple*, Sartre, in taking the position of director of *Libération*, intended to participate actively in the newspaper and write for it. He abandoned his philosophical and literary activities for six months to assist its launching.[222] Sartre shared *Libération*'s aspirations and looked forward to participating in an effort to reinvent writing so that it would better express popular speech.[223] Only the onset of blindness in the autumn of 1973 prevented him from contributing more fully to the newspaper. Where Sartre wanted to give written expression to popular speech, Foucault hoped to edit a "column on workers' memories" in *Libération* that would bring to the light of day the "fundamental experiences" of workers and uncover how these experiences taught workers, independently of any party or union, to fight the bourgeoisie.[224] Although Foucault's participation in *Libération* ultimately proved to be minimal, it marked the beginning of his interest in journalism and of his consideration of philosophy as a "sort of radical journalism."[225]

In its original incarnation, *Libération* did not last very long. The newspaper was racked by financial problems, disputes about politics that centered on the Maoist influence within it, and the difficulties encountered by any organization that tries to respect direct democracy. In the summer of 1974, Serge July, having become the director after Sartre's resignation in May 1974 and gained legitimacy with the newspaper's staff by diluting the Maoist presence within it, reorganized *Libération*, making it more like other newspapers. Although *Libération* continued to support direct-democratic politics, July installed the reign of competence, the division of labor, and professionalism in the newspaper's internal operations, thereby provoking the resignation of Vernier and others who wished to pursue the effort to produce a different, more subversive paper. July had *Libération* proclaim itself a newspaper of information, had the Liberation committees sidelined, and had a new, more conventional juridical structure adopted for the newspaper. The changes of the summer and autumn of 1974 remained in place until 1978, when *Libération* put an even more professional formula in place. One of the most prominent survivals of the *gauchiste* years, *Libéra-tion* outlasted the collapse of *gauchisme* only by abandoning many of its ideals in practice.[226]

Libération was not alone in the disjuncture between its embrace of a direct-democratic—or more generally *autogestionnaire*—politics and its failure to implement direct democracy in its own operations. A 1968 effort to institute *autogestion* at *Le Nouvel Observateur* was defeated by Jean Daniel, who held that *Le Nouvel Observateur* could only be run like a monarchy.[227] At *Esprit*, where the nature of authority relations within the journal remained on the agenda at least through 1973, Domenach resisted the extension of the critique of domination and hierarchy to his direction of the journal. In a letter to Paul Thibaud in which he explained his resis-tance to a devolution of authority, Domenach, like Daniel, compared his journal to predemocratic institutions: "'power' at *Esprit*, is me and you without omitting, of course, the existence of barons, advisors to the prince, knights, women of honor, court poets, lords, and buffoons. But above all no parliament, certainly not!"[228] The direct-democratic intellectual politics of the 1970s was, these examples would suggest, less the critique of all forms of power than its advocates suggested, if only because it spared the recently expanded power of intellectuals within the mass media.

* * *

As we have seen, as intellectuals grew disillusioned with communism and distanced themselves from the state and political parties as a result of the Algerian War and institutional change, they turned to a direct-democratic critique of hierarchy that they hoped would enable them to preserve lib-erty within the revolutionary project. Drawing on the French revolution-ary tradition and favored by intellectuals' investment in the new mass media, direct democracy came to dominate intellectual politics in the half-decade after 1968 as the events of that year appeared to prove its viability. Many intellectuals would maintain this fidelity to direct democracy in word (if not in deed) even as the impasses of its politics became apparent in the early 1970s, maintaining that any transformative politics that is not that of the people themselves, or (to put it differently) is lead by a van-guard, will end in failure. The critique of totalitarianism would emerge out of the conflict between this late *gauchiste* intellectual politics and the par-ties of the Left as they approached political power in the 1970s.

Notes

1. Megan Koreman, *The Expectation of Justice: France, 1944-46* (Durham, N.C., 1999).

2. For a reading of postwar intellectual politics that emphasizes its historicist, violent, and Manichean qualities see Tony Judt, *Past Imperfect: French Intellectuals, 1944-1956* (Berkeley, 1992). On intellectual political engagement in general see David L. Schalk, *The Spectrum of Political Engagement: Mounier, Benda, Nizan, Brasillach, Sartre* (Princeton, 1979).

3. James D. Wilkinson, *The Intellectual Resistance in Europe* (Cambridge, Mass., 1981), 21-22, 54; Ariane Chebel d'Appollonia, *Des lendemains qui déchantent*, vol. 1 of *Histoire politique des intellectuels en France, 1944-1954* (Brussels, 1991), 72. Sartre cited in Arthur Hirsh, *The French New Left: An Intellectual History From Sartre to Gorz* (Boston, 1981), 42.

4. For an elaboration with particular relevance to intellectual politics see Emile Durkheim, "Individualism and the Intellectuals," in Emile Durkheim, *On Morality and Society: Selected Writings*, ed. Robert N. Bellah (Chicago, 1973), 43-57.

5. The classic early left-wing attack on Third Republic Kantianism is Paul Nizan, *Les Chiens de garde* (1932; reprint, Paris, 1971).

6. The key texts are Jean-Paul Sartre, *Qu'est-ce que la littérature?* (Paris, 1948); Simone de Beauvoir, *Pour une morale de l'ambiguïté* (Paris, 1947); and Maurice Merleau-Ponty, "La Guerre a eu lieu," in his *Sens et non-sens* (Paris, 1966), 245-69.

7. See De Beauvoir's discussion of Kant's failure to adequately address evil will in her *The Ethics of Ambiguity*, trans. Bernard Frechtman (New York, 1996), 33-34.

8. Merleau-Ponty, "La Guerre a eu lieu," 251 and 268 for the quotes.

9. Jean-Paul Sartre, "What is Literature?" in *"What is Literature?" and Other Essays*, trans. Steven Ungar (Cambridge, Mass., 1988), 222-23. Translation altered. Emphasis in the original.

10. On the importance of virtue in French republicanism see Carol Blum, *Rousseau and the Republic of Virtue: The Language of Politics in the French Revolution* (Ithaca, N.Y.: Cornell University Press, 1986). The moral virtue that the historian Maurice Agulhon, steeped in republicanism, saw in the PCF was key to his joining the party. Maurice Agulhon, "Vu des coulisses," in *Essais d'ego-histoire*, ed. Pierre Nora (Paris, 1987), 20-23.

11. On the PCF in 1945-47 see Irwin M. Wall, *French Communism in the Era of Stalin: The Quest for Unity and Integration, 1945-1962*, Contributions in Political Science, no. 97 (Westport, Conn., 1983), chapter 2.

12. In May 1945, 56 percent of the French held that the USSR was the nation that had contributed the most to the defeat of Germany in 1945. Immediately after the war, the USSR was viewed more favorably by public opinion in France than in Northern Europe and the Anglo-Saxon countries. Although French opinions of the USSR worsened considerably after the onset of the Cold War in 1947, the French view of the importance of the Soviet war effort continues to differ from that of others fifty years later. In May 1994, 25 percent of the French believed that the USSR was the nation that had contributed the most to the defeat of Germany in World War II as compared with 9 percent of the British, 21 percent of the Germans, and 11 percent of the Americans. Jean-Jacques Becker, with the collaboration of Catherine Simon and Jean Loignon, "Le Modèle soviétique et l'opinion française," in *La France en voie de modernisation, 1944-1956. FNSP colloque des 4 et 5 décembre 1981*, vol. 2, no pagination. *Le Monde*, 31 May 1994, 15.

13. Edgar Morin, *Autocritique* (1958; reprint, Paris, 1975), 47.

14. Cited in Guillaume Malaurie in collaboration with Emmanuel Terrée, *L'Affaire Kravchenko* (Paris, 1982), 190.

15. Emmanuel Le Roy Ladurie, *Paris-Montpellier: P.C.-P.S.U. 1945-1963* (Paris, 1982), 96 for the quote. Even an intellectual on the Right like the Gaullist Claude Mauriac recognized the power of this reading of Koestler by noting that he was not "converted" by Rubashov's sacrifice (Kerry H. Whiteside, *Merleau-Ponty and the Foundation of Existential Politics* [Princeton, 1988], 170). See also Jeannine Verdès-Leroux, *Au service du parti: le*

parti communiste, les intellectuels et la culture (1944-1956) (Paris, 1983), 80 and the remarks of Jean Chaintron in *Staline à Paris*, ed. Natacha Dioujeva and François George (Paris, 1982), 195.

16. Alexandre Kojève, *Introduction à la lecture de Hegel: leçons sur la Phénoménologie de l'Esprit professées de 1933 à 1939 à l'École des Hautes Études réunies et publiées par Raymond Queneau* (Paris, 1947) and Maurice Merleau-Ponty, *Humanisme et terreur: essai sur le problème communiste* (1947; reprint, Paris, 1980). Merleau-Ponty had attended Kojève's lectures on Hegel in the 1930s. On the importance of Kojève's reading of Hegel in postwar France see Michael Roth, *Knowing and History: Appropriations of Hegel in Twentieth-Century France* (Ithaca, 1988); Vincent Descombes, *Le Même et l'autre: quarante-cinq ans de philosophie française (1933-1978)* (Paris, 1986); and David Macey, *The Lives of Michel Foucault: A Biography* (New York, 1993), 33.

17. Verdès-Leroux, *Au service du parti*, 14-18.

18. Jean-François Sirinelli, "Les Normaliens de la rue d'Ulm après 1945: une génération communiste?" *Revue d'histoire moderne et contemporaine* 32 (Oct.-Dec. 1986): 574. See also Jean-Philippe Mochon, "Les Élèves de l'École Normale Supérieure de la rue d'Ulm et la politique, 1944-1962" (Masters Thesis, Université Charles de Gaulle, Lille III, 1993).

19. Philippe Buton and Laurent Gervereau, *Le Couteau entre les dents: 70 ans d'affiches communistes et anticommunistes* (Paris, 1989), 143.

20. Chebel d'Appollonia, *Le Temps de l'engagement*, vol. 2 of *Histoire politique des intellectuels en France, 1944-1954* (Brussels, 1991), 92-97; Irwin M. Wall, *The United States and the Making of Postwar France, 1945-1954* (New York, 1991), 149-51.

21. The preceding paragraph draws on Wall, *French Communism in the Era of Stalin*.

22. Malaurie, *L'Affaire Kravchenko*, 25; Chebel d'Appollonia, *Le Temps de l'engagement*, 96.

23. "Plant an apricot orchard so the Russians and Americans can use it as a battlefield? Thanks. Not so dumb." offered a peasant in Roussillon in 1950. Laurence Wylie, *Village in the Vaucluse*, 3rd ed. (Cambridge, Mass., 1974), 33.

24. *L'Observateur* was the predecessor of *France observateur* and *Le Nouvel Observateur*. Chebel d'Appollonia , *Le Temps de l'engagement*, 110-16 and 121-41; Olivier Le Cour Grandmaison, "Le Mouvement de la paix pendant la guerre froide: le cas français (1948-1952)," *Communisme* 18-19 (2nd and 3rd quarter 1988): 120-38; Pierre Grémion, *Intelligence de l'anticommunisme: le Congrès pour la liberté de la culture à Paris* (Paris, 1995), 82-87.

25. Chebel d'Appollonia , *Le Temps de l'engagement*, 77.

26. Intellectuals like Georges Friedmann who refused to reject such a politics were for that reason not invited to the Congress for Cultural Freedom's 1955 International Congress in Milan. Grémion, *Intelligence de l'anticommunisme*, 164. Laurent Gardinier, "Liberté de l'Esprit 1949-1953: un exemple de sociabilité gaulliste au temps de la Guerre froide" (DEA Thesis, Paris IEP, 1993).

27. The following discussion of the Kravchenko affair is based on Malaurie, *L'Affaire Kravchenko*; Jean-Pierre Rioux, "Le Procès Kravchenko," in Dioujeva and George, *Staline à Paris*, 148-64; Wall, *The United States and the Making of Postwar France*, 151-53.

28. Mainstream publishers had rejected the manuscript, presumably for political reasons. Malaurie, *L'Affaire Kravchenko*, 19.

29. Grémion, *Intelligence de l'anticommunisme*, 86; Malaurie, *L'Affaire Kravchenko*, 203, 146. Camus's judgment dates from 1953.

30. Malaurie, *L'Affaire Kravchenko*, 83; David Caute, *Communism and French Intellectuals 1914-1960* (London, 1964), 124-25.

31. Judt claims that "the impression left [by the Kravchenko trial] was of a Communist moral victory" (*Past Imperfect*, 113). An avalanche of works on the camps came out in 1948 and 1949. Pierre Rigoulot, *Les Paupières lourdes: les français face au goulag: aveuglements et indignations* (Paris, 1991), 60.

32. According to contemporary polls 35 percent agreed with Kravchenko and 15 percent with *Les Lettres françaises*; 24 percent had no opinion. Among workers, 27 percent agreed

with Kravchenko and 23 percent with *Les Lettres françaises*. Malaurie, *L'Affaire Kravchenko*, 204.

33. Chebel d'Appollonia, *Le Temps de l'engagement*, 66-67. Maurice Merleau-Ponty, "The U.S.S.R. and the Camps," in his *Signs*, trans. Richard C. McCleary (Evanston, Ill., 1964), 263-73.

34. Malaurie, *L'Affaire Kravchenko*, 197; Emile Copfermann, *David Rousset: une vie dans le siècle* (Paris, 1991), 117.

35. On the decline of the PCF press see Bernard Legendre, *Le Stalinisme français: qui a dit quoi? (1944-1956)* (Paris, 1980), 44-46.

36. For Sartre's position in the early 1950s see Jean-Paul Sartre, *The Communists and Peace with a Reply to Claude Lefort*, trans. Martha H. Fletcher with the assistance of John R. Kleinschmidt (New York, 1968).

37. Chebel d'Appollonia, *Le Temps de l'engagement*, 146-47.

38. Whiteside, *Merleau-Ponty and the Foundation of Existential Politics*, chap. 8.

39. Roth, *Knowing and History*.

40. Although possessing less intellectual capital than its rival on the Left, *Les Temps modernes*, *Esprit* may have touched a wider audience. It was more deeply implanted in the provinces and enjoyed a higher circulation. Although intellectual journals did not keep very good circulation data, it appears that *Les Temps modernes* peaked at a print run of 10,000 per issue in the late 1940s and that *Esprit*'s average annual print run per issue was at 12,000 in 1950 and reached its highest (around 15,000) in the decade 1962-72. *Esprit*'s circulation declined beginning in early 1973, but appears not to have dipped below 10,000, even during the crisis of intellectual journals in the early 1980s. Circulation data is taken from Peter Deli, *De Budapest à Prague: les sursauts de la gauche française* (Paris, 1981), 78-79; Dominique Vernaudon, "'Esprit' de la mort d'Emmanuel Mounier à la fin de la guerre d'Algérie: enquête socio thématique" (Masters Thesis, Paris VII, 1978), 81; Michel Winock, *Histoire politique de la revue "Esprit": 1930-1950* (Paris, 1975), 241-42; John Hellman, *Emmanuel Mounier and the New Catholic Left 1930-1950* (Toronto, 1981), 207 and fn. 6 on page 323; Howard Davies, *Sartre and 'Les Temps Modernes,'* (New York, 1987), 217; and IMEC ESP2 B4-02 .04, the Esprit archives of the *Institut Mémoires de l'Édition Contemporaine* (IMEC), folder ESP2 B4-02 .04. The comparison of the cultural capital of *Les Temps modernes* and *Esprit* is made by Anna Boschetti, *The Intellectual Enterprise: Sartre and* Les Temps Modernes, trans. Richard C. McCleary (Evanston, Ill., 1988).

41. The most important of *Esprit*'s challenges to the PCF was its publication in November 1949 of François Fejtö's article "L'Affaire Rajk est une affaire Dreyfus internationale." See Fejtö's account of the politics of its publication in his *Mémoires: de Budapest à Paris* (Paris, 1986), 211-16; and in his *Où va le temps qui passe? Entretiens avec Jacqueline Cherruault-Serper* (Paris, 1991), 148-62.

42. For different perspectives on these and other questions regarding the period 1932-1950 see especially Winock, *Histoire politique de la revue "Esprit"*; Hellman, *Emmanuel Mounier and the New Catholic Left*; and Chebel d'Appollonia, *Des lendemains qui déchantent* and *Le Temps de l'engagement*.

43. Michel Crozier, "Les Intellectuels et la stagnation française," *Esprit* 209 (Dec. 1953): 771-82 and Jean-Marie Domenach, "Redressement," *Esprit* 210 (Jan. 1954): 63-65. Jean-Marie Domenach became co-director of *Esprit* in 1956. For the years 1950-1956 at *Esprit* see Chebel d'Appollonia, *Le Temps de l'engagement*; Jacques Rollet, "Histoire politique de la revue 'Esprit' 1950-1956" (DEA Thesis, Paris IEP, 1981) and Dominique Vernaudon, "'Esprit' de la mort d'Emmanuel Mounier à la fin de la guerre d'Algérie."

44. Gisèle Sapiro, "La Politique culturelle d'Elsa Triolet au CNE (1949-1951)," in *Elsa Triolet un écrivain dans le siècle: Actes du colloque international 15-17 novembre 1996 Maison Elsa Triolet-Aragon Saint-Arnoult-en-Yvelines*, ed. Marianne Gaudric-Delfranc (Paris, 2000), 205.

45. Sapiro, "La Politique culturelle d'Elsa Triolet au CNE (1949-1951)," 205-21; Vincent Feré, "Le Comité national des écrivains et les compagnons de route du parti communiste français (février 1946-avril 1953)" (DEA Thesis, Paris IEP, 1998).

46. This was, for example, *France observateur*'s initial reaction to the report. Deli, *De Budapest à Prague*, 225-26.
47. Ibid.
48. Grémion, *Intelligence de l'anticommunisme*, 251-54.
49. For Sartre's analysis see his article in *L'Express* (9 Nov. 1956) and his *The Ghost of Stalin*, trans. Marta H. Fletcher with the assistance of John R. Kleinschmidt (New York, 1968) as well as the comments in Deli, *De Budapest à Prague*, 132-35. See also *Esprit*'s critique of Sartre's *The Ghost of Stalin*: Jean Conilh, "Staline, le fantôme de Sartre," *Esprit* 248 (March 1957): 499-501. Grémion, *Intelligence de l'anticommunisme*, 260-61 evaluates Sartre's position as "against the current."
50. Maurice Merleau-Ponty, "On De-Stalinization," in his *Signs*, 303, originally published in *L'Express* in November 1956 in response to Sartre's article.
51. Gilles Martinet, "1956 et le renouvellement de la gauche française," in *1956 Varsovie-Budapest: la deuxième révolution d'Octobre*, ed. Pierre Kende and Krzysztof Pomian (Paris, 1978), 150-51.
52. De Gaulle invoked the threat of "totalitarian communism" in his 30 May 1968 radio speech. Laurent Joffrin, *Mai 68: histoire des événements* (Paris, 1988), 296. For Left intellectuals' use of the word with regard to the U.S. see Etiemble's charge that *Readers' Digest* is totalitarian propaganda (in Chebel d'Appollonia, *Des lendemains qui déchantent*, 149) and Jean-Marie Domenach's assertion that American society is totalitarian (in Richard F. Kuisel, *Seducing the French: The Dilemma of Americanization* [Berkeley, 1993], 115). When defending neutralism, Pierre Emmanuel claimed that both the United States and the USSR were totalitarian (in Kuisel, *Seducing the French*, 44). For an example of capitalism as totalitarian see André Gorz, *Strategy for Labor: A Radical Proposal*, trans. Martin A. Nicolaus and Victoria Ortiz (Boston, 1967; first French edition 1964), 119. The PCF used the word "totalitarian" to describe the Fifth Republic. Jeannine Verdès-Leroux, *Le Réveil des somnambules*, 168.
53. Grémion, *Intelligence de l'anticommunisme*, chap. 7.
54. Raymond Aron, *Démocratie et totalitarisme* (Paris, 1965), 288, 15, and 16 for the citation. On the 1957 essay see Robert Desjardins, *The Soviet Union Through French Eyes, 1945-85* (London, 1988), 65.
55. Cécile Richard-Nicolas, "1956 – l'escamotage du rapport Khrouchtchev," in Dioujeva and George, *Staline à Paris*, 61-74.
56. Michel Dreyfus, "1956: l'année terrible," *Communisme* 29-31 (1st to 3rd quarter 1991): 237-47. David Caute, *Communism and French Intellectuals*, 233-34. On the assaults on the PCF see Jean-Pierre A. Bernard, "Novembre 1956 à Paris," *Vingtième siècle* 30 (April-June 1991): 68-81 and Grémion, *Intelligence de l'anticommunisme*, 229-30.
57. Dreyfus, "1956: l'année terrible." On the CNE see Grémion, *Intelligence de l'anticommunisme*, 245-46; Caute, *Communism and French Intellectuals*, 232-33; Copfermann, *David Rousset*, 138-39; Sapiro, "Comité national des écrivains," in Julliard and Winock, *Dictionnaire des intellectuels français*, 299-300; and Michael Scott Christofferson, "French Intellectuals and the Repression of the Hungarian Revolution of 1956: The Politics of a Protest Reconsidered," in *After the Deluge: New Perspectives on French Intellectual and Cultural History*, ed. Julian Bourg (forthcoming).
58. This position was in *Esprit*, for example, first articulated in October 1956 by Jean-Marie Domenach and continually reaffirmed thereafter. Jean-Marie Domenach, "Le P.C. et le mal français," *Esprit* 243 (Oct. 1956): 548-50; Jean-Marie Domenach and Jacques Julliard, "Réveiller la France," *Esprit* 246 (Jan. 1957): 70-82; Paul Fraisse, "Refaire la gauche," *Esprit* 250 (May 1957): 768-76; Jean Lacroix, "Critiques nécessaires et tâches positives," *Esprit* 250 (May 1957): 746-67.
59. James D. Le Sueur, *Uncivil War: Intellectuals and Identity Politics During the Decolonization of Algeria* (Philadelphia, 2001), 52-53.

60. Jacques Tati's classic statement on French modernization, "Mon oncle," dates to 1958. Cornelius Castoriadis' faith in the revolutionary role of the French working class was shattered by the referendum vote. Hirsh, *The French New Left*, 127.

61. On communist opposition to the Indochinese War see Alain Ruscio, "Les Intellectuels français et la guerre d'Indochine: une répétition générale?" *Les Cahiers de l'IHTP* 36 (June 1996): 113-32, which emphasizes French intellectuals' lack of interest in the Indochinese War, and Edward Rice-Maximin, *Accommodation and Resistance: The French Left, Indochina and the Cold War, 1944-1954*, Contributions to the Study of World History, no. 2 (New York, 1986). The shortcomings of the PCF's positions in relation to the French resistance to the Algerian War are discussed intelligently in Pierre Vidal-Naquet, "Une fidélité têtue: la résistance française à la guerre d'Algérie," *Vingtième siècle* 10 (April-June 1986): 3-18 and in Martin Evans, *The Memory of Resistance: French Opposition to the Algerian War (1954-1962)* (New York, 1997), 212-19 and passim.

62. See Alain Monchablon, *Histoire de l'UNEF de 1956 à 1968* (Paris, 1983) on the role of the UNEF in the opposition to the Algerian War; see Michel Winock, "La Gauche non communiste en France: la coupure de 1956," in Kende and Pomian, *1956 Varsovie-Budapest*, 141-48 on the impact of the voting of full powers for Mollet.

63. Evans, *The Memory of Resistance* emphasizes the importance of the analogies with World War II drawn by the resistance against the Algerian War and the resistors' disgust, even decades after the events, with the conduct of the parties of the Left during the war. A sense of the impact of the war on evaluations of the state can be discerned from the history of torture during the Algerian War by one of the leading opponents of it, Pierre Vidal-Naquet. Vidal-Naquet writes: "All *dissidence*, whatever its nature, can push the modern state, however liberal it might be, to use torture." Pierre Vidal-Naquet, *La Torture dans la république: essai d'histoire et de politique contemporaine (1954-1962)* (Paris, 1983), 10. Julliard discussed the impact of the Algerian War on his itinerary in Jacques Julliard, interview with the author, Paris, 21 June 1994. Jacques Julliard, "La Répartition des clercs," in *La Guerre d'Algérie et les intellectuels français*, ed. Jean-Pierre Rioux and Jean-François Sirinelli (Brussels, 1991), 394 for the quotation.

64. Judt, among others, makes this claim in his *Past Imperfect*, 282-85.

65. Paul Clay Sorum, *Intellectuals and Decolonization in France* (Chapel Hill, 1977); Rita Maran, *Torture: The Role of Ideology in the French-Algerian War* (New York, 1989); Claude Liauzu, "Les Intellectuels français au miroir algérien," in Claude Liauzu, Nora Benallegue, and Salah Hamzaudi, *Les Intellectuels français au miroir algérien: mouvements sociaux maghrebins*, Cahiers de la Méditerranée, no. 3 (Nice, 1984), 1-180; Claude Liauzu, "Intellectuels du tiers monde et intellectuels français: les années algériennes des Éditions Maspero," in Rioux and Sirinelli, *La Guerre d'Algérie de les intellectuels français*, 155-74.

66. Evans, *The Memory of Resistance*, 5, 31-44, and passim.

67. Sorum, *Intellectuals and Decolonization in France*, 166-70; Michel-Antoine Burnier, *Choice of Action: The French Existentialists on the Political Front Line*, trans. Bernard Murchland (New York, 1968), 122-23; H. Rodrigues da Silva, "Le Temps de l'action. Le discours d'Esprit et des Temps modernes sur les réseaux de soutien au FLN et le mouvement des 'Insoumis'," *Hermès* 8-9 (1991): 179-87; David L. Schalk, *War and the Ivory Tower: Algeria and Vietnam* (New York, 1991), chap. 3; Jean-Marie Domenach, "'Les Damnés de la terre' I. Sur une préface de Sartre," *Esprit* 304 (March 1962): 454-63; Michael Scott Christofferson, "François Furet Between History and Journalism, 1958-65," *French History* 15, 4 (Dec. 2001): 428-29; Cornelius Castoriadis, "Suspension de la publication de *Socialisme ou Barbarie*," in *Prolétariat et organisation*, vol. 2 of his *L'Expérience du mouvement ouvrier* (Paris, 1974), 423.

68. Liauzu, "Les Intellectuels français au miroir algérien," 161-63. For example, Jean-Marie Domenach, "L'Après-guerre," *Esprit* 310 (Oct. 1962): 353-56 offers a general rejection of *tiers-mondisme* and calls for energies to be employed in the advancement of reform in France. I do not wish to argue that *Esprit* was indifferent to the third world. On the contrary, it often spoke of the need for solidarity with it. But such solidarity was to proceed

from a renovated France (*Esprit*'s first task) and did not entail blind approval of third-world revolutionary movements.

69. Burnier, *Choice of Action*, 148, 150.
70. Michel Contat and Michel Rybalka, *A Bibliographical Life*, vol. 1 of *The Writings of Jean-Paul Sartre*, trans. Richard C. McCleary (Evanston, Ill., 1974), 520.
71. Liauzu, "Intellectuels du tiers monde et intellectuels français," 173. Liauzu concludes (p. 160) from his study of publication data that *tiers-mondisme* was never a "ground swell of opinion."
72. Liauzu, "Les Intellectuels français au miroir algérien," 166.
73. Jean-Marie Domenach, "Cuba, révolution menacée," *Esprit* 294 (April 1961): 529. Here, as elsewhere, I cite Domenach's statements as evidence of the positions broadly shared by the *Esprit* community of intellectuals. As the director of the journal, he set its editorial policy in consultation with others. Statements such as this one were meant to represent *Esprit* as a whole and generally did despite the dissent of some intellectuals from any given position.
74. Jean-Marie Domenach, "Guerre et paix au Vietnam," *Esprit* 356 (Jan. 1967): 125-27. Ieme van der Poel, who systematically analyzed articles in *Esprit* on China from the years 1971 to 1975, summarizes its position as being characterized by a "prudent benevolence" in his *Une Révolution de la pensée: maoïsme et féminisme à travers* Tel quel, Les Temps modernes, *et* Esprit, Faux titre no. 65 (Amsterdam, 1992), 63.
75. Contat and Rybalka, *A Biographical Life*, 511, 520; Jean-Paul Sartre, "Sartre par Sartre," *Situations, IX: Mélanges* (Paris: Gallimard, 1972), 125-29. *Les Temps modernes* showed little interest in China and had no clear editorial policy on it during the Cultural Revolution according to van der Poel, *Une révolution de la pensée*, 69-70 and 70 for the citation.
76. When Sartre went to Cuba in 1960 he saw in its revolution the realization of his group-in-fusion. The revolution appeared to be a direct democracy without dogmatism. Contat and Rybalka, *A Bibliographical Life*, 376-77.
77. Hervé Hamon and Patrick Rotman, *Les Années de rêve*, vol. 1 of *Génération* (Paris, 1987), 93-94, 286-87, citation on 287.
78. See also the discussion of the Gauche prolétarienne's relationship to China and the Chinese Cultural Revolution below in this chapter and that of *Tel quel*'s Maoism in chapter 5.
79. This analysis is suggested by Paul Thibaud, "Génération algérienne?" *Esprit* 161 (May 1990): 46-60.
80. Robert J. Smith, *The Ecole Normale Supérieure and the Third Republic* (Albany, N.Y., 1982); Jean-François Sirinelli, "The Ecole Normale Supérieure and Elite Formation and Selection During the Third Republic," in *Elites in France: Origins, Reproduction, and Power*, ed. Jolyon Howorth and Philp G. Cerny (London, 1981), 66-77; and Jean-Michel Gaillard, *L'ENA, miroir de l'État: De 1945 à nos jours* (Brussels, 1995).
81. Louis Pinto, *L'Intelligence en action: Le Nouvel Observateur* (Paris, 1984); Niilo Kauppi, *French Intellectual Nobility: Institutional and Symbolic Transformations in the Post-Sartrian Era* (Albany, N.Y., 1996), especially the epilogue; Régis Debray, *Le Pouvoir intellectuel en France* (Paris, 1979); and Christofferson, "François Furet Between History and Journalism, 1958-65." The history of *France Observateur* and the creation of *Le Nouvel Observateur* is recounted in great detail in Philippe Tétart, "*France Observateur* 1950-1964: histoire d'un courant de pensée intellectuel," 6 vols. (Ph.D. Thesis, Paris IEP, 1995).
82. Christophe Charle, "Academics or Intellectuals? The Professors of the University of Paris and Political Debate in France from the Dreyfus Affair to the Algerian War," in *Intellectuals in Twentieth-Century France: Mandarins and Samurais*, ed. Jeremy Jennings (New York, 1993), 94-116. Charle's article should be read in the context of his *Naissance des "intellectuels": 1880-1900* (Paris, 1990).
83. Debray, *Le Pouvoir intellectuel en France*, 277-82 and passim.
84. Jean-Paul Sartre, *Critique of Dialectical Reason. I. Theory of Practical Ensembles*, trans. Alan Sheridan-Smith (London, 1976). The following discussion of Sartre's *Critique of Dialecti-*

cal Reason draws on Hirsh, *The French New Left*, chap. 3; Khilnani, *Arguing Revolution*, chap. 3; and Mark Poster, *Existential Marxism in Postwar France: From Sartre to Althusser* (Princeton, 1975), chap. 7.

85. Poster, *Existential Marxism in Postwar France*, 291.
86. Jean-Paul Sartre, *Critique of Dialectical Reason, vol 2. (Unfinished): The Intelligibility of History*, trans. Quintin Hoare (New York, 1991).
87. See his comments in Philippe Gavi, Jean-Paul Sartre, and Pierre Victor, *On a raison de se révolter* (Paris, 1974), 252, 350.
88. The word *"gauchisme"* is used here in both the general sense of "to the left of Bolshevism" and more specifically to refer to a rejection of Leninist ideas of working-class consciousness and of the vanguard role of the party. On *gauchisme* see Richard Gombin, *The Origins of Modern Leftism*, trans. Michael K. Perl (Baltimore, 1975). On the Cercle International des Intellectuels Révolutionnaires and the continued importance of workers' councils for *Arguments* see Sandrine Treiner, "La Revue Arguments: 1956-1962. Un lieu de rencontre d'itinéraires intellectuels et politiques" (DEA Thesis, Paris IEP, 1987), 36-37, 88-92, 100-4.
89. My analysis of *Arguments* draws on Hirsh, *The French New Left*, chap. 4; Poster, *Existential Marxism in Postwar France*, chap. 6; Treiner, "La Revue Arguments"; Gilles Delannoi, "Arguments, 1956-1962 ou la parenthèse de l'ouverture," *Revue française de science politique* 34, 1 (Feb. 1984): 127-45; Fejtö, *Où va le temps qui passe?* 178-88; Fejtö, *Mémoires: de Budapest à Paris*, 252-56.
90. In 1958, for example, *Arguments* opened up to the liberal *Preuves*, noting it to be worthy of interest to its readers. Grémion, *Intelligence de l'anticommunisme*, 258-59.
91. This was a general trend in French Marxism after 1956. George Lichtheim, *Marxism in Modern France* (New York, 1966), chap. 3.
92. Gorz, *Strategy for Labor*. Gorz's position was that of *Les Temps modernes* as a whole. On the new working class in general see Poster, *Existential Marxism in Postwar France*, 361-69.
93. Lefebvre cited in Poster, *Existential Marxism in Postwar France*, 245.
94. Éliane Brau, *Le Situationisme ou la nouvelle internationale* (Paris, 1968), 36-37.
95. Poster, *Existential Marxism in Postwar France*, 245.
96. A. Belden Fields, *Trotskyism and Maoism: Theory and Practice in France and the United States* (New York, 1988), 100-1. The fate of *Arguments* parallels, although only broadly, that of Vive la Révolution! a decade later. Here too, Marxist revisionism had the effect of dispersion, leading the core intellectuals of the journal in very different directions. The divergent interests of its members ultimately undermined the group's cohesion and was a major factor in the decision to cease publication of *Arguments* in 1962. Some, like Edgar Morin, had moved so far beyond Marxism that they were bothered by its use as a label for their thought. This occurred as early as 1959 for Morin. Fejtö, *Où va le temps qui passe?* 184.
97. See the discussion of this issue in the Gauche prolétarienne in van der Poel, *Une révolution de la pensée*, 25-26.
98. Diana Orieta Pinto, "Sociology as a Cultural Phenomenon in France and Italy: 1950-1972" (Ph.D. Thesis, Harvard University, 1977) and Rémy Rieffel, *La Tribu des clercs: les intellectuels sous la Ve République* (Paris, 1993), 205-9. Jean-Marie Domenach, director of *Esprit* after Béguin's death in 1957, committed the journal to a concrete reformist politics in 1958 ("A propos de la 'Nouvelle Série'," *Esprit* 260 [April 1958]: 659) and reaffirmed that commitment at the end of the Algerian War in 1962 ("Le Réalisme politique," *Esprit* 310 [Oct. 1962]: 430-46). For a concrete example of *Esprit*'s interest in reformist planning see Jean-Marie Domenach's positive appraisal of the Club Jean Moulin's *L'État et le citoyen*, "Le Club Jean Moulin et la réforme démocratique," *Esprit* 302 (Jan. 1962): 115-19. Domenach was not impressed with either the new Marxism based on the concept of alienation or structuralism. See his essays "Pour en finir avec l'aliénation" and "Le Requiem structuraliste" in his *Le Sauvage et l'ordinateur* (Paris, 1976; first published in

1965 and 1973 respectively). He wrote at length of the need for a more modest conception of politics rethought along the lines of the tragic in his *Le Retour du tragique* (Paris, 1967).

99. *Esprit* spoke of the bankruptcy of the French Left and of the need for intellectuals to end the subordination of their politics to that of the parties as early as 1957 in Jean-Marie Domenach and Jacques Julliard, "Réveiller la France," *Esprit* 246 (Jan. 1957): 70-82, a position maintained in Michel Winock, "Sans illusions," *Esprit* 355 (Dec. 1966): 739-49. The turn to a project of civilization against productivism appears in internal position papers in late 1967: Paul Thibaud, "Rapport introductif à la journée politique du 11 novembre," *Journal Intérieur: Groupes "Esprit"* (11 Nov. 1967) IMEC ESP2 .B3-03 .07, published in part as Paul Thibaud, "Un Pacte avec la richesse," *Esprit* 373 (Aug.-Sept. 1968): 142-62 and Jean-Marie Domenach, "Perplexités avant la journée politique du 11 novembre," *Journal Intérieur: Groupes "Esprit"* (Dec. 1967), 2, IMEC ESP2 .B3-03 .07. See also Jean-Marie Domenach, "L'Ancien et le nouveau," *Esprit* 372 (June-July 1968): 1026.

100. Philippe Forest, *Histoire de Tel quel, 1960-1982* (Paris, 1995), 51ff; Michel Winock, *Chronique des années soixante* (Paris, 1987), 65-72; François Dosse, *L'Histoire en miettes: des "Annales" à la "nouvelle histoire"* (Paris, 1987); Kristin Ross, *Fast Cars, Clean Bodies: Decolonization and the Reordering of French Culture* (Cambridge, Mass., 1995).

101. Pierre Victor (the alias of Benny Lévy) in Michèle Manceaux, *Les Maos en France* (Paris, 1972), 185-86. Daniel Cohn-Bendit cited in Jean-Pierre Le Goff, *Mai 68: l'héritage impossible* (Paris, 1998), 50.

102. Treiner, "La Revue Arguments," 107-8; Castoriadis, "La Suspension de la publication de *Socialisme ou barbarie*," 418; Hamon and Rotman, *Les Années de rêve*, 251-52, 293-97; Sartre in Gavi, Sartre, Victor, *On a raison de se révolter*, 68-69.

103. Marianna P. Sullivan, *France's Vietnam Policy: A Study in French-American Relations*, Contributions in Political Science, no. 12 (Westport, Conn., 1978), 71-79 on the parties, press, and opinion and 78 for polling data. In 1967, only Finnish, Swedish, and Brazilian citizens were, among those polled, more in favor of the United States's withdrawal from Vietnam.

104. Among the founders of the CVN were Henri Bartoli, Alfred Kastler, Jean-Paul Sartre, Laurent Schwartz, and Pierre Vidal-Naquet. See the reproduction of the "Appel à la création d'un Comité Viet-nam national" and the discussion of the CVN in Nicolas Pas, "Sortir de l'ombre du Parti communiste français: Histoire de l'engagement de l'extrême gauche française sur la guerre du Vietnam, 1965-1968" (DEA Thesis, Paris IEP, 1998), 305 and *passim*. This thesis, the most important work to date on the French movement against the American war in Vietnam, is summarized in Nicolas Pas, "'Six heures sur le Vietnam': Histoire des comités Vietnam français 1965-1968," *Revue historique* 613 (Jan.-March 2000): 157-85. Other useful discussions of the antiwar movement include: Jean-François Sirinelli, *Intellectuels et passions françaises: manifestes et pétitions au xxe siècle* (Paris, 1990), chap. 11; Bernard Droz, "Vietnam (guerre de)," in *Dictionnaire des intellectuels français: les personnes, les lieux, les moments*, ed. Jacques Julliard and Michel Winock (Paris, 1996), 1159-61; Jean Lacouture, "L'Opinion française et la seconde guerre du Vietnam," *Le Monde*, 13 Dec. 1966; Hamon and Rotman, *Les Années de rêve*, 308-9, 338, 336-37, 410-17, 425-29; Laurent Jalabert, "Aux origines de la génération 1968: les étudiants français et la guerre du Vietnam," *Vingtième siècle* 55 (1997): 69-81.

105. Sirinelli, *Intellectuels et passions françaises*, 249 for the Sartre citation. Macey, *The Lives of Michel Foucault*, 292; Philippe Forest, *Histoire de Tel quel*, 271-72; interview with André Glucksmann, *La Croix*, 7 Jan. 1978.

106. Pas, "Sortir de l'ombre du Parti communiste français"; Jalabert, "Aux origines de la génération 1968."

107. Issuing death certificates for structuralism were notably Jean Duvignaud and Épistémon (aka Didier Anzieu). See François Dosse, *The Sign Sets, 1967-Present*, vol. 2 of *History of Structuralism*, trans. Deborah Glassman (Minneapolis, 1997), chap. 11, entitled

"Jean-Paul Sartre's Revenge." Dosse explains how, after the initial shock, May '68 led to the medium-term triumph and long-term disintegration of structuralism.

108. See Le Goff, *Mai 68*, chap. 5.

109. At least Touraine and Mallet believed this. See Alain Touraine, *The May Movement*, trans. L. F. X. Mayhew (New York, 1971) and Serge Mallet, "May-June 1968: First Strike for Control," in *Essays on the New Working Class*, ed. and trans. Dick Howard and Dean Savage (St. Louis, 1975), 56-86.

110. Recent historical analyses are skeptical of claims that workers expressed revolutionary, qualitative demands. See Michael Seidman, "Workers in a Repressive Society of Seductions: Parisian Metallurgists in May-June 1968," *French Historical Studies* 18 (spring 1993): 255-78.

111. On the "general staff" of May '68 see especially Hamon and Rotman, *Les Années de rêve*, 465.

112. Daniel Cohn-Bendit and Gabriel Cohn-Bendit, *Obsolete Communism: The Left Wing Alternative*, trans. Arnold Pomerana (New York, 1968), 133.

113. See Daniel Cohn-Bendit's comments in Daniel Cohn-Bendit, Jean-Pierre Duteuil, Alain Geismar, and Jacques Sauvageot, *The French Student Revolt: The Leaders Speak*, trans. B. R. Brewster (New York, 1968), 58.

114. Those accepting his proposal included the Trotskyist JCR and the UNEF. Laurent Joffrin, *Mai 68*, 106-8.

115. There were 2,000 wounded, 200 seriously, in the demonstrations of May-June 1968 in Paris. Le Goff, *Mai 68*, 107-16.

116. Alain Schnapp and Pierre Vidal-Naquet, *The French Student Uprising*, trans. Maria Jolas (Boston, 1971), 231, 234, 307; and Richard Gombin, *Le Projet révolutionnaire* (The Hague, 1969), 24.

117. See Cohn-Bendit's interview with Sartre in Cohn-Bendit and others, *The French Student Revolt*, 73-83.

118. Cohn-Bendit cited in Alfred Willener, *The Action-Image of Society: On Cultural Politicization*, trans. A. M. Sheridan Smith (New York, 1970), 163.

119. Cohn-Bendit cited in Cohn-Bendit and others, *The French Student Revolt*, 79.

120. Ibid., 27-28, 35-38, 45.

121. In 1970 the antihierarchical Maoist organizations Vive la Révolution! and the Gauche prolétarienne had respectively only several hundred and about fifteen hundred members. Fields, *Trotskyism and Maoism*, 52, 100.

122. Antoine Artous and Daniel Bensaïd, "'Que faire?' (1902) et la création de la Ligue communiste (1969)," in *Retours sur Mai*, ed. Antoine Artous (Montreuil, 1988), 149. (The essay is dated March 1976.)

123. Davies, *Sartre and 'Les Temps Modernes,'* 191; André Gorz, "What are the Lessons of the May Events?" in *Reflections on the Revolution in France: 1968*, ed. Charles Posner (Baltimore, 1970), 264-65 for the citations; Deli, *De Budapest à Prague*, 158-59; André Gorz, "Détruire l'université," *Les Temps modernes* 26, 285 (April 1970): 1553-58. This latter article precipitated the resignation of Bernard Pingaud and Jean-Bertrand Pontalis from the editorial board of *Les Temps modernes*. Sartre agreed substantially with Gorz. See the discussion of Sartre's post-1968 politics below.

124. Edgar Morin, "Une révolution sans visage," in Edgar Morin, Claude Lefort, and Cornelius Castoriadis, *Mai 68: la brèche suivi de vingt ans après* (1968; reprint with additional material, Brussels, 1988), 86-87. For his critique of the movement for being insufficiently liberal see his "La Commune étudiante," in *Mai 68*, 30-32.

125. Claude Lefort, "Le Désordre nouveau," in *Mai 68*, 47, 54, 60-62; Cornelius Castoriadis, "La Révolution anticipée," in *Mai 68*, 95, 116-18, 131-41.

126. Lefort, "Le Désordre nouveau," 47, 53, 62.

127. Castoriadis, "La Révolution anticipée," 101.

128. Ibid., 108. See pages 107-12 for his "Propositions pour la constitution immédiate d'un mouvement révolutionnaire."

129. Jean-Marie Domenach, "Les Enragés de Nanterre," *Esprit* 371 (May 1968): 876. Paul Thibaud and Jean-Marie Domenach, "La Fin des tranquillités," a *projet d'éditorial* that was sent to members of the *Esprit* community on 14 May and was to be discussed at the *Comité directeur* meeting of 16 May. The document was never published. IMEC ESP2 B4-01 .05.

130. Jean-Marie Domenach, "Reflets de mai," *Esprit* 376 (Dec. 1968): 737; Jean-Marie Domenach and Paul Thibaud, "Pour (re)commencer," *Esprit* 378 (Feb. 1969): 323-24. Before the June 1968 legislative elections an internal *Esprit* document said the following about Gaullism: "All of a sudden, all that was positive in Gaullism disappeared or went over to the radical camp. Since 30 May, we have returned to the RPF with all its dangers, including that of fascism." "A propos des élections," June 1968, 3. IMEC ESP2 E3-03 .16.

131. Jean-Marie Domenach, "Disparaître ou se rénover," *Journal intérieur: groupes "Esprit,"* November 1968. IMEC ESP2 B2-01 .05. Esprit, "Mai 68," *Esprit* 372 (June-July 1968): 961-69, citations pages 965 and 969.

132. Domenach and Thibaud, "Pour (re)commencer," 324.

133. "A propos des élections," 4.

134. Esprit, "Mai 68," 965.

135. Jean-Marie Domenach's "L'Impasse de la gauche," *Esprit* 383 (July-Aug. 1969): 56. The citation is from Jean-Marie Domenach, "L'Idéologie du mouvement," *Esprit* 373 (Aug.-Sept. 1968): 50. For Domenach's belief in the importance of Marcuse see also his "Le Discours du bonheur," originally published in 1969 and reprinted in his *Le Sauvage et l'ordinateur* (Paris, 1976), 47-73.

136. Jean-Marie Domenach, "L'Idéologie du mouvement," 50. *Esprit* continually reminded its readers of the lessons to be learned from the Eastern European experience about the importance of preserving liberty. See the following and the further discussion of this issue in chapter 3: "And since young people do not want to know anything about our historical experience, may they turn their eyes toward Czechoslovakia; there are worse servitudes than those of consumer society. Europe is still too close to totalitarianism—Nazi and Stalinist—to allow itself to be whimsical with liberty." Jean-Marie Domenach, "Reflets de Mai," *Esprit* 376 (Dec. 1968): 740.

137. Jacques Julliard, "Questions sur la politique," *Esprit* 378 (Feb. 1969): 340.

138. As stated earlier, A. Belden Fields estimates GP membership at 1,500 in 1970. The review *Est et Ouest* (May 1971) estimated its membership at 2,000, according to Jean-Pierre Rivenc, "Le Mouvement maoïste français" (Troisième Cycle Thesis, University of Toulouse, 1982), 294.

139. David Drake, "*On a raison de se revolter*: The Response of *la Gauche prolétarienne* to the Events of May-June 1968," in *Violence and Conflict in the Politics and Society of Modern France*, ed. Jan Windebank and Renate Günter, *Studies in French Civilization*, vol. 5 (Lewiston, N.Y., 1995), 61-62.

140. Hervé Hamon and Patrick Rotman, *Les Années de poudre*, vol. 2 of *Génération* (Paris, 1988), 37.

141. The following discussion of the early history and prehistory of the UJCML draws on Hamon and Rotman, *Les Années de rêve*, 229-319 and Rivenc, "Le Mouvement maoïste français," parts one and two.

142. They left the UEC in January 1966 and founded the UJCML after the failure of this effort to take over the former organization.

143. Before the Cultural Revolution they had seen two things in Maoism: a refusal of passive coexistence and socialism in one country in favor of proletarian internationalism, and a critique of Stalinism superior to that of Khrushchev. On this transition to *gauchisme* see Pierre Victor (the alias of Benny Lévy), " Être prêts pour une crise sociale ouverte," in Michèle Manceaux, ed., *Les Maos en France* (Paris, 1977), 186; Jean-Pierre Le Dantec, *Les Dangers du soleil* (Paris, 1978), 86-98; Rivenc, "Le Mouvement maoïste en France," 157-232; Hamon and Rotman, *Les Années de rêve*, 319-55.

144. On these points see Hamon and Rotman, *Les Années de rêve*, 263, 268, 279; Jean-Pierre Le Dantec, *Les Dangers du soleil*, 171, 275-76; Jean-Paul Sartre, "Autoportrait à soixante-dix ans," in *Situations X: politique et autobiographie* (Paris, 1976), 182.

145. Le Dantec, *Les Dangers du soleil*, 94.

146. About one hundred of the few hundred members of the UJCML became *établis* in the autumn of 1967. Ibid., 98. Although the GP had more *établis* than any other group, *établissement* (and the populist, direct-democratic vision it entailed) became a widespread phenomenon after 1968. Marnix Dressen estimates that there were as many as 1,200 to 2,500 *établis* between 1967 and the writing of his thesis, "Les Étudiants à l'usine. Mobilisation et démobilisation de la gauche extra-parlementaire en France dans les années 1960-1970. Le cas des établis maoïstes," vol. 1 (Doctoral Thesis, FNSP, 1992), 3.

147. Ironically, the least hierarchical and most countercultural of the Maoist groups, Vive la Révolution!, would emerge in 1969 from those who had joined the PCMLF.

148. Le Dantec, *Les Dangers du soleil*, 143-44.

149. On the central importance of Flins and Sochaux in the GP's revolutionary mythology see Le Goff, *Mai 68*, 173-76.

150. Alain Geismar, Serge July, and Erlyne Morane, *Vers la guerre civile* (Paris, 1969). Erlyne Morane is a pseudonym for Herta Alvarez and Evelyne July.

151. Victor, "Être prêts pour une crise sociale ouverte," 232.

152. Guy Lardreau, *Le Singe d'or: essai sur le concept d'étape du marxisme* (Paris, 1973); Le Dantec, *Les Dangers du soleil*, 168; Antoine Liniers (the alias of Olivier Rolin), "Objections contre une prise d'armes," in François Furet, Antoine Liniers, and Philippe Raynaud, *Terrorisme et démocratie* (Paris, 1985), 165-66.

153. Lardreau, *Le Singe d'or*, 86, 87, 89, 123-24, 135-36, 142.

154. Liniers, "Objections contre une prise d'armes," 156.

155. Victor, "Être prêts pour une crise sociale ouverte," 230.

156. Hamon and Rotman, *Les Années de poudre*, 32-37.

157. The intensification of repression was not only directed at the Gauche prolétarienne. See Le Goff, *Mai 68*, 179-84.

158. For stylistic reasons I will continue to use the term GP to discuss the organization after its first, partial dissolution.

159. Hamon and Rotman, *Les Années du poudre*, 342-44, 358, 380-81, 390-91. See also Le Dantec, *Les Dangers du soleil*, 225-34.

160. It should be noted that the OPS seriously considered assassinating Paul Touvier, a member of Vichy's *milice* eventually convicted of crimes against humanity, who had been pardoned by President Pompidou in November 1971. It might well have committed murder in this case if it had found Touvier. The lack of a murderous outcome in general was also somewhat dependent on luck. See on this: Liniers, "Objections contre une prise d'armes;" David Drake, "*On a raison de se révolter;*" Alain Geismar, *L'Engrenage terroriste* (Paris, 1981); and Le Dantec, *Les Dangers du soleil*, 237-58. For a more complete analysis of the issue of terrorism after 1968 see Isabelle Sommier, *La Violence politique et son deuil: l'après 68 en France et en Italie* (Rennes, 1998).

161. "Illégalisme et guerre," first published in *Cahiers prolétaires* of January 1971 and reproduced in Geismar, *L'Engrenage terroriste*, 161-79; 177 and 179 for the quotes. Emphasis in the original.

162. Liniers, "Objections contre une prise d'armes," 156.

163. Hamon and Rotman, *Les Années de poudre*, 414. See also page 417.

164. Hamon and Rotman, *Les Années de poudre*, 389-91, 420-21, citation on page 421 and Jean Loignon, "Un mouvement maoïste en France, la Gauche prolétarienne, 1968-1973" (DEA Thesis: Paris IEP, 1982), 21-32.

165. Boulte's self-criticism was demanded. GP militants hounded him. Perhaps for this reason, Boulte took his life.

166. Pierre Victor in Gavi, Sartre, and Victor, *On a raison de se révolter*, 156-57. Other events in 1972, notably the Bruay-en-Artois affair (in which the GP called for the lynching of a

bourgeois notary accused, without evidence, of the brutal murder of a young working-class woman), and the killing of Israeli athletes by Palestinian terrorists at the Munich Olympic games, contributed to this abandonment of exemplary action and turn away from terrorism. On the former see Hamon and Rotman, *Les Années du poudre*, 428-39. On the latter, the importance of which is magnified by the Jewish origins of much of the GP leadership, see Yaïr Auron, *Les Juifs d'extrême gauche en mai 68: une génération marquée par la Shoah*, trans. Katherine Werchowski (Paris, 1998), 227-40.

167. Ibid., 234.
168. Pierre Victor in Gavi, Sartre, and Victor, *On a raison de se révolter*, 234. True to the GP's total disregard for real social relations, it believed that Lip could and would be copied elsewhere. But Lip was a revolt more reminiscent of the struggles of late nineteenth-century artisans resisting deskilling than representative of twentieth-century labor conflicts. For a nineteenth-century case with similarities to Lip see Joan Wallach Scott, *The Glassworkers of Carmaux: French Craftsmen and Political Action in a Nineteenth-Century City* (Cambridge, Mass., 1974).
169. Pierre Victor in Gavi, Sartre, and Victor, *On a raison de se révolter*, 12-13. Posthumous analyses of this sort by the GP were only possible because the GP was continuously vigilant in its critique of Leninism.
170. Hamon and Rotman, *Les Années de poudre*, 481-529; Gavi, Sartre, and Victor, *On a raison de se révolter*, 312-21, 249-55.
171. The GP gave the following reason for its dissolution in its *Cahiers prolétariens* of January 1974: "That all *organizations must continuously learn to die*, to refuse to persevere in their being, when they are out of tune with the demands of the mass movement." Cited in van der Poel, *Une révolution de la pensée*, 54.
172. Hamon and Rotman, *Les Années de poudre*, 528-29, 552-56. Despite their efforts, on 23 March 1977 Antoine Tramoni, the Renault security guard who had killed Overney, was executed by a band of former *gauchistes* turned terrorists.
173. Rivenc, "Le Mouvement maoïste français," 297; Hamon and Rotman, *Les Années de poudre*, 515, 529, 608; Gavi, Sartre, and Victor, *On a raison de se révolter*, 254-55; Geismar, *L'Engrenage terroriste*, 9-14, 109, 127-30.
174. Van der Poel, *Une révolution de la pensée*, 39-41, 53-54; Liniers, "Objections contre une prise d'armes," 147-48; Hamon and Rotman, *Les Années de poudre*, 362-64.
175. For a list of intellectuals involved see Hamon and Rotman, *Les Années de poudre*, 189.
176. Ibid., 192; Loignon, "Un mouvement maoïste en France," 37-38.
177. Gavi, Sartre, and Victor, *On a raison de se révolter*, 63-64.
178. Michel Contat and Michel Rybalka, *A Bibliographical Life*, 494.
179. Claude Francis and Fernande Gontier, *Simone De Beauvoir: A Life … A Love Story*, trans. Lisa Nesselson (New York, 1987), 329 and Annie Cohen-Solal, *Sartre 1905-1980* (Paris, 1985), 755.
180. Jean-Paul Sartre, "Le Socialisme qui venait du froid," in *Situations, IX: mélanges* (Paris, 1972), 275-76. (First published as a preface to A. Liehm, *Trois générations*, 1970.)
181. Jean-Paul Sartre, "Les Communistes ont peur de la Révolution," in *Situations, VIII: Autour de 68* (Paris, 1972), 210; Jean-Paul Sartre, "Masses, spontanéité, parti," in *Situations VIII*, 282.
182. Sartre's greatest reservation about French Trotskyism, which he valued intellectually, was its political inefficacy. See Ian H. Birchall, "Sartre and Gauchisme," *Journal of European Studies* 19, 1 (March 1989): 21-53. See also Sartre's retrospective comments on the PCF and on *Socialisme ou barbarie*, Jean-Paul Sartre, "Autoportrait à soixante-dix ans," in *Situations, X: politique et autobiographie* (Paris, 1976), 181-83.
183. Gavi, Sartre, and Victor, *On a raison de se révolter*, 30-31; Simone de Beauvoir, *Adieux: A Farewell to Sartre*, trans. Patrick O'Brian (New York, 1984), 28; *Sartre, un film réalisé par Alexandre Astruc et Michel Contat avec la participation de Simone de Beauvoir, Jacques-Laurent Bost, André Gorz, Jean Pouillon* (Paris, 1974), 135.
184. Sartre, "Masses, spontanéité, parti," 262-90.

185. Jean-Paul Sartre, "Les Bastilles de Raymond Aron," in *Situations VIII*, 175-92; Jean-Paul Sartre, "L'Idée neuve de Mai 1968," in *Situations VIII*, 193-207, page 204 for the citation.

186. Cohen-Solal, *Sartre*, 793, 803-4; *Sartre, un film*, 100-102; Jean-Paul Sartre, "Les Maos en France," in *Situations X*, 38-47.

187. De Beauvoir, *Adieux*, 14, 38; Jean-Paul Sartre, "L'Ami du peuple," in *Situations VIII*, 474; Sartre, "Autoportrait à soixante-dix ans," 213. David Drake, *Intellectuals and Politics in Post-War France* (New York, 2002), 141.

188. Sartre, "L'Ami du Peuple;" *Sartre, un film*, 124-29, and 128 for the citation.

189. Foucault cited in Didier Eribon, *Michel Foucault (1926-1984)* (Paris, 1991), 227. Michel Foucault, "Le Grand Enfermement," in *1970-1975*, 301-2. Unless otherwise noted, information on Foucault's life in the following paragraphs is drawn from Didier Eribon, *Michel Foucault*; Macey, *The Lives of Michel Foucault*; and James Miller, *The Passion of Michel Foucault* (New York, 1993).

190. Alienation is considered to be the root of revolt in Sartre, "Masses, spontanéité, parti," 272.

191. Michel Foucault, "De la nature humaine: justice contre pouvoir," in his *1970-1975*, 502-3 for the will to power and 506 for the citation.

192. Chomsky cited in Miller, *The Passion of Michel Foucault*, 203.

193. Michel Foucault, "Prisons et asiles dans le mécanisme du pouvoir," in *1970-1975*, 524.

194. Note of the editors, Daniel Defert and François Ewald, before Michel Foucault, "(Manifeste du G.I.P.)," in *1970-1975*, 174.

195. Foucault, "(Manifeste du G.I.P.)," 174-75.

196. The *casier juridiciare* is the record of a person's criminal convictions. Available to any prospective employer, it constituted a major obstacle to a former prisoner's reintegration into society.

197. Michel Foucault, "Enquêtes sur les prisons: brisons les barreaux du silence," in *1970-1975*, 177.

198. Ibid., 177-78 and Michel Foucault, "(Sur les prisons)," in *1970-1975*, 175 for the citation.

199. Michel Foucault, "Un problème m'intéresse depuis longtemps, c'est celui du système pénal," in *1970-1975*, 208.

200. Ibid., 207.

201. Macey, *The Lives of Michel Foucault*, 288; citation from Michel Foucault, "Le Grand Enfermement," in *1970-1975*, 304. Jean-Marie Domenach explains the demise of the GIP in the following terms in a letter dated 25 June 1976: "GIP dissolved itself because, its goal being to make it possible for the prisoners themselves to talk, it did not want to substitute itself for the prisoners once some of them took on responsibilities." IMEC ESP2 E4-01 .02

202. Michel Foucault, "Sur la justice populaire. Débat avec les maos," in his *1970-1975*, 340-69. According to the editorial note in this edition "Gilles" in this debate is André Glucksmann.

203. Pierre Victor in ibid., 347-49.

204. Ibid., 340-42, 352-53, 357, 364 and 346 for the citation.

205. Eribon, *Michel Foucault*, 316-17.

206. Interview with Jean-Paul Sartre, "La Justice populaire," *J'accuse*, 15 Jan. 1971, 17-19. See also the verdict of the Lens tribunal: Jean-Paul Sartre, "Premier procès populaire à Lens: réquisitoire," in *Situations VIII*, 319-31.

207. Gilles Deleuze in "Les Intellectuels et le pouvoir," in *1970-1975*, 307-8.

208. Foucault in idem.

209. Ibid., 310.

210. Michel Foucault, "L'Intellectuel sert à rassembler les idées mais son savoir est partiel par rapport au savoir ouvrier," in *1970-1975*, 421-22.

211. For indications of the attractiveness of the GIP's idea of politics for *Esprit* see Jean-Marie Domenach, "Le Détenu hors la loi," *Esprit* 411 (Feb. 1972): 166; Jean-Marie Domenach, "En finir avec les prisons," *Esprit* 415 (July-Aug. 1972): 39-54; and Philippe Meyer, "Bilan

provisoire d'une mission momentanée," IMEC ESP2 B3-04 .08. *Esprit* had appointed Philippe Meyer to a paid position as *"délégué à la recherche agitation"* beginning on 1 November 1972 and lasting until 31 August 1973. This report summarizes his activity and analysis of the militant action of the time.

212. Georges V. Santoni, "Les Intellectuels: entretien avec Jean-Marie Domenach," *The French Review* 47, 4 (March 1974): 701. The interview was conducted in June 1972.

213. According to Eribon, *Michel Foucault*, 299.

214. This analysis of the success and politics of the other *groupes d'information* is drawn from Philippe Meyer, "Bilan provisoire d'une mission momentanée."

215. *Tout!* and *Cahiers de mai*, for example. See François-Marie Samuelson, *Il était une fois Libération: reportage historique* (Paris, 1979), 52-53, 84.

216. Le Dantec, *Les Dangers du soleil*, 173-76.

217. Among them were Alexandre Astruc, Simone de Beauvoir, Maurice Clavel, Michel Foucault, Gérard Fromanger, Jean-Luc Godard, Catherine Humblot, Marin Karmitz, Katia Kaupp, Michèle Manceaux, Mariella Righini, Jean-Paul Sartre, and Agnès Varda. Samuelson, *Il était une fois Libération*, 102.

218. As indicated by the date of its birth, the APL, like the GP in general, tried to appropriate the legacy of the Resistance to legitimize itself. The GP's efforts were somewhat successful. The intellectual and Resistance leader Maurice Clavel approved of and facilitated the use of this rhetoric. He organized the placing of a wreath to the "old and new victims of fascism" on Mont Valérien on 18 June 1970 by representatives of the GP, himself, and three other famous resistors, Jacques Debu-Bridel, Professor Vladimir Jankélévitch, and Jean Cassou. Hamon and Rotman, *Les Années de poudre*, 355-56; Monique Bel, *Maurice Clavel* (Paris, 1992), 253-54.

219. Michel Foucault, "Rapports de la commission d'information sur l'affaire Jaubert," in *1970-1975*, 199-203.

220. Samuelson, *Il était une fois Libération*, 109-12.

221. *Libération* manifesto cited in ibid., 141-45. The emphasis is in the original.

222. According to Cohen-Solal, *Sartre*, 804-6.

223. Interview dated 7 February 1973 of Jean-Paul Sartre with Jacques Chancel in *Radioscopie*, 3 (Paris, 1973), 238-39.

224. Michel Foucault, "Pour une chronique de la mémoire ouvrière," in *1970-1975*, 399-400.

225. Michel Foucault, "Le Monde est un grand asile," in *1970-1975*, 434.

226. Samuelson, *Il était une fois Libération*, passim.

227. Jean Daniel, *L'Ère des ruptures* (Paris, 1979), 68-76; Louis Pinto, *L'Intelligence en action*, 69-70.

228. Letter from Domenach to Thibaud dated 14 August 1973, IMEC ESP2 B4-02 .02, in preparation for *Esprit*'s 22-23 September 1973 meeting. See IMEC ESP2 B4-02 .03 on the latter.

Chapter 2

THE GULAG AS A METAPHOR

The Politics of Reactions to Solzhenitsyn and *The Gulag Archipelago*

According to most analyses, *The Gulag Archipelago* was a decisive, revelatory text in the transformation of French intellectual politics in the 1970s.[1] For example, in his synthesis *Political Traditions in Modern France* Sudhir Hazareesingh, a historian of French intellectual politics in the 1970s, writes, "long after the rest of the Western world had seen through the pompous veneer of Soviet-style socialism, French intellectuals remained fascinated by the Leninist experience. Their awakening was brought about by the publication of Aleksandr Solzhenitsyn's *Gulag Archipelago* in 1974."[2] Pierre Grémion, another influential historian of this period, finds that *The Gulag Archipelago* was a revelatory text whose impact was "proportional to the extent of the Left's denegation of and disinterest for the Soviet concentration camp system since the David Rousset/*Les Lettres françaises* trial" of 1950 regarding the question of whether concentration camps existed in the USSR.[3] From this understanding of *The Gulag Archipelago*'s significance emerges the question that has come to dominate histories of postwar French intellectual politics: how could intellectuals have been blind for so long to the extent and significance of repression in the Soviet Union and other socialist régimes?

Contrary to this line of interpretation, I argue that the vast majority of French intellectuals of the noncommunist Left were already acutely aware of the failures of Soviet socialism and had already rejected it as a political model by the time the French translation of *The Gulag Archipelago* was published beginning in June 1974.[4] Consequently, although French intellectuals certainly found *The Gulag Archipelago* impressive, few found it so new or shocking as to induce them to fundamentally revise their political per-

---

Notes for this section begin on page 106.

spectives. The critique of totalitarianism of the late 1970s was not effected by supposed revelations about the gulag. The structure of domestic political and ideological debates explains, much more than supposed blindness to Soviet repression, why the publication of *The Gulag Archipelago* was followed a few years later by a critique of totalitarianism that took on the appearance of a "gulag effect." The critique of totalitarianism was most fundamentally the response of intellectuals of the noncommunist Left, informed by their post-1968 politics, to the dangers that they saw in the PCF as it approached political power in an alliance with the Socialist Party (the Union of the Left) based on a Common Program of Government. For this reason, I argue in chapter 3, it was in 1975, subsequent to serious disputes within the Left over both the PCF's ideological offensive beginning in October 1974 and the crisis of the Portuguese Revolution in the summer of 1975, that the critique of totalitarianism was inaugurated. Only in 1977-78, a period of tense ideological confrontation rooted in the expectation that the Left would win the 1978 legislative election, would the gulag become an omnipresent theme of French intellectual politics.

Solzhenitsyn and *The Gulag Archipelago* initially became objects of controversy less because of the contents of the book than because of the PCF's vitriolic attack on him, his writings, and his defenders. This Solzhenitsyn affair of 1974 was the first in a series of ideological conflicts within the Left between 1974 and 1977 that fueled the emerging critique of totalitarianism. Crucially, the two most influential readings of *The Gulag Archipelago* that fed into the critique of totalitarianism and helped create the appearance of a late-breaking "gulag effect," those of André Glucksmann and Claude Lefort, were catalyzed by this debate with the PCF and used Solzhenitsyn's text as a pretext for the elaboration of political philosophies long under gestation that resonated with post-1968 intellectual politics.[5]

In the ideological debates of the late 1970s, the gulag was less a revelation than a metaphor, the one word that could represent and legitimize the emerging radical repudiation of communism and revolutionary politics. The thesis that intellectuals were blind to the gulag before 1974 and, as Glucksmann and Lefort would have us believe, consequently initially resistant to Solzhenitsyn and his message before seeing the light emerged for two reasons. For one, to paraphrase Alexis de Tocqueville, a grievance becomes intolerable only when it is on the verge of being eliminated.[6] By 1974, the *progressisme* of the late 1940s and early 1950s was largely dead and buried. For that reason, those few intellectuals who supported the PCF in the Solzhenitsyn affair of 1974 and the larger number of those individuals and institutions that made marginal concessions to the PCF in the interest of Left unity were that much more unbearable. Second, the thesis that intellectuals had been blind to Soviet repression was the keystone of the case made by intellectuals, afraid of the arrival of communists in power, against the PCF and the Socialist Party's (PS's) alliance with it. Once the PS had displaced the PCF as the largest party on the Left,[7] those opposed to or critical of the Union of the Left could no longer attack it on the grounds that the PCF dominated it electorally. Increasingly, they argued that ideology was the issue and that communist ideological domination over the Left made the Union of the Left a dangerous adventure. Although they could cite as evidence the PCF's ideological offensive beginning in the autumn of 1974 and a number of concessions that the PS made to the PCF, the claim, grounded in the assertion that *The Gulag Archipelago* was a revelation, that the French Left had a congenital failure to see the reality of totalitarianism was essential to establishing this thesis. Without the blindness thesis, the PS's relative unwillingness to confront the PCF on the terrain of ideology could be taken for what it most often was, a tactical maneuver designed to sustain the life of the political alliance from which the PS's electoral benefit was evident. The corollary of the blindness thesis was the argument that only a special effort (i.e., a confrontation with the PCF and an absolute refusal of its ideology) could prevent the French Left from succumbing to the "totalitarian temptation."[8]

Finally, the reference to Solzhenitsyn and *The Gulag Archipelago* fulfilled one other crucial function in the debates of the 1970s: it allowed French intellectuals to identify their antitotalitarian politics with the universal. By appropriating Solzhenitsyn to their cause, antitotalitarian intellectuals identified with a prophetic figure of extraordinary courage. Cast as a new Dreyfus or Dostoyevsky who had additionally revealed to intellectuals the truth about the Soviet Union, communism, and revolution, Solzhenitsyn and the propositions that were said to have been derived from his work were unassailable. This identification with Solzhenitsyn, the universal truth-bearing Dreyfusard intellectual who shocked French intellectuals out of their ideological slumber, allowed antitotalitarians to disguise the origins of their positions in the mundane reality of French politics and make the claim that what they said was also universal in significance. In this manner, antitotalitarians successfully claimed that they, and not their opponents, were true to the vocation of the intellectual and, therefore, deserved to be listened to by the public.

A brief review of how domestic political and ideological debates elsewhere in the West structured the reception of *The Gulag Archipelago* helps clarify the specific character of the French case and the relationship between the French encounter with *The Gulag Archipelago* and the critique of totalitarianism. The French reception of *The Gulag Archipelago* differed from that in the United States, West Germany, Britain, and Italy in ways that echo the differences in the reception of the concept of totalitarianism explained in this book's introduction. In Britain and the United States, where domestic communism was not an issue, Solzhenitsyn and his book became pawns in the debate over détente and subjects of controversy insofar as Solzhenitsyn was considered a reactionary vis-à-vis liberalism. In the German Federal Republic the debate over *Ostpolitik* and the New Left's rejection of the theory of totalitarianism because of its status as the quasi-official ideology of the state led intellectuals who in France might have been antitotalitarian to abandon their initial support for Solzhenitsyn and become increasingly hostile to him as he took political positions on the Cold War with which they strongly differed.[9] In Italy the presence of a strong communist party made the situation apparently analogous to that in France, but the Italian Communist Party's (PCI's) "historic compromise," launched in October 1973 by Enrico Berlinguer, differed profoundly from the French Union of the Left of the 1970s in emphasizing not radical change but the consolidation of democratic institutions against the threat of fascism. Further, the PCI was significantly more critical of the USSR than the PCF. In contrast to the PCF's campaign against anti-Sovietism, the Italian communists responded to Solzhenitsyn's expulsion from the USSR by openly dissenting from Soviet policy. Consequently, neither Solzhenitsyn nor *The Gulag Archipelago* became major issues in internal Italian politics. Indeed, French intellectuals specifically pointed to the Italian communists' positions on the USSR and Solzhenitsyn as evidence of the archaism of the PCF.[10] The French antitotalitarian moment was, as French intellectuals at the time understood, a product of France's particular domestic political scene in the 1970s.

The PCF Offensive Against Solzhenitsyn and his Defenders

Already a figure of some controversy for his novels and political pronouncements, Solzhenitsyn became the object of heated debate in early 1974 when, subsequent to the 28 December 1973 Russian-language publication in Paris of his *The Gulag Archipelago*, the PCF violently attacked him and his book.[11] The PCF claimed that *The Gulag Archipelago* was part of a vast anti-Soviet campaign aimed at discrediting détente, isolating the PCF, undermining the Union of the Left, and diverting attention from the crisis of capitalism. Furthermore, the PCF held that the facts in Solzhenitsyn's book were not new, having been disclosed at the twentieth and twenty-second congresses of the Communist Party of the Soviet Union, and did not speak to present Soviet reality. Solzhenitsyn had, the PCF argued in appealing to antifascism, "disqualified himself" by his effort to "rehabilitate" General Vlasov (a Soviet general who had fought with the Germans against the Soviet Union in World War II). "All of France's Resistance members and patriots" were called upon to condemn this "rehabilitation" and fight off anti-Sovietism.[12]

The PCF's attack on Solzhenitsyn developed into a full-scale affair when on national television Gilles Martinet, the general representative of the PS for ideological questions and a member of the *conseil d'administration* of the highly influential left-wing weekly *Le Nouvel Observateur*, criticized PCF General Secretary Georges Marchais's exposition of his Central Committee's position. The Communist Party of the Soviet Union, Martinet said, did not have the last word on the Stalinist period, and the PCF's assertion that Solzhenitsyn had "disqualified himself" brought into question the PCF's commitment to fundamental liberties. The PCF responded immoderately to Martinet by attacking *Le Nouvel Observateur* in whose name Martinet had, it claimed, spoken. The PCF called off efforts then underway to patch up relations between itself and the weekly after a conflict dating back to the summer of 1973, canceled *Le Nouvel Observateur*'s invitations to one of its press luncheons, and pressured Jean Daniel, the director of *Le Nouvel Observateur*, as well as the PS to disavow Martinet.[13]

Finding the communist position on Solzhenitsyn and *The Gulag Archipelago* unacceptable, Jean Daniel actively sought a confrontation with the PCF on the issue. Believing, Daniel said, that "the core of the affair" is to "know if the unity of the Left forces one to participate in the appalling calumnious campaign against Solzhenitsyn," Daniel intended to prove that this was not the case.[14] He defended Solzhenitsyn against the charge that he had sought to rehabilitate Vlasov and ridiculed the PCF campaign against anti-Sovietism, since nothing menaced the Soviet Union and anti-Sovietism was at a historic low. He also demanded a "great debate in the Left on Stalinism," specifically calling for it to answer the question implicitly posed by Solzhenitsyn as to whether socialism and Stalinism can be separated.[15] After the French translation of *The Gulag Archipelago* came out in June 1974, Daniel took up the defense of Solzhenitsyn on an episode, dedicated to the book, of Bernard Pivot's literary television talk show "Ouvrez les guillemets" (the predecessor of "Apostrophes") that pitted Daniel and André Glucksmann against Francis Cohen, director of the communist journal *La Nouvelle Critique*, and Mal-Pol Fouchet, who allied with the PCF on this matter.[16] Before appearing on television, Daniel explained that he had agreed to participate, despite the fact that the program threatened to result in a confrontation between himself and the PCF, because he would not "sacrifice on the altar of electoral strategy essential principles" including "the battle against all totalitarianisms."[17] During the program, Daniel expressed frustration with "the tragic disproportion between what Solzhenitsyn brings us and the mediocrity of the reactions that he arouses." Leaving the response to Cohen to André Glucksmann, Daniel took issue with Fouchet for his emphasis on anti-Sovietism, his complaint that Solzhenitsyn focused solely on the Soviet régime without denouncing capitalist régimes, and his criticism of Solzhenitsyn for what he wrote on Vlassov.[18]

After Daniel's initial defense of Martinet and Solzhenitsyn, the attack on *Le Nouvel Observateur* became a daily affair in the communist press. The *Bureau politique* of the PCF commanded the party's federations, sections, and cells to mobilize against anti-Sovietism, and the party tried to enlist the support of noncommunists.[19] The PCF declared *Le Nouvel Observateur* to be an "organ that is above all anti-Soviet, anticommunist, and a divisive influence on the Left" and discreetly pressured the left-wing intellectual journals *Esprit* and *Les Temps modernes* to fall into line.[20] The PCF tried to make the case that the Soviet Union was gradually democratizing and liberalizing, only to be frustrated by its inability to convince French intellectuals that, as the Central Committee member Pierre Juquin said, not putting Solzhenitsyn in prison was already immense progress for the Soviets. More importantly, the PCF continued to maintain that the USSR was socialist; as a consequence, it considered any attack on the USSR to be an attack on communism and on the Union of the Left.[21]

The ferocity of the communist campaign and the archaism of its arguments shocked many intellectuals and led them to greater vigilance with regard to the PCF. The PCF's methods raised the specter of Stalinism, and its insistence that the USSR was socialist revealed the distance separating the party's idea of socialism from that of the noncommunist intellectual Left. Jean Daniel, reacting to the attacks on *Le Nouvel Observateur*, wrote, "all the tricks, the old tricks of the oldest Stalinisms are used.... One already hears everywhere: 'They will never change!'" Just before the suspension of the debate over Solzhenitsyn during the 1974 presidential elections, Daniel, like many others, found himself asking why "the French Communist Party is the only communist party in the world to make the struggle against anti-Sovietism a condition of membership to the Left."[22] The PCF's campaign reminded Jean-Marie Domenach, director of the influential left-wing journal *Esprit*, of the anti-Titoist campaign of 1949, with the exception that in 1974 "these excommunications now impress only a few socialists obsessed by the promise of electoral success." Most importantly, the affair revealed the Union of the Left to be "poisoned by the cadaver of Stalinism." Domenach drew the conclusion that "it must be made clear that we have left totalitarianism behind us forever."[23] For Serge July, director of *Libération*, the debate about Solzhenitsyn was a debate about the future of socialism in France, and the Soviet socialism to which the PCF was trying to commit the Union of the Left through its campaign against anti-Sovietism was not the socialism he wanted. Indeed, it was not even socialism, "unless socialism is power plants plus work camps."[24]

Jean Daniel and *Le Nouvel Observateur* received considerable support from the Left, contrary to what Daniel maintained in his memoirs.[25] Journalists boycotted the PCF press luncheon from which *Le Nouvel Observateur* had been excluded. The newspaper *Témoignage chrétien*, although *progressiste* enough to respond to the affair with anti-anticommunism, also found the PCF's attacks on *Le Nouvel Observateur* excessive.[26] Jean-Marie Domenach, director of *Esprit*, wrote *Le Nouvel Observateur* to express his solidarity "in this resistance to the mini-terror."[27] In *Libération*, which had rallied to the defense of Solzhenitsyn after some debate in the winter of 1973-74 over whether or not he was reactionary, Serge July, analyzing the affair in the wake of Daniel's appearance on "Ouvrez les guillemets," found the communist arguments to be simply "incredible, intolerable."[28] Jean-Marie Domenach agreed, he wrote in a second letter to *Le Nouvel*

Observateur, "sentence for sentence, word for word" with Daniel's defense of Solzhenitsyn on the program.[29]

Signs of hesitancy by the PS and *Le Monde* were noticed by some at the time and later used to create the myth that only a heroic few had dared to stand up against the PCF and Solzhenitsyn. *Le Monde*, which Daniel accused in his memoirs of coddling the PCF, did nothing of the sort. The PCF's reprisals against *Le Nouvel Observateur* left *Le Monde* questioning the communists' claim to be democratic; and a *Le Monde* analysis, provoked by the affair, of the relationship between Stalinism and French communism regretted that the desire to reflect on Stalinism within the PCF was a "marginal, if not to say underground [*confidentiel*]" current.[30] *Le Monde* made a minor concession to Left unity by balancing its review of *The Gulag Archipelago* with a review of six books advertised as having "positive views" of the USSR. Yet, *Le Monde*'s review of *The Gulag Archipelago* was glowing, and the newspaper defended Solzhenitsyn against the accusation that he tried to rehabilitate Vlasov. The PS, to be sure, did not wish to trigger a crisis in its relations with the PCF; for that reason its *Bureau exécutif* did not adopt Martinet's positions as its own and declared his televised declaration "untimely," but it also reminded the PCF that it needed to respect freedom of the press and opinion.[31] Later, in defending *Le Nouvel Observateur*, François Mitterrand wrote, "I am persuaded that that which is most important is not what Solzhenitsyn says, but that he be able to say it."[32] While Mitterrand certainly did not wish to address directly, for example, Solzhenitsyn's general condemnation of communism, this and Mitterrand's other carefully weighed statements should not be taken as a refusal to open the issue of Stalinism or, as one historian concluded, an "agreement with the communist view that the Soviet Union was moving towards democracy."[33] On this and other occasions, Mitterrand demanded that the PCF go further in the logic of its denunciation of Stalinism.[34] Jean Daniel told Mitterrand at the time: "Your credit is due in large part to the manner that you have known how to ally yourself with the Communist Party without ever making it a concession on the essential and in resisting it each time that it is necessary."[35]

Both inside and outside the PCF, the communist campaign failed. In accordance with the tendency of propaganda to spark interest in that which it is trying to discredit, the PCF helped put *The Gulag Archipelago* on summer reading lists and make it an enormous best-seller.[36] The support *Le Nouvel Observateur* received mirrored the PCF's failure to rally many to its positions beyond *Témoignage chrétien* and a handful of individuals.[37] Most remarkable was the PCF's singular inability to profit from allegiances to the USSR rooted in its role in World War II. The only intellectual of any standing to buy into the PCF's effort to discredit Solzhenitsyn for his analysis of Vlasov was Max-Pol Fouchet. Few accepted his "Ouvrez les guillemets" argument, which echoed those of the immediate postwar period, that Solzhenitsyn used the failures of the Soviet régime to excuse

Vlasov's actions and thereby opened the door to the rehabilitation of French collaborators who had been disappointed by France's failures. The failure of the PCF to rally former resisters other than Fouchet, who was subject to relentless scorn for his position,[38] indicates how much 1968 and the departure of de Gaulle marked the disintegration of the political culture forged in the Resistance.[39]

Put on the defensive, the PCF had to take action to prove its good will. Georges Marchais clarified his ambiguous statement that Solzhenitsyn would be free to publish his work in a socialist France "if he finds a publisher," and *L'Humanité* allowed Pierre Daix to publish an article on the Solzhenitsyn affair that reproached René Andrieu, the newspaper's editor, for using "polemical tricks of conflating diverse political currents and of manipulating texts and ideas" that were in the "Stalinist tradition."[40] In the autumn of 1974 the PCF sold *The Gulag Archipelago* at its annual *Fête de l'Humanité*,[41] and by late 1975, further pressure from within the Left forced it to condemn present-day Soviet labor camps and psychiatric hospitals and take action in favor of Soviet dissidents.[42]

The PCF's campaign fared no better within the party. Dissension emerged in the party leadership over the decision to exclude *Le Nouvel Observateur* from the press luncheon. According to Pierre Juquin, "one should not have deprived them of their meal ticket."[43] More importantly, some communist intellectuals echoed Jean Daniel's and Jean-François Revel's interpolations of the party.[44] Communist journalists sent to the USSR to research articles designed to improve its image came back disillusioned, without the expected copy.[45] And, significantly, the communist electorate did not follow the PCF's positions in the affair: 61 percent of it believed that Solzhenitsyn was right to recall the repression of the Stalinist period.[46]

Initial Reactions to *The Gulag Archipelago* and Solzhenitsyn's Politics

A close reading of reactions to *The Gulag Archipelago* reveals a seeming paradox: despite the later critique of totalitarianism there is little sign of significant revision of the politics of left-wing intellectuals or of their analyses of Soviet history in the first year or two after *The Gulag Archipelago*'s publication. To be sure, intellectuals of the Left recognized *The Gulag Archipelago* as a challenge insofar as it dated the birth of the camps to the beginning of the Russian Revolution and implicated Marx and Marxism in it. At *Le Nouvel Observateur*, for example, it was accepted that Solzhenitsyn forced them to prove that socialism could be separated from Stalinism and offer a solution to its monstrosities.[47]

There were a few intellectuals who would later play an important role in the critique of totalitarianism who treated *The Gulag Archipelago* as something of a revelation or drew radical political conclusions from it, but all of these cases represent limited or qualified reactions by moderate left-wing intellectuals who had neither believed in Soviet socialism nor embraced *tiers-mondisme*. Jean Daniel announced on "Ouvrez les guillemets" that reading *The Gulag Archipelago* "tormented him … like the discovery of a second Holocaust" and claimed that he "could no longer think the same thing after reading *The Gulag Archipelago*." Yet Daniel had hardly glorified the Soviet Union in the recent past and already knew, as he said on the program, a great deal about repression in the Soviet Union. Further, Daniel would not use such strong language to describe the impact of *The Gulag Archipelago* in his *Le Nouvel Observateur* editorials. Maurice Clavel claimed to have "almost" believed before *The Gulag Archipelago* came out that there were no purges in the Soviet Union before 1937, yet Clavel, who had been a member of the right-wing anticommunist Resistance, had never been attracted to the Soviet Union and had turned to revolutionary politics only after 1968 for his own peculiar spiritual reasons. His use of the word "almost" would seem to indicate that this claim was one of his rhetorical excesses. Bernard-Henri Lévy found in a July 1974 commentary that *The Gulag Archipelago* is "the finally blinding proof that terror in the USSR is everywhere…. the irrefutable proof that there is not good and bad, socialism and the camps, the conquests and the failures, but that … terror is nothing more than the inside lining of sacrosanct socialism…. The gulag is everywhere; in other words, over there socialism is dead." Although Lévy clearly anticipated the direction taken by the French intellectual Left, he himself had never been a militant or believed in Revolution, despite his later effort to present himself as the spokesperson for disabused revolutionaries in *La Barbarie à visage humain* of 1977. Further, his 1974 reading of *The Gulag Archipelago*—unlike the conclusions that he and others would later claim to draw from the book—did not, any more than those of Daniel or Clavel, deny that socialism was possible outside of the USSR.[48]

Outside of these few examples, reactions to *The Gulag Archipelago* were moderate; reviews often compared it to other books on the Soviet camps, concluding that although it was an unparalleled work, it was not entirely new in either its facts or interpretation. Indeed, it was probably more out of a sense of déjà vu than anything else that many intellectual circles did not comment extensively on *The Gulag Archipelago*. Hostility or blindness certainly did not explain it, given the quick and nearly unanimous criticism of Solzhenitsyn's expulsion from the USSR. Intellectuals clearly did not hesitate to defend Solzhenitsyn. A protest against Solzhenitsyn's expulsion was signed by hundreds of intellectuals from across the political spectrum.[49] In the pages of *Les Temps modernes* there was no discussion of the gulag or of *The Gulag Archipelago* until July 1976.[50] Yet it published extracts from the Soviet dissident Eduard Kuznetsov's *Journal d'un condamné à mort* in the spring of 1974; and Jeannette Colombel, a regular contributor to *Les Temps modernes*, published a "defense of Solzhenitsyn from the Left" in *Libération* that marked the beginning of the newspaper's rallying to his cause.[51] Sartre certainly did not hold *Les Temps modernes* back from criticizing the Soviet Union. He not only signed the protest against Solzhenitsyn's expulsion, but criticized Solzhenitsyn for not sufficiently contesting the Soviet system![52] *Esprit*, which organized the protest against Solzhenitsyn's expulsion and would later be one of the principle vectors of the critique of totalitarianism, did not, with the exception of an unexceptional book review, discuss *The Gulag Archipelago* in the first year after the French-language publication of volume one.[53] Not until after André Glucksmann had published his *La Cuisinière et le mangeur d'hommes* would *Esprit*, in reaction to the PCF ideological offensive beginning in the autumn of 1974 and the Portuguese affair of the summer of 1975, launch its own critique of totalitarianism.[54]

Because it is a weekly and because of its clash with the PCF, *Le Nouvel Observateur* was more inclined to discuss *The Gulag Archipelago*. Yet, with the exception of a polemical article by André Glucksmann[55] and occasional comments in the television reviews of Maurice Clavel, *Le Nouvel Observateur* tended to separate what it saw as Solzhenitsyn's uniquely admirable testimony and work as a chronicler of the horrors of the gulag from his questionable historical interpretations and the philosophical and political conclusions that he drew from them. K. S. Karol, who testified that his experience of thirteen months in the gulag was similar to that described by Solzhenitsyn, found his caustic and ironic analysis of Soviet political history to be totally inadequate; he agreed substantially with the Marxist critique of Solzhenitsyn's work by the dissident Soviet historian Roy Medvedev. Both Karol and Claude Roy criticized Solzhenitsyn for drawing too direct a line between 1917 and Stalin's camps. And for Jean Cathala, volume two of *The Gulag Archipelago* had an "incontestable greatness," "but resentment often blurs its vision."[56]

Solzhenitsyn's politics was initially no more acceptable than his historical analysis. For Solzhenitsyn, repression in the Soviet Union was incomparably worse than elsewhere, détente was a cover for Soviet repression at home and advances abroad, and socialism and revolution were doomed to end in the gulag. Solzhenitsyn wanted to judge all politics by their conformity to Christian ethics, the only justifiable politics being that which emerges out of the moral transformation of the individual soul. Solzhenitsyn's political formulae for Russia were undemocratic and conceptualized within a traditionalist, authoritarian framework.[57] While supporting Solzhenitsyn against the PCF and the USSR, intellectuals at *Esprit* and *Le Nouvel Observateur* carefully distanced themselves from his politics. Most felt that Solzhenitsyn had overstated his case. There was a "gulag" in South Africa and a "bloodbath archipelago" created by the Americans in Vietnam.[58] The West had not been deceived and defeated by the USSR since Yalta; its alliance with Stalin against Hitler was not a moral failure.[59] Socialism and liberty were not irreconcilable.[60] Not only the Left criticized Solzhenitsyn's politics. Raymond Aron, for example, spoke out against

Solzhenitsyn's apocalyptic interpretation of Western policy toward the USSR since Yalta.[61]

Intellectuals who rejected Solzhenitsyn's politics often excused him for them, most fundamentally because he had an "extraordinary presence," an enormous moral authority gained by his uncompromising and successful opposition to the Soviet régime, that they wished to use in their debates within the French Left.[62] In their effort to appropriate Solzhenitsyn, they emphasized that his lack of information about the West and the repression to which he had been subject helped explain his retrograde political positions. Solzhenitsyn had to be educated about political realities outside of the Soviet Union, especially the reality of oppression in the West. Jean Daniel's pedantic interrogation of Solzhenitsyn about colonialism on the widely-watched "Apostrophes" television program of 11 April 1975 was the culmination of this effort.[63] Before the program, Daniel feared that Solzhenitsyn, who had "multiplied declarations in all directions," was "in danger of being appropriated by our worst enemies." It seemed to Daniel that Solzhenitsyn's defenders, like those of Dreyfus before him, were going to "be faced with a difficult defendant, with an ungrateful innocent person."[64] At first hesitant to appear on "Apostrophes" because of the political positions that Solzhenitsyn had taken, Daniel finally accepted the invitation after Claude Durand, Solzhenitsyn's contact at his publisher Éditions du Seuil, had Daniel's friends K. S. Karol and Max Gallo convince him that he was best placed to save Solzhenitsyn from himself.[65] By eliciting a statement from Solzhenitsyn on the evils of colonialism, Daniel felt that he had delivered Solzhenitsyn from reaction.[66] When Raymond Aron criticized his television performance, Daniel fought hard to retain the mantle of Solzhenitsyn, claiming that *Le Nouvel Observateur* had been "a thousand times more frank, more welcoming, and more enthusiastic with regard to Solzhenitsyn than *Le Figaro*."[67]

Yet, despite Daniel's intervention, Solzhenitsyn showed no signs of changing his politics. When asked in his second, 9 March 1976, appearance on French television about false news reports that he was planning to go to Pinochet's Chili, Solzhenitsyn complained that he heard the word Chili more than he heard about the Berlin Wall and claimed that "if Chile hadn't existed, it would have been necessary to invent it."[68] Faced with the obstinacy of this "difficult defendant," left-wing intellectuals sympathetic to Solzhenitsyn increasingly argued that he was a new Dostoyevski, forged into a prophetic, moral figure by the camps, who along with his message escaped the narrow bounds of contemporary politics.[69] Criticized by Raymond Aron for failing to recognize this during his interrogation of Solzhenitsyn on "Apostrophes," Daniel himself adopted this approach to Solzhenitsyn on the occasion of Solzhenitsyn's March 1976 television appearance.[70] Intellectuals, like those at *Esprit*, who wished to enlist Solzhenitsyn in the emerging critique of totalitarianism, emphasized that his circumstantial statements on contemporary politics were irrelevant to understanding his significance.[71]

Solzhenitsyn Tamed: Late-Gauchiste Readings of Solzhenitsyn by André Glucksmann and Claude Lefort

Whereas differences with Solzhenitsyn in politics and historical analysis distanced many intellectuals from him, Glucksmann and Lefort claimed to embrace Solzhenitsyn's message. In fact, though, they succeeded in doing so only by plastering their own political philosophies onto *The Gulag Archipelago*. By writing the most important French commentaries on *The Gulag Archipelago*, reprimanding other intellectuals for not listening to Solzhenitsyn, and developing political philosophies proclaimed in the name of Solzhenitsyn that were highly influential in the developing critique of totalitarianism, Glucksmann and Lefort helped create the myth of French blindness to the gulag and the impression of a "gulag effect."

Despite irreconcilable differences between them and their work, Lefort and Glucksmann's trajectories and interpretations of Solzhenitsyn are in significant respects congruous. Both are political philosophers, *agrégés* in philosophy, who wrote theses under the direction of Raymond Aron in the 1960s.[72] Both had been involved in communist and revolutionary politics and subsequently, reacting against communism, evolved toward libertarian or anarchistic positions of which they tried to be the theorists.

Lefort, born in 1924, had been a Trotskyist from 1942 to 1947 and later, with Cornelius Castoriadis, one of the founders and leading intellectuals of the journal *Socialisme ou barbarie* and the minuscule political movement associated with it. Upon leaving *Socialisme ou barbarie* in 1958, when his long-standing criticisms of revolutionary vanguardism clashed with *Socialisme ou barbarie*'s newly heightened emphasis on building a revolutionary movement, Lefort felt liberated from the constraints of the group dynamic within *Socialisme ou barbarie* and free to develop ideas latent in his political philosophy. In subsequent years Lefort superseded his existing Marxist critiques of Soviet totalitarianism and of revolutionary leadership by reconceptualizing totalitarianism in opposition to democracy and elaborating a general critique of revolutionary politics and Marxism.[73] By the mid 1970s, Lefort—like many of his contemporaries—had come to refuse any politics that was organized or hierarchical enough to create "the conditions for a dominating-dominated division." And in Lefort's mind, even the model of a society of workers' councils risked doing this. Totally rejecting the position of power, Lefort's ideal politics was that of a "struggle on all terrains, against the current or potential forms of domination" that would neither "imagine its outcome in reality" nor "reduce the power with which it clashes to something real, limited to a unity of empirically determinable apparatuses that are effectively destructible."[74]

André Glucksmann, born in 1937, grew up in a communist milieu in the shadow of World War II. During the war his father had died trying to escape the Nazis, his mother had participated in the Resistance, and young André Glucksmann himself had been in personal danger by virtue of his

Jewish identity. After the war, Glucksmann was a member of communist youth organizations and a reader of *L'Humanité* before the age of ten. He joined the party in due course, only to break with it in the late 1950s in reaction to the Soviet intervention in Hungary and the PCF's Algerian War policy.[75] From his departure from the PCF until 1968, Glucksmann's militancy was limited to occasional participation in anticolonial and anti-Vietnam War demonstrations. After finishing his thesis and becoming an assistant to Raymond Aron, he seemed far from a future in revolutionary politics. Yet, May '68 persuaded Glucksmann that revolution was possible. Having appointed himself theorist of the revolution, he wrote political tracts, became involved in the launching of leftist periodicals like *Action* and *J'accuse*, and agitated, first in a Comité de base pour l'abolition du salariat et la destruction de l'Université at Vincennes and later in the Gauche prolétarienne.

Glucksmann's post-1968 revolutionary politics, although peppered with references to Marx, Lenin, and Mao, was clearly more in an anarchist tradition informed by the failure of the Russian Revolution and hostility toward the "reactionary" politics of the PCF in 1968. Classic Marxist analyses in terms of the relations of production or class structure were either secondary or irrelevant to Glucksmann. In 1968 Glucksmann proclaimed the situation to be revolutionary simply because there was a heightened class struggle. In his later analysis, the different revolts of the people, including "the authentic revolt of the middle classes," were said to be unifiable in the struggle against "fascism" because "classes determine their political identity in the class struggle."[76] Not only was the Russian Revolution an unacceptable model for Glucksmann, but he believed that the PCF and the elite in the East (as well as that in the West) were united against revolution in France because it would spark a revolution in socialist countries.[77] Following the model of the Paris Commune, the revolution must fully develop democracy "not in replacing the machinery of state by another (party) hierarchy, but in instituting universal eligibility to positions of power and the removability of the people in charge on all levels."[78] As for the forms of revolutionary organization and struggle, Glucksmann believed Leninist models to be inappropriate; exemplary action sufficed to spark a revolution. The task of the revolutionary movement "does not consist of directing, but of coordinating in a network the autonomous centers" of revolution that develop. Sprouting from below and nurtured by the revolutionary movement, the socialist revolution will not be a "seizure of power by a revolutionary party."[79] Although the revolutionary politics of Glucksmann had both a Leninist and a populist, anarchistic side, the latter was dominant, and increasingly so over time.[80] As for Mao, he was, says Glucksmann, significant for the Maoists as a critic of Soviet communism, a "sort of successful Daniel Cohn-Bendit."[81] After the dissolution of the Gauche prolétarienne, Glucksmann's politics, like Lefort's, would move away from revolution and abandon all efforts to seize power. Following

Foucault, Glucksmann shifted the terrain of combat to the field of microp-owers, the disciplines that are at "the root of the force of the state."[82]

Glucksmann and Lefort's books on Solzhenitsyn were born out of broadly similar circumstances. Both started as articles written in protest of Solzhenitsyn's reception in France.[83] On the basis of these articles, Claude Durand commissioned the two to write books for the Combats collection that he edited at Éditions du Seuil. Durand was also Solzhenitsyn's contact and indefatigable promoter at Éditions du Seuil, and Éditions du Seuil not only was the publisher of *The Gulag Archipelago* in French translation, but also had gained the worldwide rights to it. Although *The Gulag Archipelago* needed no help to become an enormous international success, Éditions du Seuil and Durand had much to gain if what remained of the international influence of the Parisian intellectual scene could be parleyed into a world-wide "gulag effect."[84]

André Glucksmann first enjoined French intellectuals and the French Left to listen to "Solzhenitsyn's" message in a *Nouvel Observateur* article of early March 1974. Written well before Glucksmann could have had any more than a very incomplete knowledge of *The Gulag Archipelago*—since it was not yet fully translated into French—his article offered a reading of Solzhenitsyn's earlier texts under the influence of his populist and anar-chist politics and his anger with activists and politicians who still situated the USSR on the Left and were hesitant to embrace Solzhenitsyn.[85] Solzhen-itsyn, Glucksmann argued, had managed by virtue of his time in the camps to close the gap between the people and the writer and recover the authen-tic voice of the former. Further, Solzhenitsyn's Ivan Denisovich, this "epit-ome of the immigrant worker, the absolute *ouvrier spécialisé*," saw the truth of the Soviet régime, proved that "the eye of the peasant sees justly."[86] If the French Left refused to listen to Solzhenitsyn it was not only because they did not want to "despair of [*désespérer*] the 'Common Program.'" More fundamentally, "the central committee operates in our heads." The lan-guage of Marxism is a language of power that makes it impossible to take the side of the persecuted in the USSR. The authoritarian Marxist state, which is only a perfected version of the Western bourgeois authoritarian state, is limited only by popular resistance, by Solzhenitsyn's Matryona and "others who stand up to power without giving in to its idiotic and demeaning logic." To understand Solzhenitsyn, Glucksmann concluded, your heart must "elude the state."[87]

Before reading *The Gulag Archipelago*, Glucksmann already knew about the Soviet camps. *The Gulag Archipelago* impressed him less for its infor-mation on repression than for what it said about popular resistance, a cen-tral theme of the Gauche prolétarienne's politics in the early 1970s.[88] In Glucksmann's mind of 1975, "Lip and Matryona clarify each other."[89] In reprimanding the French Left for not buying "Solzhenitsyn's" message, Glucksmann was effectively attacking those who did not share his late-*gauchiste* political perspectives.

Glucksmann developed these same themes in detail in *La Cuisinière et le mangeur d'hommes*. Marxism, he asserted, is a language of power used to govern the pleb and fuel the will not to see Soviet repression. The point of view of the pleb is that of truth; its resistance is the only acceptable politics. Russian dissidents and the workers at Lip are fighting the same battle. In his book, even more than in his article, Glucksmann developed a reading of Solzhenitsyn in accordance with his anarchistic and populist politics that supported a general critique of the state and the point of view of power. The gulag is a repetition of the history of the West—a development out of Foucault's great confinement, Marx's primitive accumulation, and even Western conceptions of politics since Plato. If the West is not shocked by the gulag, argued Glucksmann, it is not only due to the influence of Marx, but also because the West invented the camps and the politics that sustain them. Thus, while Glucksmann found the "simple people" of his quarter and at Lip to be moved by the arrest and expulsion of Solzhenitsyn, reading the press he felt "transported back a quarter of a century." Although he offered little in the way of evidence, Glucksmann claimed that reflection on the Soviet camps had not progressed beyond the efforts of Merleau-Ponty and Sartre in their 1950 article "Les Jours de notre vie." Because it is Marxist, the USSR is still considered, despite the camps, to be a socialist workers' and revolutionary state that shares the values of the French intellectual Left.[90]

Not surprisingly, Claude Lefort's article on Solzhenitsyn touches on many of the same themes and questions in postwar French politics as Glucksmann does. He too was enraged by the French Left's unwillingness to adopt "Solzhenitsyn's" analyses, reopened *Les Temps modernes* of 1950 to ponder Merleau-Ponty and Sartre's reflections on the significance of the camps, and argued, with no more evidence than Glucksmann, that "the social phenomenon of denial of facts relative to the Soviet universe subsists."[91] Although Lefort insisted that *The Gulag Archipelago*'s contents were "no *revelation*, except for those who are new to politics," he also contended that the book conveys a crucial perspective on Soviet history that is ignored only due to "the ravages of ideology."[92] Solzhenitsyn, the intellectual of the pleb for Glucksmann, became for Lefort a "libertarian"[93] whose *The Gulag Archipelago* is "marked by the sign of anti-authoritarianism" and owes its conception to Solzhenitsyn's identification with the "slogger." Not only does Solzhenitsyn's work come "from down below," but because it "excludes the illusion of a possible overview of the social arena" and "is created out of the experience of the dominated" it is able to rise "to the universal."[94] As for concerns that some statements by Solzhenitsyn may contradict this image of his work, Lefort contended that anything that Solzhenitsyn said or wrote outside of *The Gulag Archipelago* is only "opinion," a "*secondary* discourse." *The Gulag Archipelago*, on the other hand, is "a work conceived and written in line with an experience, following a thirst for knowledge that extracts thoughts from its author and imposes upon him a course and a line of questioning the necessity of which the man Solzhenitsyn does not follow when he judges, condemns, indignantly protests, and questions in reaction to the twists and turns of events."[95]

Having isolated *The Gulag Archipelago*, Lefort proceeded to read it as a work presenting a coherent theory of totalitarianism that follows the lines of the political thought that he himself had been developing over the past twenty years. In effect, Lefort used the occasion of *The Gulag Archipelago* to expound his own political philosophy disguised as Solzhenitsyn's. While pretending that he was only elaborating Solzhenitsyn's ideas, Lefort extracted from the multiplicity of arguments—some of which contract each other—in Solzhenitsyn's three hefty tomes a few key ones that served as points from which he could launch his own theses. Only when, as in his polemic with Marx, Solzhenitsyn's work proved to be hopelessly inadequate to the task did Lefort abandon the pretense of clarifying Solzhenitsyn and proceed to openly elaborate his own ideas—in this case, on the relationship between Marx and totalitarianism.[96]

Lefort analyzed totalitarianism as a negation of democracy and a "symbolic constitution of society"—incomprehensible from either a sociological or an economic perspective—such that society is deemed to be indivisible and the state (and ultimately the Egocrat, Stalin) considered to coincide with society and be the agent and visible manifestation of its unification.[97] This denial of the internal division of society engenders imaginary enemies.[98] The terror, undertaken in the name of the people, that is, the undifferentiated society, is the constant rooting out of imaginary enemies, the necessary instrument of the effort to unify society and achieve the dedifferentiation of civil society and the state.[99] Yet, only within the camps does the dream of ultimate domination, unattainable outside of them, tend to be realized. This dream of a unified society and the application of industrial organization to the camps explain their brutality.[100] Despite the use of industrial techniques, the camps are, contrary to some of Solzhenitsyn's statements, the result of this symbolic constitution of society and not of economic necessity.[101] As for Stalin, he is a necessary One who unifies and announces the unity of society.[102]

A final, essential part of Lefort's analysis is his explanation of why the "commissar-interrogators put so much zeal into cases that they knew to be full of 'hot air.'"[103] Although Solzhenitsyn concentrated nearly all of his attention on the question of villainy, Lefort claimed that the "ideology of granite" that Solzhenitsyn briefly mentioned is the key.[104] This ideology of granite is nothing less than the total identification of the individual communist with the ideology of the party, such that the distinction between subjects disappears.[105] This submersion of the individual in the totalitarian symbolic constitution of society and the consequent inability of the individual to have a *savoir* outside of the party explains, contrary to Koestler and Merleau-Ponty, the conduct of Bukharin and the other defendants at the Moscow trials and that of the communists in the camps.[106] While

Solzhenitsyn supposedly led the way to an analysis of communist discourse, Lefort added that "we did not need to read Solzhenitsyn to identify it" because "we know it by heart; it is constantly spoken in our own society by communist militants" and "by numerous eminent representatives of our *progressiste* Left."[107] Indeed, Lefort had little need to read Solzhenitsyn for most of his analysis.

La Cuisinière et le mangeur d'hommes and *Un homme en trop* were foundational texts for two main currents of the left-wing critique of totalitarianism of the late 1970s and early 1980s: that articulated by the "new philosophers" and that rooted in Lefort's understanding of totalitarianism in opposition to democracy as a symbolic constitution of society. Glucksmann's book, written in an accessible (and often vulgar) language and widely read, probably did more to undermine Marxism and the politics of the party-political Left than Lefort's. It also inaugurated French intellectuals' fascination with dissidence both in Eastern Europe and as a model for French intellectual politics.[108] Lefort's more difficult work probably had a deeper impact on French political and historical thought, influencing the antitotalitarian currents that emerged within the "Second Left" and would find a home at the École des hautes études en sciences sociales in the 1980s.[109] Beyond their differences—notable in Glucksmann's effort to make the gulag the culmination of Western civilization—both Glucksmann and Lefort placed ideology at the center of their analyses and emphasized the blindness that it produces. This emphasis on ideology became one of the constituent elements of French antitotalitarianism.

No less importantly, Glucksmann and Lefort tamed the wild Russian from the taiga for the French intellectual Left by forcing his account of the gulag into categories that French intellectuals could understand and accept. Because of these efforts by Glucksmann, Lefort, and others, Solzhenitsyn could serve for French intellectuals as a symbol of uncompromising resistance to the Soviets, an exemplary victim of the PCF and the *progressistes*, a prophet of anticommunism, and a Cassandra for the Union of the Left. Although, as we have seen, *The Gulag Archipelago* was no revelation when first published, by 1977 many intellectuals were claiming that it was responsible for totally transforming intellectual politics by opening the eyes of French intellectuals to the totalitarian nature of communism. For Bernard-Henri Lévy *The Gulag Archipelago* was, he wrote in *La Barbarie à visage humain* (1977), a text "that, barely said and published, sufficed to overturn our ideological landscape and reference points."[110] Pierre Rosanvallon and Patrick Viveret, the authors of the influential *Pour une nouvelle culture politique* (1977), claimed that "we receive the gulag today like German philosophy received the French Revolution in its time: as a radical questioning of received knowledge marking a watershed."[111] François Furet wrote in his seminal *Penser la Révolution française* (1978) that "the work of Solzhenitsyn raised the question of the gulag everywhere in the depths of the revolutionary design…. Today the gulag leads to a rethinking of the Terror by virtue of an identity in their projects."[112] The gulag became an important motif in these and other important texts of the late 1970s and early 1980s, but not because of the alleged revelatory impact of *The Gulag Archipelago*. Rather, intellectuals instinctively understood, as Charles Péguy had said in his commentary on the Dreyfus affair, that in the French intellectual scene "all parties live by their *mystique* and die from their politics."[113] Solzhenitsyn and *The Gulag Archipelago* were the *mystique* of antitotalitarian politics.

Notes

1. Although my analysis and conclusions differ from it, I benefited from Sandrine Hubaut, "L'Effet Soljénitsyne sur les intellectuels français" (Masters Thesis, Université Charles de Gaulle, Lille III, 1992).
2. Sudhir Hazareesingh, *Political Traditions in Modern France* (New York, 1994), 33. Hazareesingh is also the author of *Intellectuals and the French Communist Party: Disillusion and Decline* (Oxford, 1991).
3. Pierre Grémion, *Intelligence de l'anticommunisme: le Congrès pour la liberté de la culture à Paris* (Paris, 1995), 602. Grémion is also the author of *Paris-Prague: la gauche face au renouveau et à la régression tchécoslovaques (1968-1978)* (Paris, 1985). See also the evaluations along these lines by Sunil Khilnani, *Arguing Revolution: The Intellectual Left in Postwar France* (New Haven, 1993), 128; and Pierre Rigoulot, *Les Paupières lourdes: Les français face au goulag: aveuglements et indignations* (Paris, 1991), 10, 123.
4. Volume one of *The Gulag Archipelago* appeared in French translation in June 1974, volume two in December 1974, and volume three in March 1976.
5. André Glucksmann, *La Cuisinière et le mangeur d'hommes: essai sur les rapports entre l'État, le marxisme et les camps de concentration* (Paris, 1975); Claude Lefort, *Un homme en trop: réflexions sur "L'Archipel du Goulag"* (1976; reprint, Paris, 1986).
6. Alexis de Tocqueville, *The Old Régime and the French Revolution*, trans. Stuart Gilbert (Garden City, N.Y., 1955), chap. 4 of part 3.
7. Usually dated to the partial legislative elections of 29 September and 6 October 1974.
8. Thus, for example, Jean-François Revel, *La Tentation totalitaire* (Paris, 1976).
9. Robert Conquest, "Solzhenitsyn in the British Media," John B. Dunlop, "Solzhenitsyn's Reception in the United States," Brigit Meyer, "Solzhenitsyn in the West German Press Since 1974," all in *Solzhenitsyn in Exile: Critical Essays and Documentary Materials*, ed. John B. Dunlop, Richard S. Haugh, and Michael Nichelson, Hoover Press Publication, no. 305 (Stanford, Calif., 1985), 3-79.
10. Jean Daniel, "Soljénitsyne, les communistes français et nous," *Le Nouvel Observateur* 481 (28 Jan. 1974): 19; Jean Daniel, "L'Espoir et le programme," *Le Nouvel Observateur* 484 (11 Feb. 1974): 23.
11. The PCF's reaction to Pierre Daix's *Ce que je sais de Soljenitsyne* (Paris, 1973) had already created a minor affair in 1973.
12. Citation of a 1 February 1974 *L'Humanité* article by Léo Figuères in Pierre Daix, "Solzhenitsyn in France After 1974," in *Solzhenitsyn in Exile*, 80. This issue of *L'Humanité* also included a compilation of citations from the West German press under the title "Neo-Nazis in Ecstasy." See also *Le Monde*, 1 Jan. 1974, 16; the summary of PCF Central Committee resolution "Repousser l'antisoviétisme c'est l'affaire de tous" in *Le Monde*, 20-21 Jan. 1974, 6; and the articles of Serge Leyrac in *L'Humanité*, 31 Dec. 1973 and 17 Jan. 1974.

13. *Le Monde*, 23 Jan. 1974, 10; Jean Daniel, *L'Ère des ruptures* (Paris, 1979), 229-31.
14. Daniel, "Soljénitsyne, les communistes français et nous," 18.
15. Ibid., 19.
16. Other participants included Olivier Clément, author of a book about the spiritual sources of Solzhenitsyn's work, the writer Alain Bosquet, and Nikita Struve, editor of the Russian edition of *The Gulag Archipelago*.
17. Jean Daniel, "Explication," *Le Nouvel Observateur* 502 (24 June 1974): 20.
18. "Ouvrez les guillemets" episode broadcast on the 1e chaîne on 24 June 1974, consulted at the archives of L'Institut national de l'audiovisuel (INA).
19. *Le Monde*, 3-4 Feb. 1974, 5.
20. The PCF asked that its subscription to *Esprit* be canceled in a letter of 24 Jan. 1974 according to Casa, "'Esprit' interdit," *Esprit* 434 (April 1974): 694-97. PCF pressure on *Esprit* and *Les Temps modernes* is referred to in Jean-Marie Domenach, "Soljenitsyne et le destin de l'Europe," *Esprit* 433 (March 1974): 393.
21. The citation is from *Le Monde*, 3-4 Feb. 1974, 5. Jean-Marie Domenach, "Soljenitsyne et le destin de l'Europe," *Esprit* 433 (March 1974): 393. Jean Elleinstein and Claude Frioux, "Les Intellectuels dans la société soviétique," *France nouvelle* 1475 (19 Feb. 1974): 20-22; Jacques de Bonis, "Variantes et constantes de l'anti-soviétisme," *France nouvelle* 1473 (5 Feb. 1974): 6-8; André Harris and Alain de Sédouy, *Voyage à l'intérieur du Parti communiste* (Paris, 1974), 18 and passim.
22. Jean Daniel, "L'Espoir et le programme," 23; the explicit comparison was with the PCI. Jean Daniel, "Anti-éditorial," *Le Nouvel Observateur* 490 (1 April 1974): 16. See also Jean Daniel, "Pour en finir avec l'antisoviétisme," *Le Nouvel Observateur* 487 (11 March 1974): 18-19.
23. Jean-Marie Domenach, "Soljenitsyne et le destin de l'Europe," 393, 394; Jean-Marie Domenach, *Le Nouvel Observateur* 484 (11 Feb. 1974): 5.
24. Serge July, "Le Fantôme de Soljenitsyne sur la 1e chaîne face à la pensée morte," *Libération*, 25 June 1974, 3.
25. Daniel, *L'Ère des ruptures*, 234-45.
26. See Daniel's indication of the support that *Le Nouvel Observateur* received from *Le Monde*; *Témoignage chrétien*; journalists at *Point*, *L'Express*, and *Europe no. 1*; and the *Comité exécutif* of the PS in his "Soljenitsyne, les communistes français et nous," 18. See also the criticisms of the excessiveness of the PCF's attacks by Claude Gault, editor in chief of *Témoignage chrétien*, in *France nouvelle* 1475 (19 Feb. 1974): 19.
27. Jean-Marie Domenach, letter in *Le Nouvel Observateur* 483 (11 Feb. 1974): 5.
28. July, "Le Fantôme de Soljenitsyne," 3. For *Libération*'s rallying to Solzhenitsyn's cause see notably the following editorials: Philippe Gavi, "Lin Piao, Soljenitsyne…," *Libération*, 14 Feb. 1974, 1 and 12; Philippe Gavi, "L'Exil de Soljenitsyne: un écrivain entre deux prisons," *Libération*, 15 Feb. 1974, 1 and 8; and Marcel Delorme and Maren Sell, "Pour Soljenitsyne la vérité est révolutionnaire," *Libération*, 27 Feb. 1974, 1 and 12. The editorial position taken by *Libération* is criticized in, for example, M. F., P. R., and P. B., "Soljenitsyne et la démocratie," *Libération*, 6 March 1974, 7.
29. Jean-Marie Domenach, letter in *Le Nouvel Observateur* 504 (8 July 1974): 5.
30. Daniel, *L'Ère des ruptures*, 236, 244-45. *Le Monde*, 23 Jan. 1974, 10; *Le Monde*, 14 Feb. 1974, 5. I found no evidence of Daniel's claims in my systematic reading of *Le Monde*'s coverage of the PCF-*Le Nouvel Observateur* altercation.
31. *Le Monde*, 26 Jan. 1974. To claim as Pierre Grémion does (*Paris-Prague*, 284) that the PS had disavowed ("désavouer") Martinet is inexact, if only because Martinet himself had declared that he spoke "in a private capacity." *Le Monde*, 24 Jan. 1974, 12.
32. François Mitterrand, *L'Unité* (9 Feb. 1974) cited in Jean Daniel, *L'Ère des ruptures*, 237.
33. Citation from Khilnani, *Arguing Revolution*, 154. Khilnani misconstrues ideological debates in the PS, in part because he fails to recognize their instrumental role in intra-party power struggles. He takes the *Projet socialiste pour les années 80* (1980) as representative of the PS view of the USSR throughout the 1970s. Despite being the official party

position in 1980, it was in effect a sop given to the CERES current by Mitterrand and was destined to be ignored by the rest of the party and by Mitterrand himself in his 1981 election campaign. See Thomas R. Christofferson, *The French Socialists in Power, 1981-1986: From Autogestion to Cohabitation* (Toronto, 1991), 60-61.

34. Mitterrand interviewed in *Le Nouvel Observateur* 484 (11 Feb. 1974): 24-25. Mitterrand defended *Le Nouvel Observateur* in this interview.

35. Jean Daniel, "L'Espoir et le programme," *Le Nouvel Observateur* 484 (11 Feb. 1974): 23.

36. Six hundred thousand copies of volume one had been sold by the end of 1974. *Le Monde*, 13 Dec. 1974, 17. Koestler's *Darkness at Noon* and Kravchenko's *I Chose Freedom*, which were also enormous publishing successes, undoubtedly had had their French circulation boosted by PCF campaigns against them. Rigoulot, *Les Paupières lourdes*, 56; Ariane Chebel d'Appollonia, *Le Temps de l'engagement*, vol. 2 of *Histoire politique des intellectuels en France, 1944-1954* (Brussels, 1991), 64.

37. Philippe Robrieux, *(1972-1982)*, vol. 3 of *Histoire intérieure du Parti communiste* (Paris, 1982), 180-81. Alain Decaux, a historian, Claude Gault, the editor of *Témoignage chrétien*, and Max-Pol Fouchet, a writer, contributed brief articles to *France nouvelle* 1475 (19 Feb. 1974): 19. Yet, Decaux and Gault wrote critical appraisals of some of the PCF's positions. The editor of *Le Monde diplomatique*, Claude Julien (see his "Du bon usage de l'antisoviétisme," *France nouvelle* 1479 [19 March 1974]: 19) and the writer Robert Escarpit also rallied to the communist positions. The writer Alain Bosquet was also hostile to Solzhenitsyn, but for reasons that largely escape the confines of the French ideological debates of the time. On "Ouvrez les guillemets" he accepted Solzhenitsyn's "catalog of accusations" but attacked him for lacking literary talent and abandoning his aesthetic responsibilities to become a political partisan. See also his pamphlet, *Pas d'accord Soljenitsyne!* (Paris, 1974).

38. Maurice Clavel's attacks on Fouchet (*Le Nouvel Observateur* of 25 Feb. 1974 and of 25 Nov. 1974) were particularly ferocious. Fouchet responded to the first Clavel article with a letter in *Le Nouvel Observateur* 487 (11 March 1974): 6, 9. See also Jean Lacouture, *Sud Ouest* (Bordeaux), 7 July 1974, 7.

39. Grémion, *Paris-Prague*, 294. Henry Rousso, *The Vichy Syndrome: History and Memory in France Since 1944*, trans. Arthur Goldhammer (Cambridge, Mass., 1991), chap. 3.

40. Reported in *Le Monde*, 9 March 1974, 9.

41. Rigoulot, *Les Paupières lourdes*, 126.

42. See the discussion in chapter 4.

43. Harris and Sédouy, *Voyage à l'intérieur du Parti communiste*, 78.

44. Ibid., 142-43. Jean-François Revel, "Si Soljenitsyne était français ..." *L'Express* 1178 (4 Feb. 1974): 30.

45. Robrieux, *(1972-1982)*, 178-79.

46. Sofres opinion poll of 27 Feb. 1974 published in *Le Nouvel Observateur* 486 (4 March 1974): 36-37.

47. Jean Daniel, "Pour en finir avec l'antisoviétisme," 19; K. S. Karol, "U.R.S.S.: le système B.," *Le Nouvel Observateur* 485 (18 Feb. 1974): 28-29.

48. "Ouvrez les guillemets" episode broadcast on the 1e chaîne on 24 June 1974; Maurice Clavel, "'Vingt millions!...' Une émission-choc sur Soljenitsyne," *Le Nouvel Observateur* 503 (1 July 1974): 29; Bernard-Henri Lévy, "Soljenitsyne un ethnologue," *Le Quotidien de Paris*, 3 July 1974. Curiously, Lévy, who would later claim that *The Gulag Archipelago*'s impact was due to its literary quality, wrote in this article that it was not a "a great piece of literature" and that Solzhenitsyn was a "second-rate writer." More information on the biographies of Clavel and Lévy can be found in chapter 5.

49. *Le Nouvel Observateur* 485 (18 Feb. 1974): 31. See IMEC ESP2 E4-03 .09, the *Esprit* archives of the *Institut Mémoires de l'Édition Contemporaine*, folder ESP2 E4-03 .09, for a long list of signatures. The protest, organized by *Esprit*, read:

> Arrested by the police on 12 February 1974, Aleksandr Solzhenitsyn was expelled from the USSR twelve hours later. This sudden measure was motivated

by the appearance in foreign bookstores of works by this writer the publication of which was denied to him in his own country.

All this is in contempt of the Geneva Convention that the USSR has just signed and that, as its preamble says, is dedicated to the goals of "assuring respect for human dignity" and of "facilitating the diffusion of the works of the mind."

It is in the name of this respect and in the name of this liberty that the undersigned protest against the measures of which Aleksandr Solzhenitsyn, Nobel Laureate for literature, has been victim.

Prominent left-wing signatories to the protest include, among others: Jean Daniel, Jean-Marie Domenach, Claude Roy, Pierre Daix, Philippe Sollers, Marcelin Pleynet, "le Comité de Rédaction de *Tel quel*," Jean-Paul Sartre, Jacques Derrida, Jacques Julliard, Germaine Tillion, Jacques Le Goff, Jean Cassou, Hélène Cixous, Dominique Desanti, Jean-Toussaint Desanti, Jean-Pierre Faye, Georges Friedmann, Roger Garaudy, Francis Jeanson, Madeleine Rebérioux, Maxime Rodinson, Alain Touraine, Pierre Vidal-Naquet, Michel Winock, Olivier Todd, Daniel Mothé, Paul Thibaud, Jacques Ozouf, Alexandre Astruc, Claude Bourdet, and—last but not least—Max-Pol Fouchet.

50. Pierre Rigoulot, "Le Goulag et la crise du marxisme," *Les Temps modernes* 31, 360 (July 1976): 2306-33.

51. Jeannette Colombel, "Pour une défense de gauche de Soljenitsyne," *Libération*, 22 Oct. 1973, 2.

52. See Sartre's comments in Philippe Gavi, Jean-Paul Sartre, and Pierre Victor, *On a raison de se révolter* (Paris, 1974), 348-50. Sartre had gone blind by the time *The Gulag Archipelago* was published, but he had Simone de Beauvoir read it to him in the summer of 1974 according to Simone de Beauvoir, *Adieux: A Farewell to Sartre*, trans. Patrick O'Brian (New York, 1984), 73.

53. Hélène Zamoyska, "L'Archipel du goulag," *Esprit* 437 (July-Aug. 1974): 139-47.

54. See chapter 3.

55. Discussed below.

56. The citation is from Jean Cathala, "Socialisme: le démon dans le sang," *Le Nouvel Observateur* 533 (27 Jan. 1975): 52. Jean Cathala, "L'Archipel du diable," *Le Nouvel Observateur* 478 (7 Jan. 1974); K. S. Karol, "Soljénitsyne n'a rien inventé," *Le Nouvel Observateur* 481 (28 Jan. 1974); Claude Roy, "Vingt millions de morts," *Le Nouvel Observateur* 505 (15 July 1974); K. S. Karol's introduction to Roy Medvedev, "Lettre ouverte à Soljenitsyne," *Le Nouvel Observateur* 524 (18 Nov. 1974).

57. French intellectuals could be informed of these elements of Solzhenitsyn's thought by his *The Gulag Archipelago, Letter to the Soviet Leaders* (available in French in early March 1974), articles in *From Under the Rubble* (available in French in January 1975), and the extensive press coverage of his political pronouncements.

58. "Les Goulags sud-africains," *Le Nouvel Observateur* 616 (30 Aug. 1976): 30; Jean-Paul Enthoven, "L'Amérique et le sang des autres," *Le Nouvel Observateur* 542 (29 March 1975): 52-53, a review of Noam Chomsky and Edward S. Herman, *Bains de sang constructifs: dans les faits et dans la propagande* (Paris, 1974), with a preface, "L'Archipel bloodbath," by Jean-Pierre Faye.

59. Jean-Marie Domenach, "'Continent' et Soljéntisyne," *Esprit* 452 (Dec. 1975): 860-61; K. S. Karol, "Soljénitsyne n'a rien inventé," 70.

60. K. S. Karol, introduction to Roy Medvedev, "Lettre ouverte à Soljénitsyne," 87, 89; Jean Daniel, "Les Prophéties de Soljénitsyne," *Le Nouvel Observateur* 545 (21 April 1975): 39. For other criticisms of Solzhenitsyn's politics see Jean-Marie Domenach, "Soljénitsyne et le destin de l'Europe," *Esprit* 433 (March 1974): 387; Paul Thibaud, "Soljénitsyne en occident," *Esprit* 447 (June 1975): 1019-21; Jean Daniel, "Pour en finir avec l'antisoviétisme," 19; K. S. Karol, "U.R.S.S.: le système B.," 29; Jean Cathala, "Socialisme: le démon dans le sang"; Jean Daniel, "Moscou contre Mitterrand," *Le Nouvel Observateur* 544 (14 April 1975): 40; Jean Daniel, "La Faiblesse des forts," *Le Nouvel Observateur* 591 (8 March 1976):

20; Jean Daniel, "Du Goulag au Maghreb," *Le Nouvel Observateur* 592 (15 March 1976): 28-29.

61. Raymond Aron, "La IIIe guerre mondiale n'a pas eu lieu," *Le Figaro*, 12 June 1975, 32, in response to Solzhenitsyn's "Troisième guerre mondiale?" *Le Monde*, 31 May 1975, 8.

62. Citation of B. F., "Soljénitsyne à Paris," *Le Monde*, 12 April 1975, 4.

63. For a partial transcript of this episode of "Apostrophes" watched by more than half of all French possessing a television, see "Soljénitsyne en direct," *Contrepoint* 21 (May 1976): 143-62. The tape of this broadcast at the INA lacks a French translation of Solzhenitsyn who spoke in Russian.

64. Daniel, *L'Ère des ruptures*, 258.

65. Daniel, *L'Ère des ruptures*, 259-60.

66. Jean Daniel, "Les Prophéties de Soljénitsyne," 38-39. In his "Soljénitsyne en Occident," Paul Thibaud also displayed his pleasure that Solzhenitsyn had been saved from reaction. Michel Foucault congratulated Daniel for having led Solzhenitsyn "to the essential." Daniel, *L'Ère des ruptures*, 264.

67. Jean Daniel, *Le Figaro*, 24 April 1975, 31, in response to Raymond Aron, "Le Message," *Le Figaro*, 18 April 1975, 2.

68. "Les Dossiers de l'écran" broadcast on 9 March 1976 on Antenne 2, consulted at the archives of the INA. Citation taken from Michael Scammell, *Solzhenitsyn: A Biography* (New York, 1984), 939.

69. Portrayals of Solzhenitsyn as a new Dostoyevski or prophetic figure include: Jean Daniel, "Explication"; Jean-Marie Domenach, "Soljénitsyne et le destin de l'Europe"; and Guy Durand, "Soljénitsyne," *Esprit* 456 (April 1976): 752-54. Solzhenitsyn did not see it this way. When he agreed to appear on French television on 9 March 1976, he did so with the hope of expressing his views about relations between Moscow and foreign communist parties. Thus, the accusation that he was trying to influence the French cantonal elections by scheduling his 9 March 1976 broadcast between the two rounds might not be unfounded. Scammell, *Solzhenitsyn*, 940-41. Solzhenitsyn publicly rejected this claim by saying on television that he had not known about the French elections when the program was scheduled. "Les Dossiers de l'écran," broadcast on 9 March 1976 on Antenne 2.

70. Raymond Aron, "Le Message," 2; Daniel, "Du Goulag au Maghreb," 28-29.

71. Note on Solzhenitsyn, *Esprit* 456 (April 1976): 836; Guy Durand, "Soljénitsyne"; Lefort, *Un homme en trop*, 8, 31.

72. Published as Claude Lefort, *Le Travail de l'œuvre Machiavel* (Paris, 1972) and André Glucksmann, *Le Discours de la guerre* (Paris, 1967).

73. Claude Lefort, "Préface," in *Éléments d'une critique de la bureaucratie* (Paris, 1979), 7-28; "Entretien avec C. Lefort," *L'Antimythes* 14 (Nov. 1975): 1-30.

74. "Entretien avec C. Lefort," 12-13.

75. On his trajectory see especially, "L'Itinéraire d'André Glucksmann," *La Croix*, 7 Jan. 1978; Lucien Bodard, "André Glucksmann," *Le Point* 495 (25 March 1982): 157-66; "De la violence: entretien avec André Glucksmann," *Actuel* 54 (May 1975): 14-18; Jürg Altwegg, "Von der Mai-Barrikade zur Atomstrategie. Der weiter Weg des Andrés Glucksmann – ein Gespräch," *Dokumente* 40, 1 (March 1984): 39-48; and Hervé Hamon and Patrick Rotman, *Génération*, 2 vols. (Paris, 1987, 1988).

76. André Glucksmann, *Stratégie et révolution en France 1968: introduction* (Paris, 1968), chap. 2; André Glucksmann, "Fascismes: l'ancien et le nouveau," *Les Temps modernes* 310 bis (1972): 294, 297.

77. Glucksmann, *Stratégie et révolution*, chap. 4.

78. Ibid., 59.

79. Ibid., 106, 114.

80. Although he continually undercut it, Glucksmann initially believed that some form of revolutionary organization was necessary. In 1968 he accepted Lenin's (originally Karl

Kautsky's) argument that workers cannot arrive at revolutionary consciousness on their own. In France, the students would bestow it upon them. Ibid., 83-84.

81. "L'Itinéraire d'André Glucksmann."

82. "De la violence: entretien avec André Glucksmann," 17.

83. André Glucksmann, "Le Marxisme rend sourd," *Le Nouvel Observateur* 486 (4 March 1974): 80; Claude Lefort, "Soljénitsyne (Commentaire sur *l'Archipel du goulag*)," *Textures* 10-11 (1975): 3-38. Glucksmann also wrote a response to a *Le Monde* review of Solzhenitsyn's *Letter to the Soviet Leaders* in which he contested the interpretation of this work as naïve and reactionary. André Glucksmann, "Soljenitsyne gênant? Lettre ouverte à Michel Tatu du 'Monde,'" *Libération*, 15 March 1974, 1, 10.

84. Scammell, *Solzhenitsyn*, 905; Antoine Spire, "Le Chat solitaire de la rue des Saint-Pères," *Le Matin* no. spécial, Salon du Livre, 17 March 1986, 6; "Un Bestseller," *Le Monde*, 13 Dec. 1974, 17; Rémy Rieffel, *La Tribu des clercs: les intellectuels sous la Ve République*, (Paris, 1993), 305, 487-88; Claude Durand, interview with the author, Paris, 16 June 1994.

85. Jean Daniel confirms that neither he nor Glucksmann had read *The Gulag Archipelago* when Glucksmann published his article. Daniel, *L'Ère des ruptures*, 248. Glucksmann relates his conflicts with *gauchiste* militants over the evaluation of the USSR in "L'Itinéraire d'André Glucksmann."

86. Immigrant and unskilled workers were privileged in the populist pantheon of the Gauche prolétarienne. "The eye of the peasant sees justly" (*"L'œil du paysan voit juste"*) was one of the Gauche prolétarienne's favorite populist citations from Mao.

87. Glucksmann, "Le Marxisme rend sourd."

88. "L'Itinéraire d'André Glucksmann"; Altwegg, "Von der Mai-Barrikade zur Atomstrategie," 43.

89. "De la violence: entretien avec André Glucksmann," 17. The same point is made in André Glucksmann, *La Cuisinière et le mangeur d'hommes*, 11.

90. Glucksmann, *La Cuisinière et le mangeur d'hommes*, 35-37.

91. Lefort, *Un homme en trop*, 20. The first chapter of this book is essentially a republication of his 1975 article.

92. Ibid., 10, 27, 30.

93. Lefort defined "libertarian" in a 1977 interview as "the critique of all constraining authority from wherever it comes and, at the core, the demand in relation to all power, whatever the nature, of one's liberty, of liberty itself as soon as it is menaced." Interview of Claude Lefort by Gilbert Grand, *Le Devoir* (Montreal), 19 Nov. 1977.

94. Lefort, *Un homme en trop*, 31, 32, 37. Lefort's assertion that the position of the dominated is universal conflicts with his claim to have learned from his teacher Merleau-Ponty "the critique of all pretensions to occupy the place of absolute knowledge or to maintain a discourse on the totality." "Entretien avec C. Lefort," 5.

95. Lefort, *Un homme en trop*, 8, 31.

96. Ibid., 180-204. See also his rejection of Solzhenitsyn's arguments on the relationship between economics and the camps (99-108) and his rather rigid rejection of Solzhenitsyn's contention that the reconstruction of the system of camps after 1956 was the work of the penitentiary bureaucracy. For Lefort, this could not be the case because "no particular group, whether it be managers of repression or managers of the Plan concerned with the exploitation of forced labor, is, in a totalitarian society, capable of making his interests prevail independently of the Party" (245).

97. This summary of Lefort's argument is from his 1986 "Avertissement pour l'édition de poche." Ibid., 6.

98. Ibid., 54.

99. Ibid., chap. 2.

100. Ibid., 63-64, 115-16.

101. Ibid., 108. Lefort argues that Solzhenitsyn's description disagrees with his conclusions.

102. Ibid., chap. 3. Stalin, however, exceeds his necessity by his madness.

103. Ibid., 127.

104. Ibid., 127-36.
105. Ibid., 140.
106. Ibid., 140-79.
107. Ibid., 179.
108. See chapter 4. Some twenty thousand copies of *La Cuisinière et le mangeur d'hommes* were sold in one year. Gérard Petitjean, "Les Nouveaux Gourous," *Le Nouvel Observateur* 609 (12 July 1976): 65.
109. See chapter 5. From 1977 to 1985, François Furet was president of the EHESS, where he helped elect Claude Lefort, Cornelius Castoriadis, and Lefort's students Marcel Gauchet and Pierre Rosanvallon to positions.
110. Bernard-Henri Lévy, *La Barbarie à visage humain* (Paris, 1977), 165.
111. Pierre Rosanvallon and Patrick Viveret, *Pour une nouvelle culture politique* (Paris, 1977), 79.
112. François Furet, *Penser la Révolution française* (Paris, 1978), 29.
113. "*Tout parti vit de sa mystique et meurt de sa politique.*" Charles Péguy, *Men and Saints: Prose and Poetry*, trans. Anne and Julien Green (New York, 1944), 100.

Chapter 3

INTELLECTUALS AND THE POLITICS OF THE UNION OF THE LEFT

The Birth of Antitotalitarianism

The significance of Solzhenitsyn's *The Gulag Archipelago* in the emergence of French antitotalitarianism has—as the preceding chapter has argued—been misconstrued. *The Gulag Archipelago* was not a revelatory text; it was the PCF's attacks on it and its author that gave it a special prominence in French debates. Still, *The Gulag Archipelago* was eventually attributed a decisive influence in the evolution of the politics of the French intellectual Left because doing so allowed French intellectuals to critique the Union of the Left in universal terms, harshly condemn communism, and magnify the threat that communism posed in France by highlighting intellectuals' past blindness to totalitarianism. As the following discussion should demonstrate, this attribution of influence to *The Gulag Archipelago* was, given the dynamics of the politics of the Left between 1974 and 1978, an essential claim for those critical of the Union of the Left. This chapter will, following the preceding chapter's effort to dismantle the critique of totalitarianism's myth of origins, offer the first elements of an explanation of the origins of French antitotalitarianism in the encounter of French intellectuals of the noncommunist Left and their particular concerns with the politics of the Union of the Left.

In brief, this chapter argues that certain intellectuals developed the critique of totalitarianism in response to the intensification of political struggle within the Union of the Left in 1974 and 1975. This critique of totalitarianism was not an abrupt reversal of the noncommunist left-wing intellectuals' positions on the parties of the Left, but rather a radicalization of their existing criticisms. Many intellectuals, particularly those discussed in chapter 1, who had developed sharply critical attitudes toward communism after 1956 and had participated in the direct-democratic political currents central to intellectual politics in the half-decade after 1968, were extremely wary of the PS-PCF alliance behind a Common Program of Government from its inception. Beginning in 1975, the increased electoral viability of the united Left and the multiplication of competition and invective within it sparked these same intellectuals to amplify and intensify their criticism of it. Fearful that the PCF might dominate the Union of the Left and wishing to forestall the Left's revival of political formulae that were, in their eyes, too close to those that they had already rejected in the 1950s and 1960s, these intellectuals developed a critique of communism and, to a lesser degree, of the related politics of the Union of the Left as totalitarian.[1]

If the elaboration of the critique of totalitarianism was primarily prompted by domestic political concerns, French antitotalitarianism necessarily reflected the diversity of positions on the domestic political scene. Within the field of party politics there were disputes between the PCF and the PS, within these same parties, between the independent Left and the parties of the Union of the Left, and, of course, between the Right and the Left—all of which contributed to the emerging critique of totalitarianism. The positions staked out by intellectuals echoed, but did not slavishly follow, those within the strictly political field. Intellectuals drew on their political reflections of the preceding two decades in formulating their evaluations of the Union of the Left and its relationship to totalitarianism. And although antitotalitarian intellectuals drew closer to each other as their critiques became more radical in 1976 and 1977, important differences remained between their reflections on totalitarianism. This and the succeeding chapters will offer a history of this moment in French intellectual politics that respects and explains these differences while underscoring the fundamental unity of the concerns and analyses of French antitotalitarians.

"The Union is a Struggle": The Socialist-Communist Alliance to 1975

The Union of the Left was a child of the bipolar logic of politics in the Fifth Republic. In the Fourth Republic, by contrast, the PCF had been a political pariah after 1947, and the socialists (SFIO) had gained access to political power through "Third Force" centrist coalitions directed against the ostracized parties of the extreme Left (PCF) and extreme Right (de Gaulle's RPF). In the Fifth Republic, the SFIO first tried to construct a "Third Force" alternative to De Gaulle, but after the poor performance of the *"Cartel des 'non'"* in the October 1962 referendum on the election of the president by universal suffrage, it could not avoid the conclusion that the new régime had brought an end to its pivotal political position. De Gaulle's imposing presence and the Fifth Republic's presidentialism, capped off by the direct popular election of the president beginning in 1965, all contributed to the formation of a bipolar political system.

The PCF, seeking to escape its Cold War isolation, took advantage of the opportunities offered by the Fifth Republic first to forge limited electoral agreements and then to campaign, beginning in 1964, for a close alliance with the socialists on the basis of a Common Program of Government. The electoral efficacy of socialist-communist cooperation proved itself in the November 1962 and especially the December 1967 legislative elections, as well as in Mitterrand's impressive showing in the 1965 presidential election. By contrast, the failure of Gaston Defferre's effort to put together a center-left coalition in support of his candidacy in the 1965 presidential election and the poor showing of the Left when divided in the 1968 legislative and 1969 presidential elections reinforced the conclusion that the Left could return to political power only if its diverse forces worked together. When the PS replaced the SFIO at the historic June 1971 Épinay congress, the party's new leader François Mitterrand resolutely committed it to pursuing a programmatic deal with the PCF, without which any PS-PCF electoral alliance would, it was believed, be fragile and uninspiring. A year after Épinay, the Union of the Left on the basis of the Common Program of Government had been achieved.[2]

The Common Program of Government was, as the name suggests, more than an electoral alliance. It was a governmental program for the length of one five-year legislature that promised sweeping reforms that would greatly augment the French welfare state and, by nationalizing key sectors of the economy, open "the path to socialism."[3] Published in separate editions by the PCF and the PS, the Common Program circulated in millions of copies; it was the most widely publicized political program in French history.[4] It gave the left-wing electorate hope and gave the Union of the Left an irresistible *élan*. It justifiably occupied the center stage of French politics in the 1970s.

The result of a long series of discussions and negotiations between socialists and communists, Left unity on the basis of a Common Program required that important, long-standing differences between the two parties on liberty and democracy, foreign policy, evaluations of Soviet-bloc socialism, and the extent of nationalization to be undertaken by a Left government be overcome, or at the very least, skillfully papered over.[5] Although the PS prevailed on most points, the Common Program was a compromise document that made some concessions to the communists and contained some significant ambiguities. For example, although the Common Program's guarantees of liberty and democracy were, at the PS's insistence, concrete and straightforward, there were potentially contradictory statements on the crucial question of *alternance* (the change-over of political power). The program guaranteed regular elections "by universal direct and secret suffrage" and committed its signatories to respect "the verdict expressed by universal suffrage," but the text immediately qualified this commitment with the following passage, which might seem to deny the possibility of such an outcome by asserting the inevitability of the Left's electoral success: "If the confidence of the country were refused to the majority parties they would renounce power to take up the struggle in the opposition. But democratic power, the existence of which implies the support of a popular majority, will have as its principal task the satisfaction of the laboring masses and will therefore be strengthened with the ever increasingly more active confidence that they will bring it."[6] Also, although the PS succeeded in limiting the extent of nationalization, the Common Program allowed for nationalizations other than those explicitly mentioned in the text "in the event that the workers decide that they want to see their firm enter into the public or nationalized sector."[7] The PS and PCF could not agree on a common position on the question of worker control of nationalized firms. The former made known its preference for *"autogestion,"* and the latter betrayed its Leninist political line by rejecting *autogestion* in favor of *"gestion démocratique."*[8] Finally and most importantly, the Common Program failed to address the signatories' appreciation of existing socialist régimes. The PCF was, as the Solzhenitsyn affair later revealed, clearly attached to the Soviet model. This silence within the text cast doubt on the communists' commitment to building a form of socialism freer and more democratic than that behind the iron curtain.[9]

The PS clearly understood the limits of the PCF's commitment to political freedom. In the years following the signing of the Common Program it continually pushed the PCF to offer a clear and acceptable position on the issue while simultaneously seeking to distance itself from the communist stance and reassure the electorate of the intentions of the Left. Indeed, the PS used the issue of repression in communist Czechoslovakia to this end.[10] In February 1972 Mitterrand proposed to the PCF that they "protest together against the dangerous evolution in Czechoslovakia," and in July 1972 he told the communists in no uncertain terms what he thought of the Czechoslovak normalization and the PCF silence about it: "I will believe in the chances of liberty in the world when I see ideological and political solidarities take a second seat to truth…. The Czechoslovak leaders are putting international communism on a regressive course."[11] An official PS representative, Robert Pontillon (in charge of the PS's international relations), participated in a 26 October 1972 "meeting of solidarity" with victims of repression in Czechoslovakia organized by the Comité du 5 janvier pour une Tchécoslovaquie libre et socialiste.[12] A few months later, the PS sponsored a colloquium on "Czechoslovakia: socialism and democracy" in which Prague Spring and the significance of normalization were discussed.[13] In large part because of the attention that the PS gave to these issues, the PCF would find itself continually on the defensive on the issue of liberties as it sought to broaden its appeal in the 1970s.

While the public debate on liberty under socialism was politically important, in Mitterrand's analysis communist behavior would be determined by relations of force within the Left and not communist professions of intent.[14] Mitterrand's goal, first exposed in his *Ma part de vérité* (1969) and repeated on numerous occasions, was to create a "political movement [i.e., the Socialist Party] able to balance at first, and then dominate the Communist Party and finally to obtain a majority of its own."[15] The PS would dominate within the Left by attracting the *nouveau salariat* (new employees), and the united Left would eventually emerge victorious by appealing to the Left with its economic program and—presumably after the subordination of the communists had rendered the question of liberty moot—to the Right with its political liberalism.[16]

Like Mitterrand, who openly spoke of seeking a *rééquilibrage de la gauche* (rebalancing of the Left) in favor of the PS through the Union of the Left, Georges Marchais, the general secretary of the PCF, had few illusions about his party's alliance with the PS. In his "Rapport au Comité central" of 29 June 1972—which was not made public until July 1975—Marchais clearly stated that the Common Program was only a first step forward "allowing us to create the most favorable conditions for mobilizing the masses around *our* ideas, *our* solutions, and *our* objectives." Although the Common Program only outlined a "régime of advanced democracy," it created favorable conditions for a socialist transformation of society that would be possible if the PCF were to outflank the "reformist social democratic" PS by using its resources to "invigorate, direct, organize, and fully develop the mass movement."[17] Like the PS, the PCF sought to win the support of new social groups (engineers, technicians, *cadres*) that went by the appellation *"nouvelles couches sociales"* within the party. To attract them, it emphasized the commonality of their interests with those of the working class, eased the conditions of adherence to the party, and tried to demonstrate that the PCF was not a closed bureaucratic sect or a countersociety, but rather an open and dynamic party that posed no threat to freedom.[18]

The PCF's efforts were imperfect and ultimately failed. Its attempts to reassure the public that freedom would be safe with the communists in power were undermined by its own attempt to focus debate on anticommunism and anti-Sovietism during the Solzhenitsyn affair of 1974 and during the debate over the Portuguese Revolution in the summer of 1975. Its attacks on *Le Nouvel Observateur* during these episodes, evidently intended to neutralize or garner to its benefit this weekly's considerable influence with the *nouvelles couches sociales*, totally backfired. They only served to increase opinion-makers' hostility to the party and to spark the intellectuals' critique of totalitarianism. The PCF's much less ambiguous embrace of Soviet dissidence in late 1975 and 1976 and its abandonment of the dictatorship of the proletariat in early 1976 were, at least for most noncommunist intellectuals, too little, too late.

The PCF's bid to win the battle of opinion within the Left was probably fatally flawed. It is hard to imagine how in the 1970s the PCF could have simultaneously convinced the public that it was not a threat to freedom and asserted, as it did, the necessity of electing communists because only the PCF was radical enough to ensure that the Common Program would be implemented. Similarly, it would have been difficult for the PCF to entirely abandon the Soviet model and Leninist politics while maintaining an independent identity within the Left. In the final analysis, the PCF's efforts to recast its image were undermined by its own half-hearted embrace of change and the enduring suspicion of intellectuals unwilling to abandon on such short notice their deep-seated hostility to the PCF based on a long experience of French communism. The PCF's Union of the Left strategy did, in the end, transform the party, but in the direction of division and weakness, culminating in its internal crisis after the 1978 legislative elections.

Despite the communist and socialist leaderships' keen awareness of the competitive nature of the Union of the Left, there was little open conflict between the two parties in the first two years after the signing of the Common Program. Both parties were encouraged by their growth in the early 1970s, and both limited disputes within the alliance in order to prove its efficacy during the 1973 legislative and 1974 Presidential elections.[19] After the 1974 presidentials there would be ample time to jockey for position within the Left because no elections were scheduled until the March 1976 cantonals. Further, communist leaders considered it necessary to coddle the PS and went to extraordinary lengths in the 1973 and 1974 elections in order to win it over to the alliance. In the 1973 legislatives, for example, when Mitterrand rejected the PCF's call for a joint campaign, Marchais accepted it *faute de mieux*. In the 1974 presidentials, the PCF likewise accepted Mitterrand without quid pro quo as the candidate of the Left for the first round of the election and made few demands on him during the campaign. Mitterrand, in turn, neglected the communists and ran on what he called his "options"—a word used to avoid evoking the Common Program. Mitterrand gained support from outside the Union of the Left, notably from the Confédération française démocratique du travail (CFDT) and Michel Rocard, PSU national secretary from 1967 to 1973 and its presidential candidate in 1969. Neither did Mitterrand's campaign team reflect the Union of the Left. It was composed of his loyal supporters from his 1965 effort; Claude Perdriel, the owner of *Le Nouvel Observateur*; and a few new men, notably the economists Jacques Attali, Christian Goux, and Michel Rocard.[20]

The 1973 and 1974 elections started to bring about the *rééquilibrage de la gauche* sought by Mitterrand and the PS. In the 1973 legislatives, the PS and its close ally, the Mouvement des radicaux de gauche, received some 20.8 percent of the vote, a significant increase over the scores of their predecessors in the 1967 and 1968 elections; and the PS made its first significant inroads into the Catholic electorate. The PCF, on the other hand, stagnated at 21.4 percent of the vote, worse than its 1968 score, but better than that of 1967. Furthermore, the communists suffered a considerable erosion of their support in the red belt around Paris. In the 1974 presidential elections Mitterrand's first-place finish in the first round and loss with 49.3 percent of the vote in the second round were perceived as moral victories and proved to be mobilizing.[21] Large numbers of new party members began to flow into the PS, and Mitterrand soon laid the ground with his *appel* of 25 May 1974 for the Assises nationales du socialisme of 12-13 October 1974, which would integrate into the PS those elements of the Left that, although critical of the Common Program, had supported him in the presidential election.

The Assises du socialisme brought a significant part of the Christian and *soixante-huitard* Left into the PS. Although both the PSU and the CFDT maintained their autonomy from the PS, large numbers of PSU and CFDT militants and some prominent politicians (Michel Rocard and Jacques Delors, for example) entered the PS at this time. Through the Assises the PS also forged bonds with the diverse social movements that had emerged after 1968. The *Projet de société* (programmatic statement) of the Assises integrated the new post-1968 movements (including, for example, challenges to hierarchy in production, the state, churches, the army, and schools; the revolt of the prisoners; and the demands of minorities and immigrants) into the PS's definition of socialism and gave *autogestion*— labeled the "keystone of a democratic socialism" and broadly defined as the greatest possible democratization and decentralization of power that still respects the needs of the collectivity— a central place within it. While the Assises led the PS to recognize the importance of these new issues, it was also the occasion for the Assises participants to confirm their need for the PS as the unifier of their disparate struggles in a "global transformative project," at the center of which was the "conquest of the State." With the Assises the PS intensified its effort to become the dominant force within the Left and began its shift to the center of the political spectrum, where elections ultimately had to be won.[22]

By gathering under one tent the diverse socialist currents that had gone their separate ways in the 1950s and 1960s, the Assises effected a second Union of the Left that would prove to be almost as significant and conflictual as the first. The PS's Assises current was critical of the Common Program and, the 1974 presidential election campaign notwithstanding, also of Mitterrand. Indeed, very few loyal Mitterrandists emerged out of the Assises current, which would fall behind Rocard when he challenged Mitterrand's leadership of the party after the 1978 legislative elections. The Assises also marked the beginning of an important conflict within the PS—ultimately mediated by Mitterrand—between the Centre d'études, de recherches et d'éducation socialiste (CERES), one of the PS currents that was part of the majority coalition formed at Épinay, and the Assises current.[23] Last but not least, the Assises was a major factor in the PCF's adoption of a more critical posture toward its socialist ally in October 1974. The Assises was one of the main turning points in the history of the French Left in the 1970s.

Following the PS's success in the 1973 and 1974 elections and coinciding with the Assises, the six legislative by-elections on 29 September and 6 October 1974 sparked the PCF's launching of a yearlong polemic with the socialists. Although the Left as a whole progressed over the Right in these elections, it was the PS that gained, while the PCF's share of the vote declined in five of the six cases. On 7 October 1974 the *Bureau politique* of the PCF issued a statement in reaction to the election results that asserted that the PCF's influence had played an essential role in removing the PS from the path of the "injurious politics of class collaboration" and further charged that the socialists' call for a redistribution of power within the Left was an effort on the part of the bourgeoisie to undermine the PCF.[24] Subsequent PCF attacks on the PS targeted the Assises as evidence of the PS's centrist inclination. By casting doubt on the PS's commitment to the Common Program and advancing the argument that only a strong Communist Party could guarantee that the Union of the Left would remain on the Left, the PCF hoped to recapture the ground recently lost to the socialists. This offensive against the PS was accompanied by the PCF's reassertion of its traditional political themes: the revolutionary nature of the working class and the vanguard role of the Communist Party.[25]

The socialists initially met the communist polemic with protestations of their loyalty to the Union of the Left and the Common Program. Believing that a break with the communists would undermine socialist gains subsequent to the signing of the Common Program (especially because it would demobilize activists and close socialist access to the communist electorate), the PS refrained from launching a hard-hitting counterattack. Mitterrand said little until 14 January, when he urged Marchais to "reflect on the fact that a democratic party represents an immense advantage," to which Marchais crudely replied by calling Mitterrand "sure of himself and domineering [*sûr de lui et dominateur*]," the same words that de Gaulle had used in his infamous 1967 characterization of the Jewish people.[26] As Mitterrand's exchange with Marchais indicates, the PS response to communist invective may have been restrained, but it was also acute and to the point. The reports of Lionel Jospin, the head of the PS commission charged with analyzing PS-PCF relations, lucidly attributed the polemic to the PCF's refusal of *rééquilibrage* and challenged the PCF to accept pluralism within the Left.[27] Although the dispute was beginning to peter out in the spring of 1975, it lasted through the summer because the positions taken by the PCF on the Portuguese Revolution gave it new life, refocusing it on the question of liberty.

Beyond ending the honeymoon of the Union of the Left, the polemic with the PCF opened up an ideological conflict within the PS. CERES, one of the strongest supporters of the Common Program and the Union of the Left within the PS, echoed many of the communist critiques of the recent evolution of the PS.[28] Hostile to reformist tendencies within the PS but also critical of the PCF's Leninist analysis of politics and conception of the party, CERES hoped that the Union of the Left would both turn the PS into a revolutionary party and force the PCF to embrace democracy. If the parties of the Left were to evolve along these lines, they would eventually fuse, erasing the division of the Left that dated back to the 1920 Congress of Tours.

In CERES's analysis, the Assises du socialisme threatened the chances for a favorable evolution of the Left. It agreed with the communists that the Assises marked the PS's turn away from the Common Program in a more reformist direction. CERES's differences with the current of the Assises were particularly marked on the question of *autogestion*. CERES had been one of the original proponents within the PS of *autogestion*, which it understood as a democratization of decision-making to be achieved *after* the Left had arrived in power and collectivized the economy. Although, like many others on the Left, it promoted *autogestion* as a solution to the shortcomings of Soviet socialism, it accepted heterogeneity between means and ends in its application. Its *autogestionnaire* slogan was "struggle today in order to exercise control tomorrow," in contrast to the PSU's "exercise control today in order to decide tomorrow." CERES feared that radical *autogestionnaire* sentiments such as those expressed by the PSU, which were common in the Assises current, would sidetrack the Left from the essential and immediate tasks of coming to power and collectivizing the economy.[29]

CERES's criticism of the Assises in the autumn of 1974 resulted in it being pushed out of the majority within the PS when Mitterrand forged an alliance with the Assises current at its expense at the party's Pau Congress in early 1975. CERES's criticism of the PS's new direction did not lessen in intensity after the Pau Congress. At the Convention nationale du Parti socialiste of 3-4 May 1975 dedicated to the PCF polemic, it denounced "social democracy" within the PS and called for an end to the division of the Left between the socialist and communist parties. Then and during the subsequent months, it defended positions on the Portuguese Revolution close to those of the PCF.[30]

The conflict between CERES and the Assises current kept the PS ideologically divided right up to Mitterrand's election in 1981. With Rocard's speech on the two political cultures of the French Left at the April 1977 Nantes Party Congress, differences within the party became more explicit.[31] Ideological clashes within the PS would reach their greatest level of intensity when Rocard mounted his challenge to Mitterrand's leadership after the 1978 legislative elections. Mitterrand retaliated at the Metz Party Congress of April 1979 by casting Rocard into the minority and bringing CERES back into the majority with the appointed task of attacking Rocard. Although this intraparty ideological jousting of the late 1970s was somewhat superficial insofar as it was above all an instrument in the power struggle between Mitterrand and Rocard, it provided inspiration for French intellectuals' reflections on totalitarianism.[32]

Intellectuals and the Union of the Left: Criticism and Suspicion

Although the direct-democratic intellectuals discussed in chapter 1 were never indifferent to the Union of the Left, it did not enter into the forefront of their concerns until 1974, after its electoral success made it the central phenomenon in French politics. The coincidence of the rise of the Union of the Left with the decline of *gauchisme* further highlighted the former as it began to attract many former *gauchiste* militants—if not intellectuals—impressed by its dynamism and efficacy. The Assises consummated the collapse of *gauchisme* and, by bringing many of its remnants into the PS, focused the intellectual Left's attention on the Union of the Left. Even though some intellectuals associated with post-1968 *gauchiste* currents greeted the Assises with enthusiasm, they mostly maintained a critical perspective on the Union of the Left. The Common Program was far too state-centered for their taste, and the Union of the Left was additionally suspect for offering a precious political opportunity to the communists. In the criticism and suspicion of left-wing intellectuals, the parties of the Left had—as the following discussion of *Esprit, Le Nouvel Observateur*, and *Libération* demonstrates—a serious problem on their hands.

Esprit, one of the first voices of the critique of totalitarianism of the 1970s, had articulated criticisms of the politics of Left unity well before the Common Program was signed. The opportunism of Mitterrand, resigned to work with the communists as they were, was unacceptable to *Esprit*. As long as the PCF failed to de-Stalinize (and *Esprit* incessantly asserted that this had not happened), any Union of the Left would, *Esprit* argued, be stillborn or, if it gained power, either build nothing of lasting value or result in authoritarian socialism.[33] Finding the politics of Michel Rocard to be the most attractive option in the electoral arena after 1968,[34] *Esprit* emphasized that the mainstream Left had to move further from the Soviet socialist model and renovate itself before making a bid for power.[35] To drive home the former point, *Esprit* continually exposed and protested repression by East European communist régimes.[36] For *Esprit* renovation meant adopting an antiproductivist *autogestionnaire* socialist program that would provide firm guarantees of liberty and democracy. The intellectuals at *Esprit* had little tolerance for a Left that failed to take their prescription. After the Left's abysmal showing in the 1969 presidential election, Domenach warned: "If the Left is incapable of translating into political propositions these aspirations that have emerged among us, it has nothing more to say, and we will leave it to die in its corner."[37] As it happened, the Left neither died in its corner nor recast itself along the lines favored by *Esprit*. *Esprit* soon found itself having to adapt to a new and rapidly rising PS allied with an unreconstructed PCF and led by François Mitterrand, who, next to Guy Mollet, was probably the most disliked of all socialist politicians by the intellectuals at *Esprit*.[38]

The Common Program fell far short of *Esprit*'s hopes for the Left. In Paul Thibaud's analysis its conception of democracy was "formal," "ossified," and "static." Instead of promising decentralization and institutional change that would open up a space for initiatives on the part of individuals and groups, it favored a bureaucratic form of politics, "a representative, instituted, and marshaled democracy, that of the great political and union organizations." Its idea of socialism was infused with technocratic productivism that focused on redistribution and did not challenge the existing conception of needs. Its *autogestionnaire* elements were weak because they applied only to production and, Thibaud feared, were probably nothing more than "insincere additions." In short, Thibaud considered the Common Program to be "underlain by that good old state socialism" that he and *Esprit* rejected. Believing that the program abandoned Eastern Europe and favored the Finlandization of Western Europe, Thibaud held that it was an "ideological triumph of the PCF" that was balanced only by its guarantees of liberties. Perhaps because he believed at this point that the Stalinist PCF did not have the power to undermine liberty in France, Thibaud was willing to offer some minimal and highly qualified support for the united Left:

> The socialism of the day before yesterday that is proposed to us will bring about at least a change in the crews in power and the opening up of the situation. The illusory ideas that this program contains can only be superseded through an initial attempt to realize them. Only a danger of political dictatorship or a pressing menace in foreign policy might make stagnation without end preferable to the freeing up of initiatives that will allow in spite of everything an experiment in a socialist direction.[39]

Domenach, even more than Thibaud, found that the PCF's politics made the Union of the Left profoundly problematic.[40] For Domenach the programmatic statement of the Union of the Left was of secondary importance to the question of confidence in the PCF, of whether "it can participate in the government without seriously endangering liberties and national independence." More specifically, Domenach asked whether the PCF had the same ideas of democracy, liberty, and the rights of man as its allies. "If not, it is useless to unite." Demanding that the PCF be judged from its internal party practice, Domenach gave examples from the party's history that led the reader to the conclusion that the PCF could not be trusted with power.

While *Esprit* did not abandon its criticisms of the united Left, its support for it became more substantial in 1973 and 1974 as it proved its durability and efficacy on the electoral front. Paul Thibaud's article "Avant les élections" of January 1973 reiterated his criticisms of the Common Program, but seemed more enthusiastic about the prospects that victory of the Left would offer by opening up a contest between "state socialism, political liberalism, and *autogestionnaires* ferments." And while the orientation of the Common Program toward bureaucratic socialism made the repression of liberties a possibility, he found it "ridiculous to evoke with regard to it the prospect of Siberian-style concentration camps." He found significant guarantees against this outcome: the likely *rééquilibrage* of the Left by the PS, without which the Left could not win, the promises of the Common Program regarding liberties, and the *autogestionnaire* currents in society that "offer a basis for opposing bureaucratization and superseding paternalistic socialism."[41] Thibaud's expectation of PS *rééquilibrage* came true in the 1973 legislative elections, after which *Esprit*, prefiguring the Assises of the next year, argued that the PS should become the focal point of their efforts.[42]

The Assises made *Esprit* an insider to the PS and the Union of the Left. The event marked the entry into the PS of forces (from the CFDT and PSU, for example) with which intellectuals at *Esprit* were close and gave them hope that the PS was moving toward the *autogestionnaire* and antiproductivist socialism that they advocated. Jean-Marie Domenach, who attended the Assises, considered that its *Projet de société* "testifies to the evolution of the Left since 1968 and brings about some remarkable innovations" that he wholeheartedly supported. Previously one of the harshest critics of the united Left at *Esprit*,[43] Domenach, speaking in the name of the "leaders of *Esprit*," now argued that they should work within it, that "actions undertaken outside of the terrain of classical politics must now link up with an effort to conquer power."[44] Soon Domenach was speaking of *autogestion* and the assault on technocratic productivism as "our serious contribution to the Union of the Left."[45] Domenach had—contrary to the more measured and politically realistic opinion of Michel Rocard—vigorously demanded that the Assises mark nothing less than the beginning of a thorough transformation of the Left; [46] and for a moment, he seemed to believe that this was possible. In any event, his rising expectations would soon be sorely disappointed by the Assises's failure to make his priorities those of the PS.[47] Disillusionment with the Assises and the PS-PCF polemic beginning in October 1974 induced *Esprit* to radicalize its critique of the politics of the Union of the Left and even more firmly assert the necessity of its ideas. The result would be the elaboration of a critique of totalitarianism beginning in the late summer of 1975.

The coincidence of the inauguration of *Esprit*'s effort to bring its "serious contribution" to the Union of the Left and the launching of the PS-PCF polemic in October 1974 reinvigorated *Esprit*'s reflection on the PCF and its place in the Union of the Left. In a January 1975 article Domenach asserted that the PCF's recent return to invective in the style of the Cold War and its

effort to firmly establish its Leninist relationship to the working class indicated that it had hardly abandoned Stalinism. Domenach was spooked—
yet again—by the specter of a communist seizure of power in France along
the lines of the Prague coup of 1948. Although the weakening of the PCF's
electoral strength and legitimacy offered some hope for a positive evolution, the PCF's ideological offensive and the PS's muted response to it
raised a possibility that had previously been only a secondary theme of
Esprit's analysis: that the PCF was establishing its ideological hegemony
over the Left. In Domenach's analysis the PS had a choice: "either it will go
ahead with the ritual exorcisms that are asked of it—and it will thereby get
used to putting up with its destiny of subordination—or, in turn, it will
have to speak up and ask the essential questions."[48]

Michel Winock and Paul Thibaud also developed the theme of PCF ideological hegemony over the PS at this time. Both saw (not entirely incorrectly) the PCF's ideological offensive as an effort to preserve an
ideological hegemony over the Left that was threatened by the entry of the
autogestionnaire currents into the PS. For Winock, "the PS was nonetheless
right up to these last years a sort of empty vessel from the point of view of
ideas. It did not have a truly definite line, and in these conditions the PCF
could impose its line and assume the ideological leadership of the Union
of the Left. However, what worries the PCF is nonetheless that large-scale
entrance into the PS of people who define socialism in a radically different
manner."[49] Thibaud, who once found hope in the *rééquilibrage* of the Left,
was no longer much impressed by it. The key question was now ideological. He argued: "The PCF's intention is certainly not to take power on its
own, nor even within a majority, while the dynamics of the electoral
alliance are unfavorable to it. Its means of influence are different: militancy and ideological tenacity. And it is on that terrain that it now takes up
the acknowledged offensive to prevent the Socialist Party and the Union of
the Left from drifting in a manner doctrinally unacceptable to it."[50] In
short, intellectuals at *Esprit* imagined that the politics of the Union of the
Left had turned into a battle between themselves and the PCF for the soul
of the PS. They consequently embarked on the task of articulating their
vision of *autogestionnaire* socialism and clarifying their fundamental differences with the communists.[51]

Esprit was not alone in its political evolution in the year after the *Assises*.
Le Nouvel Observateur, for example—although it published a broader
spectrum of political opinion than *Esprit*—adopted a similar, if more flexible and realistic, political line represented notably by Jean Daniel's editorials. *Le Nouvel Observateur* supported the Common Program and the
Union of the Left, but with qualifications that dated back to their inception. Gilles Martinet's response to early critiques of the Common Program by Pierre Uri and Jean-François Revel in *L'Express*, for example,
although arguing against Uri and Revel that the Common Program
should be corrected rather than denounced, admitted that it "has many

weaknesses."[52] In Jacques Julliard's analysis there was a limited risk to democracy in France posed by the PCF's Leninism, but it could be held in check by "the critical, but active intervention of the dynamic forces of the country" in favor of "the decentralizing and *autogestionnaires* tendencies of the socialist Left."[53] *Le Nouvel Observateur* clearly wanted the parties of the Left to become more *autogestionnaire* and to take into account the demands of those who are "prosperous yet dissatisfied,"[54] but, at least initially, was careful to ensure that the debate within the weekly over the Union of the Left did not alienate any significant segment of its readership. For example, when Jean Daniel first mentioned the Common Program in the pages of *Le Nouvel Observateur*, he was careful to portray the weekly as the home of "all those men who [despite their differences] have the Left as a common homeland."[55] While supporting the Union of the Left from this critical standpoint, it organized the debate within the Left about it and gave expression to voices as diverse as François Mitterrand and Alain Geismar.[56]

Come the 1974 presidential election, Jean Daniel adopted toward Mitterrand's candidacy a position of "critical support." Daniel, who regretted that the unexpected electoral campaign interrupted the debate on Solzhenitsyn and anti-Sovietism, [57] implicitly demanded that Mitterrand take the concerns raised by this affair seriously. Mitterrand had to explain, Daniel wrote at the beginning of the campaign, "how, free of all affective links and all dependencies, the candidate of the Left intends to become the President of a republic with a socialist and antitotalitarian calling."[58] Daniel further complained that Mitterrand's economic program was "contrary to the obvious facts of modernity" and demanded more audacity, imagination, and combativeness in the Left's ideas on a host of issues including ecology, the Atlantic alliance, *moeurs*, immigration, and the status of women.[59] After Mitterrand had established his candidacy on the left-center of the political spectrum, Daniel praised him for going beyond the archaic Common Program to take into account modern realities, adopt a more realistic economic plan, and move closer to the *autogestionnaire* current that *Le Nouvel Observateur* supported. "Our 'critical support,' however great its vigilance, now," Daniel wrote, "has much to support and little to criticize."[60] Still, Daniel maintained a certain distance from Mitterrand right up to the eve of the second round of the election, when he echoed Jean-Marie Domenach's less than enthusiastic endorsement of Mitterrand, which held that his victory would open up a "space of freedom."[61]

Not surprisingly, Daniel applauded the Assises du socialisme, qualifying its *Projet de société* "a great text, an historic charter, a doctrinal turning point." He bragged that its principal authors were "our friends" Gilles Martinet and Jacques Julliard and that its ideas had almost all been developed in the pages of *Le Nouvel Observateur*. Beyond the program, Mitterrand and Rocard were a winning combination that gave the Left a good chance at gaining power.[62]

Come the communist polemic of the autumn of 1974, Jean Daniel was considerably more sympathetic toward the strategy of Mitterrand and the PS than most intellectuals at *Esprit* were, but on the other hand, he was also deeply marked by his own battle with the PCF over Solzhenitsyn and fearful of a potential PCF threat to liberty. After the 1974 presidentials, Daniel noted his preference for the PCF's rather submissive behavior during the campaign (behavior that he dubbed "of an exemplary discretion and efficacy") and admiringly congratulated the socialists on the success of their strategy of dealing with the PCF in terms of relations of force.[63] Come October, Daniel proved to be understanding of Mitterrand's tactical silence in the face of PCF invective,[64] but in early 1975 the dynamics of the polemic began to disturb him. He complained that in the face of PCF pressure, leading socialists were protesting their fidelity to the Common Program, socialist elected officials were repudiating their compromised past political alliances, and masochist intellectuals were anxiously questioning their innocence.[65] Daniel found the PS Congress of Pau troubling because the party had, he believed, "debated on the terrain and on the themes imposed solely by the Communist Party."[66] While not as clearly developed by Daniel as by *Esprit*, criticisms of the PS's opportunism and worries about PCF ideological domination were beginning to emerge in the pages of *Le Nouvel Observateur* as well in early 1975.

On the extreme Left, at *Libération* and in the ex-Gauche prolétarienne, direct hostility toward the Union of the Left was considerably more intense and sustained than elsewhere on the Left. Still, there are some broad similarities between the evolution of this current and that of the more moderate ones discussed above. Whereas *Esprit* and *Le Nouvel Observateur* offered critical support to Mitterrand's candidacy, *Libération* was never able to fully rally behind it (for many of the same reasons that *Esprit*'s and *Le Nouvel Observateur*'s support remained critical). And whereas *Esprit* and *Le Nouvel Observateur* were enthusiastic about the Assises and identified with it for a time, *Libération* rejected it almost immediately as insufficiently *autogestionnaire*—a conclusion at which *Esprit* would arrive only some time later. In short, although *Libération* was always more extreme in its judgments, its critiques of the Union of the Left were, like those of *Esprit* and *Le Nouvel Observateur*, rooted in an *autogestionnaire*, direct-democratic perspective.

Pierre Victor, Philippe Gavi, and Jean-Paul Sartre, in their reflections on politics at the end of the Gauche prolétarienne adventure, had nothing but contempt for the Union of the Left. It contributed nothing to their ongoing effort to rethink socialism and cultural revolution. Sartre could not see anything positive coming out of a Left victory. If anything, the Union of the Left endangered liberty, which Sartre now considered perhaps even more important than socialism. For them, as Victor put it, "the Union of the Left is first of all the Communist Party; the Communist Party is the cultural counter-revolution. As for … the Socialist Party, it functions as the principal machine harnessing the cultural revolution to its ends." Versus the Right and the Union of the Left, they hoped to put forward a third alternative, that of an anticapitalist and antibureaucratic cultural revolution.[67]

During the 1974 presidential campaign Sartre sustained this analysis in all its direct-democratic extremism. The Union of the Left was, in his words, "a joke," "a false unity of an old Left that we oppose." Against this old Left that wanted "socialism with hierarchy," Sartre supported the candidacy of Charles Piaget, the hero of Lip. Piaget's candidacy would, he argued, offer an occasion to develop and present the ideas of the new Left, portray the old Left as "an old demonic thing," and advance the revolutionary process. Sartre rejected the argument that Mitterrand should be supported in either the first or the second round of the election because a victory of the Left would open up space for the new social movements. Cooptation would result in this case, Sartre argued by analogy, just as those who entered "the Marshal's movement" during the occupation in order to turn it to the Left were "turned into Pétainists [*pétainisés*]."[68]

Like Sartre and much of the rest of the extreme Left, *Libération* initially rallied behind the candidacy of Piaget. Piaget's candidacy, *Libération* stressed, was not the work of extreme-Left groups, but "born simultaneously in the head of loads of people."[69] His was a "collective candidacy" of the direct-democratic movement, of the "Lips."[70] In other words, "he will be the spokesman for downtrodden France. He will not speak for us; with him we will all speak."[71] Although Lip's "dual concern for permanent democracy and for collective and united expression" was understood to be incompatible with electoral politics, Piaget's candidacy would, it was argued, give "body" to the movement and challenge the logic of the system.[72]

After this phantom candidature of Piaget-Lip collapsed on 15 April 1975 when the PSU—following Michel Rocard—backed Mitterrand instead of Piaget, the *Libération*-associated Left fell into disarray. Everyone writing in the pages of *Libération* agreed that real change could only come about through the development of the movement of *contestation* (protest) exemplified by Lip. They saw a danger of authoritarian socialism in the Union of the Left and the Common Program (which in any case did not reflect the workers' "desire to take their destiny in hand"[73]) and considered elections to be, at best, a "stopgap of democracy."[74] Yet, although some leading former Gauche prolétarienne figures such as Alain Geismar, Pierre Victor, and Serge July argued vehemently against voting for Mitterrand,[75] voices still emerged in his favor. Most seemed to agree with Philippe Gavi that they did not have a "credible alternative to the Union of the Left and to elections."[76] There was, it was argued, something to gain from his election: some concrete, if limited, gains for workers; possibly a new political dynamic; and, at the very least, the satisfaction of defeating the Right. Although it ultimately refused to endorse Mitterrand, *Libération* announced that the majority of the newspaper's team would vote for him in the second round.[77] Leading extreme-Left intellectuals signed a manifesto against abstention by revolutionaries,[78] and Daniel Cohn-Bendit hijacked the 1968 slogan against elections to dub abstention in 1974 a "trap for idiots [*piège à cons*]."[79] In Serge July's bitter and exaggerated post-election analysis, "the unorganized extreme Left had gone crazy, as if possessed by Mitterrand."[80]

The 1974 presidential election marked the end of *gauchisme*'s dynamism as electoral politics consumed its militants, later to be digested by the PS at the Assises. At first, *Libération* adopted a distant neutrality toward the Assises, refusing to choose between the social movements and the Assises, but also firmly warning that "there can be no question of separating the nature of the project of a socialist society from its mode of elaboration."[81] When *Libération* reappeared in mid November after the suspension of its regular publication at the end of June 1974, its analysis was, along the lines of its earlier warning, uniformly critical of the Assises. The Assises had failed "to reconcile worker protest" with the "parliamentary Left," and the promise of *autogestion* had not materialized. For these direct democrats the strife within the Union of the Left was epiphenomenal to the Left's "obsessions with political maneuvers" and its failure to promote popular initiative.[82] As Lip faded into the mythical past, *gauchisme* lost the initiative to the Union of the Left, and *Libération* began its transformation into a more professional newspaper, the *gauchistes* at *Libération* maintained their direct-democratic critique of the Union of the Left. As their own political possibilities shrank, they increasingly focused on warning their audience of the dangers of the Union of the Left and of any politics that accepted representation. André Glucksmann's *La Cuisinière et le mangeur d'hommes* and the antitotalitarian politics that it prefigured emerged out of this evolution of late *gauchisme*.

The Portuguese Revolution in French Politics and the Birth of Antitotalitarianism

In the spring of 1975 the PS-PCF polemic was quieting down[83] when the radicalization of the Portuguese Revolution gave new life to disputes within the Left. The Salazarian régime—weakened by economic difficulties, protracted colonial war, and mediocre political leadership after Salazar fell into a coma in 1968—was overthrown in a coup of 25 April 1974 by an Armed Forces Movement (MFA) comprised of radical junior officers critical of the existing Portuguese socioeconomic order and opposed to Portugal's colonial war. The fall of the authoritarian old régime unleashed repressed political expression, pent-up social discontent, and underground cultural life and inaugurated an intense struggle to determine the future of Portugal. Following an initial phase that ended with the resignation of President General António Spínola on 30 September 1974 subsequent to the defeat of his efforts to slow the pace of decolonization and modernize the economy with the help of old régime oligarchies, Portuguese politics moved decisively to the Left. Soon, though, the alliance of the summer of 1974 between the Portuguese Socialist Party (PSP) and the Portuguese Communist Party (PCP) fell apart, and the MFA split along similar lines with the dominant faction drawing close to the PCP. These latent conflicts within the Left became explicit in the debate over a law of January 1975 that made Intersindical, the PCP-dominated labor union, the sole legal labor union. They reached a new intensity after a failed right-wing coup of 11 March 1975.

After 11 March the revolution entered its most radical phase. Social unrest spread: a wave of workers' takeovers of factories and peasant land seizures followed the coup. Economic policy turned to the Left: the pace of nationalizations intensified, and a radical land redistribution plan was adopted. The MFA deepened its alliance with the PCP, notably by allowing it a greater voice in the government. In addition, the Left strengthened its hold over the MFA as moderates were purged from it. This more radical MFA was institutionalized as the center of state authority. It forced the delay of scheduled elections until 25 April and the diminution of their significance. The elections were limited to the designation of a Constituent Assembly that would draw up and ratify the new constitution; they were not to affect the composition of the Provisional Government. These provisions notwithstanding, the elections conferred democratic legitimacy on the parties of the moderate Left and Center (the PSP, which finished first in the voting with 37.9 percent of the vote, and the Popular Democratic Party, which finished second with 26.4 percent) while revealing the limited support of the PCP (which won 12.5 percent of the vote with an additional 4.2 percent going to its close ally, the Portuguese Democratic Movement). Thus, the elections gave the moderate political forces (above all, the PSP) a foundation for rallying resistance to an increasingly contentious radicalization of the revolution. Because the ruling faction of the MFA and especially the PCP showed considerable contempt for parliamentary democracy and freedom of speech, the PSP was able to successfully frame the political struggle around those issues, arguing that the PCP was actively trying to establish a Leninist dictatorship in Portugal. Although this conclusion is contestable, a number of political controversies, the most important of which was the *República* affair, lent credence to the PSP's case.[84]

República was a Lisbon daily newspaper that gave expression to socialist opinion and had been an important forum for opposition to the Salazarian régime. During the course of the revolution, its socialist editorial staff clashed with the *gauchiste* newspaper workers, culminating in the *gauchistes'* 19 May 1975 occupation of the newspaper, upon which they named a new director and began to publish the paper on their own. When the socialists protested the action, the Council of the Revolution—the supreme state authority and institutional embodiment of the power of the MFA after the

11 March coup—closed down the paper. Although the PCP was probably not at the root of the *República* affair, its refusal to condemn the workers' actions, its formal monopoly of the labor movement, and its disproportionate influence in the Portuguese mass media suggested that the action was part of a communist effort to muzzle the opposition before seizing power. Beyond the *República* affair, the PCP's maximalist rhetoric, sustained mobilization, infiltration of institutions, and disregard for the results of the April elections fed fears of a PCP takeover in the summer of 1975.

A month of political crisis began in the second week of July, when the PSP left the government (followed a week later by the Popular Democratic Party) in protest of the Council of the Revolution's decision to have *República* reappear with a new military director and the MFA's plan to institute a form of direct democracy that would bypass the political parties. In opposition, the PSP vociferously demanded freedom for the press, elections in localities and in the central trade union, and the formation of a government that reflected the results of the 25 April election. It presented the political choice as one between a free society and communist dictatorship. In the following weeks the PCP continually lost ground. The PSP was able to prove further its legitimacy by organizing massive demonstrations in its support in the big cities. Beginning in late July the PCP came under physical attack from Catholic peasants of central and northern Portugal, who turned against it and radical revolution out of fear of losing their land and discontent with fixed prices for agricultural goods. At least forty-nine local PCP offices were burned and sacked, virtually driving the communists out of these areas. These events of the summer of 1975 led to the organization of opposition within the MFA to the communist-influenced Prime Minister General Vasco Gonçalves and his politics, culminating in President General Costa Gomes's dismissal of Gonçalves as prime minister. Subsequently, the PSP was brought back into the provisional government in alliance with moderates who had taken control of the MFA. The Portuguese extreme Left was finally decisively defeated with the failure of the 25 November coup attempt by radicals within the army.[85]

Although the end of the Salazarian régime and the entry of communists into the government (for the first time in Western Europe since 1947) were of considerable interest to the French and sparked American Secretary of State Henry Kissinger's fear of Mediterranean dominos, the Portuguese Revolution did not become a major preoccupation of the French Left until its radicalization in the spring of 1975. Even then, as in the Solzhenitsyn affair of early 1974, it became involved because of the PCF's reflexive support of the PCP's politics. Also similar to the earlier Solzhenitsyn affair is the striking contrast, notable to contemporaries, between the positions taken by the PCF and those of the Italian Communist Party (PCI). Whereas the PCF supported the PCP's most controversial stances (its effort to gain a monopoly on labor representation, its alliance with the MFA, its minimization of the importance of the elections to the Constituent Assembly, its position on the *República* affair, and its blaming of the northern Portuguese peasants' anticommunist riots of July and August on the fascists), the PCI distanced itself from the PCP on all of these points. In keeping with its strategy of historic compromise it urged the PCP to consolidate liberal democratic institutions. At each turning point in the Portuguese Revolution it recommended moderation, if only to parry the effort by the right wing of the Italian Christian Democratic Party to use the occasion to scuttle the PCI's overtures to its party with the argument that all communists are "totalitarians, twin brothers of fascists and stupid militarists."[86] The PCI's strategy and calculations were not those of the PCF, which was still in its phase of ideological retrenchment when the Portuguese Revolution radicalized in the spring of 1975. By uncritically supporting the PCP, the PCF opened itself up to the same sort of antitotalitarian arguments that the PCI was working so hard to neutralize. The PCF's positions on the Portuguese Revolution appeared even more troubling because they coincided with the party's effort to convince the public that freedom would not be endangered if it came to power. The presentation of the PCF's *Déclaration des libertés* on 15 May 1975 was followed only a few days later by the beginning of the *República* affair. Like Marchais's earlier statement that Solzhenitsyn could be published in a France with communists in the government "if he found a publisher," this PCF profession of good intentions seemed insincere in the context of the party's position on developments in Portugal in the spring of 1975.

The French controversy over the Portuguese Revolution began at the end of May 1975 with the *República* affair. The PCF tried to deny the PCP's responsibility in the incident and minimize its importance. It put the emphasis on the PSP's effort to exploit the affair and claimed that the turmoil at the newspaper had nothing to do with freedom of the press. It was, said Confédération générale du travail (CGT) General Secretary Georges Séguy upon returning to France from Portugal on 27 May, only a "classic workplace conflict."[87] The PS, which had just been courted by the PSP leader Mario Soares at a meeting of southern European socialist parties held at Mitterrand's house in the Landes, vigorously contested the PCF's interpretation and gave its full support to the PSP. Mitterrand proclaimed defiantly that the affair was about liberty; and Claude Estier, the editor of the PS weekly *L'Unité*, recalling the PCF's recent statement on liberties, admonished it for holding that there can be "one truth in Paris and another in Lisbon."[88] This vigorous PS response elicited from the PCF its well-worn accusation that the socialists were participating in the current anticommunist campaign. This quarrel within the French Left over the Portuguese Revolution continued well into the summer of 1975 as the French socialists and communists lent moral support to their Portuguese homologues at every turn. Efforts by the PCF to rally PS support against attacks on the PCP in July and August resulted in little more than an anodyne "Communiqué Commun" calling for an antifascist alliance in Portugal and failed to alter the PS's judgment that the PCP was largely to blame for the hostility directed toward it.[89]

The dispute over the Portuguese Revolution acquired new dimensions with the entry of *Le Monde* and *Le Nouvel Observateur* into the fray. *Le Monde* created quite a stir with its "Bulletin de l'étranger" (effectively an editorial) of 21 June 1975 on the *República* affair, which, while not adopting the communist position, defended a relativist position on freedom of the press in Portugal by arguing that the weight of Portugal's recent past made its immediate application problematic. Furthermore, *Le Monde* seemed to adopt a Marxist critique of formal liberties by suggesting that the true question is "to know if, in allowing everyone to exercise freedom of expression, one does not in fact allow some to abuse it."[90] *Le Monde*'s editorial prompted an immediate response from Edgar Morin in *Le Nouvel Observateur* (and also from Raymond Aron in *Le Figaro*).[91] Morin was troubled by the opposition that he saw *Le Monde* establishing between "the revolutionary process and freedom of the press." *Le Monde*'s treatment of the question was, he argued, "exemplary of a structure of thought and of a logic of reasoning that have manifested themselves in a thousand ways since the *República* affair." Further, the French were, he believed, very receptive to this dichotomy between revolution and liberty because it was "in resonance with the idea, ingrained on the school benches, that the republic of 1789 in danger saved itself by answering its enemies with the Terror." The French had to rethink this issue and "revolutionize the idea of revolution." Otherwise, Morin concluded, "not only are we not ready to exit one of the greatest tragedies in history, but we are ready to resume it" because restrictions on the freedom of the press undertaken in the name of revolutionary self-defense were the first step toward a Leninist-styled dictatorship.

Le Monde's treatment of the *República* affair gave, as Morin's piece implied, further evidence of the growing ideological hegemony of the PCF over the French Left. That *Le Monde*, the most professional and objective of French dailies, could play fast and loose with the freedom of the press was certainly troubling. *Le Monde*'s "Révolution et liberté" editorial damaged the newspaper's reputation over the short term.[92] The publication in early 1976 of *Le Monde tel qu'il est*, an attack on *Le Monde* by the disgruntled former *Le Monde* journalist Michel Legris, sparked further discussion of biases in the newspaper's reporting on China, Cambodia, Portugal, and the Union of the Left.[93]

At *Le Nouvel Observateur* Jean Daniel questioned Séguy's interpretation of the *República* affair well before *Le Monde*'s infamous 21 June "Bulletin de l'étranger." His 16 June editorial challenged Séguy on almost all points and concluded that the real reason for the conflict at *República* was that the newspaper "did not humor the communists," unlike the rest of the press, "which the communists practically control."[94] Furthermore, Daniel took the opportunity to challenge the legitimacy of Séguy holding a leadership position in the PCF while heading the CGT. The CGT's response was characteristically hostile, accusing Daniel of making calumnious statements.[95] Daniel's rejoinders conceded nothing. In subsequent articles that kept the debate alive into late July, he protested the CGT's questioning of his intellectual and journalistic honesty and its refusal to openly debate the issue. He also demanded that Séguy admit that his interpretation of the *República* affair was erroneous and that the French communists revise their position on liberty in Portugal.[96]

Daniel's skirmish of June and July with Séguy, the CGT, and the PCF over the *República* affair was followed in August by a more serious clash with the PCF over the course of the Portuguese Revolution in that crucial month. In his editorial of 11 August 1975 Daniel rallied behind Antunes and Soares against the PCP in reaction to the conflict within the MFA occasioned by the Antunes-led moderate opposition to Gonçalves and the crisis of the revolution to which it corresponded.[97] He agreed with their analysis that the PCP was a danger, not only if it came to power but also because its extremism was paving the way for a fascist reaction. That Daniel's editorial immediately preceded violent attacks on the PCP was quickly seized upon by the PCF. *L'Humanité* of 12 August reported the PCF *Bureau politique*'s conclusion that *Le Nouvel Observateur* had delivered an "odious justification in advance of a possible massacre of communists" and published an article by Yves Moreau claiming that what Daniel had written "amounted to justifying the pogroms."[98]

The communists' accusations quickly achieved the dimensions of an affair. Daniel, who claimed that he had never before been "the object of such a revolting libel," demanded his right of reply in the pages of *L'Humanité*, and when this was denied him, he took his case to *Le Monde*, where he announced his intention to sue *L'Humanité* for defamation.[99] A declaration of solidarity with Daniel and *Le Nouvel Observateur* in this dispute appeared in *Le Nouvel Observateur* of the following week and was eventually signed by some ninety-six figures of political, intellectual, and professional note.[100] The PCF organized its own campaign in support of Yves Moreau,[101] and Georges Marchais entered the fray on 18 August on France-Inter. He repeated the accusations against Daniel—despite Daniel's clear condemnation of anticommunist violence in Portugal in *Le Nouvel Observateur* of the same day—whom he designated "a specialist of anticommunism," and offered a specious justification of *L'Humanité*'s refusal of Daniel's right of reply. He also wildly tried to turn the tables on Daniel and the socialists with regard to the question of liberties by evoking seizures of *L'Humanité* by socialist governments during the Algerian War and expressing his concern that this would happen again were the noncommunist Left to return to power. All this was, Daniel responded on France-Inter the next day, "grotesque," "vile," and "sad."[102] Although this second conflict of the summer of 1975 between Daniel and the PCF came to an end in early September 1975 with both sides declaring victory,[103] it, in conjunction with the other disputes over the Portuguese Revolution and the long PS-PCF wrangle of 1974 and 1975, altered perceptions of the Union of the Left.

For Daniel, the questions raised by the clashes over the Portuguese Revolution were important because they were not "theoretical," but rather "prefigure our future."[104] The *República* affair, he wrote, had become a French affair "because it provokes several essential debates."[105] More generally, he believed that "if the Left does not come to an agreement on Portugal it negates itself. It does not suffice to say that Portugal is not France. One must enumerate and confront all of the revolutionary problems that are posed in a society in transition toward socialism."[106] This, Daniel concluded, the communists had refused to do.

One of the central questions raised in the summer of 1975 was that of the freedom of the press. Like Estier and Mitterrand, Daniel demanded that Marchais understand that "this liberty that he promises to defend in France and in the future, he must defend it today in Portugal." The PCF's failure on liberties in this case was, Daniel emphasized, not exceptional, but rather fell into a pattern. Recalling Marchais's statement that *The Gulag Archipelago* could be published under a government with PCF participation "if this book found a publisher," Daniel ironically commented that "Georges Marchais and Max-Pol Fouchet can put their minds at ease. Solzhenitsyn found a publisher in Lisbon. Simply, he did not find a printer."[107] The pattern was confirmed by the second Portuguese affair over Daniel's 11 August editorial, in which, Jean-Denis Bredin's analysis in *Le Nouvel Observateur* concluded, there was a troublesome distance between "words and things," that is, between the rights that the PCF claimed to support (in this case the right of reply) and its behavior.[108] As a result of these positions taken by the PCF (as well as *Le Monde*'s "Bulletin de l'étranger"), Daniel became, according to his memoirs, increasingly obsessed by the question of liberty as the 1978 elections approached.[109]

The Portuguese affairs brought the Union of the Left into question by raising the specter of communist ideological domination of the Left. "The blackmail of anticommunism," Daniel wrote in response to the PCF's use of it in the *República* affair, "must cease becoming this dominant ideology that makes non-communists feel guilty and prevents them from asserting themselves. What do electoral victories matter if on the ideological and constructive level these non-communist forces become only secondary or obstructionist forces."[110] Positively, Daniel proposed, again with a certain irony, new slogans for the Common Program: "the struggle against the Stalinist mind is the concern of all democrats. Anti-socialism, whether it be simple-minded or not, on the Right or on the Left, is a manifestation of the reactionary mind."[111] Communist intimidation of *Le Nouvel Observateur* in August was, stressed Daniel, a concern not only of *Le Nouvel Observateur*, but for "the very practice of democracy within the concrete struggle for socialism." Both the PCF's positions on the Portuguese Revolution and its behavior toward the noncommunist Left in France raised serious questions about the feasibility (and even the desirability) of the Union of the Left at the end of the summer of 1975 in the minds of Daniel and other intellectuals.[112]

Gilles Martinet, for example, believed that the Portuguese Revolution had raised important questions about what the Left would do when it arrived in power. More generally, he added, "the French Left cannot be content with patching up a union that was so gravely compromised by the polemics of the last months and even more by those of these last weeks.... To recover its credibility the Left must have the courage to openly confront the problems that it has deliberately ignored until now. Portugal is not that far from France."[113] The concerns of Martinet and others within the PS led to the creation of the journal *Faire*, the first issue of which appeared in October 1975. Bringing together Mitterrandist and Rocardian politicians and intellectuals, but not subject to party discipline, *Faire* promised to be the vehicle for the PS's assertion of its own independent, *autogestionnaire* identity. It explicitly rejected "the negotiation of artificial compromises" and dedicated itself to opening up a "true debate" on issues like the Portuguese Revolution and especially on what the French Left would do in power. It was in *Faire* that the critique of totalitarianism would be articulated within the PS.[114]

Intellectuals associated with *Esprit* were particularly concerned about the events of the summer of 1975. Jean-Marie Domenach, writing in *Le Nouvel Observateur*, considered the August affair to be "very serious," an affair in which "truth and politics are linked in an extremely concrete manner and which involves all of us." The battle against "falsification" and "libel" on the part of the PCF was one against fascism and also totalitarianism—which "always begins by taking control of language."[115] Jacques Julliard also demanded that the PCF learn to debate politics without resorting to excommunications for reason of a hidden hostility to the Left or anticommunism. The communists' actions, especially if successful, would undermine the credibility of the Union of the Left. Julliard explained, "if by fear of opening itself up to the accusation of anticommunism the Socialist Party were in the long run to give the impression that it will end up resigning itself to the political and intellectual hegemony of the PCF, then not only the centrist temptation so feared by the communists might well revive in its heart, but moreover the Union of the Left would risk remaining indefinitely in the minority in the nation." It was, Julliard emphasized, necessary to the health of the Union of the Left and certainly not anticommunist "to put at the center of our concerns this immense historic divorce of socialism and liberty that insults the hope of millions of workers in this country." One had to "ask why the gulag happened and how to prevent others from emerging" without, of course, attributing to the French communists "responsibility for the gulag."[116]

The connection between the events of the summer of 1975 and *Esprit*'s development of a critique of totalitarianism, already evident in Julliard's and Domenach's *Le Nouvel Observateur* articles, can be clearly seen in the writings of Paul Thibaud, who soon became the directing force behind *Esprit*'s antitotalitarianism. Already in *Esprit* of May 1975, Thibaud expressed his concern over the PCF's support for the MFA, which, he argued, brought into question the French communists' acceptance of parliamentary democracy and, as a consequence, the feasibility of the Union of the Left.[117] In its analysis of the subsequent events in Portugal *Esprit*, like Jean Daniel's *Le Nouvel Observateur*, feared a Leninist takeover by the PCP, supported the PSP, and blamed the counterrevolutionary threat on the PCP's excesses.[118] Paul Thibaud argued in his final analysis of the crisis of the Portuguese Revolution that the PCP was ultimately unable to establish a popular democracy primarily because of popular resistance or, to be more precise, because "a certain libertarian practice that resists authoritarian integration is since 1968 part of the repertoire of the peoples of Europe." The PSP, because it defended parliamentarianism (labeled "the keystone of the other liberties"), was able to give this popular movement a much needed outlet. A "libertarian critique of social democracy" was, Thibaud concluded, the most fruitful political formula.[119]

That *Esprit*'s critique of totalitarianism was primarily a response to debates within the French Left and not external events or revelations is most clearly evident in Thibaud's exchange with Pierre Guidoni (a CERES representative on the *Bureau exécutif* of the PS) in a *Quotidien de Paris* debate on Marxism that focused on Glucksmann's *La Cuisinière et le mangeur d'hommes*.[120] Guidoni delivered a sharp critique of Glucksmann's book that showed considerable understanding of both its relationship to *gauchisme* and its rhetorical techniques. Solzhenitsyn, Guidoni argued, was no revelation, and it was inadmissible for those who claimed that he was to ask others to "throw out the baby with the bathwater, Marxism with the Terror, on the pretext that for such a long time you did not know how to distinguish between them, and that you justified one with the other." Secondly, it was an imposture for former Maoists like Glucksmann to "present as a discourse addressed to everyone—and above all to others—that which is only a self-criticism," especially when there is little relationship between the "populist delirium of the Maoists" and Marxism. In Guidoni's analysis, Glucksmann, faced with the failure of post-1968 *gauchisme*, had to choose: "Either it was all false from the beginning, *gauchisme* an impasse, and reality elsewhere, in the PS and the PCF, in the battles around the Common Program, in the historically constituted working-class movement with its reading of Marxism—the only one that is operational, here and now. Or it was all true, and above all the fundamental treason of the Left. In that case, one must go further, 'go full circle,' and show that none of the battles make any sense once one has lost one's own." Glucksmann, like many *gauchiste* intellectuals but unlike most *gauchiste* militants, preferred the later option, remaining true to the impossible revolution promised by May '68.

For Thibaud, Guidoni had simply evaded addressing the heavy past of socialism. The real question was to "know … if the same causes produce the same effects, if the use of a certain corpus of concepts does not lead inescapably to totalitarianism." Guidoni, Thibaud argued, was blind to this question because of his adherence to Marxism, "the most formidable mystifying machine," and, more fundamentally, because of his "adoration of revolutionary power." Guidoni had accepted the "essential Stalinist argument" that "the organized historical agent is right on principle, that power is the criterion of truth."

Refusing the alternatives offered by Guidoni, Thibaud held that the choice was between "power" and "the people," "precarious and uncertain liberty" and "the state as the holder and organizer of good." According to Thibaud's circular reasoning—which indicates the extent to which the critique of totalitarianism emerged out of a struggle within the French Left—Guidoni's lack of receptiveness to Glucksmann's argument was "proof [!] that the essential thesis of Glucksmann's book is correct: power and the people are two incompatible realities." For Thibaud, Glucksmann's book had inaugurated the "critique of the entire twentieth century that we need" by uncovering the root of totalitarianism in the "belief in the goodness of the state" that is identified with the people. Henceforth, "one must explain the perversion of the project, demonstrate the mechanisms of blindness." Unlike François Mitterrand, who, Thibaud argued, repressed "'mental reservations' that injure the Union of the Left" only to find them returning in the form of Freudian slips, they had to "reflect on that which in truth haunts us."

This *Esprit* promised to do beginning with its September 1975 issue, the introduction to which clearly established the connection between *Esprit*'s inauguration of a critique of totalitarianism and the debates within the Left:

> The political debate internal to the Left does not cease to flare up despite, or because of the precautions that are taken to avoid having the radical stakes of it appear directly. This persistent malaise goes far beyond the events that gave rise to it. The ground upon which the Left has traditionally established itself appears to be undermined. The time has come—one senses it from many directions—to check and reconstruct the foundations. It is this foundational work that we intend to undertake here in a systematic manner.[121]

Thibaud's lead article "Contre la prise de pouvoir … et pour l'autogestion," laid radical foundations for this reflection. Echoing his reply to Guidoni, Thibaud held that "a social struggle conducted in accordance with the principles that were (and that still are) those of socialism produces a totalitarian state precisely because the state was imaginarily invested with an unreal competence in the struggle and because it was loved and desired as the place where the good of society would become visible and realizable." It was, Thibaud argued on the authority of Cornelius Castoriadis and André Glucksmann, Marxism that made this possible by giving the illusion of a "total knowledge that allows one to govern humanity." More generally though, Thibaud added, "the absolute legitimization of absolute power is provided, beyond Marxist doctrine, by the revolutionary passion of identifying power and the people and by the dream of a final solution to the political problem."

Thibaud's alternative to totalitarianism was, not surprisingly, *autogestion*. This time *autogestion* took on a new and more radical form. It was "a revolt that paralyzes and questions the rulers more than it seeks to replace them," something that "brings into question the very legitimacy of the authorities, their pretension to represent a central rationality," whether it be Stalinist or the "totalitarian" logic of capitalism. *Autogestion* became here "a castration of the desire for power, ... the condition of the struggle for real autonomy." In a world being crushed under the weight of totalitarianism, the best hope for the development of *autogestion* was the *groupes d'information*[122] that could "inform people on their fate and undo the coupling of irrational domination and technological rationalism."[123]

With its "colloque politique" of 29 and 30 November 1975,[124] *Esprit* consciously began its transformation into a locus of the critique of totalitarianism. Thibaud's "Exposé des motifs" for the colloquium even more bluntly established the connection between the emerging critique of totalitarianism and concerns regarding the Union of the Left. The first draft held, citing the examples of the Solzhenitsyn and Portuguese affairs,[125] that the bipolarization of French politics prevented dissident voices within the Left from getting a fair hearing. Thibaud argued that although the exile of Solzhenitsyn was deplored in France, his book was not read and his "radical investigation of Stalinism" was countered by the invocation of "a few superficially interpreted opinions of its author." Likewise, "the spontaneous collusion in the name of revolution of the Portuguese Leninists and Bonapartists can not be tackled directly." In these and other cases, censorship is undertaken in the name of the "necessities of the alliance," behind which is hiding "an ideological vulgate of which the PCF is the manager and the interested guarantor and through which the Left gives itself the image that it desires of the world and of itself." Thibaud continues: "If the Union of the Left leads to collective censorship, it is that a certain political practice generates a certain type of blindness, in particular (but not only) blindness before totalitarianism.... How and why does the anti-capitalist struggle produce and reproduce (given the current norms of thought and action) the conditions for totalitarianism? That is the question that the established Left avoids." For Thibaud, "one can not do anything as long as the critique of the concepts that perpetuate blindness has not been imposed, as long as one will not have made the effort to understand that which biases the common language of the Left." If the Left chooses not to undertake this critique of itself, "as short term political advantages and habits encourage it to do," it will be condemned to repeat the errors of the past. Thibaud concludes, "one must attempt a critique of the presuppositions of the Left that liberates a new opposition to capitalism." [126]

Thibaud's final "Exposé des motifs" proposed that the colloquium address notably the emergence of "the question of totalitarianism as the inevitable product of the revolutions of the twentieth century." Can one, Thibaud asked, have a revolution that does not lead to a "reinforcement of power?" If so, how does one "exit from the Jacobin model," that is, "from the increasingly tight vicious circle that links revolution to the reinforcement of power and to the 'civilizing' action of the modern state against all autonomies?" Following Glucksmann, can the idea of resistance replace that of revolution? And if one renounces the idea of ending oppression, how does one avoid falling into "classical liberal skepticism or pseudo-Christian resignation"? Perhaps, Thibaud suggested, *autogestion* could be the antidote to totalitarianism. If so, they needed to define its relationship to power and the state. Additionally, Thibaud suggested that they try to go beyond thinking of liberty in terms of real and formal liberties and consider whether the idea of class struggle was still fruitful given the integration of the working class and the dangers of the dream of bringing an end to class society. Thibaud had clearly located some of *Esprit*'s themes for the coming years, but it appears that Glucksmann's book and the status of Marxism dominated the colloquium's proceedings, with some calling for a liquidation of Marxism and others, evidently following the position staked out by Domenach in a September 1975 article, wishing to retain certain elements of it.[127]

The first antitotalitarian gathering of intellectuals, the November 1975 colloquium was only the beginning of *Esprit*'s work in forging the critique of totalitarianism.[128] *Esprit* organized further meetings of intellectuals around the theme of totalitarianism that resulted in texts published in two 1976 issues of *Esprit*.[129] *Esprit* soon began publishing articles on and by the hitherto "marginal" antitotalitarian intellectuals Cornelius Castoriadis, Claude Lefort, and Marcel Gauchet (a student of Lefort), giving their ideas more exposure than ever before.[130] Although *Esprit* was hardly alone in the thrust of its critique of the Left, the critique of totalitarianism as a collective phenomenon of French intellectual life was largely a result of *Esprit*'s organizational efforts.

Within *Esprit* Paul Thibaud was the force behind the development and organization of the critique of totalitarianism. He wrote the "Exposé des motifs" for the November colloquium, and he put together *Esprit*'s 1976 issues on totalitarianism. Jean-Marie Domenach, although *Esprit*'s director in 1975 and 1976, allowed Thibaud free rein to develop *Esprit*'s critique of totalitarianism. Apparently limiting his own role to that of offering constructive criticism,[131] Domenach was preparing Thibaud to succeed him as the journal's director.[132]

When Domenach resigned from the directorship of *Esprit* at the end of 1976, he gave as his reasons fatigue and especially his belief that the older generation should make way for the new, journals being "a generational affair." Domenach supported his successors' elaboration of the critique of totalitarianism and for that very reason believed that he and his peers should not weigh them down with their "too heavy experience." He explained: "No doubt the men of my generation are poorly placed for that [understanding the twentieth century], waylaid as they are by resentment and by self-justification. It is therefore for our young comrades to take up the struggle from the place we reached with difficulty and from which we can perceive the unity of totalitarianisms. We would not have been of our time if we had not conceded something to that frenzy that shook Europe between 1930 and 1950.... The new generation at *Esprit* is immunized against totalitarianism."[133] Indeed, Domenach's ideas on totalitarianism and the remedy for it in the late 1970s did not match those of Thibaud. Unlike most of the analyses published in *Esprit* under Thibaud's directorship, Domenach maintained that *déracinement* (uprooting), not ideology, was the fundamental cause of totalitarianism and was rather skeptical of *autogestion* as an alternative politics.[134] Domenach maintained that Charles Péguy was "the antidote to totalitarianism" and held onto the truth that he had drawn from the Resistance, namely that "liberty depends less on legal constraints that define it than on the courage of those who live it."[135]

When Paul Thibaud took over the direction of *Esprit* with its issue of January 1977, he devoted the journal to the critique of totalitarianism; for years every issue of *Esprit* under Thibaud's direction began with a title page manifesto against totalitarianism. By the end of 1976 Thibaud had moved somewhat away from his radical refusal of power developed in the summer of 1975,[136] and, evidently influenced by the writings of Claude Lefort, called for *Esprit* to develop a political philosophy of democracy that would focus, in particular, on the question of democracy's institutional bases, understood here in relationship to totalitarianism as a "recognition of social division" that "prevents the system from closing in on itself."[137] In giving *Esprit* the task of developing a new political culture, Thibaud consciously distanced the journal from personalism insofar as it had failed to reflect on the properly political and institutional because it tended to "define itself according to a vision of man and a representation of ultimate ends." *Esprit*'s intervention on the level of civilization had, Thibaud believed, served as an alibi for its failure to develop a credible political project. And its "transposition of the form of religious belief ... to the socio-political order" had, especially given the poverty of *Esprit*'s reflection on the political, resulted in complaisance toward revolutionary régimes.[138] Thibaud hoped that *Esprit* would develop a realistic democratic political alternative, but as we shall see in chapter 5, *Esprit*'s politics in the following years became increasingly negative, dominated by the defensive struggle against the totalitarian menace.

Jean-François Revel's *The Totalitarian Temptation*

Although the critique of totalitarianism was primarily a phenomenon of the noncommunist intellectual Left, denunciations of communism and the politics of the Union of the Left as totalitarian were not limited to these circles. Rhetoric of this sort had been the daily bread of the Right since the beginning of the Cold War. Coming from the extreme-right press or the right-wing *Le Figaro*, these critiques were almost entirely ignored by the intellectual Left, but from the pen of Jean-François Revel, a center-left editorialist at the influential news magazine *L'Express*, they were a more serious matter.[139] In his *La Tentation totalitaire*, published in January 1976, Revel denounced the dangers of totalitarianism lurking in the Union of the Left using many of the same arguments developed in the pages of *Le Nouvel Observateur* and *Esprit*. But, by casting his net wider and concluding that the Union of the Left had to be abandoned, Revel pushed his argument further than other budding antitotalitarians were willing to go in 1976. His position and the reactions to it reveal much about the contours of antitotalitarian politics.

A *normalien* of the *promotion* of 1943 and an *agrégé* in philosophy (1953), Revel had been a professor in *lycées* in Algeria, Mexico, Italy, and metropolitan France from 1947 until 1963, when he resigned his teaching position to concentrate on his work as a writer, journalist, and editor. After the success of his *Pourquoi les philosophes?* (1957) catapulted him into journalism, he worked as the director of the cultural pages of *France observateur* from 1959 to 1963 and then at *Figaro littéraire* before becoming a permanent member of the editorial staff at *L'Express* in 1966. At *L'Express* he was first a cultural editorialist and then became the political editorialist in 1971 when Jean-Jacques Servan-Schreiber gave up the position so as to concentrate on his political career. Although he has defined himself as an intellectual and writer who also does journalism—and not as a journalist who also writes books—it would be more accurate to see Revel as an intellectual working within the tradition of the French polemical essayist.[140]

After the war and through the 1960s Revel was firmly on the Left. According to his memoirs, he was anticolonial from the late 1940s, against the European Defense Community, and convinced in the 1950s that Marxism could "offer responses in all domains of reality," but he was never a fellow traveler and was never tempted to become one. Between 1960 and 1970 Revel had "cordial, if not amicable relations" with Mitterrand. Considered to be part of Mitterrand's inner circle, he was part of his "brain trust" in 1965, a member of his "shadow cabinet" in 1966, and a candidate from the Fédération de la gauche démocrate et socialiste—Mitterrand's political formation—in the 1967 legislative elections. Although Revel claims in retrospect that Mitterrand was the active agent in their relationship and that his participation in Mitterrand's schemes was purely formal, he was, he admits, clearly attracted to Mitterrand's virtuoso performance in opposition to de Gaulle.[141]

Revel did not disapprove of purely electoral agreements with the PCF, but he refused to believe that a Common Program was necessary for the Left to come to power, and he maintained that the only alternative to Gaullism was a center-left coalition—despite the collusion of the Gaullists and communists against it.[142] By the early 1970s Revel clearly preferred European social democracy and the politics of the American Left to the direction then taken by the French Left.[143] He considered the Common Program to be a complete capitulation of republican socialism to bureaucratic centralism and of the PS to the PCF, especially because he believed that nationalizations were both economically senseless and politically dangerous. After his criticisms of the Common Program were met with hostility by the socialists and they denounced him as being on the Right, Revel concluded that the Left had adopted the Gaullist majority's pretension to infallibility. He very quickly became an implacable enemy of the Union of the Left and indignantly insisted that he remained true to the values of the Left whereas the PS's close alliance with the communists betrayed them.[144]

La Tentation totalitaire, broadly about the world advance of Stalinism, offered Revel's critique of the Union of the Left as it reached maturity. At the core of Revel's book was the argument that there are only two possible alternatives to capitalism: social democracy and communism, the essence of which is Stalinism: "The real struggle is between these two systems. Those dissatisfied with capitalism as it is who fail to choose one system are in effect choosing the other. And those who claim not to chose either while saving their harshest attacks for social democracy's 'class collaboration' are in fact choosing Stalinism. All the more so because Stalinism uses such brutally efficient methods to gain power that neutrality in the face of them amounts to abdication."[145] Thus it was established that the French socialists, who claimed to be on the road to a French socialism that was neither Stalinist nor social democratic, were, to use that "Stalinist" epithet, "objectively" Stalinist.

Socialists, Revel argued, indirectly justified totalitarianism by their excessive critiques of capitalism and liberalism and their failure to analyze the reasons for their own failures. They had become submissive to Stalinism because they persisted in believing that communist régimes had taken a first step toward socialism. Consequently, they were susceptible to the communist argument that any criticism of the politics of the communists is anticommunism and therefore inadmissible. This docility toward Stalinism undermined resistance to its advance and made its triumph inevitable at the moment of crisis when the choice must be made between democracy and totalitarianism.

Revel selectively chose his evidence and wildly misinterpreted its significance to make the case that France was subject to the political dynamic that he described. Thus, for example, in his discussion of the Portuguese affair, on which he dwelt at some length, Revel claimed that Mitterrand's August 1975 attribution of responsibility to the PCP for the disintegration of the situation in Portugal was the socialists' first criticism of the communist position and therefore "too late in the day"—an analysis that ignores the dispute over the *República* affair.[146] And Revel contended that Mitterrand's expression of indignation upon the July 1975 release of Marchais's "Rapport au Comité central" of 29 June 1972—which laid out the communist strategy to dominate the Union of the Left—revealed that he had believed that the communists had been transformed into loyal partners, something other than Stalinists. But did Revel, who knew Mitterrand the political opportunist and realist so well, really believe that he could be so naïve? Mitterrand had, after all, always understood his relations with the communists as relations of force and had, in an interview with Revel himself, stated clearly that "my problem is not to know if they [the communists] are sincere; my problem is to have everything happen as if they were."[147] Is it not more reasonable to assume that Mitterrand, in playing at being indignant, was trying to score political points by highlighting the disingenuousness of the communists? Revel, having "demonstrated" the noncommunist Left's submissiveness to communism that he postulated in his dichotomous presentation of the available political choices, concluded that the Union of the Left was dominated by the communists and that it would necessarily end in their triumph because, although the socialists had more electoral support, they were ideologically submissive to the communists.[148] Indeed, Revel would later argue in response to his critics, the electoral triumph of the socialists was, given their adoption of Stalinist ways, actually a communist victory: "That they [the socialists] are more numerous than before only makes the operation more profitable for the communists."[149]

Not surprisingly, most supporters of the Union of the Left saw Revel's book as a polemical attack on the alliance and responded to it in kind. *Le Monde* editor Jacques Fauvet, reacting to the advance copy published in *L'Express* under the title "Suicide socialiste," countered that the real suicide of the socialists had been their long refusal of an alliance with the PCF.[150] Claude Estier argued in very Mitterrandist terms that the Union of the Left was a success because the PS had become the "premier French political force" and the PCF had been obliged "to reject the ossified representational frameworks that were theirs not too long ago."[151]

The reaction at *Le Nouvel Observateur* and *Esprit* is particularly interesting because Revel's perspective converged on certain crucial points with their own. Whatever their opinion of Revel's specific political analyses, they could agree with his general conclusion that there was a real danger of communist ideological domination over the Union of the Left. What they could not accept was Revel's argument that everyone who accepted the Union of the Left—and he specifically included *Le Nouvel Observateur* among them—was a dupe of the communists, a practitioner of what he called "enlarged Stalinism." Nor could they accept Revel's argument that there was no alternative to social democracy and Stalinism. *Autogestion,* their mantra, was, argued Revel, an illusion.[152] *Esprit* ignored Revel's book although a bit more than a year later, Jacques Julliard—increasingly worried by the direction taken by the Left—confessed his admiration for Revel's analysis.[153] *Le Nouvel Observateur* received *La Tentation totalitaire* poorly, never reviewing it and—with the exception of a couple of semi-supportive articles by Maurice Clavel—only mentioning it briefly in order to repudiate it.[154] Daniel responded to Revel with the argument that "the Union of the Left always consisted for us in marrying the current of the parties to better turn them away from the 'totalitarian temptation.'" Revel, because he rejected all alliances with the communists as suicidal, had no influence with them; *Le Nouvel Observateur*, by contrast, did have a hold over the communists and could "occasionally shake them out of their certainties."[155] In a letter to Revel of 15 January 1976 Daniel was more conciliatory. He confessed that "your problem is mine for the last fifteen years, and it monopolized all of my time in 1975." They differed, Daniel explained, in that "my ambition and my adventure consisted of working for the triumph within the socialist camp of almost the same ideas." Still, Daniel was not happy that Revel had attacked him and his weekly. He wrote to Revel: "I regret that you did not believe it necessary to consider the dimensions of the polemic that placed me in opposition to the PCF. The lessons of it would perhaps have caused you to correct certain of your conclusions."[156] In sum, Daniel agreed that there was a "totalitarian temptation" but disagreed with Revel's conclusion that the Union of the Left need necessarily fall victim to it. Gilles Martinet, the PS's national secretary, who—it should be recalled—had urged at the end of the summer of 1975 the socialists to confront the communists on these issues, agreed substantially with Daniel. Revel, he wrote, "is in the wrong era. It is no longer [unlike in the 1950s] Stalinism that intimidates, revolts or terrorizes the socialists; it is events and also the pressure of the socialists that progressively leads the communists to denounce Stalinism."[157]

Revel was not impressed by these objections to his argument. Daniel was, he believed, deluding himself in thinking that he was able to influence the communists or even resist their pressures. And, like Thibaud in response to Guidoni, Revel held that the polemical responses to his own polemic were proof of his thesis. After analyzing in obsessive, book-length detail the responses to *La Tentation Totalitaire*, Revel concluded: "With the generalized refusal of debate, with the fear of the disturbing idea, with the concealment of undesirable facts, and with the habitual use of slander have been put in place the constituent elements of the *totalitarian mentality* which only need to come to political power to become a totalitarian system."[158]

*   *   *

At the origin of all varieties of the critique of totalitarianism was an encounter of intellectuals with the Union of the Left. Although French intellectuals have never been very comfortable with party and electoral politics, the chasm between intellectual politics and the politics of the parties of the Left widened considerably when left-wing intellectuals, in their effort to find an alternative to Soviet communism, turned toward direct-democratic (or in the case of Revel, social-democratic) solutions at the same time that the Union of the Left was being forged around a rather old-fashioned state-centered Common Program. The effort, represented by the Assises, to bridge the distance between the two failed in 1974-75, and intellectuals, angry that the Left had not listened to them and fearful that the communists had effectively gained control of the French Left, researched, developed, and then deployed their political equivalent of an atomic bomb: the critique of totalitarianism.

Designed to deny the legitimacy of political competitors, the critique of totalitarianism simplified the political terrain. In particular, by focusing on the question of ideology the critique of totalitarianism denied the legitimacy of the Mitterrandist understanding of the dynamics of the Union in terms of relations of force and indeed of any understanding of French politics of these years in terms of real social, political, or institutional forces or structures. While argumentation along these lines produced an effective weapon for use in the quarrels within or against the Left, it was very hard to prevent its proliferation in a chain reaction of political denunciation. At the extreme, any failure to confront the communists became a sign of their ideological domination over the Left and of the totalitarian danger that France would face were the Left to come to power. Therefore, while Jean Daniel believed that he was helping fend off the drift toward totalitarianism within the Union of the Left, Revel considered Daniel to have succumbed to the totalitarian temptation because he had dropped his defamation suit against *L'Humanité*.[159] Once Mitterrand's reasoning in terms of relations of force was disqualified, one man's tactical concession to the communists became the next man's proof of communist ideological domination. The same problem emerged when it came to evaluating the origins of totalitarianism when understood as the sole product of ideology. Was totalitarianism a product of Leninism; or, as Morin and an increasing number of intellectuals suspected, of revolutionary ideology; or even more broadly, as Glucksmann suggested, of Western Reason since Plato? Once the origins of totalitarianism had been circumscribed to the realm of ideas, there was no limit to such arguments except perhaps the gumption of their authors and length of the daisy chain of ideas that the intellectual community could digest before it became nauseous. The success of the "new philosophers," analyzed in chapter 5, must be understood in this context.

After its birth in the crisis of the summer of 1975, antitotalitarianism spread quickly throughout the French noncommunist intellectual Left, acquiring the dimensions of a movement in the mobilization in support of East European dissidents. It became the focus of national attention in mid 1977 as the Union of the Left, universally expected to win the 1978 legislative elections after its March 1977 municipal election triumph, began to fall apart and the "new philosophers" emerged to capitalize on the crisis atmosphere. In these years of its maturity French antitotalitarianism became progressively more radical and began to cover up its mundane political origins by making the claim that it represented the abrupt awakening of intellectuals from decades of illusions about communism to embrace a politics of democracy and human rights. The story is, as the next chapter will further demonstrate, quite a bit more complicated.

Notes

1. My interpretation runs totally contrary to that of Pierre Grémion's influential work on the period. Grémion claims that the "liberal *progressiste* cultural milieu autonomous from the political parties" that emerged after 1956 was eclipsed in 1968 and during the years of the Common Program in favor of left-wing intellectuals' "subservience to the party spirit." Pierre Grémion, *Paris-Prague: la gauche face au renouveau et à la régression tchécoslovaques (1968-1978)* (Paris, 1985), 201.
2. Particularly useful on politics within the Left in the decade before Épinay are Robert Verdier, *P.S./P.C.F.: une lutte pour l'entente* (Paris, 1976) and Jean Poperen, *La Gauche française: le nouvel âge 1958-1965* (Paris, 1972).
3. *Programme Commun de Gouvernement du Parti Communiste Français et du Parti Socialiste (27 Juin 1972)* (Paris, 1972), 112.
4. According to Bernard E. Brown, "The Common Program in France," in Bernard E. Brown, ed., *Eurocommunism and Eurosocialism: The Left Confronts Modernity* (New York, 1979), 16.
5. When it committed itself to pursuing a Common Program with the communists, the PS demanded that the PCF give "clear and public answers to questions concerning national sovereignty, democratic liberties and ... submission to the will of the people as expressed through universal suffrage." D. S. Bell and Byron Criddle, *The French Socialist Party: The Emergence of a Party of Government*, 2nd ed. (Oxford, 1988), 131.
6. *Programme Commun de Gouvernement*, 149.
7. Ibid., 115.
8. Ibid., 111. This is the only point in the text where there is an openly expressed disagreement between the PS and the PCF.
9. This analysis of the Common Program draws on Robert Verdier, *P.S./P.C*; Bernard E. Brown, "The Common Program in France," 14-66; and Albert du Roy and Robert Schneider, *Le Roman de la rose: d'Épinay à l'Élysée, l'aventure des socialistes* (Paris, 1982).
10. This contention goes contrary to Pierre Grémion, who claims that "the price to pay for the signing of the Common Program" was the socialist Left's "silence on Prague winter." Grémion, *Paris-Prague*, 234.
11. Mitterrand cited in Franz-Olivier Giesbert, "Les Mauvais coups de Prague," *Le Nouvel Observateur* 403 (31 July 1972): 18.
12. *Le Monde*, 22-23 Oct. 1972, 8.
13. Pierre Daix, in particular, intervened on the question of the significance of normalization. See "Socialistes français et anciens du printemps de Prague ont recherché le sens de la 'normalisation'," *Le Monde*, 28 Nov. 1972, 7.
14. Du Roy and Schneider, *Le Roman de la rose*, 217.
15. Mitterrand's *Ma part de vérité* cited in Bell and Criddle, *The French Socialist Party*, 143. Mitterrand reiterated this point a few days after the signing of the Common Program at the twelfth congress of the Socialist International held in Vienna.

16. Hughes Portelli, *Le Socialisme français tel qu'il est* (Paris, 1980), 104-5.

17. Georges Marchais, "Rapport au Comité central, Paris, 29 juin 1972," in Etienne Fajon, ed., *L'Union est un combat: textes et documents de M. Thorez – W. Rochet – G. Marchais* (Paris, 1975), 88-89, 112, 117, 94.

18. On the PCF's strategy of openness see Philippe Robrieux, *(1972-1982)*, vol. 3 of *Histoire intérieure du Parti communiste* (Paris, 1982), especially pages 196-98 and Alex Macleod, *La Révolution inopportune: les partis communistes français et italien face à la Révolution portugaise (1973-1975)* (Montreal, 1984), chap. 2.

19. On the growth of PCF membership see Robrieux, *(1972-1982)*, 151-54 and Macleod, *La Révolution inopportune*, 54-55.

20. Du Roy and Schneider, *Le Roman de la rose*, 120, 136-44.

21. Election results in Hughes Portelli, *La Ve République* (Paris, 1994), 540, 542, and 543.

22. "Projet de société: pour le socialisme," in Assises du socialisme, *Pour le socialisme: Paris 12-13 octobre 1974* (Paris, 1974), 11-45 and pages 23, 24, and 29 for the citations.

23. This new division replaced that over *démollétisation*.

24. Robrieux, *(1972-1982)*, 216.

25. Ibid., 212-13 and Verdier, *P.S./P.C.*, 288.

26. Verdier, *P.S./P.C.*, 287; citations from du Roy and Schneider, *Le Roman de la rose*, 170; Brown, "The Common Program in France," 31. This Marchais-Mitterrand exchange prompted *Le Monde* to begin a regular rubric on PS-PCF relations.

27. On the Jospin reports see Brown, "The Common Program in France," 46-48; du Roy and Schneider, *Le Roman de la rose*, 173-74 and 202-3; and Bell and Criddle, *The French Socialist Party*, 133.

28. On CERES see David Hanley, *Keeping Left? Ceres and the French Socialist Party: A Contribution to the Study of Fractionalism in Political Parties* (Manchester, 1986).

29. Jacques Rollet, "Le PS et l'autogestion" (Thesis: Paris IEP, 1982), citations on page 279.

30. *Le Monde*, 6 May 1975, 10-11. See, for example, the opinion piece of Didier Motchane, CERES member of the PS *Bureau exécutif:* "Ne pas se tromper d'adversaire," *L'Unité* 167 (18-24 July 1975): 9.

31. Reproduced as "Les Deux cultures politiques" in Michel Rocard, *Parler vrai* (Paris, 1979), 76-84.

32. This point is further elaborated below in this chapter and in chapter 5. On the crucial, and instrumental, role of ideology in the PS see Portelli, *Le Socialisme français tel qu'il est*, 158-63.

33. Paul Thibaud ("Sur place ou innovation?" *Esprit* 392 [May 1970]: 865-69) mentioned the prospect of a "drift toward an oriental model of socialism" (866) were a united Left to come to power, while Michel Winock ("La Contradiction du P.C.F.," *Esprit* 392 [May 1970]: 884-97) argued that the union would break up before achieving power because the socialists would fear an outcome like the Prague coup of 1948. Jean-Marie Domenach ("Notre affaire Tillon ou la vitrine et l'appareil," *Esprit* 404 [June 1971]: 1253) held that a united Left could not win if the PCF did not de-Stalinize. In his reflections on a film on Czechoslovak history since World War II ("Le Bonheur dans vingt ans," *Esprit* 410 [Jan. 1972]: 68-69), Domenach also raised the specter of a Prague coup in France and concluded that "there will not be a solid Union of the Left" as long as this remained a possibility. Jacques Julliard ("Le Socialisme à l'ordre du jour," *Esprit* 412 [March 1972]: 450-69), in contrast to Domenach, found the Czechoslovak situation of 1948 to be substantially different from the contemporary French one, but argued that as long as the PCF remained attached to existing socialist societies, any victory of the Left would be the result of an "electoral coalition without principles and without hope" (469) that would be incapable of building a new society.

34. Michel Winock, "En un combat douteux," *Esprit* 382 (June 1969): 1003; Jacques Julliard, "L'Après-gaullisme," *Esprit* 383 (July-Aug. 1969): 154.

35. Jacques Julliard's "Le Socialisme à l'ordre du jour" is particularly clear on this point.

36. After the crushing of Prague Spring, Jean-Marie Domenach pledged to force French communists to face the truth about the USSR ("Que pouvons-nous pour la Tchécoslovaquie?" *Esprit* 375 [Nov. 1968]: 506-9). Domenach later demanded ("Dites-moi, M. Marchais," *Esprit* 398 [Dec. 1970]: 949-50) that Georges Marchais denounce repression in Czechoslovakia and held that his failure to do so made a true dialogue with the communists impossible. Christophe Calmy ("Le Défi démocratique," *Esprit* 428 [Oct. 1973]: 445-46) argued that the Union of the Left could not advance if the communists were to continue to defend the USSR and denounce its critics as anticommunists.

37. Jean-Marie Domenach in Thomas Molnar and Jean-Marie Domenach, "L'Impasse de la gauche," *Esprit* 383 (July-Aug. 1969): 62.

38. After the 1968 legislative elections, Domenach reveled in Mitterrand's failure, calling him "rancid" in his "Tu l'as voulu ...," *Esprit* 373 (Aug.-Sept. 1968): 166. Domenach revealed his hesitation to support Mitterrand in 1974 in his "Agenda électoral," *Esprit* 436 (June 1974): 1019-26. He finally offered lukewarm support for Mitterrand's candidacy in his "Ne pas se dérober," *Le Nouvel Observateur* 496 (13 May 1974): 43.

39. Thibaud, "Le Socialisme au programme," *Esprit* 416 (Sept. 1972): 288-93. For further elaboration of *Esprit*'s critiques of the Common Program see Daniel Mothé, Jean-Marie Domenach, Philippe Meyer, and Paul Thibaud, "Éléments pour un programme commun," *Esprit* 421 (Feb. 1973): 570-79.

40. Jean-Marie Domenach, "Les Idées et les mots," *Le Monde*, 27 Sept. 1972, 10.

41. Paul Thibaud, "Avant les élections," *Esprit* 420 (Jan. 1973): 205-13, citations on pages 211 and 212. Jacques Julliard's "Après Pompidou," *Esprit* 435 (May 1974): 771-81 similarly finds the dangers of seven more years of rule by the Right to be greater than those in the case of a victory of the Left.

42. Julliard argued that the PSU militants could help turn the PS into a "genuine socialist force" in his "Les Élections et le reste," *Esprit* 423 (April 1973): 995, and Michel Winock argued that it was within the PS that "one will increasingly be able to debate the issues" in his "Renouveau du Parti socialiste," *Esprit* 423 (April 1973): 940.

43. See, for example, Jean-Marie Domenach, "Mépris du peuple," *Esprit* 422 (March 1973): 711-13 and Domenach, "Agenda électoral."

44. Jean-Marie Domenach, "Les Assises du socialisme," *Esprit* 440 (Nov. 1974): 676-79 and pages 676 and 678 for the citations.

45. Jean-Marie Domenach, "Avec quoi faut-il rompre?" *Esprit* 440 (Nov. 1974): 625.

46. Jean-Marie Domenach argued in articles in the summer of 1974 that the Left could successfully respond to Giscard's liberal, technocratic neocapitalism only if it adopted antiproductivist and *autogestionnaire* perspectives. See his "La Mutation la plus difficile," *Le Nouvel Observateur* 506 (22 July 1974): 32-33 and his "Gens de gauche secouez-vous!" *Le Nouvel Observateur* 510 (19 Aug. 1974): 24-25. The later article gave rise to a debate in the pages of *Le Nouvel Observateur* in which Rocard upbraided Domenach for his lack of political tact. He wrote that by giving short shrift to the doctrinal renewal of the Left in recent years "Domenach erodes confidence and reinforces the adversary. Furthermore, Domenach totally neglects the fact that our problem is less to advance at any price toward the proposals that are best adapted to the latest ideas than to assure that we all advance together." Michel Rocard, "Le Dernier tremplin de la gauche," *Le Nouvel Observateur* 515 (23 Sept. 1974): 70.

47. For Domenach's later disappointment see his comment in "Autoportrait du sociologue, entretien avec Alain Touraine," *Esprit* 451 (Nov. 1975): 601 and Jean-Marie Domenach, *Lettre à mes ennemis de classe* (Paris, 1984), 139-40.

48. Jean-Marie Domenach, "Questions essentielles," *Esprit* 443 (Feb. 1975): 163-72, citation on pages 170-71. A rare earlier articulation of the theme of the PCF's ideological domination over the Union of the Left can be found in Paul Thibaud, "Le Socialisme au programme," 292.

49. Paul Thibaud, "Crise, gestion de la crise, autogestion ...," *Esprit* 442 (Jan. 1975): 3-4 and Michel Winock's comments in "Table ronde," *Esprit* 443 (Feb. 1975): 188 and 199, citation

on page 188. In this roundtable discussion Georges Lavau, a regular political commentator at *Esprit*, offered a Mitterrandist analysis of the politics of the Union of the Left in terms of power relations that rejected the claim that the question of ideology was crucial. His analysis gained no traction at *Esprit*.

50. Thibaud, "Crise, gestion de la crise, autogestion …," 3.
51. See ibid.; Daniel Mothé, "Où en est le courant autogestionnaire?" *Esprit* 442 (Jan. 1975): 16-33; Jean-Marie Domenach, "Au nom de l'autogestion," *Esprit* 447 (June 1975), 1037; and the articles on *autogestion* in *Esprit* 448 (July-Aug. 1975) and *Esprit* 449 (Sept. 1975).
52. Gilles Martinet, "Une mauvaise cible," *Le Nouvel Observateur* 404 (7 Aug. 1972): 13.
53. Jacques Julliard, "Faut-il redouter un Prague français?" *Le Nouvel Observateur* 407 (28 Aug. 1972): 13.
54. Jean Daniel, "Des insatisfaits prospères," *Le Nouvel Observateur* 414 (16 Oct. 1972): 30. André Gorz, who published under the name Michel Bosquet in *Le Nouvel Observateur*, was an important spokesman within the weekly for this position. See, for example, his defense of the *autogestionnaire* politics of the PSU and CFDT in light of the shortcomings of the Common Program in his "Au-delà des élections," *Le Nouvel Observateur* 417 (6 Nov. 1972): 38-39.
55. Jean Daniel, "Les Rendez-vous du 11 septembre," *Le Nouvel Observateur* 408 (4 Sept. 1972): 17.
56. The debate within *Le Nouvel Observateur* was launched by a lengthy two-part article beginning in the issue of 13 Nov. 1972 that explored the collapse of *tripartisme* in 1947 and its lessons for the Union of the Left. For Alain Geismar's statement in the name of *La Cause du peuple* against the Union of the Left see his "Pourquoi nous ne voterons pas," *Le Nouvel Observateur* 425 (30 Dec. 1972): 25.
57. Jean Daniel, "Qui peut battre Mitterrand?" *Le Nouvel Observateur* 492 (15 April 1974): 22.
58. Jean Daniel, "Un mois pour changer la France," *Le Nouvel Observateur* 491 (8 April 1974): 20.
59. Daniel, "Qui peut battre Mitterrand?" 22.
60. Jean Daniel, "Le Nouveau 'Plan Mitterrand'," *Le Nouvel Observateur* 493 (22 April 1974): 28 for the citation and Jean Daniel, "Le Salut par le risque," *Le Nouvel Observateur* 494 (29 April 1974): 28-29.
61. Jean Daniel, "Un espace de liberté," *Le Nouvel Observateur* 496 (13 May 1974): 36-37 echoing Domenach, "Ne pas se dérober," published in the same issue. Domenach committed a revealing slip between the two rounds of the election. On 6 May, after the first round, he circulated a petition calling upon people to "put everything into the effort to assure the failure of Giscard d'Estaing's candidacy" but failing to mention Mitterrand. In a second letter of 10 May he corrected what he called the petition's "unintentional equivocation." The corrected petition ended with a call to "assure François Mitterrand's success." Letters in IMEC ESP2 E4-03 .04, that is, the *Esprit* archives of the Institut Mémoires de l'Édition Contemporaine, folder ESP2 E3-03 .04.
62. Jean Daniel, "La Chance du 12 octobre," *Le Nouvel Observateur* 517 (7 Oct. 1974): 38-39 and Jean Daniel, "Le Clan," *Le Nouvel Observateur* 518 (14 Oct. 1974): 40. Daniel's contemporary enthusiasm for the Assises is reiterated in his later reflections on the period, Jean Daniel, *L'Ère des ruptures* (Paris, 1979), 271.
63. Jean Daniel, "Giscard face au peuple français," *Le Nouvel Observateur* 497 (21 May 1974): 23.
64. Daniel, "Le Clan," 40.
65. Jean Daniel, "La Campagne communiste contre Mitterrand," *Le Nouvel Observateur* 531 (13 Jan. 1975): 23.
66. Jean Daniel, "Les Deux Paris," *Le Nouvel Observateur* 535 (10 Feb. 1975): 12.
67. Philippe Gavi, Jean-Paul Sartre, and Pierre Victor, *On a raison de se révolter* (Paris, 1974), 252, 348-60, citation on page 355.
68. Jean-Paul Sartre in a dialogue with Pierre [Victor] and Philippe [Gavi] in *Libération*, 13-14 April 1974, 4.

69. "Piaget-Lip porte-parole du nouveau monde?" *Libération*, 6-7 April 1974, 3.
70. "Piaget une candidature collective," *Libération*, 10 April 1974, 1 and 3.
71. "Piaget-Lip porte-parole du nouveau monde?" 3.
72. "Piaget candidat?" *Libération*, 5 April 1974, 1; "Le Mouvement populaire à la recherche de son expression politique," *Libération*, 4 April 1974, 1.
73. "La Mystification du 1er tour et la candidature Piaget," *Libération*, 12 April 1974, 1.
74. Ph.[ilippe] Gavi, "Tribune du 19 Mai," *Libération*, 18-19 May 1974, 3.
75. Alain Geismar and Pierre Victor, "Aujourd'hui le risque c'est de perdre les acquis de Mai 68," *Libération*, 4-5 May 1974, 3; and, retrospectively, Serge July, "De l'éloge de François Mitterrand à celui de la bêtise," *Libération*, 4 June 1974, 2.
76. P.[hilippe] Gavi, "De Mai 68 à Mai 74: ces gauchistes qui votent Mitterrand," *Libération*, 13 May 1974, 2.
77. Libération, "*Libé* et les élections," *Libération*, 15 May 1974, 1, 3.
78. "Contre l'abstention des révolutionnaires," *Libération*, 15 May 1974, 3. The manifesto called for voting "with those who want to drive the Right out of power" and said nothing about Mitterrand or the Union of the Left. Listed here as signatories are: Simone de Beauvoir, Hélène Gixous [*sic*], Jean Chesneaux, Marguerite Duras, Michel Foucault, Daniel et Marie Guérin, Raymond et Geneviève Guglielmo, Pierre Halbwachs, Alain Jaubert, Raymond Jean, Julia Kristova [*sic*], Robert Lapoujade, Henri Leclerc, Henri Lefebvre, Michel Leiris, Jean-Marc Lévy-Leblond, Charles Malamoud, Dyonis Mascolo, Maurice Nadeau, Claudine Romeo Laudi, Philippe Sollers, and Pierre Vidal-Naquet.
79. Daniel Cohn-Bendit, "Tribune libre: abstention piège à cons," *Libération*, 18-19 May 1974, 1.
80. July, "De l'éloge de François Mitterrand à celui de la bêtise," 2.
81. "Libé et le débat sur le socialisme," *Libération*, 15-16 June 1974, 1. Note also the matter-of-fact reporting of the *Assises* initiative in "Contre-attaque du PS," *Libération*, 27 May 1974, 2.
82. "PC-PS: les jaloux," *Libération*, 21 Nov. 1974, 3; "Dis, p'pa, l'autogestion, ça commence quand?" *Libération*, 26 Nov. 1974, 4; Michel Chemin, "Contre Lip, pour les Assises," *Libération*, 27 Nov. 1974, 6; M. K., "Où en est le regroupement des socialistes," *Libération*, 2 Dec. 1974, 3.
83. In April the two parties cooperated in a campaign protesting unemployment and inflation, and in early May preparations began for the first "summit meeting," held on 19 June, between the two parties since the end of September 1974. T.[hierry] P.[fister], "Neuf mois de controverse," *Le Monde*, 20 June 1975, 8.
84. Macleod, *La Révolution inopportune* makes a strong case for the PCP's limited ambitions.
85. On the Portuguese Revolution I have relied on Kenneth Maxwell, *The Making of Portuguese Democracy* (New York, 1995). Helpful on the PCP was Macleod, *La Révolution inopportune* and Alex Macleod, "The French and Italian Communist Parties and the Portuguese Revolution," in *In Search of Modern Portugal: The Revolution and Its Consequences*, ed. Lawrence S. Graham and Douglas L. Wheeler (Madison, Wis., 1983), 297-320. Also useful was Robert Harvey, *Portugal: Birth of a Democracy* (London, 1978).
86. Remo Gasperi, *Il Popolo*, 16 March 1975, cited in Macleod, *La Révolution inopportune*, 158.
87. *Le Monde*, 29 May 1975, 2.
88. Claude Estier, "Une vérité à Paris une autre à Lisbonne?" *L'Unité* 160 (30 May 1975): 2. François Mitterrand, "Ma part de vérité," *L'Unité* 160 (30 May 1975): 32.
89. See François Mitterrand's letter of 13 August and the "Communiqué Commun" of 13 August of the three parties signatory to the Common Program reproduced in *L'Unité* 169 (5-11 Sept. 1975): 12-13.
90. The defense of relativism is as follows: "The cultural backwardness of a country and a long past of dictatorship and obscurantism make difficult the immediate, unnuanced application of a freedom of expression that often tends to be exercised to the profit of

those nostalgic for the past who are still installed in the 'apparatus.'" "Révolution et liberté," *Le Monde*, 21 June 1975, 1.

91. Edgar Morin, "La Liberté révolutionnaire," *Le Nouvel Observateur* 555 (30 June 1975): 22-23 and his "Une précision d'Edgar Morin," *Le Nouvel Observateur* 556 (7 July 1975): 30. Raymond Aron, "Il n'y a pas de quoi rire," *Le Figaro*, 23 June 1975, 1 and 5, and his follow-up articles, "La France n'est pas la Portugal," *Le Figaro*, 5-6 July 1975, 1 and 2, and "De la crise portugaise au débat français," *Le Figaro*, 25 July 1975, 1 and 3. Jacques Fauvet, the director of *Le Monde*, responded to their initial articles with his "Révolution et liberté," *Le Monde*, 1 July 1975, 1 and 11.

92. *Le Monde*'s coverage of the Portuguese Revolution and the related French affair came under attack at *Esprit*. Gilbert Padoul ("L'Impasse portugaise," *Esprit* 449 [Sept. 1975]: 251) held that the analyses of the Portuguese Revolution by the PCF and CERES were "gently echoed by the special correspondent of *Le Monde*," and Jean-Marie Domenach ("Le Premier Front," *Le Nouvel Observateur* 563 [25 Aug. 1975]: 18) criticized *Le Monde* for suggesting that Daniel's August altercation with the PCF was nothing more than a dispute among journalists.

93. See, for example, Jean-Marie Domenach, "'Le Monde' en question," *Esprit* 456 (April 1976): 769-78 and Pierre Nora, "Se le sel perd sa saveur …," *Le Nouvel Observateur* 596 (12 April 1976): 42-43. The questioning of *Le Monde* is analyzed in Jean-Noël Jeanneney and Jacques Julliard, *Le "Monde" de Beuve-Méry ou le métier d'Alceste* (Paris, 1979), 279-309.

94. Jean Daniel, "Pour que la lutte soit claire," *Le Nouvel Observateur* 553 (16 June 1975): 18.

95. See the CGT declaration cited in Daniel, *L'Ère des ruptures*, 303, note 6.

96. Jean Daniel, "Les Choses par leur nom," *Le Nouvel Observateur* 554 (23 June 1975): 14; Jean Daniel, "Les Points sur les 'i'," *Le Nouvel Observateur* 555 (30 June 1975): 14; Jean Daniel, "La Réponse de Jean Daniel au communiqué du bureau confédéral de la C.G.T.," *Le Nouvel Observateur* 557 (12 July 1975): 22; "La C.G.T. et 'Le Nouvel Observateur'," *Le Nouvel Observateur* 558 (21 July 1975): 25.

97. Jean Daniel, "Portugal face à l'anticommunisme," 561 *Le Nouvel Observateur* (11 Aug. 1975): 16-17.

98. Reported in *Le Nouvel Observateur* 563 (25 Aug. 1975): 18. Their evidence was the following statement by Daniel: "If the Communist Party diabolically perseveres in a Bolshevik logic implying the elimination of the other worker parties is there anything else to do other than to fight it in becoming the 'objective' ally of the reactionaries, clericalists, and fascists who still reigned over Portugal yesterday." Daniel, "Portugal face à l'anticommunisme," 17.

99. Daniel's article in *Le Monde* of 13 Aug., reproduced in *Le Nouvel Observateur* 563 (25 Aug. 1975): 19.

100. "La Déclaration des 35," *Le Nouvel Observateur* 562 (18 Aug. 1975): 18. A final list of signatories is given in *Le Nouvel Observateur* 565 (8 Sept. 1975): 8.

101. See *L'Humanité*, 15 Aug. 1975, 1, and subsequent issues.

102. Georges Marchais and Jean Daniel on France-Inter as cited in *Le Nouvel Observateur* 563 (25 Aug. 1975): 19. Marchais's legal argument is analyzed by Jean-Denis Bredin, "Georges Marchais et le sens des mots," *Le Nouvel Observateur* 563 (25 Aug. 1975): 20.

103. Michel Cardoze "Jean Daniel avec ses guillemets," *L'Humanité*, 28 Aug. 1975, 5 published extensive excerpts of Daniel's editorial of 11 August, after which Daniel abandoned the defamation suit and declared victory in the postscript to his "Les Français doutent la France," *Le Nouvel Observateur* 564 (1 Sept. 1975): 16. "La Déroute de Jean Daniel," *L'Humanité*, 2 Sept. 1975, 2 claimed that Daniel, by renouncing his suit, was "routed" because *L'Humanité* had maintained its interpretation of his text.

104. Daniel, "Les Choses par leur nom," 14.

105. Daniel, "Les Points sur les 'i'," 14.

106. Jean Daniel, "Lettre à un militant communiste," *Le Nouvel Observateur* 563 (25 Aug. 1975): 17.

107. Daniel, "Les Choses par leur nom," 14.

108. Bredin, "Georges Marchais et le sens des mots," 20.
109. Daniel, *L'Ère des ruptures*, 302.
110. Daniel, "Pour que la lutte soit claire," 19.
111. Daniel, "Les Points sur les 'i'," 14. Similar suggestions parodying communist rhetoric can be found in Daniel, "Pour que la lutte soit claire," 19.
112. Note, for example, Daniel's discussion of the Union of the Left in the past tense. In "Les Français doutent la France" Daniel wrote that the communists "were supposed to have governed" with the socialists. According to the *L'Humanité* article "La Déroute de Jean Daniel," Daniel wrote in a "circular" to people who had rescinded their subscriptions to *Le Nouvel Observateur*: "The French communists—yesterday still our allies in the Union of the Left." Neither Daniel nor *Le Nouvel Observateur* denied this.
113. Gilles Martinet, "Et si la France était le Portugal ..." *Le Nouvel Observateur* 564 (1 Sept. 1975): 35.
114. For statements on the orientation of *Faire* see: editorial statement, *Faire* 1 (Oct. 1975): 2; Patrick Viveret, editorial statement, *Faire* 2 (Nov. 1975): 2; Patrick Viveret, editorial statement, *Faire* 3 (Dec. 1975): 2. Analyses of the Portuguese Revolution include: Alain Touraine, "Portugal: la révolution difficile," *Faire* 1 (Oct. 1975): 3-9, which interprets the crisis of the summer of 1975 in Portugal as a rejection of a communist seizure of power, and Gilles Martinet, "En France que ferions nous?" *Faire* 2 (Nov. 1975): 31-35, which reflects on the danger of putting one's trust in workers' councils. Jean-Pierre Cot, "L'Union est un combat," *Faire* 1 (Oct. 1975): 35-39 calls for the PS to be more assertive.
115. Jean-Marie Domenach, "Le Premier Front," *Le Nouvel Observateur* 569 (25 Aug. 1975): 18.
116. Jacques Julliard, "Les Inconvénients de l'union," *Le Nouvel Observateur* 557 (12 July 1975): 18-19.
117. He wrote: "If the Common Program has a meaning, it is in the acceptance by the communists of the parliamentary framework for social transformation. Can this acceptance appear serious if at the first opportunity the communists find the best of justifications for those who do what they like with formal liberties?" *Esprit* 446 (May 1975): 855.
118. Gilbert Padoul, "L'Impasse portugaise," *Esprit* 449 (Sept. 1975): 249-52; Alfredo Margarido, "Le M.F.A. condamné à éclater," *Esprit* 449 (Sept. 1975): 253-56.
119. Paul Thibaud, "Les Apories du Léninisme," *Esprit* 449 (Sept. 1975): 258-259. The article is dated 8 August.
120. Paul Thibaud, "D'où vient l'aveuglement?" *Le Quotidien de Paris*, 16 July 1975, in response to Pierre Guidoni, "La Nouvelle Trahison des clercs," *Le Quotidien de Paris*, 8 July 1975.
121. Introduction to *Esprit* 449 (Sept. 1975): 161.
122. Discussed in chapter 1.
123. Paul Thibaud, "Contre la prise du pouvoir ... et pour l'autogestion," *Esprit* 449 (Sept. 1975): 163-83, citations on pages 164, 169, 171, 172, 174, 183.
124. The November colloquium was evidently being prepared at least as early as the beginning of August 1975, as evidenced by the letters of Daniel Mothé of 9 Aug. 1975 and René Pucheu of 25 Aug. 1975 criticizing the preparatory text. IMEC ESP2 B2-02 .11.
125. The final "exposé des motifs" bemoaned that the Assises du socialisme did not have "decisive results" on the Union of the Left and that "a libertarian politics has hardly been formulated" out of the renewal of militancy and the new struggles that emerged out of 1968. Instead, 1968 had mostly furnished "new fodder for the old politics." In sum, "the methods and the objectives of the politics of the Left have been able to change, but not its conceptual framework." [Paul Thibaud], "Un exposé des motifs et une indication de programme concernant un colloque politique qu'*Esprit* organise les 29 et 30 nov. prochains au village de vacances de Dourdan." IMEC ESP2 B2-02 .10.
126. [Paul Thibaud], "Colloque de l'automne 1975," in IMEC ESP2 B2-02 .11.
127. According to J. P. Siméon's analysis of the conference in the document entitled "Esprit de l'escalier." IMEC ESP2 B2-02 .10. Jean-Marie Domenach, "Idéologie et marxisme," *Esprit* 449 (Sept. 1975): 197-212.

128. Participants in the "colloque politique" as per the list "Assisteront au Congrès des 29-30 novembre 1975" in IMEC ESP2 B2-02 .10: Marie-Louise Beaumont, J. C. Besson-Girard, Eliane Boucquey, Hubert Brochier, Claude Cadart, Jacques Caroux, Pierre Caussat, Philippe Courrège, M. and Mme. Delpeleire, Axos Ditroï, M. and Mme. Gautrat, Luce Girard, Pierre Hassner, Jean Irigaray, Jacques Julliard, Pierre Kende, Stéphane Khémis, Hubert Lafont, Richard Marienstras, Pierre Mayol, Olivier Mongin, Maurice Mounier, Marc Paillet, Bernard Pingaud, M. Pomian, Henri Provisor, René Pucheu, Marie-Clair Ropars, M. Rosanvallon, Guy Roustang, Joseph Rovan, Philibert Secretan, J. P. Siméon, Alfred Simon, Alex Smolar, Antoine de Tarlé, Georges Thill, Pierre Vidal-Naquet, Paul Virilo, Michel Winock, Catherine Vourch, J.-M. Domenach, P. Thibaud, Chalin, Mme. Marie Denis, Alex Derczansky, J. P. Dupuey, Esson, Eslin, Andrée Gérard, Robert Leroy, Majewska, Patrice Mignon, J. Moreau, Fernande Schulmann.

    Also listed on a presumably earlier "Liste des participants inscrits" are: Christiane Barrier-Lynn, Michèle Bouvier, Jean Duvignaud, Serge Karsenty, Jean Mayer, Philippe Meyer, M. Molitor, Jacques J. Natanson, Marc Richir, Jean-Pierre Rioux.

    Some intellectuals of general prominence or of importance in the critique of totalitarianism who were invited to the "colloque politique" but who apparently did not attend include: Miguel Abensour, Cornelius Castoriadis, Michel de Certeau, Marcel Gauchet, André Glucksmann, Pierre Grémion, Georges E. Lavau, Claude Lefort, Edgar Morin, Jacques Ozouf, Paul Ricoeur, Philippe Robrieux, Alain Touraine, Patrick Viveret, and Alfred Willener.

    Some who could not attend noted their interest in the colloquium. Alain Touraine wrote that he read the presentation of it "with great interest." Edgar Morin noted his desire to speak on all the questions that were to be addressed at the colloquium. See their letters in IMEC ESP2 B2-02 .11

129. Marcel Gauchet's influential "L'Expérience totalitaire et la pensée de la politique," *Esprit* 459 (July-Aug. 1976): 3-28 was, according to the note on page 3, a "revised version of an oral presentation in the reading group on political texts that met at the journal." Thibaud's correspondence (in IMEC ESP2 S16-08 .01.) regarding the articles in *Esprit* of September 1976 on "Révolution et totalitarisme" indicates that they emerged out of a debate organized by *Esprit*. This debate is probably the meeting of January 1976 on "La Révolution, idée et expérience" referred to by Pierre Grémion, *Paris-Prague*, 308. Grémion notes other meetings organized by *Esprit* on "Soljenitsyne" (Oct. 1975), "La Liberté" (April 1976), and "La Révolution hongroise" (Dec. 1976).

130. Beginning with Olivier Mongin, "Penser la politique contre la domination, sur quelques travaux de Lefort et Gauchet," *Esprit* 450 (Oct. 1975): 511-16.

131. See Domenach's marginal comments on Thibaud's "Colloque de l'automne 1975."

132. René Pucheu's letter of 25 Aug. 1975 makes it clear that the Nov. 1975 colloquium was supposed to be an important step toward the passing of *Esprit*'s directorship from Domenach to Thibaud. IMEC ESP2 B2-02 .11

133. Jean-Marie Domenach, "Sans adieu," *Esprit* 463 (Dec. 1976): 743, 750.

134. Jean-Marie Domenach, *Ce que je crois* (Paris, 1978), 108-16, 265-67. In his marginal notes on Thibaud's draft of the "Exposé des motifs" for the November 1975 colloquium Domenach commented: "Julliard said one day '*autogestion*? An unrealizable utopia.' Is not *Esprit* going to play the (idealist) fool of the (labor union) kings?" Jean-Marie Domenach's note on Thibaud's "Colloque de l'automne 1975," 5.

135. Domenach, *Ce que je crois*, 223; Domenach, "Sans adieu," 746.

136. As early as 1976 Paul Thibaud, in criticizing the efforts to establish "popular power" in Portugal, had concluded that without an institutional reflection and practice, "the libertarian movements are condemned either to 'succeed' in a totalitarian manner, that is to say perversely, or to vanish. Institutional reflection is obstructed, if not rendered impossible, by the fantasy of the absence of power that is mixed up with the idea and the practice of popular power." P.[aul] Th.[ibaud], "A propos du pouvoir populaire," *Esprit* 454 (Feb. 1976): 334.

137. Paul Thibaud, "Réunion des 25-26 septembre 1976," 5. IMEC ESP2 B2-03 .01 This theme is also developed in Paul Thibaud, "Aujourd'hui," *Esprit* 463 (Dec. 1976): 755-75.

138. On the other hand, personalism's emphasis on community and reciprocity (recast as "democratic reciprocity") remained relevant, especially in opposition to the liberal individualism that Thibaud rejected. Thibaud, "Réunion des 25-26 septembre 1976," 2. Thibaud, "Aujourd'hui," 763, 770 and 764 for the citations.

139. For example, Gilles Martinet focused his response to critiques of the Common Program on those published in the pages of *L'Express* by Jean-François Revel and Pierre Uri. Martinet, "Une mauvaise cible," 12-13. At the time, *L'Express* was the largest circulating French weekly and, like Revel, on the center-left.

140. Jean-François Revel, *Mémoires: le voleur dans la maison vide* (Paris, 1997), see generally on his career and pages 313-14 for his self-definition as an intellectual and writer.

141. Ibid., 295-99 on his politics (citation page 297) and 366-83 on his relations with Mitterrand.

142. Jean-François Revel, "Le Jeu P.C.-U.D.R.," *L'Express* 1100 (7 Aug. 1972): 13.

143. Jean-François Revel, "Les Deux socialismes," *L'Express* 1095 (3 July 1972): 29, an evaluation of the Common Program, makes clear his preference for Swedish socialism; and his *Ni Marx, ni Jésus* (Paris, 1970) makes the case for the American Left.

144. See his editorials, "Les Deux socialismes;" "Que veulent les socialistes?" *L'Express* 1097 (17 July 1972): 19 and "Réponse à François Mitterrand," *L'Express* 1099 (31 July 1972): 13.

145. Jean-François Revel, *The Totalitarian Temptation*, trans. David Hapgood (New York, 1977), 148.

146. Ibid., 100. Recall that the PS not only refuted the communists' interpretation of the affair, but protested vigorously against the PCF's claim that the PS was engaging in "anticommunism."

147. Ibid., 71-72 and interview of François Mitterrand by Jean-François Revel, *L'Express* 1121 (1 Jan. 1973): 19.

148. Revel, *The Totalitarian Temptation*, 95, 330.

149. Jean-François Revel, *La Nouvelle Censure: exemple de mise en place d'une mentalité totalitaire* (Paris, 1977), 234.

150. J.[acques] F.[auvet], "Suicide socialiste?" *Le Monde*, 13 Jan. 1976, 34. André Fontaine's review of the book in *Le Monde* was no more generous. André Fontaine, "Brejnev maurrassien," *Le Monde*, 17 Jan. 1976, 1 and 6.

151. Estier's review of *La Tentation totalitaire*, published in *France-Soir* of 16 Jan. 1976 and cited in Revel, *La Nouvelle Censure*, 206.

152. Revel, *The Totalitarian Temptation*, 146-47 for his opinion of *autogestion* and footnote 10, pages 92-93, for example, for his evaluation of *Le Nouvel Observateur*.

153. See Julliard's letter cited in Revel, *La Nouvelle Censure*, 252-53.

154. Maurice Clavel, "Mes repas avec René Andrieu," *Le Nouvel Observateur* 585 (26 Jan. 1976): 62; Maurice Clavel, "L'Échec d'un best-seller," *Le Nouvel Observateur* 611 (26 July 1976): 53.

155. Jean Daniel, "Une libération exemplaire," *Le Nouvel Observateur* 584 (19 Jan. 1976): 16.

156. Daniel, cited in Revel, *La Nouvelle Censure*, 233 and 255.

157. Gilles Martinet, "L'Amérique et les fronts populaires," *Le Nouvel Observateur* 591 (8 March 1976): 24.

158. Revel, *La Nouvelle Censure*, 270.

159. Ibid., 235-40.

Chapter 4

DISSIDENCE CELEBRATED

Intellectuals and Repression in Eastern Europe

By 1977 the shifts in intellectual politics induced by the debate over the Union of the Left and manifested in the emerging critique of totalitarianism became plainly visible to even the most casual of observers. The year 1977 was a year of dissidence in French intellectual politics. At the 21 June reception for Soviet dissidents at the Théâtre Récamier in Paris, and at the Biennale de Venise on East European dissidence of 15 November to 15 December, the leading figures of the noncommunist French intellectual Left visibly and firmly manifested their support for their persecuted confreres beyond the iron curtain and in exile in the West. Committees mobilizing support for dissidents proliferated. Further, French intellectuals began to theorize a politics of dissidence that would be applicable in France itself. It was also the year of the new philosophers, notably Bernard-Henri Lévy, author of *La Barbarie à visage humain*, and André Glucksmann, author of *Les Maîtres penseurs*. Although their books offered rather simplistic and extraordinarily pessimistic political philosophies, they were enormously successful and sparked an important debate about intellectual politics and the Union of the Left that clearly revealed the widening gulf between the politics of French intellectuals of the noncommunist Left and that of the communist and socialist parties. Finally, 1977 was the year of the crisis of Marxism. Although clearly visible in the debates over the new philosophers, themselves dubbed "magnificent Marx-haters" by the liberal British weekly *The Economist*, it became undeniable once Louis Althusser, France's premier Marxist philosopher, announced its arrival at *Il Manifesto*'s conference on "Power and Opposition in Post-Revolutionary Societies," held concurrent to and in competition with the Italian socialists' Biennale de

---

Venise. As the location of Althusser's intervention reveals, the new promi-nence of dissidence and the crisis of Marxism were closely related.[1]

The phenomena of the new philosophers and dissidence in French intel-lectual life were no less intertwined. Not only did Lévy and Glucksmann support East European dissidence, but they represented themselves as dis-sident intellectuals before a leviathan state and an ideological politics that threatened to engulf France if and when the Left came to power. In the dis-course on French politics proffered by Lévy, Glucksmann, and some of their supporters in 1977, new philosophers were dissidents and vice versa. The attraction of dissidence in 1977 followed directly from the intense anx-ieties of many noncommunist intellectuals over the prospects of the Left coming to power in 1978.

This chapter on East European dissidents in French intellectual politics and the next on the new philosophers seek to put the extraordinary year 1977 in perspective by thoroughly explaining the place of East European dissidence in French intellectual politics and evaluating the significance of new philosophy and the debate that it sparked. The current chapter focuses on French intellectuals' mobilizations against repression by communist régimes in the 1970s, notably those of the Comité du 5 janvier pour une Tchécoslovaquie libre et socialiste, and the Comité international des math-ematicians. Contextualizing the 1970s by briefly considering protests against the repression of the Hungarian Revolution and in support of the first Soviet dissidents, this chapter shows that French intellectuals did not miss their chance to protest repression in Eastern Europe after 1956 and that the politics of this protest was clearly inscribed within domestic debates and agendas.[2] Whether from the Left or from the Right, French mobiliza-tions against repression by communist régimes were designed to have an impact on domestic politics or, at the very least, articulate and express a political community. The language of manifestos and petitions, the list of signatories to them, and even the specific instances of human rights viola-tions protested were carefully selected to these ends. Like most French intellectuals since the Dreyfus affair, those who took action against human rights violations by communist régimes claimed to be intervening in the name of truth and justice, but much of their action consisted of convincing their compatriots that their politics best served these eternal verities.[3]

Because these protests were inscribed in domestic political debates and agendas there is a direct correlation between the amount of interest in them and the extent to which they could be used in French political strug-gles. In particular, interest was closely related to the intensity of the domestic debate about the PCF and the dangers that it represented to lib-erty and democracy. Although the connection between the debate over French communism and that over repression under "really existing social-ism" was already evident in the late 1940s and early 1950s in the Kravchenko affair and the politics of Rousset's commission on Soviet camps, it took a new turn after the crushing of the Hungarian Revolution in 1956. After 1956, intellectuals of the noncommunist Left generally did not refrain from protesting human rights violations under communism for fear of such protests' domestic anticommunist political uses. On the contrary, they emphasized the need to speak out in order to highlight the difference between their vision of a socialism that respects liberty and the socialism then being practiced in the East. The domestic incentive to protest grew in the 1970s with the rise of the Union of the Left and reached a new plateau in 1977, when it looked likely that the Union of the Left would win the 1978 legislative elections and the PCF would consequently share in the exercise of political power. In fact, precisely because of its position on socialism intellectuals on the Left may have been *more* likely than intellectuals on the Right to protest and campaign against repression beyond the iron curtain. The Right, because it considered communism entirely noxious and utterly incorrigible, was probably more inclined to denounce and combat communist régimes in general than to protest their specific actions.

Although left-wing intellectuals framed their protests in the two decades after 1956 in terms of their desire to reconcile socialism and liberty, the extent to which they considered that "really existing socialism" could potentially reconcile the two changed considerably in response to events in Eastern Europe and as liberty grew in importance in their politics. To judge from representative protests, between 1956 and 1968 they imagined that the liberalization begun by Khrushchev might bring about such a reconciliation to the East. Hopes for a favorable evolution were questioned as a result of the Daniel-Siniavski affair of 1965 and 1966 and the subsequent repression of dissidence, and evaporated after the Warsaw Pact intervention in Czechoslovakia in 1968. After 1968, although left-wing intellectuals continued to protest in the name of reconciling socialism and liberty, they were increasingly doubtful that this could be achieved in Eastern Europe. In the course of the 1970s their protests became increasingly hostile toward communist régimes, and toward 1977 they began to disassociate their protests from the socialist project and embrace human rights dissidence as such.

There is, as this chronology indicates, some merit to the argument, advanced by Paul Thibaud, that French intellectuals followed the lead of Eastern European intellectuals themselves (who moved from Marxist revisionism to human rights dissidence in the years after 1968) in the evolution of their engagements vis-à-vis communist régimes and dissent within them.[4] And to be sure, the French intellectuals' enthrallment with dissidence in the late 1970s would not have been as significant as it was if the movement in Eastern Europe had been less important or there had not been a substantial community of refugee dissidents in Paris. But the openness of the French intellectual Left to East European dissidents living under communism or in exile in the West in the late 1970s was above all a consequence of the uses of dissidence in the domestic battle over the Union of the Left.

Protests to Reconcile Socialism and Liberty, 1956-68

The crushing of the Hungarian Revolution was, as we saw in chapter 1, a profound shock to many French intellectuals. It decisively undermined double standards in the evaluation of the Soviet Union and led many left-wing intellectuals to vow not to remain silent in the face of repression under communism. Indeed, French intellectuals responded to the Soviet intervention in Hungary with a flurry of protests and petitions that culminated in the period from 1958 to 1960 with the campaign of the Comité Tibor Déry—led by Jean-Marie Domenach, Louis de Villefosse, and François Fejtö—to liberate Tibor Déry and other imprisoned Hungarian intellectuals. This mobilization, like all those that followed, was—as the following examples clearly indicate—aimed as much at imposing an interpretation of the event, settling accounts, and establishing the limits of acceptable politics as at impacting the course of events in Hungary. Anticommunist intellectuals were the first to raise their voices in petitions published in *Le Monde* on 6 November. The Congress for Cultural Freedom called upon the United Nations to take action "in the name of universal conscience" to protect the Hungarian people, their liberty, and their independence from "the brutal repression and the terror of the Soviet armies." A petition of French intellectuals, including Albert Camus, Gabriel Marcel, André Breton, and Jules Romains, compared the USSR to czarist Russia in the days of the Holy Alliance and called Moscow "the capital of world absolutist reaction." The petition added that its signatories "consider these butchers to be pariahs of humanity and denounce the communist leaders of free countries, who ... cover their hands with the blood of the Hungarian people." Denis de Rougemont, one of the signatories of the Congress for Cultural Freedom's petition, was even more direct in *Le Figaro littéraire* of 10 November, where he called for action "against those who applaud the crime, who try to have it forgotten or who seek to excuse it."[5]

Vercors, hearing on French radio on the evening of the fourth what he described as "the overzealous protest of a group of old enemies of communism, to which rally other men carried away by their disappointment and bitterness," decided to draw up a protest of his own that would "bring together outraged consciences without coming to the aid of Western imperialism and its hypocritical condemnations." The petition, written by Vercors and signed by leading *progressiste* and communist intellectuals including Jean-Paul Sartre, Simone de Beauvoir, André Spire, Laurent Schwartz, Claude Roy, and Claude Morgan, established their right to protest the Soviet government's actions because they had never "shown unfriendly feelings toward the USSR or socialism" and denied the right to protest the Soviet intervention to those, labeled hypocrites, who had been silent on the American intervention in Guatemala. Protesting "against the use of guns and tanks to break the revolt of the Hungarian people and their desire for independence, even if certain reactionary elements were mixed in with the revolt," the petition proclaimed that neither socialism nor liberty could be brought about at the point of bayonets, expressed concern that Hungarian writers—who had played a major role in the origins of the revolution—not be punished, and demanded that the Soviet government tell the truth about the affair.[6]

The connection made between the defense of an ideal socialism reconciled with liberty and the protests of repression under communism evident in the Vercors protest petition also emerges clearly in the reactions of the French intellectual Left to the repression of Soviet dissidence from the trial and conviction of Iuli Daniel and Andrei Siniavski in February 1966 through the early 1970s. Further, a study of the language of the protests demonstrates that the French intellectual Left was attentive to developments in the East and evolved in its positions along lines that broadly paralleled those of Soviet dissent.[7] Soviet dissent, which emerged in the aftermath of the Daniel-Siniavski trial, generally assumed until 1968 that Soviet law was just, although improperly applied, and demanded the application of "socialist legality." French protests of the same period also assumed the general legitimacy of the Soviet Union while gently reminding Soviet authorities that socialism and liberty should be inseparable. After 1968 Soviet dissidents increasingly abandoned their hopes that Soviet authorities would respect "socialist legality" and concentrated on widening the sphere of civil liberties and political expression, which they now assumed the system rejected. Likewise, after 1968 and as the phenomenon of dissidence and its repression multiplied, the French intellectual Left believed that Soviet socialism was fundamentally divorced from liberty, and although they often protested in the name of a true socialism, they increasingly assumed that the Soviet system no longer incarnated it in reality or even in potentiality. Not surprisingly, as we shall see in the case of the Comité du 5 janvier pour une Tchécoslovaquie libre et socialiste, French intellectuals made the transition from protest in the name of socialism to support for East European dissidents who concentrated exclusively on human rights (and either were hostile or indifferent to the socialist content of the régime) with relative ease.

The trial and conviction of Daniel and Siniavski for spreading "anti-Soviet propaganda" in their works published in the West was a turning point in Soviet history, marking the end of the Khrushchevian era's thaw of Soviet cultural life and the emergence of Soviet dissent in reaction to the verdict. Significantly, the trial broke with the formula of the Stalinist era, with its prearranged scripts and confessions of guilt, and reverted to czarist forms in which the accused used the trial to defend their views, in this case the right to freedom of expression. The defense of freedom of expression and the infringement of legal due process in the trial became the focus of subsequent protests in the Soviet Union.[8]

In France intellectuals issued numerous protests of the trial and the conviction.[9] The most famous of these was the post-trial letter published in

L'Humanité of 16 February 1966 by Louis Aragon, a member of the PCF's Central Committee and the party's most renowned writer.[10] Aragon's letter offered a variation on the theme of the protests of noncommunist intellectuals: the necessary marriage of socialism and liberty. After reminding the reader that "we can in no way forget that which we owe to the Soviet Union and to the peoples that compose it," it concluded that to convict Daniel and Siniavski was "to make difference of opinion a crime, this is to create a precedent that is more harmful to the interest of socialism than the works of Siniavski and Daniel could be." While respectfully requesting that the verdict be appealed, Aragon revealed his concern for the significance of this trial for socialism in France: "It is to be feared in effect that one might think that this type of procedure is inherent in the nature of communism and that today's decision prefigures what justice will be in a country that will have abolished exploitation of man by man. It is our duty to proclaim that that is not so and can not be so in France, at least, where it is our responsibility."

Aragon's letter was widely understood by contemporaries as a statement on French socialism as well as a protest of the trial. Claude Roy, welcoming a chance to further the reconciliation of socialism and liberty, applauded it as a "declaration of principle the consequences of which can only be favorable for the future of democracy and of socialism in France—and elsewhere." Henri Lefebvre was less impressed. He feared that this was only Aragon's personal statement and did not engage the Communist Party itself. Further, anticipating an analysis that would become more common in the 1970s, he judged the problem to be more profound than Aragon allowed as "each political régime has the scandals that it deserves."[11]

Other protests against the trial and conviction were, not surprisingly, as concerned as Aragon's with the threat that this verdict represented for the effort to reconcile socialism and liberty. The Comité national des écrivains, which claimed to have "always defended the right of the writer to freely express himself," protested "not only against the rigor of the sentence but also against the very principle of legal proceedings." It hoped, it stated in a post-1956 French version of the Soviet dissidents' demand for the application of socialist legality, that "it will be possible to review such a serious decision that risks to alter the Soviet Union's image amongst its best friends."[12] An open letter of protest sent to *Pravda* by seventeen writers and artists demonstrated less enthusiasm for the Soviet Union's version of socialism while defending socialism in the abstract. It called the imprisonment of Daniel and Siniavski "insulting for the idea that innumerable men have of socialism" and called upon the Soviet press to inform the Soviet people of the international reactions to the trial.[13]

In the late 1960s and early 1970s few petitions and protests were as optimistic as those in reaction to the Daniel-Siniavski trial of 1966. A January 1968 protest of the trial and conviction of Alexander Ginzburg, Iury Galanskov, Andrei Dobrovolsky, and Vera Lashkova explicitly noted the continuity between this repression and the Daniel-Siniavski trial and the Soviet authorities' unresponsiveness to the earlier protests.[14] Demanding the "revision of the trial of Ginzburg and the liberation of all the intellectuals imprisoned for the crime of non-conformism," the protesters also said that they "regret that fifty years after the October Revolution, and despite a certain amount of progress in the liberalization of the régime, Soviet power shows such an evident contempt for the rights of the person and gives such a deplorable example of 'socialist legality.'" As the scare quotes indicate, the notion of socialist legality was losing a legitimacy that the intervention in Czechoslovakia would more decisively discredit.[15] In November 1972, when the West received news of the death of Iury Galanskov in prison, the Fédération de l'éducation nationale demanded greater attention to the fate of political prisoners in the USSR and underlined "the permanency and the gravity of the attacks on democratic liberties committed in the USSR in the very name of socialism."[16] The new perspective might best be summarized by the name of one of the committees active in the early 1970s: the Comité pour la défense des libertés dans les pays se réclamant du socialisme (Committee for the defense of liberties in countries calling themselves socialist).

From Protesting in the Name of Socialism to Supporting Human Rights Dissidence: the Comité du 5 janvier

In the early 1970s the permanence of repression of dissidence in Eastern Europe and the significance of this repression for the Left's self-definition led to a multiplication of protest and the formation of durable committees staffed by left-wing intellectuals and militants devoted exclusively to action on behalf of dissidents. These included, for example, the Comité international contre la répression, the Comité contre les hôpitaux psychiatriques spéciaux en URSS, the Comité pour la défense des libertés dans les pays se réclamant du socialisme, the Comité pour la libération des enfantsotages tchécoslovaques, the Comité pour la libération immédiate des emprisonnés politiques dans les pays de l'Europe de l'Est, the Comité du 5 janvier pour une Tchécoslovaquie libre et socialiste, and the Comité international des mathématiciens. The following pages examine the latter two initiatives.

The Comité du 5 janvier was a sustained effort that mobilized a substantial number of militants and numerous intellectuals to give practical aid to victims of the Czechoslovak "normalization" and rally French opinion in their favor—all in the interest of reconciling socialism and freedom. The history of the Comité du 5 janvier demonstrates that the attempt to reconcile socialism and freedom did not prevent French intellectuals from speaking up against normalization; on the contrary, it provided them a powerful motivation to do so. French intellectuals did not wait until the appearance of human rights dissidence in the form of Charter 77 to speak and act against repression in Czechoslovakia. Furthermore, the Comité du 5 janvier's later mobilization in defense of Charter 77 and human rights dissidence followed seamlessly from the committee's support of the Czechoslovak revisionist opposition victimized by normalization earlier in the 1970s.

The Comité du 5 janvier, founded in January 1970, plainly identified with Prague Spring and abhorred its repression by the Warsaw Pact invasion of August 1968 and the subsequent normalization of Czechoslovakia. It was named after 5 January 1968, the day that Alexander Dubček replaced Antonín Novotný as the First Secretary of the Communist Party of Czechoslovakia, inaugurating Prague Spring. The committee declared in its first bulletin that Prague Spring had demonstrated "for the first time … that there was no contradiction between liberty and justice, that constraint was not the necessary price of equality." But after August 1968 this new socialism "was submerged by a more powerful obsolete, archaic socialism" and now socialism itself "is sick from Czechoslovakia and will be truly cured only when the mute Czechoslovak people are allowed to speak up." They hoped that their protest would contribute to this outcome and help "fend off the executioner."[17]

The committee's "Déclaration du 5 janvier 1970," signed by committee members and effectively constituting the committee's statement of purpose and belief, specified the relationship between the committee's actions and the effort to forge a free and democratic socialism in France. The statement explicitly renewed their condemnation of the armed intervention of August 1968. While judging the "disapproval" of the invasion by "an important part of the communist movement"[18] to be "a positive act," it declared that "to save over the long term in the consciousness of the workers the hope that they may place in the coming of a truly socialist society, this disapproval, for fear of appearing as an inconsequential and platonic gesture for the use of the other parties of the Left and public opinion, must be prolonged by the condemnation in our country of a so-called 'normalization.'" Consequently, the declaration denounced "the current efforts tending to hide, minimize, or have forgotten in France the effects of the military intervention against socialist Czechoslovakia" and reaffirmed the signatories' "solidarity with those who are trying to create a socialist society in which power is transferred from the hands of the bureaucrats to those of the workers." The committee would "make known in France the truth on Czechoslovakia and notably the content of the declarations of the leaders deposed by order of the occupying power and currently prevented from publicly presenting their defense."[19] For Roger Garaudy, recently excluded from the PCF for his position on normalization, it would be "playing the game of all the anticommunists to support normalization with our silence."[20] In a word, where the PCF failed to speak and act against normalization and thereby discredited communism, the Comité du 5 janvier would not.

Later declarations made even more explicit the Comité du 5 janvier's close linkage of the defense of the victims of repression in Czechoslovakia and the battle for a socialism reconciled with liberty in France. As the committee stated in January 1973, "this battle [against repression in Czechoslovakia] … is not only one of solidarity, but also concerns our own future."[21] In a *Le Monde* advertisement of the same month the committee asked people to join their effort "if for you socialism is inconceivable without liberty."[22] Later that year the committee specified that "one can not be a partisan of a true, democratic and *autogestionnaire* socialism for France and be silent on the caricature of socialism that is offered us by the transformation of the Czechoslovak popular democracy into a protectorate of the USSR. One can not demand liberty for the victims of repression in the imperialist countries and forget the militants of 'Prague Spring.'"[23]

The first signatories to the Comité du 5 janvier's "appeal" were mostly current and former members of the PCF who were evidently dissatisfied with the party's failure to follow up on its initial "disapproval" of the invasion with a vigorous condemnation of normalization, but the committee consciously sought to expand its membership beyond these circles. It called upon others to join and sent out letters to a wide variety of socialist and revolutionary Marxist organizations because, it said, the fate of Czechoslovakia concerns "all socialists, all revolutionaries."[24] The committee was, it emphasized in its November 1970 bulletin, not "a movement of internal—or even external—opposition to the PCF" and was "open to everyone in the sole goal of making it possible for the Czechoslovak people to speak up."[25] The Comité du 5 janvier's Mutualité meeting against normalization of late November 1970, presided over by Charles Tillon, was correspondingly supported by many diverse organizations, including the Ligue communiste and the PSU.[26]

The Comité du 5 janvier's most significant effort to broaden its appeal was its campaign against repression in 1972. In December 1971 and January 1972 the most important Czechoslovakian opposition group, the Socialist Movement of Czechoslovak Citizens, was decapitated when its leaders—mostly ex-communists who had played a prominent role in Prague Spring and remained attached to the project of constructing a Socialism with a Human Face—were arrested.[27] The Comité du 5 janvier launched an "Appel pour les victimes de la répression en Tchécoslovaquie" in their support. Evidently more ecumenical in its language than the "Déclaration du 5 janvier 1970," it read:

> Will revolutionary fidelity and national pride once again—as in the era of "l'Aveu"[28]—be considered criminal in Prague and Bratislava?
>
> Men and women are suspected, watched, hounded, imprisoned, and thrown into solitary confinement in state prisons because they symbolize the hope of a people who, despite the rigors of the occupation and of the police, do not agree to renounce them.

A few among us have met some of these men and women and know them well. We admire them for having decided three years ago to continue the battle for socialism shoulder to shoulder with their people and for having preferred this risk to the solitude of exile.

If you assist our efforts, we will not allow them to be either discredited or broken.

To shield their honor and their lives from the persecutions that menace and strike them we refuse to allow them to be caught in the trap of silence, of our silence.

Must one—on the pretext of not providing fodder to any campaign[29]—accept to be silent? Some will undoubtedly think so. But many others will say with us that their liberty and, in part, their ideal depends on our openly expressed solidarity.

We, who sign and will sign this Appeal by the thousands, will, notably by means of these communiqués, contribute to forbidding silence on the fate of the victims of repression and will place them under the only protection that remains for them: ours.[30]

The *appel* was a success. By the end of May 1972—that is, even before the trials of the Czechoslovak opposition in the summer of 1972—it had 1,083 signatories and by the end of January 1973, some 2,730.[31] The signatories included a large number of prominent French cultural, intellectual, and political figures.[32] Among them were the three founders of the Groupe d'information sur les prisons (Michel Foucault, Jean-Marie Domenach, and Pierre Vidal-Naquet) and other intellectuals associated with Gauche prolétarienne initiatives (Maurice Clavel, Vladimir Jankélévitch, and Joris Ivens); representative intellectuals from *Les Temps modernes* (Jean-Paul Sartre, Simone de Beauvoir, Michel Leiris, Gisèle Halimi, and André Gorz), *Esprit* (Jacques Julliard, Jean Cassou, and Domenach), and the literary avant-garde (Julia Kristeva and Philippe Sollers from *Tel quel* and Jean-Pierre Faye from *Change*); prominent Marxist revisionists and post-Marxists (Henri Lefebvre, Edgar Morin, and Pierre Naville); intellectuals who had left the PCF in the 1950s (Marguerite Duras, Claude Roy, Maurice Agulhon, and Jacques Ozouf, in addition to Lefebvre and Morin) and others who had left more recently (Roger Garaudy, Paul Noiret, Madeleine Rebérioux, Victor Leduc, Jean-Pierre Vernant, and Charles Tillon); prominent socialists (Daniel Mayer and Jules Moch), anarchists (Daniel Guérin), and Trotskyists (Alain Krivine and Naville); prominent fellow travelers of the late 1940s and early 1950s (Claude Aveline and Louis de Villefosse); two founders of the neutralist *L'Observateur* of the early 1950s (Claude Bourdet and Gilles Martinet); leaders of the intellectual mobilization against torture during the Algerian War (Laurent Schwartz and Vidal-Naquet); and many others. In short, prominent representatives of most of the trajectories and tendencies within what then composed the noncommunist intellectual Left signed the *appel*.

This was, of course, an appeal in favor of socialism and against the repression of socialists. And although many of the signatories would probably have been willing to sign a blanket condemnation of human rights abuses under communism, some saw their action more narrowly in terms of the socialist project. *Tel quel*, reflecting on its support for the Czechoslovak opposition, commented in 1974: "is it a matter of demanding 'abstract liberties'? The question before us is simple: what is more favorable to socialism? *Progressiste* demands or the revisionist police dictatorship? Obviously the former." Thinking of liberties exclusively in terms of socialism might have considerably restricted the defense of liberty, but in the mid 1970s the insistent posing of the question of liberties in relation to the Union of the Left forced, as will be demonstrated below, an extension of the defense of liberty rather than its retraction.[33]

The *appel* was followed by a "meeting of solidarity" with the victims of repression in Czechoslovakia and in support of a *Jury international contre les nouveaux procès de Prague* held at the Mutualité in Paris on 26 October 1972. Organized by the Comité de 5 janvier, the meeting received support from much of the French Left outside of the PCF and Confédération générale du travail (CGT) and featured speakers such as Jirí Pelikán (the director of Czechoslovak television during Prague Spring who had emigrated to Rome, where he published the émigré socialist opposition journal *Listy*), Jan Sling (the son of a communist leader executed in 1952), and Valerio Ochetto (an Italian journalist who had been imprisoned for thirty-seven days in Prague earlier in 1972).[34] Although denounced by the PCF for taking "quite naturally its place in the current anti-Soviet and anti-communist campaign of power,"[35] the meeting was by all accounts a success. According to Geneviève Deroin's analysis for the committee the meeting was a "great attendance success"; a subscription and contributions at the door covered all expenses and additionally financed the printing of a brochure on the meeting. The "meeting of solidarity" evidently created a dynamic favorable to further activity. At a follow-up gathering of 10 November the Comité de 5 janvier decided to undertake a number of activities during the upcoming months, including a campaign to provide each child of the Czechoslovak political prisoners a gift expressing the solidarity of France, a press conference to introduce *Ici Prague* (a collection of documents by the Czechoslovak socialist opposition published in 1973 at Éditions du Seuil), and a series of provincial screenings of the film "L'Aveu" that were to be followed by debates with the audience.[36]

Over the course of the early 1970s the Comité du 5 janvier devoted considerable energy to publicizing the plight of the opposition in Czechoslovakia and extending substantial material and moral support to it. Besides sending toys to the children of the imprisoned, it sent money to their families on two occasions in 1972.[37] Some 9,500 postcards were sent to Dubček in August 1972 in a show of solidarity with him.[38] Interventions in favor of the release of political prisoners were made at the Soviet and Czechoslovak embassies in December 1974.[39] Numerous meetings were held in support of the victims of repression and to attract attention to their cause, advertisements were regularly placed in *Le Monde* to the same effect, and many of the key documents of the Czechoslovak socialist opposition were reproduced and distributed by the committee.[40] These and later efforts did not go unnoticed in Czechoslovakia. *Tribuna*, the Czechoslovak Communist Party weekly, attacked the Comité du 5 janvier as a "neo-Trotskyist organization ... of an anti-Czechoslovak spirit." When Zdenek Mlynár, a prominent oppositional ex-communist, emigrated from Czechoslovakia he wrote the Comité du 5 janvier to thank it expressly for the "moral, political, and financial assistance" that it had given the Czechoslovak opposition.[41]

As the committee broadened its perspectives and widened the scope of its activities in the course of the 1970s, it evolved along with the main currents of dissent in Czechoslovakia and in accordance with its desire to reconcile socialism and liberty. In its initial support for Prague Spring and its leaders against "normalization," the Comité du 5 janvier was defending the then dominant opposition to the régime. But in defending oppositional communists it was also, it emphasized, fighting for "Christians and other democrats of all colors" and preparing "the way for democratic socialism in our country."[42] Although it had long recognized the need to defend liberty everywhere, in the summer of 1975 the committee decided to work with other groups to this end.[43] Committed, it said, to defending pluralism within the socialist movement and the rights of creation, assembly, and expression for everyone, the Comité du 5 janvier supported the Comité international des mathématiciens' campaigns of 1975 and 1976.[44]

The evolution away from the committee's earlier exclusive concentration on the defense of Prague Spring and Marxist revisionism, already visible in 1975 and 1976, emerged more clearly in its support for Charter 77. Its engagement in favor of Charter 77 was certainly eased by the Czechoslovak ex-communist opposition's important role in the emergence of the Charter and its appeals for support from the West European Left.[45] Prominent ex-communists[46] like Jirí Hájek and Zdenek Mlynár were among the first to demand that the Czechoslovak state respect international human rights agreements, and reform communists participated to some degree in the elaboration of the Charter 77 document.[47] Over half, about 150, of the first 243 initial signatories to the Charter were "reform communists of various hues,"[48] and one of the first three spokesmen for the Charter was a reform communist (Jirí Hájek). Although some noncommunist Chartists were suspicious of them, reform communists were an integral part of the Charter movement and participated in the general consensus on the basic orientation of Charter 77: concentration on the questions of legality and human rights rather than oppositional political activity, political programs, and formal organization. The repression of 1971 and 1972 had taught the ex-communists the impossibility of forming a structured opposition and the importance of assuring basic human rights.[49] Charter 77 was, in its origins, as much the product of their experience as anything else.

No doubt partially as a consequence of this evolution of the Czechoslovak ex-communist opposition, the Comité du 5 janvier was quick to pick up on the new focus on human rights in Czechoslovakia. It publicized an appeal of the last quarter of 1975 by Czechoslovak ex-communists to "European democrats," calling upon them to work to ensure that the Helsinki Accords were respected in Czechoslovakia, and it simultaneously protested the violation of human rights in the case of noncommunist Czechoslovak students refused visas and foreign exchange that they needed to travel to countries beyond the iron curtain. In 1977 it fully supported Charter 77 in the spirit of the Chartists. Come the October 1977 conviction of Chartists, it defended noncommunists like Vaclav Havel. The petition that the committee sent to Czechoslovak President Husák on this occasion focused its protest on the violation of human rights without even mentioning socialism. The Comité du 5 janvier also diffused "Le Testament de Jan Pantocka," one of the first three spokesmen of the Charter, despite the fact that he had never been a Marxist or communist and was not known to be political. [50] The Comité du 5 janvier's positions of 1977 were reflected in the changing composition of its leadership. Oppositional communists no longer dominated it as in 1970. As of 27 October 1977 its president was Claude Bourdet.[51]

The Comité du 5 janvier's shift from protests for liberty and socialism to protests that focused primarily on human rights was, like that in Czechoslovakia, a gradual one. The Comité du 5 janvier had, like many Czechoslovak ex-communists, arrived at support for the Charter through a trajectory that had begun with an identification with Prague Spring. Seven of the ten French members of the Comité international de soutien à la Charte—incorrectly identified by Pierre Grémion as a break with the past in French intellectuals' relationship with East European dissidence—had signed the Comité du 5 janvier's "Appel pour les victimes de la répression en Tchécoslovaquie" of 1972 or were otherwise involved with the Comité du 5 janvier.[52] Well before 1977 French intellectuals had established a tradition of protest against repression under communism in the name of defending human rights within the socialist project. Because their demands for liberty only increased over time, it was not difficult for them to switch to defending human rights in themselves. Key to this evolution is the place that dissidence took in the politics of the Union of the Left.

Protest in the Shadow of the Union of the Left: The Comité international des mathématiciens

The link in the second half of the 1970s between the rising prominence of East European dissidence for the French intellectual Left and the struggle over the Union of the Left emerges clearly in the campaigns led by the Comité international des mathématiciens to liberate first Leonid Plyushch and then Vladimir Bukovski and other victims of repression. These campaigns of 1975 and 1976 forged a strong link between French political concerns and East European dissidence and made it possible for human rights dissidence to emerge as a central theme in French intellectual politics in 1977. They show how the concern to secure liberty in the face of growing fear of the PCF's potential threat to it led intellectuals to adopt a more demanding position on the question of liberties and eventually divorce it from the socialist project.

Leonid Plyushch, born in 1939, was a mathematician at the Institute of Cybernetics of the Ukrainian Academy of Sciences in 1968, when his life as a dissident began. That year Plyushch's protest of the January 1968 trial of the dissidents Alexander Ginzburg and Iuri Galanskov cost him his job. Cast out of his profession, Plyushch became further involved in dissident activities in the following years. While maintaining his Marxist convictions, Plyushch was a founding member and active participant in one of the first human rights efforts by Soviet dissidents, the Initiative Group for the Defense of Human Rights, until his arrest in January 1972 for "anti-Soviet agitation and propaganda." In January 1973 Plyushch was tried and condemned for his actions, but judged to be a schizophrenic and therefore not held responsible for them. In July 1973 he was admitted to the psychiatric hospital at Dnepropetrovsk, where he was subject to a repressive application of psychiatric medications.[53]

French mathematicians organized in support of Plyushch and Yuri Chikanovitch, another Soviet mathematician, in the winter of 1973-74. An appeal of December 1973 for the liberation of Chikhanovitch signed by more than five hundred French mathematicians and addressed to "all those who are attached to democratic liberties" was followed by the formation of a Comité international des mathématiciens pour la défense de I. Chikanovitch et L. Pliouchtch in January 1974.[54] The Comité international des mathématiciens' members engaged in all the usual activities of committees against repression. For example, they held press conferences and issued press releases informing the public of the condition of their charges, wrote newspaper articles, launched an *appel* addressed "to jurists and psychiatrists," asked Mitterrand and Jacques Chirac to intervene when they went to Moscow, sent a delegation with an appeal in hand to the Soviet embassy, telegraphed Brezhnev and Kosygin, and organized a "Journée internationale L. Pliouchtch."[55] The French committee's activities were sustained by the release of Chikanovitch on 5 July 1974, appeals in favor of Plyushch by other Soviet dissidents, the solidarity of the international mathematics community at its August-September 1974 conference in Vancouver, and the organizational experience and skills of the mathematician Laurent Schwartz.

Schwartz had been a leading figure in the politics of petitions and protests since the Algerian War, second only to Jean-Paul Sartre as the most frequent signatory to petitions in the period from 1958 until Sartre's death in 1980. A brilliant mathematician, Schwartz was also a man of the Left. He had been a Trotskyist from 1936 to 1947 and a leading member of the PSU at its founding. As the thesis director of Maurice Audin, a communist militant and mathematician tortured and killed by the French police in Algeria in 1957, Schwartz was at the forefront of the efforts of the famous Comité Audin against the Algerian War. In 1966 Schwartz took a leading role in the mobilization against the American war in Vietnam, participating in the Russell Tribunal and the Comité Vietnam national. He organized interventions in favor of Soviet dissidence at least as early as 1968.[56]

As a man of the Left, Schwartz was not indifferent to the problems posed by the Union of the Left. He undoubtedly hoped that the mobilization in favor of Plyushch would not only contribute to his liberation, but also encourage the PCF to loosen its connections to the USSR and firmly commit itself to the defense of liberties under socialism. The choice of Plyushch was perfect for such a maneuver. It would be difficult for the PCF to refuse its solidarity with this Marxist, whose only crime was to speak out against violations of Soviet law and human rights. He was, according to the title of Schwartz's 21 April 1975 *Le Nouvel Observateur* article, "Un 'fou' exemplaire" (an exemplary "madman").[57]

The high point of the French campaign for Leonid Plyushch and its use in French politics was the meeting for the liberation of Plyushch of 23 October 1975 in the Mutualité. The flier announcing the meeting made the two points essential to the domestic debate: that Plyushch was a Marxist and that "liberty is to be defended everywhere." The meeting was supported by human rights organizations, other committees against repression, prominent left-wing personalities, and the major forces of the Left with the exception of the PCF and CGT.[58] *Le Nouvel Observateur*, which had twice already favorably reported on the efforts of the Comité international des mathématiciens,[59] directly calling upon its readers to attend, while making clear to them the significance of the issue for the Left. The communist "national leader" of the Syndicat national de l'enseignement supérieur, "in which the PCF current has a large majority," had, *Le Nouvel Observateur* added, supported the meeting and the liberation of Plyushch. His position and those taken by the noncommunist Left were, the weekly further remarked, "among those that really advance the unitary battle for liberty, and we would congratulate ourselves on it if the case of Plyushch were not so tragic."[60]

The meeting was a success in all respects: in terms of attendance, its domestic political repercussions, and perhaps even its impact on Plyushch's fate. According to Marco Carynnyk, the editor and translator of the English-language edition of Plyushch's autobiography, with 5,000 people in attendance it was "the largest rally ever sponsored for a Soviet prisoner of conscience."[61] Someone arriving late to the meeting would have found that the only empty seats were those evoked by Louis Astre, secretary of the Fédération de l'éducation nationale, when speaking of the absence of the PCF and the CGT at the meeting. The "empty seats" of the communists were a favorite theme at the meeting, especially because the rally in favor of Plyushch was, by what Astre held to be an "unfortunate coincidence," on the same evening as an important PCF "rally for liberties" attended by several tens of thousands of people at the Porte de Versailles's Parc des Expositions. At the podium in the Mutualité, Roger Pannequin, representing the Comité du 5 janvier, explicitly repudiated the anticipated PCF claim that their meeting was anti-Soviet in nature and challenged "our communist comrades" to "demand with us liberty for Leonid Plyushch" on "these days [that] one has you speak so much about liberty." Jean-Jacques Marie from the Comité pour la libération immédiate des emprisonnés politiques en Europe de l'Est called for the unity of all democrats and worker organizations to save Plyushch and "all the victims of a repression that is the very contrary of socialism." Vercors emphasized that it was necessary to protest not only to assure Plyushch's liberty, but also to assure the victory of socialism, and Claude Roy maintained that denouncing the treatment inflicted on Plyushch "does not make one an enemy of a régime of people's Soviets. It ... makes one a revolutionary or liberal democrat, enemy in any case of despotism and of the pseudo-psychiatry of the police state." Finally, Dominique Taddéï, the representative of the PS,[62] laid down the political law. On the one hand, he emphasized that "we do not accept in this battle" those who failed to fight for human rights in Chili, South Africa, or Spain. On the other hand, he questioned those who fought these other battles but had not yet engaged in favor of Plyushch: "do they not see that [their silence on Plyushch] muffles their cries in these other dramatic circumstances?" Presiding over the meeting, Laurent Schwartz said that he would submit the Plyushch dossier to Marchais in hope of gaining the PCF's adhesion to the cause. Ending with the singing of the "International," the rally for Plyushch had served its domestic political purposes well, exposing and critiquing the PCF's position while not excluding the hope for a reconciliation—on the PS's terms of course—of the quarreling parties within the Union of the Left. *Le Nouvel Observateur* celebrated the occasion by publishing the text of Claude Roy's speech at the meeting. *Libération* gave its interpretation in a cartoon that it published next to Christian Jelen's article on the event. It featured an ogre-like figure representing the PCF counting ballots and exclaiming: "Now is not the time to give myself a pain in the ass over Plyushch. I am recounting the vote."[63]

Contrary to *Libération*'s understanding of the impact of electoralism, the PCF did not let the questioning of its commitment to liberties go unanswered precisely because it was concerned about its image with the voting public. In *L'Humanité* of 25 October René Andrieu wrote that it was not indifferent to the case of Plyushch and had been trying to obtain information about it for some time. Moreover, he added that "if it is true—and unfortunately the contrary has yet to be proven—that this mathematician is interned in a psychiatric hospital solely because he took a stand against certain aspects of Soviet politics or against the régime itself, we can only confirm our total disapproval and demand that he be liberated as rapidly as possible." Entitled "De grâce! Pas de leçon!" (For God's sake! No Lesson!) Andrieu's article claimed that the PCF had never been given an invitation to the meeting and ended with a review of the SFIO's less than stellar record on liberties and human rights during the Algerian War. A few days later Marchais publicly supported Andrieu's position and added that they had asked the USSR for an explanation. The hoped-for reconciliation of the Left followed soon thereafter. A delegation of the Comité international des mathématiciens met with Pierre Juquin, a member of the PCF's central committee, on 14 November. On the same day Tatyana Plyushch, the wife of Leonid, revealed to the Western press in Moscow her letter to Georges Marchais, in which she thanked the PCF for its interest in her husband's case and urged it to take further action. On 8 January 1976 Leonid Plyushch left the psychiatric hospital in Dnepropetrovsk, and on 11 January he and his family arrived in Paris.[64]

The PCF's position on the Plyushch affair was only one of a series of important developments within French communism in the period between the 23 October Mutualité meeting and the liberation of Plyushch. On 11 December excerpts of a clandestinely made film of a contemporary work camp in the USSR were shown on French television. The next day the PCF's *Bureau politique* declared that "if reality corresponds to the images that were diffused and if it is not publicly refuted by the Soviets, it will express its profound surprise and its most definite disapproval."[65] When *Pravda* denounced the film as a fabrication and reprimanded the PCF for its failure to defend the USSR, the PCF did not back down. While defending its willingness to combat anti-Sovietism, the PCF responded that the struggle against anti-Sovietism could "neither serve to mask nor to justify the errors and the mistakes that can be committed and are used by the adversaries of socialism." This was a spectacular shift from the PCF's position on anti-Sovietism in the early 1970s, notably during the Solzhenitsyn affair of 1974. It was confirmed in early January when Marchais pronounced: "If the camps did not exist we would not have published the communiqué of the *Bureau politique*. The French Communist Party did not wait for the position of anyone to give its opinion on this question. We gave it, and nothing invalidates our position." A few days thereafter, Marchais announced on French television to the surprise of everyone that the PCF would abandon the concept of the dictatorship of the proletariat at its twenty-second congress in early February. The PCF was in the midst of a precipitous Eurocommunist evolution intended to neutralize doubts about its position on liberties that hindered its progress in electoral politics.[66]

The PCF's new positions on the question of liberties and repression in the USSR were a cause for celebration for the noncommunist intellectual

Left. For Jean Daniel, the affair of the *"'fou' exemplaire"* had ended in "an exemplary liberation." This liberation, which "no right-wing exploitation and no stain tarnished," had been the result of a campaign undertaken exclusively by "men of the Left ... who are not turned off of socialism by the internment of Plyushch." Further, it proved, contrary to Jean-François Revel, that the socialist's alliance with the PCF was not suicidal; they have been able "occasionally to shake the communists out of their certitudes."[67]

Libération and *Esprit* were somewhat less impressed by the PCF's evolution,[68] but the main point for them as well as *Le Nouvel Observateur* and presumably the rest of the noncommunist Left was that they had to continue challenging the PCF on these questions. *Esprit* announced that it would only become more demanding of the PCF as the 1978 legislative elections approached: "To the degree that by means of the Union of the Left its participation in the government becomes more plausible, arises more insistently the question of knowing to what the specificity of the communist consciousness and practice is attached and toward what it aims." The PCF's recent evolution was not sufficient. The PCF had to issue a "fundamental critique of the USSR" and "give itself a perspective other than that of constructing something here that already exists elsewhere." *Libération* highlighted the need to defend others against the repressive Soviet state. It called for more action to save the "other Plyushches." For Daniel as well, the liberation of Plyushch needed to be followed by new mobilizations against repression that would challenge the PCF.[69]

The uses of the Plyushch campaign in French politics did not end with his liberation. His first press conference was held on 3 February 1976, the day before the opening of the twenty-second congress of the PCF. Further, a letter that Plyushch had sent to Pierre Juquin asking the PCF to intervene on behalf of other dissidents was anonymously sent to the press on the same day as his press conference. Whether or not the date of Plyushch's press conference was a coincidence, the leaking of his letter was not. None of this, it should be noted, was Plyushch's doing; he specifically repudiated any effort to use his case in French politics. During his press conference he emphasized on several occasions his friendship with French communists and said that he considered the disclosure of his letter to Juquin to be "a provocation" by someone who wanted to "set me at odds with my communist friends." Plyushch added that "these methods recall to a great extent those of the KGB."[70]

Plyushch's usefulness in French politics was limited by precisely that which made him an attractive rallying point in 1975: his Marxism. In their reflections on the campaign to liberate Plyushch, Michel Broué, Henri Cartan, and Laurent Schwartz of the Comité international des mathématiciens recognized that Plyushch was able to become a symbol of the cause of victims of repression in the USSR for the entire French Left largely because he was a Marxist. His cause had functioned, they added, like that of Maurice Audin, the sole European to have "disappeared" in the Battle of Algiers and yet "a symbol of torture during the Algerian War." The campaign for Plyushch had brought down taboos, but the Comité international des mathématiciens wanted others, notably those of the PCF, to be overcome.[71] This battle within the Union of the Left would be furthered by the Comité international des mathématiciens' next campaign: that for the liberation of six political prisoners, three from Eastern Europe (Vladimir Bukovski, Semyon Gluzman, and Jirí Müller) and three from Latin America (José-Luis Massera, Victor Lopez Arias, and Edgardo Enriquez).[72]

As an effort to force the PCF's evolution or, failing that, force its hand on liberty, this campaign was well conceived. By indiscriminately lumping together victims of fascist and communist repression, the Comité international des mathématiciens, while ostensibly only reacting to the PCF's earlier criticism that they were interested only in critiquing injustices in the USSR, implied the equivalency of two repressions and the two régimes, fascist and communist.[73] Further, by pushing forward the case of an individual like Bukovski, the committee was breaking away from its earlier focus on Marxist dissent. This time the committee did not advertise the Marxism of its charges.

While not a Marxist, Bukovski—who turned out to be the focus of the campaign—was a major figure in Soviet dissent and victim of its repression. Born in 1942, Bukovski was arrested in 1963 for possessing two photocopies of Milovan Djilas's *The New Class*. Classified as mentally ill, he spent two years in psychiatric detention. Released in February 1965, he was arrested once again in December while participating in a demonstration in support of Daniel and Siniavski. Freed in August 1966, he was sent back to prison six months later for demonstrating in favor of the dissidents Alexander Ginzburg, Iury Galanskov, Andrei Dobrovolsky, and Vera Lashkova. After serving three more years in prison, he used his next period of freedom to compile his *Une nouvelle maladie mentale en U.R.S.S.: l'opposition*, an important exposé on psychiatric repression in the USSR, which cost him a sentence of two years of prison, five years of forced labor, and five years of exile—to be served consecutively. While incarcerated, Bukovski wrote with his fellow inmate Semyon Gluzman a "Guide de psychiatrie à l'usage des dissidents" dedicated to Plyushch. An indomitable opponent of repression in the USSR, by 1976 Bukovski had spent nearly one third of his life in prison.[74]

Could the PCF afford to refuse to lend its weight to the campaign in favor of Bukovski and the others? Probably not, if it wished to maintain the credibility of its commitment to liberties. When Plyushch arrived in France, *L'Humanité* had proudly reminded the readers of the positions taken by the PCF on his case, and Marchais had added that the communists "defend and will continue to defend liberty each time that it is necessary."[75] Furthermore, once Soviet citizens got word of the PCF's position on Plyushch, they began to send letters to Marchais—which they subsequently revealed to the Western press in Moscow—asking the PCF to intervene in this or that case. One of these letters asked Marchais to intervene in the cases of Vladimir Bukovski and Semyon Gluzman. It was from Nina Bukovski, Vladimir's mother![76]

Laurent Schwartz, announcing in *Le Nouvel Observateur* a Mutualité meeting of 21 October 1976 in favor of the six prisoners, would not allow the PCF to evade the issue. He bemoaned the failure of the PCF and the CGT to join their effort; there would, as in the previous year's rally for Plyushch, be "two 'empty seats' on the rostrum." Schwartz feigned not to understand why the communists took this position unless they, unlike the Comité international des mathématiciens, did not defend liberty "everywhere and without exception." Although René Duhamel, member of the *Secrétariat confédéral* of the CGT, refused to attend the meeting, saying that it was "scandalous to put the governments of socialist countries and those of the fascist countries of Latin America on the same level," the PCF's Pierre Juquin, on the other hand, accepted the invitation. Gaston Plissonnier, a member of the PCF's *Bureau politique*, explained why. Although, he said, the PCF had been placed "before a fait accompli" by the Comité international des mathématiciens and Schwartz had tried to tarnish the PCF's reputation on liberties, Juquin would rise above politics and lead a PCF delegation to the meeting because "a single thing matters to us: the battle for liberty."[77]

Although no representative of the CGT attended, the Mutualité meeting of 21 October was not marked by discussion of "empty seats." The focus of attention was Juquin. Indeed, one of the organizers complained to *Le Monde*'s reporter that whereas "the year before the audience had come to save Plyushch," this time they showed up "to see Juquin." Although Plyushch shook his hand, Juquin's presence was not universally appreciated. When he spoke he was, according to *Le Monde*, "baited by the audience, often cut off by hostile cries that alluded to his party's earlier positions." Still, although he refused to put the USSR and Chile on the same plane, Juquin said what was expected of him: that the PCF would not accept violations of human rights under socialism. For the PCF, Juquin's speech, minus the interruptions of course, was an event not to be forgotten; it was printed in six million copies.[78]

On 18 December 1976 Vladimir Bukovski and Luis Covalán, the general secretary of the Chilean Communist Party imprisoned by Pinochet, were exchanged on the tarmac of the Zurich airport like prisoners of war or characters in a Cold War spy novel. Pinochet had suggested the exchange of prisoners and, with the United States serving as an intermediary, the Soviet Union had agreed to it—perhaps because it wanted a foreign policy success for the celebration of Brezhnev's seventieth birthday. In the French context the event was astonishing. The implicit political agenda of the Comité international des mathématiciens was fulfilled, and by the Soviets themselves! Patrick Viveret, editor in chief of the journal *Faire*, said that the exchange "shows in a caricatured fashion that which can be in common between two totalitarian political systems."[79] Only two months earlier on the occasion of the Mutualité meeting Tass (the Soviet Union's official news agency) had attacked the PCF for putting a "common law criminal" like Bukovski on the same level as the "heroic victims of Chilean fascism." Now it was, René Duhamel complained, doing it itself.[80]

Duhamel's position notwithstanding, the PCF used the opportunity to consolidate its position on liberties. When "L'Aveu" was shown on French television on 14 December, *L'Humanité* had already called upon its readers to view the film and the discussion after it in which Jean Kanapa, Joseph Pasteur, Jirí Pelikán, Artur London, London's wife Lise, and Laurent Schwartz would participate. Marchais called the exchange of Bukovski and Covalán "lamentable," not for Duhamel's reasons, but because "we judge intolerable the haggling between a socialist and a fascist country over the fate of two men hounded for having exercised the inalienable human rights." Andrieu, writing in *L'Humanité*, declared that "the libera-tion of certain protesters one at a time under the pressure of international opinion does not suffice. The truth is that nobody in a socialist country should be deprived of freedom because of his opinions."[81]

Schwartz did not deny the progress made by the PCF. He wrote in a *Le Nouvel Observateur* article that "the Communist Party differentiates itself completely from the totally or partially Stalinist régimes to the East," but he demanded more. In the discussion of "L'Aveu" Schwartz had asked the PCF to give guarantees of its "new sentiments." Convinced that men like Kanapa were too compromised to carry out a complete "de-Stalin-ization" of the PCF, Schwartz now proclaimed that it could be accom-plished only after new men took over the party's leadership. Evidently, it would be nearly impossible for the PCF to satisfy men of the intellectual Left like Schwartz.[82]

Even more surprising than the Corvalán-Bukovski exchange was Bukovski himself. Ebullient and combative, Bukovski gave a press confer-ence on the day of his arrival that broke from ordinary press conference etiquette and dismantled the barrier between himself and his audience. Asked by a journalist what he wished Brezhnev on his seventieth birthday, Bukovski replied: "I wish for him to be exchanged for General Pinochet." Noting that he was not given a document attesting to his liberation from prison, Bukovski said that he considered himself to be "a political prisoner on vacation." Explaining that four hundred rubles had been taken from him in exchange for his current outfit of French origin (which Bukovski proved to be French by showing the audience the label), Bukovski joked, "I will not ask the Soviet government for the change." Bukovski's mordant humor was used in the service of a more explicit political critique two days later: asked on RTL how many political prisoners there were in the USSR, Bukovski replied, 250 million. Bukovski, unlike Plyushch, was no Marxist and had a pessimistic view of the West's relationship to the USSR that paralleled his total repudiation of the Soviet system. In his mind the

Helsinki Accords were no more than a "Soviet ruse" to provoke unilateral disarmament in the West and to hinder the West's intervention in Soviet domestic affairs.[83]

Libération was captivated by Bukovski. Even before he arrived in Geneva, it explained that "we would like to have been Bukovskis in the Soviet Union." He was an "old friend," a "rebel so close that a mysterious affection links us to him." By contrast, the Chileans and Soviets had shown by their "system of hostage taking" that states are nothing more than exceptionally powerful terrorist organizations. *Libération* was thrilled by Bukovski's claim that he was only interested in human rights. When Bukovski demanded action to help the prisoners of the Vladimir Prison, where he had been incarcerated, *Libération* headlined "Bukovski addresses you." Bukovski, *Libération* explained, challenged old political categories. He was not interested in power, philosophy, or ideology. He was a fighter whose struggle "brings into question power in its authoritarian and repressive logic." Bukovski dominated the front page of the *Libération* issues of 19, 20, 21, and 23 December. In these days *Libération* interviewed Bukovski's mother and then Bukovski himself, and even published a Christmas story by him. Through Bukovski, *Libération* decisively annexed Soviet dissidence to its anti-authoritarian late-*gauchiste* ideology. André Glucksmann was no less inspired by Bukovski. He dedicated his book *Les Maîtres penseurs* "to the madman who wants to exchange Brezhnev and Pinochet for each other."[84]

* * *

The campaigns led by the Comité international des mathématiciens gave a new resonance to dissidence in French politics. They showed how dissidence could be used to unambiguously commit the socialist Left to action against repression by communist régimes and, more impressively, force the PCF to denounce this repression and distance itself from the Soviet Union. Further, by separating the protest against repression in Eastern Europe from the socialist project, the Comité international des mathématiciens prepared the way for the politics of human rights advanced in 1977.

Rising anxieties about the Union of the Left in 1977 only increased the urgency of campaigns in favor of dissidence. As Laurent Schwartz and the directors of the major periodicals of the noncommunist Left argued in a June 1977 statement demanding that the Left rally behind Polish workers and their Polish intellectual and professional supporters in the Committee for the Defense of Workers (KOR): "It is our trial that is being prepared in Poland. And it is yours."[85] Following this logic, more committees against repression formed in 1977 to defend the latest victims in Eastern Europe, including: the Comité Borissov, the Groupe de soutien aux prisonniers de Vladimir, le Comité de soutien à la Charte, the Comité des physiciens pour la défense de Youri Orlov, and the Comité de défense d'Anatole Chtcharankski.

The campaigns of 1975 and 1976 and concern over the likely victory of the Union of the Left in 1978 led some intellectuals to adopt dissidence and the politics of human rights as a model for French intellectual politics. This identification with dissidence was encouraged by the post-*gauchiste* critique of power and the long-standing linkage of positions on repression and dissent in Eastern Europe and positions on the French socialist project.[86] Critiques of communist repression, previously used by intellectuals of the noncommunist Left to liberate the socialist project from the failures of "really existing socialism," were now used to assimilate the two. The French dissident intellectual of 1977 was, as we shall see in the next chapter, a dissident not vis-à-vis the unelected leaders of the Soviet Union, but vis-à-vis the possible future elected French Union of the Left government.

In conclusion, French intellectuals of the Left, eager to differentiate their socialist ideal from the often grim reality to the east, did not fail to protest repression under communism between 1956 and the late 1970s. To be sure, before the 1970s these protests did not mobilize large numbers or attract a great deal of attention and mostly focused on victims who were on the Left. But the low intensity of protest was probably less a measure of an unwillingness to speak out than of the minimal relevancy of protest to the most pressing political concerns until the Union of the Left brought the PCF out of its political isolation and close to the exercise of power. In any event, 1968 removed the last vestiges of legitimacy from the USSR and increased intellectuals' hostility to the PCF as they adopted an anti-authoritarian political culture. After the signature of the Common Program, noncommunist intellectuals did not hesitate to protest repression by communist régimes. On the contrary, the new political situation encouraged their protests, used as a weapon in the battles over the definition of the Left, and forced a direct confrontation with the issue of human rights. There was, in fact, little debate within the intellectual Left over using dissidence in French politics or supporting the emerging non- or anti-Marxist opposition in Eastern Europe. As a result of the battle over the Union of the Left, human rights dissidence gained a privileged place with the French intellectual Left.

Notes

1. *The Economist* 6990 (20 Aug. 1977), 54. Louis Althusser, "The Crisis of Marxism," trans. Grahame Lock, in *Power and Opposition in Post-Revolutionary Societies*, trans. Patrick Camiller and Jon Rothschild (London, 1979), 225-35.
2. Note this analysis refutes those of Tony Judt, who argues that intellectuals abandoned Eastern Europe after 1956 in favor of concentrating their energies on third-world revolutionary movements and only rediscovered Eastern European communism and its discontents once these extra-European political options had run their course, and of Pierre Grémion, who maintains that the Left was silent on the normalization of Czechoslovakia and discovered dissidence only in 1977. Tony Judt, *Past Imperfect: French Intellectuals, 1944-1956* (Berkeley, 1992), 284-85; Pierre Grémion, *Paris-Prague: la gauche face au renouveau et à la régression tchécoslovaques* (Paris, 1985), chap. 6 and passim.
3. The study of these collective actions by intellectuals has been opened up by Jean-François Sirinelli's *Intellectuels et passions françaises: manifestes et pétitions au xxe siècle* (Paris, 1990). Much of the recent research focuses, following Sirinelli's lead, on the sociability of the signatories to specific petitions. As a consequence, the diachronic perspective and the specifically political dimensions of the texts of petitions and protests have received less attention.
4. Paul Thibaud, interview with the author, Paris, 9 June 1994. For the Eastern European evolution see Vladimir Tismaneaunu, *The Crisis of Marxist Ideology in Eastern Europe: The Poverty of Utopia* (New York, 1988).
5. Sirinelli, *Intellectuels et passions françaises*, 311-12; Grémion, *L'Intelligence de l'anticommunisme*, 229.
6. Vercors, *P.P.C. ou le concours de Blois* (Paris, 1957), 119-20; *France observateur* 339 (8 Nov. 1956): 4, reproduced in Sirinelli, *Intellectuels et passions françaises*, 289-91. Further analysis of the politics of protest of the Hungarian Revolution can be found in the analysis of the Comité Tibor Déry in Michael Scott Christofferson, "The Antitotalitarian Moment in French Intellectual Politics, 1975-1984" (Ph.D. Diss., Columbia University, 1998), 297-313 and also in Michael Scott Christofferson, "French Intellectuals and the Repression of the Hungarian Revolution of 1956: The Politics of a Protest Reconsidered," in *After the Deluge: New Perspectives on French Intellectual and Cultural History*, ed. Julian Bourg (forthcoming).
7. For a succinct analysis of Soviet dissent's evolution through the 1970s see Marshall S. Shatz, *Soviet Dissent in Historical Perspective* (New York, 1980), chapters 5 and 6.
8. Ibid., chap. 5.
9. See the list, "Principales protestations hors d'U.R.S.S.," *Esprit* 357 (Feb. 1967): 277-85.
10. Republished in *Le Monde*, 17 Feb. 1966, 2.
11. Roy and Lefebvre cited in ibid.
12. *Le Monde*, 22 Feb. 1966, 3. At this time the members of the *Comité directeur* of the CNE included Arthur Adamov, Louis Aragon, George-Albert Astre, Jean-Louis Bory, Michel Butor, Georges Gozzy, Guillevic, Jacques Madaule, Albert Memmi, Robert Merle, Pierre Parraf, Wladimir Pozner, Alain Prévost, Jean Rousselot, Georges Sadoul, and Jean-Paul Sartre.
13. *Le Monde*, 27-28 March 1966, 5. It was signed by Jean-Louis Barrault, Jacques Brel, Danièle Delorme, Joris Ivens, Armand Lanoux, Michel Leiris, Yves Montand, Hélème Parmelin, Anne Philipe, Edouard Pignon, Jacques Prévert, Pierre Prévert, Madeleine Renaud, Yves Robert, Simone Signoret, Henri Spade, and Vercors.
14. This continuity was particularly evident in the case of Ginzburg, who had compiled a book on the Siniavski-Daniel trial.
15. *Le Monde*, 20 Jan. 1968, 4. The first signatories to the statement of protest were Robert Badinter, Abraham Behar, Jean Cassou, Jean Cerf, Claude Chevalley, Jean and Dominique Desanti, Jacques Tixier, Jean-Marie Domenach, André Frenaut, Roger Godement,

Francis Kahn, Alfred Kastler, Cyrille Koupernik, Daniel Lacombe, Jean-Paul Mathieu, Minkowski, Jacques Monod, Maurice Nadeau, Jacques Panigel, Perelman, Bernard Pingaud, Claude Roy, Georges and Fanny Shapira, Laurent Schwartz, Pierre Vidal-Naquet, and Robert Worms. Laurent Schwartz and Maurice Nadeau organized the protest.

16. *Le Monde*, 18 Nov. 1972, 5.
17. "Le Premier Mille," *Vérité tchécoslovaque. Bulletin du Comité du 5 janvier pour une Tchécoslovaquie libre et socialiste* 1 (July 1970): 2.
18. This is an explicit reference to the PCF Central Committee's 22 August 1968 resolution declaring that the PCF "disapproves" of the military intervention in Czechoslovakia. The *Bureau politique's* 21 August declaration was a bit stronger. It spoke of the party's "surprise" and "reprobation."
19. "Déclaration du 5 janvier 1970," in ibid., 7.
20. Garaudy's speech at the Comité du 5 janvier's November 1970 Mutualité meeting reported in *Le Monde*, 28 Nov. 1970, 11.
21. Letter of 25 Jan. 1973 in *Vérité tchécoslovaque. Bulletin du Comité du 5 janvier pour une Tchécoslovaquie libre et socialiste* 5 (Jan. 1973): 3.
22. *Le Monde*, 6 Jan. 1973, as reproduced in *Vérité tchécoslovaque. Bulletin du Comité du 5 janvier pour une Tchécoslovaquie libre et socialiste* 5 (Jan. 1973): 5.
23. Open letter announcing the inauguration of a "Campagne Sabata" in *Vérité tchécoslovaque. Bulletin du Comité du 5 janvier pour une Tchécoslovaquie libre et socialiste* 6 (1973): 2.
24. "Un appel ouvert à tous," in *Vérité tchécoslovaque. Bulletin du Comité du 5 janvier pour une Tchécoslovaquie libre et socialiste* 1 (July 1970): 14. One thousand had signed the *appel* by the middle of 1970, according to page 1 of this same bulletin.
25. *Vérité tchécoslovaque. Bulletin du Comité du 5 janvier pour une Tchécoslovaquie libre et socialiste* 2 (25 Nov. 1970): 13.
26. *Le Monde*, 28 Nov. 1970, 11.
27. Vladimir K. Kusin, *From Dubček to Charter 77: A Study of 'Normalization' in Czechoslovakia, 1968-1978* (New York, 1978), 156-68.
28. *L'Aveu* (*The Confession*) was Artur London's account of his experience as a defendant in the Czechoslovakian anti-Titoist purge trials of the early 1950s. Published in French in 1968, the book was made into a movie starring Yves Montand and Simone Signoret by Constantin Costa-Gavras in 1970.
29. This is a clear reference to the PCF's contemporary condemnation of efforts of this sort as anticommunist or anti-Soviet campaigns.
30. *Le Monde*, 28-29 May 1972, 7.
31. Idem. and *Vérité tchécoslovaque. Bulletin du Comité du 5 janvier pour une Tchécoslovaquie libre et socialiste* 5 (Jan. 1973): 2.
32. A list of the first 1,083 signatories is given in *Le Monde*, 28-29 May 1972, 7. A select list, which includes some additional signatures, is in *Le Monde*, 22-23 Oct. 1972. I draw on the analysis of the signatories of this petition in Rémy Rieffel, *La Tribu des clercs: les intellectuels sous la Ve République* (Paris, 1993), 177-78.
33. "Éditorial: Nouvelles Contradictions, nouvelles luttes," *Tel quel* 58 (summer 1974): 3. For the evolution of *Tel quel* on these questions see chapter 5 below.
34. Those present included the PS represented by Robert Pontillon (a member of the party's national secretariat who was in charge of international relations), Objectif socialiste represented by André Jeanson, the PSU represented by Michel Rocard, the Ligue communiste represented by Alain Krivine, the Centre d'initiative communiste (oppositional communists) represented by Victor Leduc, the Organisation communiste internationaliste (Lambertist Trotskyists), the Ligue des droits de l'homme, and the CFDT. *Vérité tchécoslovaque. Bulletin du Comité du 5 janvier pour une Tchécoslovaquie libre et socialiste* 5 (Jan. 1973): 2; *Le Monde*, 22-23 Oct. 1972, advertisement of the meeting; and *Le Monde*, 28 Oct. 1972, for the report on the meeting.
35. "A la mutualité: un meeting contre la répression en Tchécoslovaquie," *Le Monde*, 28 Oct. 1972, 5.

36. All according to the 27 Nov. 1972 letter of Geneviève Deroin to signers of the *appel* in the Bibliothèque de Documentation Internationale Contemporaine dossier on the Comité du 5 janvier, call number F Pièce 4063, item 1.
37. *Le Monde*, 6 Jan. 1973, 5.
38. Deroin letter.
39. Letter of 5 Dec. 1974 in the supplement to *Vérités tchécoslovaques. Bulletin d'information du Comité pour une Tchécoslovaquie libre et socialiste* 4 (April 1975).
40. Some of the more important documents published by the Comité du 5 janvier included the Sept. 1971 interview of Josef Smrkovsky with PCI central committee member David Lajolo, Anne Sabotova's 1972 letter to the communist and socialist parties of the world calling for the release of her husband and children from prison and the respect for democratic rights in Czechoslovakia, Alexander Dubček's letter of 18 Jan. 1974 on the occasion of Josef Smrkovsky's death, and Dubček's letter of 28 Oct. 1974 to the Czechoslovak Parliament.
41. *Vérités tchécoslovaques. Bulletin d'information du Comité pour une Tchécoslovaquie libre et socialiste* 5 (June-July 1975): 8. Item 15 (a photocopy of Mlynár's 26 June 1977 letter with a French translation) in the Bibliothèque de Documentation Internationale Contemporaine dossier on the Comité du 5 janvier, call number F Pièce 4063.
42. A 1973 *appel* for the liberation of Jaroslav Sabata in IMEC ESP2 E4-02 .06. Jean-Marie Domenach sent 50 francs from the "*Esprit* compte" to help the Comité du 5 janvier's "Campagne Sabata."
43. "Pour un accord général sur des propositions d'action commune est-ouest," *Vérités tchécoslovaques. Bulletin d'information du Comité pour une Tchécoslovaquie libre et socialiste* 5 (June-July 1975): 7.
44. See the discussion of these efforts below.
45. For example, on 16 Jan. 1977 Zdenek Mlynár asked West European governments, socialists, and communists to support the charter. H. Gordon Skilling, *Charter 77 and Human Rights in Czechoslovakia* (London, 1981), 101.
46. In the Czechoslovak context the denomination "ex-communist" refers to individuals who were expelled from the Czechoslovak Communist Party after 1968. They could (and in the case of Hájek and Mlynár did) remain revisionist communists committed to the reform program of Prague Spring.
47. Kusin, *From Dubček to Charter 77*, 294-95; Janusz Bugajski, *Czechoslovakia: Charter 77's Decade of Dissent*, vol. 125 of *The Washington Papers* (New York, 1987), 11.
48. Bugajski, *Czechoslovakia*, 29. The importance of reform communists within the Charter movement declined in the following years.
49. Kusin, *From Dubček to Charter 77*, 275-86.
50. See items 12 bis, 16, 17, 18, and 18 bis in the Bibliothèque de Documentation Internationale Contemporaine dossier on the *Comité du 5 janvier*, call number F Pièce 4063. On Jan Patocka see Skilling, *Charter 77 and Human Rights in Czechoslovakia*, 20-23.
51. The committee's letter of 27 Oct. 1977, item 18 bis in the Bibliothèque de Documentation Internationale Contemporaine dossier on the Comité du 5 janvier, call number F Pièce 4063.
52. Grémion, *Paris-Prague*, 315. The French members of the Comité international de soutien à la Charte were Pierre Daix, Jean-Marie Domenach, Pierre Emmanuel, Alfred Kastler, Yves Montand, Pierre Seghers, Simone Signoret, Vercors, Gilles Martinet, and Edmond Maire. Only Emmannuel, Kastler, and Seghers do not appear to have worked with the Comité du 5 janvier, but none of them had failed to protest repression under communism before 1977. Emmanuel, as president of the French PEN Club, had been particularly active.
53. On Plyushch's story see Yania Mathon and Jean-Jacques Marie, ed., comp., and trans., *L'Affaire Pliouchtch* (Paris, 1976) and Leonid Plyushch, with a contribution from Tatyana Plyushch, *History's Carnival: A Dissident's Autobiography*, ed. and trans. Marco Carynnyk (New York, 1979). A French edition of *History's Carnival* was published by Seuil in 1977.

54. See *Le Monde*, 12 Dec. 1973, 5 for the December *appel*. See also the evocation of the history of the Comité international des mathématiciens in Michel Broué, Henri Cartan, and Laurent Schwartz, "Préface," *L'Affaire Pliouchtch*, 5-16. Lipman Bers, an American mathematician, proposed the formation of this committee.

55. Activities reported in *Le Monde*, 2-3 Feb. 1974, 3; *Le Monde*, 16 Feb. 1974, 6; *Le Monde*, 27 March 1974, 38; *Le Monde*, 22 April 1974, 4; *Le Monde*, 25 April 1975, 4; *Le Monde*, 7-8 July 1974, 3; *Le Monde*, 6 Sept. 1974, 2; and in Broué, Cartan, and Schwartz, "Préface." See also Henri Cartan, "Il faut sauver Leonid Pliouchtch," *Le Monde*, 28 Dec. 1974, 3.

56. Rieffel, *La Tribu des clercs*, 166-67, 182-85. *Le Monde*, 20 Jan. 1968, 4.

57. Laurent Schwartz, "Un 'fou' exemplaire: Leonid Pliouchtch," *Le Nouvel Observateur* 545 (21 April 1975): 55.

58. For the *appel* with a list of groups and individuals supporting the meeting see *L'Affaire Pliouchtch*, 135-36. An original of the flier can be found in IMEC ESP2 .E5-02 .14.

59. Schwartz, "Un 'fou' exemplaire" and *Le Nouvel Observateur* 485 (18 Feb. 1974): 32.

60. P. L., "Pour la Libération de Leonid Pliouchtch," *Le Nouvel Observateur* 571 (20 Oct. 1975): 45.

61. Marco Carynnyk, "Marxist Metanoia," in *History's Carnival*, xii. Contemporary press accounts confirm that the Mutualité was overflowing: *Le Monde*, 25 Oct. 1975, 12; Christian Jelen, "Les Tabous meurent aussi," *Libération*, 25 Oct. 1975, 4.

62. The representation of the PS by Taddéï was itself significant. Taddéï was a PS expert on cultural affairs who tried to rally intellectuals to the PS. Pontillon, who had represented the PS at the 1972 Comité du 5 janvier meeting, was, by contrast, an expert on international relations. By substituting Taddéï for Pontillon the PS implicitly recognized that the meeting was more a matter of French politics than an international political affair. For Taddéï's role in PS relations with intellectuals see Rieffel, *La Tribu des clercs*, 147-50.

63. *Le Monde*, 25 Oct. 1975, 12; *Le Monde*, 26-27 Oct. 1975, 6; *L'Affaire Pliouchtch*, 141, 142, 145, 153, 155. Claude Roy, "U.R.S.S.: Psychiatres ou policiers?" *Le Nouvel Observateur* 572 (27 Oct. 1975): 46. *Libération*, 25 Oct. 1975, 4

64. See *Le Monde*, 26-27 Oct. 1975, 6 for Andrieu's article; *Le Monde*, 28 Oct. 1975, 9 for Marchais's comments; and *Le Monde*, 16-17 Nov. 1975, 4 for the meeting with Juquin. Tatyana Plyushch's letter is reproduced in *L'Affaire Plyushch*, 160-61. According to the Comité international des mathématiciens, it had not invited political parties as such, but had invited leading personalities from the PCF and other political parties.

65. The words "surprise" and "disapproval" were, it should be noted, the same as those used in the PCF *Bureau politique*'s 21 Aug. 1968 statement on the Soviet intervention in Czechoslovakia.

66. *Le Monde*, 14-15 Dec. 1975, 2; Philippe Robrieux, *(1972-1982)*, vol. 3 of *Histoire intérieure du Parti communiste* (Paris, 1982), 251; *Le Monde*, 6 Jan. 1976, 5.

67. Jean Daniel, "Une libération exemplaire," *Le Nouvel Observateur* 584 (19 Jan. 1976): 16. See also Jean Daniel, "Pliouchtch parmi nous," *Le Nouvel Observateur* 588 (16 Feb. 1976): 16 and K. S. Karol, "Pliouchtch l'optimiste," *Le Nouvel Observateur* 587 (9 Feb. 1976): 27.

68. See, for example, Thierry Wolton, "Le PCF face aux barbelés," *Libération*, 20 Dec. 1975, 1, 3; Pierre Michelbach, "De Grâce! Pas de Leçon!" *Esprit* 452 (Dec. 1975): 857-60; and the introductory editorial piece to *Esprit* 454 (Feb. 1976): 237-40.

69. *Esprit* 454 (Feb. 1976): 237; *Libération*, 3 Feb. 1976, 1, 4-5; *Libération*, 4 Feb. 1976, 12; and Daniel, "Une Libération exemplaire."

70. *Le Monde*, 13 Jan. 1976, 4 and *Le Monde*, 4 Feb. 1976, 1-3.

71. Michel Broué, Henri Cartan, and Laurent Schwartz, "Préface," *L'Affaire Pliouchtch*, 15-16. This statement was written immediately upon Plyushch's liberation. The book was already published by the time of Plyushch's press conference, according to *Le Monde*, 4 Feb. 1976, 1. *L'Affaire Pliouchtch* was, like many important documents on East European dissidence, published in Claude Durand's collection *Combats* at Seuil.

72. Massera was the leader of the Uruguayan Communist Party and a well-known mathematician. Lopez Arias was a union leader of Bolivian miners. Enriquez was the leader

of the Chilean MIR (Movement of the Revolutionary Left). Gluzman was a psychiatrist and personal friend of Plyushch who had gotten on the wrong side of the Soviet authorities for distributing Samizdat and, above all, for arguing that General Grigorenko was not in need of psychiatric treatment. Jirí Müller was the head of the Czechoslovak student union during Prague Spring. He was condemned for his oppositional activities to a prison term of five and a half years in 1972. See the following pages for information on Bukovski. I have taken the thumbnail sketches of these individuals from the flier announcing the 21 Oct. 1976 Mutualité meeting for their liberation. For the flier see item 8 in the Bibliothèque de Documentation Internationale Contemporaine dossier on the Comité du 5 janvier, call number F Pièce 4063.

73. Thierry Pfister, *Le Monde*, 16 Oct. 1976, 3. Unlike my presentation, the flier announcing the 21 Oct. 1976 Mutualité meeting did not list the six prisoners in any particular order.
74. I base my portrait of Bukovski on the article "Un cas exemplaire: Vladimir Boukovski," *Libération*, 3 Feb. 1976, 4 and that in *Le Monde*, 19-20 Dec. 1976, 3. A French translation of Bukovski's *Une nouvelle maladie mentale en U.R.S.S.: l'opposition* was published by Seuil in 1971. *Esprit* 405 (July-Aug. 1971) is devoted to this and other problems of repression in the USSR.
75. *Le Monde*, 13 Jan. 1976, 4.
76. The text of the letter, given to the Western press in Moscow on 6 Jan. 1976, can be found in *Le Monde*, 8 Jan. 1976, 3. Other letters reported in the French press asking the PCF for support include those from Alexandre Luntz, *Le Monde*, 23 Jan. 1976, 2; Benjamin Levitch, *Le Monde*, 4 Feb. 1976, 4; and Vira Lisova, *Le Quotidien de Paris*, 24 Dec. 1975.
77. Laurent Schwartz, "Pour libérer Boukovski, Enriquez, Glouzman, Lopez, Massera, Müller," *Le Nouvel Observateur* 621 (4 Oct. 1976): 51. Thierry Pfister, *Le Monde*, 16 Oct. 1976, 3.
78. *Le Monde*, 23 Oct. 1976, 5; T.P., *Le Monde*, 21 Dec. 1976, 2. *Lutte ouvrière*, 8 Nov. 1976.
79. Patrick Viveret, "Éditorial," *Faire* 15 (Jan. 1977): 2.
80. Jacques Amalric, *Le Monde*, 19-20 Dec. 1976, 3; *Le Monde*, 22 Dec. 1974, 4.
81. *Le Monde*, 19-20 Dec. 1976, 1, 3; *Le Monde*, 21 Dec. 1976, 2, quoting Andrieu's 20 Dec. *L'Humanité* article.
82. Laurent Schwartz, "Aux tâches nouvelles, équipes nouvelles," *Le Nouvel Observateur* 633 (27 Dec. 1976): 24-25, citation page 24. For Schwartz's comments on television see Maurice Clavel, "'Happy end' pour un cauchemar …," *Le Nouvel Observateur* 632 (20 Dec. 1976): 68.
83. *Le Monde*, 21 Dec. 1976, 1, 2; *Libération*, 20 Dec. 1976, 1, 8. For Luis Corvalán's very different viewpoint see his interview with Philippe Ganier-Raymond, *Le Nouvel Observateur* 640 (14 Feb. 1977): 62-78.
84. For the citations see *Libération*, 19 Dec. 1976, 1, 8-9; "L'Idéologie? Un luxe," *Libération*, 23 Dec. 1976, 8; and André Glucksmann, *Les Maîtres penseurs* (Paris, 1977), dedications page.
85. "A toutes les centrales syndicales, aux partis signataires du 'Programme commun'," *Le Nouvel Observateur* 657 (13 June 1977): 50. The *appel* was signed by "Jean Daniel, director of *Le Nouvel Observateur*; Claude Lefort, member of the editorial committee of *Libre*; Georges Montaron, director of *Témoignage chrétien*; Jean-Paul Sartre, director of *Les Temps modernes*; Laurent Schwartz, Professor at l'École polytechnique; Paul Thibaud, director of *Esprit*; Patrick Viveret, editor in chief of *Faire*."
86. Probably the first important application of the post-*gauchiste* critique of power to protest against repression by communist régimes was Jean-Paul Sartre and Simone de Beauvoir's *appel* to Nobel Prize winners demanding Dr. Mikhail Stern's liberation. It said in a language reminiscent of that of the GIP: "Every one of us, every one of you, can one day be a victim of a machination by a state. We never tire of recalling to the state apparatuses that their all-powerfulness has human justice as a limit." *Le Nouvel Observateur* 597 (17 April 1976): 82-83.

Chapter 5

ANTITOTALITARIANISM TRIUMPHANT

The New Philosophers and Their Interlocutors

In French intellectual politics 1977 was the year of the "new philosophers," notably Bernard-Henri Lévy and André Glucksmann, whose books attacking the revolutionary and progressive politics of the Left became runaway bestsellers, selling as many as 80,000 copies each within a year.[1] Omnipresent in the mass media, Glucksmann, Lévy, and their books were at the center of the political debates of French intellectuals in 1977. Their triumph marks the coming of age of French antitotalitarianism.

The new philosophers' critiques of the politics and ideology of the Left were, even in their exaggeration, timely. New philosophy entered the spotlight in French intellectual politics in May 1977 at precisely the moment that the final crisis of the Union of the Left began. The Left's landslide victory in the municipal elections of 12 and 20 March 1977 multiplied competition and conflict within it in expectation of its victory in the 1978 legislative elections. The PCF soon demanded an updating of the Common Program, and in May the parties of the Union of the Left began negotiations on it that ended in failure on 23 September. The PCF had, by most accounts, preferred to force an end to the Union of the Left by demanding a more radical Common Program and thereby undermine the Left's chances for victory in 1978 rather than settle for a subordinate position within a victorious but moderate Left dominated by the socialists. Indeed, as a result of the 1977 rupture of the Union of the Left, the Right won the 1978 elections.

The new philosophers were able to occupy the spotlight in the spring and summer of 1977 because they spoke to this crisis of the Left and because debating the new philosophers became another way of debating the fate of the Left. Wherever it took place, the debate on new philosophy was a debate on its politics. The episode of the television program "Apostrophes" on the new philosophers was entitled "The New Philosophers, are they on the Left?" In *Le Nouvel Observateur* the new philosophers were debated in the forum "objectif 78," created in anticipation of the 1978 elections. In *Le Monde* the new philosophers were asked about their positions on the Left.[2] New philosophy received the approval and toleration of leading intellectuals precisely because they found it politically opportune. Further, the reaction of the noncommunist intellectual Left to new philosophy reveals a near-consensus behind the proposition that totalitarianism is the inevitable product of revolutionary projects and discourses (especially those that are state-centered) and was, as a consequence of the Union of the Left's politics, on the horizon in the France of 1977.

Although new philosophy was a mass media phenomenon, its success cannot be primarily attributed to the rising importance of the mass media in French intellectual life if only because the media and political aspects of new philosophy are inextricably intertwined.[3] Although new philosophy was the creation of a publisher, Grasset, and an editor, Bernard-Henri Lévy, trying to sell their authors, it was not imposed on French intellectual debate by mass media exterior to the intellectual field. Rather, it was promoted and debated by well-established, legitimate intellectuals with access to the cultural and political press precisely because of its political repercussions. To be sure, new philosophy and its politics can and should be seen as the culmination of the development of mass media-derived cultural celebrity as a resource in strategies of intellectual legitimization and consecration.[4] Thus, although intellectuals were led by their own critiques of the politics of the Union of the Left to support or tolerate new philosophy, their politics and their acceptance of the mass media orientation of the new philosophers were partially determined by their own use of the mass media in their strategies of consecration within the intellectual field. It is certainly no accident that the extra-university market for cultural goods had played an important role in the careers of almost all of the leading intellectuals who most vigorously supported new philosophy.

The following pages explore new philosophy in order to shed light on the contours of the critique of totalitarianism at its height. The focus is on the production of the new philosophy phenomenon and its reception by the larger intellectual community. Both reveal that new philosophy expressed in all its extremes the crisis atmosphere of the year leading up to the 1978 legislative elections and the general crisis of intellectual politics as antitotalitarianism reached maturity.

Parisian Samizdat: Glucksmann's *Les Maîtres penseurs* and Lévy's *La Barbarie à visage humain*

Glucksmann's *Les Maîtres penseurs* of 1977 follows the same line of argumentation as *La Cuisinière et le mangeur d'hommes* of 1975. It offers another denunciation of the coercive state and again proposes the resistance of the pleb as the sole alternative to it. Marxism is once more presented as the ideology of the gulag, and the gulag is said to be an invention of the West and a product of Western science. But Glucksmann's new book carries the argument further.

Joining Marx in infamy are Hegel, Fichte, and Nietzsche, also presented by Glucksmann as philosophers of a coercive and normalizing state. Glucksmann argues that these "master thinkers" systematized and justi- fied the modern state's project of domination, itself put on "order of the day" by the French Revolution. They promoted an interiorization of the law that smothers the pleb's protest at its inception. While not directly responsible for the gulag and Auschwitz, they "systematized and ren- dered strategically manageable ideas and tactics largely diffused before them in societies in the process of becoming rationally disciplinarian." They are guilty for having "under the cover of knowledge ... put together the mental apparatus indispensable to the launching of the great final solu- tions of the twentieth century." Although Glucksmann would later say that the master thinkers were responsible for blindness to the gulag and not the gulag itself, he did claim that "the sixty million deaths of the gulag" are "the logical application of Marxism."[5]

Glucksmann's book is constructed around a number of homologous oppositions: the state versus the pleb, anti-Semitism versus Judaism, rev- olution and power versus resistance, and reason and science versus igno- rance. The state seeks to dominate the pleb, submit it to its will. This project leads directly to anti-Semitism, the camps, and genocide:

> *All that wanders*, there is the question. Under the cloak of the Jew one condemns an entire little world that risks to elude the state in crossing frontiers, and that, in transgressing them, upsets the disciplinary society. The Europe of states seeks to exclude the marginal. The master thinkers make way for the master purgers who mix Jews and homosexuals in the Nazi camps and all that deviates in the Russian camps. Liberal Europe wanted to assimilate and normalize more calmly; cultural genocide substitutes for physical genocide.

Although the project of domination is that of the state, intellectuals, sci- ence, and reason are all essentially complicit in it. Science and the texts of the master thinkers are simply strategies of domination, and "to think is to dominate." Conversely, behind Nazism and Stalinism lie texts and science. Neither Nazism nor Stalinism is a phenomenon circumscribed to a partic- ular time or place; they are located in the texts that form the cultural her- itage of Europe. Sociological explanations of socialist régimes are, like explanations of Nazism by German militarism, illegitimate and interested efforts to divert attention from that which is essential to them: the Euro- pean state's project of domination systematized in the texts of the master thinkers. Revolution is not an option; it does not lead to fundamental change. Mirroring that which already exists and conveyed by a science of revolution, it is above all a project of the state to increase its domination. Anti-intellectual, Glucksmann praises the merits of ignorance. Identifying reason and revolution with domination, he lauds the authenticity of unreflective self-interested action: the resistance of the pleb and the panurgic *"Fay ce que vouldras."*[6]

Glucksmann's diatribe was directed against the Union of the Left and often explicitly so. His book alluded to the "common program" of the "master thinkers" and called the inmates of the concentration camps "those not in the program." He condemned, following Maurice Clavel's *Dieu est Dieu*, the politics of the "dirty handshake" (*mains sales tendues*) between the Catholic Church and the PCF and the rallying of clergy to the Union of the Left in the name of the liberation of man.[7] The conclusion of Glucksmann's book was obvious to all in 1977: the Union of the Left was a ruse of the state and its "master thinkers" to increase their power over the pleb. Even nationalizations, Glucksmann later explained in an interview with Max Gallo, aim at the "the Jewish side of the 'private sector'... not privilege or exploitation." The Left, Glucksmann implied in his television interviews, was dangerous because it had not reflected on the gulag, specifically on the role of Marxism in it. [8]

Les Maîtres penseurs, it should be noted, rejected the concept of totalitarianism for reasons that stem from Glucksmann's Foucauldian politics and *gauchiste* past. The concept of totalitarianism was, Glucksmann argued, a means of exculpating the West. Glucksmann explained:

> Some American intellectuals tried in the name of totalitarianism to construct common explanations of Stalin and of Hitler. The trouble with such a categorization was that it justified the 'non-totalitarian' régimes to the point of becoming blind to any line of descent (intellectual or historical) as well as any kinship (practical or contemporary) between the hard methods of domination of the West and of the East. The critique of totalitarianism shows a deplorable tendency to always boil down to a critique of totalitarianism elsewhere.

Despite these reservations, Glucksmann used the word in other forums in 1977 and increasingly resorted to it in the early 1980s, especially during his vigorous campaign in favor of the deployment of Euromissiles in West Germany, for the express purpose of distinguishing between communist régimes and democracies.[9]

Bernard-Henri Lévy's *La Barbarie à visage humain* is, even more directly than Glucksmann's *Les Maîtres penseurs*, addressed to the Left on the eve of its likely electoral victory. Lévy, evidently anxious to prevent his book from being dismissed as a right-wing pamphlet, declared in his forward: "Alas! It is the Left, the instituted Left that I address here, because it is the Left at which I take aim, its passion for illusion and ignorance. It is to it, of course, that I *speak* because it is my family. I speak its language and I believe in its morality for lack of believing in its science." Lévy's preferred readers were, he stated, those nondogmatic socialists "who have the wisdom to think within History without for that believing in the certainty of its course. It is they whom I want to trouble and at least question because they will soon have our destiny in their hands." *La Barbarie à visage humain* was a word of warning to the Left by a self-described moralist who sought to "take historical pessimism to its conclusion" and feared, he would later say on television, that the French Left was on the slippery slope to totalitarianism.[10]

La Barbarie à visage humain seeks to refute the possibility of real political change for the better. Power is, it argues, omnipresent and inescapable. There is no alternative to power; revolution is impossible. Power and the state are original to society and eternal; nothing exists before them or independent of them. There is no dialectic or negativity. History exists only insofar as it ends in capitalism. Only totalitarianism is nominally "the new, the unprecedented in our era" while also being "its past that does not pass by, the face of its future." In this world of radical pessimism, Marxism, socialism, and *progressisme* are dangerous ideologies precisely because they promise to change the world. Change being impossible, politics geared toward it can only result in more repression. The gulag is "the Enlightenment minus tolerance."[11]

For Lévy, politics should focus on preventing the spread of totalitarianism, which is nothing less than the fullest development of capitalism, the Enlightenment, progress, power, and the state. The font of antitotalitarian politics is, according to Lévy, religion. Only it has held back the development of totalitarianism by forcing the state to answer to transcendental imperatives. Once true religion is destroyed, the totalitarian state emerges by laicizing religion, creating a religion of the state that allows the Prince to "take himself for the Sovereign" and reign "alone and without limit over the terrestrial kingdom." Against this development, which becomes a matter of immediate concern with the Marxization of the Left, Lévy pleads for political liberalism, but since he considers the liberal state to be "a state that censors itself" in accordance with transcendental imperatives, Lévy finds in ethics and morality the bulwark against totalitarianism. Politics can only be provisional, uncertain, and conjunctural. The new "anti-barbaric intellectual" will be a "metaphysician, artist, and moralist" who will "testify to the unspeakable and hinder the horror, save what can be saved and refuse the intolerable; we will not remake the world, but at least we can see to it that it does not fall apart."[12]

Glucksmann's *Les Maîtres penseurs* and Lévy's *La Barbarie à visage humain* share a great deal in common. Both are polemical essays written from a perspective of reflection on the gulag and Auschwitz, which they hold to be direct developments of the Western state and reason. Presenting the state and power as noncontradictory monoliths, they deny that either can be evaded, put to good use, or overthrown. Both advocate a minimalist, nonconstructive politics and denounce more ambitious political programs, notably that of the Union of the Left, as ultimately repressive. To be sure, they differ on some points. Glucksmann's book is somewhat more careful in its analysis of the relationship between ideas and the gulag. And where *Les Maîtres penseurs* places its bets on the plebs and their resistance to the state, *La Barbarie à visage humain* explicitly denies the value of resistance in itself and demands a rehabilitation of ethics as the only way of fending off the worst. Finally, Glucksmann remains favorable to some form of socialism, whereas Lévy denounces it as a dangerous form of optimism.

Although primarily a product of late *gauchiste* politics, the positions taken by Lévy and Glucksmann also reflected their Jewish identity at a time when a new awareness of French anti-Semitism and the history of the Holocaust in France was emerging. To the extent that the Holocaust was the formative event in Glucksmann's life, he was disposed to identify the state with anti-Semitism and resistance with survival. Glucksmann's father, who worked in London for Moscow during World War II died when, according to Glucksmann, he was "forcefully embarked by the English in a ship of undesirables that somebody mysteriously torpedoed." With his mother and sister, who participated in the Resistance, Glucksmann survived the war in the unoccupied zone, but not without a good dose of luck. At one point, he and his mother were seized by French gendarmes and "put in a transit camp of Jews bound for Germany"; they survived only because they were released after his mother "screamed at the cops."[13] "As a Jewish child who miraculously escaped the massacre," Glucksmann explained, "I have never had a blind confidence in the discourses of the great powers."[14] As for Lévy, his North African Sephardic Jewish origins may have distanced him from the more pronounced assimilationism of the metropolitan Ashkenazic population. While the connection between Jewish identity and the author's distrust of the state was not as clearly pronounced in Lévy's 1977 book as it was in Glucksmann's, anti-Semitism soon became the central issue of his interventions—in, for example, his 1978 accusation that Georges Marchais was anti-Semitic and his 1981 denunciation of the "French ideology."[15]

Lévy and Glucksmann adopted similar responses to their critics. While criticizing the Union of the Left and warning of the authoritarian, indeed *concentrationnaire* threat that it posed, they both parried critiques of their politics and ideas with the accusation that their opponents' attacks proved that they were already engaging in the repressive, exclusionary logic they would perfect when they came to power. This was a repetition of Paul Thibaud's argument against Pierre Guidoni and Jean-François Revel's diatribe against the Left as a whole,[16] but with a twist: against the totalitarianism that was entering the "heads" of the Left before it occupied the state, the new philosophers pretended to be dissidents.

Lévy was especially extravagant in his denunciation of the attacks on his politics. When, on "Apostrophes," Xavier Delcourt accused Lévy of working against the Common Program, Lévy responded: "You proceed like the police!"[17] In his reply to his critics in *Le Nouvel Observateur* Lévy deployed the full force of his rhetoric of repression and dissidence, claiming that because their books may contain "truths that bother it," "an army of master censors scrambles to lock up free and scattered thoughts.... Under the cover of discipline" the Left is beginning "right now to make its dissidents get in line." Lévy saw an "unavowed totalitarianism" emerging and asked "if already in some obscure agency our fate has not been sealed in the black book of exclusions." Soon they may be forced to choose between "the virtues of gallows and the charms of the guillotine." Lévy concluded: "here at the core is what distinguishes us from the intellectuals of the state: we are ready to do everything in our power so that this type of choice does not one day become inevitable; they do everything they can so that it becomes not only unavoidable, but also legitimate and reasonable." There were, Lévy tells us a year later, "small Moscow trials" "in that affair of the 'new philosophers.'" Using arguments like this, the new philosophers could, as Gilles Deleuze argued at the time, turn any and all critiques in their favor.[18]

Glucksmann, even more than Lévy, was the "dissident" intellectual in 1977. His most fantastic intervention was at Julia Kristeva's May 1977 Centre Beaubourg talk entitled "Un nouveau type d'intellectuel: le dissident," which presented dissidence as a model for Western intellectuals. Attacked by the audience for comparing the French situation to that under communist régimes, Kristeva responded that this was necessary because the Common Program was out of date. Asked further for whom she would vote, Kristeva was at a loss, at which point Glucksmann stood up and screamed: "We have finally gotten there! Control of party cards, of loyalty to the party. Here's why we already need to be dissenting in France ... the gulag has already begun."[19] Considering himself and Kristeva to be dissidents, Glucksmann denounced intellectuals like Jacques Attali, whom he considered compromised by "power," and explicitly sought to oppose the "terrorist" French state by following the example of East European dissidents, who had taught them the "methods of antitotalitarian thought" and how to resist power without imitating it.[20]

New philosophers other than Glucksmann and Lévy were quick to cast themselves as dissidents in the debates of 1977. Christian Jambet and Guy Lardreau, authors of *L'Ange*—who claimed that "the truth of the Left" was *The Gulag Archipelago* and that (especially because of the PCF) "there will be no tomorrow" if the Left won the elections—argued that the attacks that sought to relegate them to the Right proved that "the spiritual gulag is already there." Jean-Marie Benoist, who would challenge Georges Marchais for his seat in the Val-de-Marne in the 1978 legislative elections, demanded in May 1977 that he be allowed his "right to dissidence before the election and not after."[21]

The attraction of the politics of dissidence was not limited to new philosophers. Jean Daniel, presiding over the Biennale de Venise, spoke of the lessons that dissidence taught them: the sacred nature of "the right to difference and to revolt" as well as the politics of human rights, described as "a strategy more ethical than political." Likewise, as we shall see below, intellectuals associated with the journal *Tel quel* made dissidence their political model in 1977. Finally, many other intellectuals—most of whom probably did not accept Glucksmann's dissident politics—contributed to the valorization of dissidence in French politics by participating alongside Glucksmann in the Biennale de Venise and the Théâtre Récamier reception for dissidents held parallel to President Giscard d'Estaing's reception of Brezhnev at the Elysée. They all agreed that dissidence had to be given priority over state imperatives and other political demands.[22]

New Philosophy as a Mass Media Phenomenon

To the extent that new philosophy was a mass media phenomenon, Bernard-Henri Lévy was its author. Lévy was born in 1948 into a well-to-do family (his father was an industrialist) in Béni-Saf, Algeria. At the end of the Algerian War, Lévy and his family left Algeria and ultimately settled in Paris. There he attended the *khâgne* at Louis-le-Grand and was preparing for the entrance exams to the École normale supérieure (ENS) come May '68. May '68 did not find young Lévy on the streets; rather, he listened to the events on the radio and limited his activism to lobbying the educational bureaucracy to hold the ENS entrance exams despite the events. Lévy entered ENS in the autumn of 1968, obtained his *agrégation* in philosophy in 1971, and spent his last year at ENS as a reporter in Bangladesh, where he covered the Indo-Pakistani War for the newspaper *Combat*. His travels resulted in a *thèse de 3e cycle* directed by Charles Bettelheim and published in 1973.[23] Although apparently sympathetic to the Maoists of the GP in this half-decade after 1968, Lévy did not believe in revolution and never became a militant.[24]

After obtaining his intellectual credentials, Lévy set out to make his fortune in journalism, publishing, and politics. His forays into politics and journalism were at first disappointing. Having met Mitterrand while at ENS, Lévy joined his team of advisors for a time in the mid 1970s and took charge, apparently without conviction, of the portfolio on *autogestion*. In early 1975 Lévy tried to use his press experience—after leaving *Combat*, he had edited the weekly page "Idées" in *Le Quotidien de Paris* in 1974—and his connections with the PS to launch a new Parisian daily, *L'Imprévu*. Founded with Michel Butel—who had also been a journalist at *Combat*—and financed by their personal and familial capital, *L'Imprévu* promised to be, according to its founders, a "left-wing morning daily" and a "newspaper for the common man" that would contribute to the Union of the Left. Although on the Left, *L'Imprévu* was not *autogestionnaire* in its management; Butel and Lévy would not share power with the newspaper staff. They held that the liberal management practices that they had experienced at *Combat* and *Le Quotidien de Paris* were "injurious to the health of journalism" and would not allow them to be replicated at *L'Imprévu*. Despite their political connections, financial reserves, and support from individuals like Michel Foucault (who published an interview in the newspaper's first two issues) and Maurice Clavel (who believed that the newspaper had built on the errors of *Libération*), *L'Imprévu* did not sell and folded after eleven issues. The Union of the Left proved to be an inadequate terrain for Lévy's ambitions.[25]

Lévy's adventures in publishing were more successful. In 1973 he arrived at the apolitical, commercial publisher Grasset, with a recommendation by Jean-Jacques Brochier, editor of *Magazine littéraire*, a literary weekly owned by Jean-Claude Fasquelle who, with Bernard Privat, ran Grasset. After discussing his own projects for books, Lévy, who knew nothing about publishing at the time, was offered the position of director of a book collection for Grasset. Lévy asked his friends, many of whom had been students with him at the *khâgne* of Louis-le-Grand,[26] for book proposals and had twenty within two weeks, all of which were accepted by the publisher. Since the proposals were diverse, three collections were created for them: "Enjeux," "Théoriciens," and "Figures"—all directed by Lévy. For Grasset, Lévy was a link to the younger, 1968 generation of writers and readers. For Lévy, Grasset was the fast track to power within French intellectual life. Together, they would attempt to sell their new authors under the rubric "new philosophy."[27]

New philosophy was, like the "new novel" before it,[28] the creation of a promotional campaign. Born when Lévy dubbed his authors "new philosophers" in his *Les Nouvelles littéraires* dossier of 10 June 1976, new philosophy was given a noisy reception throughout the cultural press.[29] The new philosophers promoted each others' books at every possible occasion. In *Le Nouvel Observateur*, to which Lévy increasingly contributed after the failure of *L'Imprévu*,[30] new philosophy fared well. The weekly published an article on "Les Nouveaux Gourous," many of whom were Lévy's new philosophers, and otherwise gave favorable press to their books.[31] Maurice Clavel used his *Le Nouvel Observateur* columns and numerous other media appearances to praise works by new philosophers: Philippe Nemo's *L'Homme structurel* and especially *L'Ange*, by Guy Lardreau and Christian Jambet.[32] *Le Magazine littéraire* vigorously promoted the books of its owner's publishing house, to the extent of publishing a flow chart of the "Inter-fluences de la philosophie contemporaine" in which the new philosophers appeared as the sole inheritors (with the exception of the Althusserians Étienne Balibar and Lecourt) of the French philosophical tradition.[33] Lévy even had contacts in *Le Monde*, where Roger-Pol Droit, a classmate of his at Louis-le-Grand, assured that the new philosophers were well received in its revered pages.[34] The new philosophers also appeared on numerous occasions on programs on the radio station France Culture and in lecture and discussion forums in Paris such as the "Revue parlée philosophique" run by Lévy and Jean-Marie Benoist (also one of Lévy's authors) at the Centre Beaubourg.[35] These campaigns paid off immediately; *L'Ange* sold 15,000 copies in the first two months.[36]

Because new philosophy had its origin in a promotional campaign, it was never clear who the new philosophers were or what they represented.[37] In Lévy's dossier in *Les Nouvelles littéraires* they were, with one exception, authors published in Lévy's collections at Grasset.[38] After the term "new philosophers" became current in the cultural press in 1977, Grasset made the connection between its authors and new philosophy explicit in its advertisements for Lévy's collections.[39] In Lévy's presentation of the *Nouvelles littéraires* dossier the new philosophers had little in common with each other besides their iconoclasm and their enemies. Lévy wrote that they were "a new generation of philosophers [who] storm yesterday's citadels, shake their foundations and make their certitudes wobble," but did not form a school and were at most a current "without a head, without a leader, and without a principle."[40] Later Lévy and many of his authors would deny that they were new philosophers, and Lévy would himself criticize the term by declaring that "things are all the same a bit more complicated and that any effort at reduction and amalgamation would be ruinous for everyone."[41] By inventing a philosophical current comprised of his authors, postulating opposition to it and contradictions within it, and then denying its very existence and denouncing the use of the term, Lévy created a debate out of nothing that gave the impression that the new philosophers had something to say. The iconoclastic individualism of the new philosophers not only offered the generation of '68 an alternative identity to the militant one but also provided new philosophy with a ready alibi. If new philosophy did not exist (except when Lévy said so), any critique of it as a collective phenomenon in intellectual politics could be nothing more than an insidious normalizing effort aimed at discrediting the authors identified with it and denying their individuality.

The other great orchestrator of new philosophy was Maurice Clavel. Clavel was a *normalien* and *agrégé* in philosophy (1942) of conservative provincial bourgeois origins who had played an important role in the right-wing, anticommunist Resistance and made a name for himself after the war as a playwright. Active in right-wing, nationalist circles after the Liberation, he increasingly turned to the Left in the 1950s and 1960s, joining revisionist communists briefly after 1956, left-wing Gaullists after de Gaulle's return to power, and then breaking with Gaullism in 1965 to 1966 as a result of the Ben Barka affair. Clavel's rupture with Gaullism brought him into the fold of *Le Nouvel Observateur*, where he took up the critique of television in November 1966. Experiencing a religious awakening in 1965, Clavel turned to Catholicism, within which he defended the doctrine of original sin and vigorously opposed modernization.

For Clavel, May '68 was nothing less than the beginning of a new era in modern history. He interpreted it as a spiritual revolt against materialism,

an uprising of Being and Truth against the abyss of nothingness of contemporary society. After the events were over, Clavel sought to keep the
movement alive and influence it in a spiritual direction. While approving
of revolt, he disliked the violence, fanaticism, and Marxist ideology of
many *gauchiste* militants. Clavel found that the Gauche prolétarienne (GP)
approximated his idea of the legacy of May '68 and drew close to it in 1971.
It was, he would later say, the agent of "that spiritual and cultural pro-
ductivity that I had ascribed to May '68 from the beginning."[42] He
approved and legitimized with his own Resistance credentials the GP's
use of the vocabulary of resistance and was a crucial link between the GP
and left-wing Gaullists. Clavel would also play an important role in the
evolution of the GP leadership after the GP's dissolution.

In the 1970s, as the *gauchiste* years slid into those dominated by the
Union of the Left, Clavel became an increasingly visible figure on the
French intellectual scene and an implacable opponent of the established
Left. In December 1971 he became an instant hero when, after French television censored his film on May '68, he walked out on the live television
broadcast of the program "A armes égal" with the salutation *"Messieurs les
Censeurs, bonsoir!"* The notoriety gained from this appearance and his
noteworthy television reviews in *Le Nouvel Observateur* helped assure the
spectacular success of his *Ce que je crois*, which sold 100,000 copies from its
publication in May 1975 to the end of that year.[43]

Clavel had no liking for the Union of the Left. He considered the PS's
promise to *"changer la vie"* (change life) through the Common Program to
be a fraudulent co-optation of the spiritualist thrust of May '68 by a mate-
rialist program. He was very critical of Mitterrand's campaign in 1974,
arguing that one should vote for Giscard if, as the Left sometimes claimed,
the standard of living was the most important issue. He wrote an article
intended for (but refused by) *Le Nouvel Observateur* that argued in favor of
abstention in the second round of the presidential election. Later, in reaction to a January 1976 episode of "Apostrophes" in which communist
René Andrieu and Jean-François Revel debated the "totalitarian temptation," Clavel announced to his readers his total disgust for the communists
and the Union of the Left:

> Dear comrades and friends of *Le Nouvel Observateur*, yes, it is since that day in
> March 1974 that I can no longer see them [the communists] and that I can no
> longer speak to them. That they appeared to me, that they revealed themselves
> to be incurable as it were. That I can no longer believe them or try to believe
> them. That their sketches on liberties make me sick. That their Union of the
> Left—yours, excuse me—has proven to be a sinister piece of nonsense. That I
> can no longer take part in your grueling fight alongside the PCF within this
> political coalition that for me is at the very least a biological monster.

Although Jean Daniel reined in Clavel during the 1974 election and distanced *Le Nouvel Observateur* from his January 1976 repudiation of the

Union of the Left, he appreciated the role that Clavel played in *Le Nouvel Observateur* as a critic of the Union of the Left. In retrospect, Daniel says that there was "intellectual complicity" between himself and Clavel, a "complementarity" that "led us to veritable intellectual operations on the verge of politics." The place given to new philosophy in the pages of *Le Nouvel Observateur* was the best example of this.[44]

After the publication of *The Gulag Archipelago*, Clavel was quick to draw lessons from the gulag for French politics. His *Le Nouvel Observateur* columns mentioned it incessantly beginning in 1974, as did his books *Ce que je crois* of 1975 and *Dieu est Dieu, nom de Dieu!* of 1976, but Clavel was above all interested in attacking Christian Marxists who supported the Union of the Left. For Clavel, who held that the death of man proclaimed by Michel Foucault in *Les Mots et les choses* was the death of man without God and that the spiritual revolt of May '68 would mark a return to faith, the Christian supporters of the Union of the Left were the enemy. Their rejection of the doctrine of original sin, their self-assuredness, and their identification of the Left with the liberation of man were all intolerable for Clavel. Because of them the Church was divided, Clavel wrote, between "*la Chapelle*" (the chapel) and "*l'Archipel*" (the archipelago). Against them, Clavel looked hopefully to the former leaders of the GP.[45]

Clavel played a crucial role in promoting the intellectuals of the former GP. Omnipresent on television and radio and in the printed press after the publication of his *Ce que je crois*, he used his access to these forums to promote Glucksmann's *La Cuisinière et le mangeur d'hommes* in 1975 and Lardreau and Jambet's *L'Ange* in 1976.[46] Clavel, along with Michel Bosquet (aka, André Gorz), was largely responsible for bringing Glucksmann to the pages of *Le Nouvel Observateur* and ensuring that he stayed there.[47] When *La Cuisinière* came out in June 1975, Clavel gave the advance proofs to Daniel, who, although initially skeptical of Glucksmann's analysis of the relationship between Marxism and the gulag, considered the book to be very important and had *Le Nouvel Observateur* consecrate two reviews to it, a laudatory one by Bernard-Henri Lévy and a more skeptical one by François Furet.[48]

In June 1976 Clavel widened the scope of his campaign when he hosted at his house in Asquins outside of Vézelay a weekend meeting with eleven intellectuals, most of whom were former GP Maoists (Robert Devezies, François Ewald, Alain Geismar, André Glucksmann, Christian Jambet, Guy Lardreau, Michel Le Bris, Jean-Pierre Le Dantec, Jean-Claude Meunier, Jean Raguenès, and Pierre Victor), to discuss their disillusionment with political activism. Although their philosophical and political perspectives differed and Clavel was unable to convert them to the spiritualism that he shared with Lardreau and Jambet, the participants agreed on a fundamental aspiration that they defined as "the end of man's power over men" and the dangers inherent in all forms of ideology. Clavel rallied his guests behind the figure of Socrates, whom he presented as the "anti-mas-

ter thinker," and a campaign to "liberate liberty" from contemporary ideologies. He gave them two years (approximately the time between their
meeting and the 1978 legislative elections) to become famous and to convert the masses to a new Socratic or, as Clavel hoped, Christian thought.
After outlining a strategy for their conquest of the French intellectual
scene, he urged them to finish their works in progress and pushed himself
to finish his book on Socrates so that it would appear at the same time as
Glucksmann's *Les Maîtres penseurs*. By February 1977 Clavel's *Nous l'avons
tous tué ou "ce juif de Socrate! …"* was ready, and Clavel pressured Grasset
to publish it by April, that is, soon after *Les Maîtres penseurs* was scheduled
to appear. When Françoise Verney and Bernard-Henri Lévy at Grasset
failed to move fast enough, Clavel attributed the delay to political pressures coming from the Union of the Left and sold his book to Seuil, which
expedited its release. Concerned about the initially languid reception of
Les Maîtres penseurs, which he reviewed in *Le Nouvel Observateur* as "the
great book…. Finally a book for true revolutionaries," Clavel even proposed that his book be advertised with Glucksmann's under the title
"Shake the Left before use."[49]

Clavel's patronage of the young ex-GP intellectuals was a relatively successful endeavor. Clavel and his Maos continued to meet over the next few
years as the "Cercle socratique." Clavel contributed enormously to the
success of Glucksmann, Lardreau, and Jambet. Many of the other members of the circle later delivered their reflections on the impasses of revolution and the threat of totalitarianism in radical politics.[50] Further,
benefiting from the patronage of Clavel and other intellectuals and their
training in the launching of media coups by the GP's politics of exemplary
action, GP Maoists mounted a "seizure of power" in the mass media.[51]

Although Clavel was labeled the *"oncle," "tonton,"* and the *"Dr. Mabuse"*
of the new philosophers,[52] he did not promote all of the authors in Lévy's
collection. Clavel had allowed Lévy to enlist his services to promote
L'Ange, but he would do nothing in favor of the books of Jean-Marie
Benoist, with whom Clavel had, he said, nothing in common. Further,
Clavel did nothing to advance *La Barbarie à visage humain* of Lévy, from
whom he considered himself to be separated "by my intuition that May '68
is a cultural break productive of being and of thought." To the extent that
he accepted the validity of the category "new philosophers," Clavel considered them to be the former leadership of the GP. No doubt Clavel and
many of the former GP intellectuals found Lévy—who claimed to speak in
the name of disillusioned *gauchistes* without ever having been a *gauchiste*
himself—disingenuous and, for this reason, would not identify their cause
with his. *Libération*, for example, although reviewing Glucksmann's *Les
Maîtres penseurs* very favorably, took pride in its refusal to discuss "new
philosophy," which it considered it to be a commercial enterprise, and
eventually rejected Lévy as a parasite on the adventure of GP Maoism and
his *La Barbarie à visage humain* as vacuous.[53]

The highpoint of new philosophy's media extravaganza was the show-down of Glucksmann, Lévy, and Clavel against the authors of *Contre la nouvelle philosophie*, François Aubral and Xavier Delcourt, on the well-advertised "Apostrophes" broadcast of 27 May 1977. With an audience of six to seven million, this program was probably the most memorable moment in 1970s intellectual politics. Yet, it was only one of many television appearances by Glucksmann and Lévy in 1977. In addition to his "Apostrophes" appearance, Glucksmann appeared on television on at least four other occasions in 1977: discussing the anti-Semitism of German philosophers on FR3 in February; faced off against Jacques Attali on "L'Homme en question" on FR3 in April; in his FR3 "Libre opinion" in June; with Michel Foucault and Maurice Clavel in the film presented by Clavel on "La Part de vérité" on TF1 in July; and on Jean-Louis Servan-Schreiber's TF1 program "Questionnaire," as well as the FR3 program "Ils pensent pour vous" in September. Lévy seems to have appeared less often on television in 1977, perhaps only on "Apostrophes" and FR3's "L'Homme en question" in November, but compensated for his lesser television time with interviews in forums like *Playboy* and *Marie-Claire*.[54] Including interventions by and about Glucksmann and Lévy on the radio and in the more serious press (*Le Monde*, *Le Nouvel Observateur*, etc.), there was probably more mass media attention given to the new philosophers in 1977 than there had been for any other phenomenon in French intellectual life since the heyday of structuralism in the mid 1960s or the existentialist craze after the Liberation.

If Lévy and Glucksmann were so well received by the tube, one reason is that they made good television. Both were, by contemporary accounts, very telegenic. Both were skillful in presenting their cases to television audiences and not afraid to offer simple ideas and catchy formulas to this end. Presenting themselves as representatives of a new generation, that of 1968, they appeared as such on the tube, irreverent and relaxed like few, if any, French intellectuals before them. On "Apostrophes" both Lévy and Glucksmann stood out, in contrast to Maurice Clavel and the host Bernard Pivot, because of their long hair and casual dress. Glucksmann wore blue jeans and a collarless shirt, and Lévy, dressed like a dandy to seduce, had his shirt open to the third button. In their style as well as in the content of their thought, the new philosophers appealed to the generation of 1968 in favor of depoliticization and a mass media-mediated individualism. Theirs was a message that French President Giscard d'Estaing welcomed. In May, when *La Barbarie à visage humain* came out, the Elysée circulated the rumor that Giscard was very interested in Lévy's work. Later, in September 1978, Giscard invited the three heroes of the "Apostrophes" episode on the new philosophers to a lunch for intellectuals at the Elysée palace.[55]

In Praise of New Philosophy: Michel Foucault and *Tel quel*

Although promoted in the mass media, new philosophy would not have been as successful as it was if it had not received support from prominent intellectuals. Beyond the campaigns orchestrated by Lévy and Clavel there were interventions, for example, by Roland Barthes in favor of *La Barbarie à visage humain* and by Jean-François Revel in favor of new philosophy as a whole. Barthes felt close to Lévy's discussion of the "the crisis of historical transcendence" and was, he said, "enchanted" by Lévy's writing.[56] Revel supported the new philosophers as allies in the battle against the Union of the Left and presented them as following the analysis of his *La Tentation totalitaire*. Most important was Michel Foucault's consecration of André Glucksmann's *Les Maîtres penseurs* and the rallying of Philippe Sollers and his literary journal *Tel quel* behind Bernard-Henri Lévy and new philosophy in general.

Foucault endorsed Glucksmann's *Les Maîtres penseurs* without reservations in a glowing *Le Nouvel Observateur* review. Furthermore, in 1977 Foucault gave his approval to Glucksmann's use of his *Folie et déraison* to draw a parallel between the gulag and confinement during the classical age in *La Cuisinière et le mangeur d'hommes*. Foucault's support for Glucksmann was not cheap. The criticisms of it by Claude Mauriac and Gilles Deleuze led Foucault to break off his friendships with them rather than qualify his accolades for Glucksmann's work.[57]

The positions taken by Foucault are that much more enigmatic given that Glucksmann's ideas, notably his conceptions of power and reason, were, as Peter Dews argues in an article on the question, foreign to the more rigorous analyses of Foucault. Glucksmann identified power with the state and postulated the existence of a pleb that largely escapes both, whereas Foucault, at his most innovative, considered power to be diffuse and analyzed it in terms of micro-structures that he explicitly developed in opposition to a conceptualization of power in terms of sovereignty located in the state. Further, Glucksmann's complete identification of Reason (understood by him as a philosophical and Hegelian Reason) and science with domination is alien to Foucault's genealogies, which seek to explain the emergence of particular forms of reason and science "at the point of articulation of discursive and non-discursive practices." In Foucault's analysis of the great confinement, for example, "Reason" itself is not culpable.[58]

Part of the explanation of Foucault's endorsement of Glucksmann must be sought in Foucault's use of the media in his strategy of intellectual consecration. Foucault had in the 1960s converted his academic credentials into cultural celebrity by increasing his visibility in intellectual reviews and the cultural press, eventually achieving intellectual superstardom with the publication of his *Les Mots et les choses*, which was extensively discussed in the mass circulation press and became a bestseller in the summer of 1966. This cultural celebrity was, in turn, an important factor contributing to Foucault's election to the Collège de France in 1970. In the 1970s, Foucault continued to thirst for recognition in the broader intellectual scene and wrote books that were eminently relevant to contemporary issues. Although Glucksmann may have distorted Foucault's ideas, he was a useful ally in Foucault's bid for recognition—especially after Foucault's disappointment with the reception of *La Volonté de savoir* in 1976. Glucksmann praised Foucault to the sky in books that sold in large numbers and were well-promoted in the media. Glucksmann wrote, for example, that Foucault was the first since Marx to systematically interrogate "the most immediate origins of the modern world."[59]

Still, even if Foucault welcomed Glucksmann as an advertisement for himself, Foucault's support for Glucksmann was, above all, political in origin. To say this is not to deny the importance of Foucault's wager on the media or to establish a distinction between Foucault's philosophy and his politics in explaining his relationship with Glucksmann,[60] but to argue that the coherency of Foucault's positions on Glucksmann's work and related issues is perhaps best understood in terms of Foucault's politics. For one, Foucault's politics and his use of the mass media were closely related. In 1977, for example, Foucault blamed poor reception of his *Folie et déraison* of 1961, in contrast to the media-driven popular success of *Les Mots et les choses* of 1966, on the dominance of communism and Marxism in French intellectual life. Also, Foucault did not, when he spoke of philosophy as a type of radical journalism, for example, always recognize distinct boundaries between his philosophical, political, and media interventions.[61]

Foucault was vehemently anticommunist and highly critical of the Union of the Left. He identified with the movements that emerged out of May '68 and believed that a change of government would not alter the problems faced by them. Evidently fearful of the Left in power, he challenged it to "invent an exercise of power that does not frighten people." Asked on the eve of the 1978 legislatives of his opinion on the Left, he responded that it was not for him to rally to the Left but for the Left to adapt to the redefinition of the political that he and others had been undertaking over the last fifteen years. He was among those intellectuals for whom the mobilization in favor of dissidence was a means of challenging the PCF. For example, his decision when he was invited to "Apostrophes" on 17 December 1976 to discuss the transcript of the trial of the Soviet Doctor Stern, published with his encouragement at Gallimard as *Un procès 'ordinaire' en U.R.S.S.*, instead of his own *La Volonté de Savoir* followed—according to Maurice Clavel—from the failure of the PCF journal *La Nouvelle Critique* to publish his commentary on Stern's trial in its pages.[62]

Ultimately, Foucault could endorse Glucksmann because Foucault resolved important ambiguities in his mid 1970s conception of power in his political practice by falling back upon his hostility to the state and other central institutions as well as his hatred of communism. Foucault, who identified power as the question of the twentieth century, argued that it had been fatally misunderstood in the past because it had been posed exclusively in terms of the state and sovereignty and not in terms of disciplines, that is, configurations of power/knowledge that constituted the subject. To understand modern forms of power and exercise some control over them, Foucault held that one had to go beyond the conceptualization of power in terms of sovereignty and the correlative understanding of power as repression and rethink it as both diffuse—such that "we all have power in our bodies"—and productive. At this point, disciplines could be challenged by genealogies, loosely defined by Foucault as "a sort of enterprise to desubjugate historical knowledges and set them free, that is to say capable of opposition and of a battle against the coercion of a unitary, formal, and scientific theoretical discourse."[63]

From this perspective, revolution, the desirability of which Foucault had come to question by 1977, had failed to fulfill its promises because it concentrated on the question of political sovereignty without bringing the disciplines into question. Further, it was perhaps fatally flawed because sovereign power could not, Foucault argued, have a decisive impact on disciplinary power. Like Glucksmann, Foucault—perhaps carried away by his focus on disciplinary power at the expense of sovereign power—suggested at times that the most horrific exercise of power in postrevolutionary Russia paralleled the uses of power in the West. In *Surveiller et punir* Foucault consciously drew a direct parallel between the gulag and the disciplining institutions of the West by describing the latter as forming a "carceral archipelago." On another occasion, Foucault argued that the repressive use of psychiatry in the Soviet Union was not "a misuse of psychiatry; it was its fundamental project."[64]

While Foucault's challenge to the repressive hypothesis (most fully developed in *La Volonté de savoir*) and assertion, at the expense of sovereign power, of the importance of "diffuse" disciplinary power opened the door to a critique of revolution, his denial that power was shared equally allowed him to stay true to his radical direct-democratic convictions. Thus Foucault, contrary to his radical reconceptualization of power as diffuse, continually located disciplinary power in central and institutional sites and considered resistance to it to reside in the marginal and noninstitutional, which, like Glucksmann, he called the pleb. Genealogies were insurrections of "knowledges ... first and above all against the effects of centralizing power that are linked to the institution and the functioning of a scientific discourse organized at the interior of a society like ours."[65]

Foucault did not develop a well-articulated analysis of the origins or significance of the gulag. He denounced the pretension of Marxism to the status of a science as a play for power and, as we have already seen, made the analogy between the gulag and disciplines, but he also argued in one case that the Stalinist terror was the failure of discipline and that the concentration camp was a "median formula between the great terror and discipline." If Foucault never explained the specificity of the Bolshevik régime, it was because his analysis of sovereign power, the importance of which cannot be ignored in Soviet history, remained rudimentary, and because Foucault showed little interest in directly addressing the gulag question except insofar as it became an issue in French politics. When considering the rapprochement between the gulag and the great confinement, Foucault feared, above all else, that it might be used to make all persecutions appear alike, let the PCF off the hook, and allow the Left not to alter its discourse. Probably for this very reason, Foucault had references to the "carceral archipelago" suppressed from later editions of *Surveiller et punir*. Foucault believed, he said, that Glucksmann's *La Cuisinière et le mangeur d'hommes* did not fall into this political trap. Thus, perhaps it is not surprising that Foucault, lacking an analysis of his own of the gulag and its relationship to the state and finding in Glucksmann's *Les Maîtres penseurs* a denunciation of his enemies (communists, totalizing ideologies, and the state) in the name of the marginal to which he himself assigned the essential role in politics, praised the book.[66]

The support of new philosophy by *Tel quel* was, as in the case of Foucault, the product of both a strategy of intellectual legitimization that invested heavily in the extra-university market for intellectual production and a deep-seated hostility to the PCF that came to the forefront as *Tel quel* turned away from radical politics and the 1978 elections approached. The case of *Tel quel* is particularly interesting because the journal and its intellectuals, by embracing the politics of dissidence, became closely identified with new philosophy. Also, because *Tel quel*'s apparently abrupt shift from Maoism to new philosophy from the autumn of 1976 to the spring of 1977 has been presented as emblematic of the spectacular reversals in intellectual politics in this period,[67] it deserves explanation. A closer look at *Tel quel*'s politics and its use of politics in strategies of literary consecration reveals that this shift was less abrupt and less influenced by disillusionment with the Chinese Cultural Revolution than commonly recognized.

Tel quel appeared on the French literary scene in 1960. Like most other literary reviews of the period, it rejected literary engagement and refused to subordinate literature and aesthetics to politics. It distinguished itself from others by focusing on literary modernism and supporting the new novel. It defended an immanentist conception of literature and repudiated the notion of literature as a reflection of internal or external experience. Apolitical and producing literature that was largely derivative, the early *Tel quel* was most innovative in the marketing of literature. It was the centerpiece to the publisher Seuil's conscious effort to win over the rapidly expanding population of university students by selling it literature by young writers with whom it could identify. As a consequence, when *Tel quel* became a literary avant-garde later in the mid 1960s it was unlike any avant-garde that preceded it in possessing a relatively stable financial base made possible by the literary market.[68]

Between 1963 and 1968, *Tel quel* transformed itself into a literary avant-garde. In 1963 a *Tel quel* book collection edited by Philippe Sollers, the central figure in *Tel quel*'s history and the only founding member who remained with the journal by the end of that year, was established at Seuil, and in 1964 the "telquelians" began a series of public lectures that gave *Tel quel* the allure of a movement. At the same time, *Tel quel* also engaged in theoretical and philosophical investigations of literature, consciousness, and language, in the course of which it established relations with the leading figures of structuralist and post-structuralist thought (Foucault, Barthes, Derrida, and Lacan) and welcomed within its own ranks the Bulgarian émigré Julia Kristeva, who would later become the review's leading theorist. True to its long-standing immanentist conception of literature, *Tel quel* challenged the distinction between reality and fiction, defined literature as productive rather than reflective, and gave literature a role in overturning "logocentrism."

The new, active role given to literature, a changing political context, and strategies of intellectual legitimization as an avant-garde contributed to *Tel quel*'s politicization in beginning in 1966. That year, members of *Tel quel*'s *Comité de redaction*, including Jean-Louis Baudry, Jean-Pierre Faye, and Sollers, took positions against the American war in Vietnam. Sollers, who had a long-standing interest in Chinese culture, and Baudry followed the Cultural Revolution closely and formed a "political committee" within *Tel quel* in the autumn to discuss the possibility of attaching their literary enterprise to it. They were evidently attracted to the Cultural Revolution because they saw it as an anti-authoritarian movement that worked on the level of culture and thought—qualities that resonated with their self-representation as a literary avant-garde. Yet, despite this attraction to the Cultural Revolution, *Tel quel* decided in early 1967 to pursue a rapprochement with the PCF that was consummated in 1968.

The decision to work with the PCF is comprehensible from the perspective of *Tel quel*'s pursuit of an audience and legitimacy as an avant-garde. A Maoist turn at this point would, the telquelians reasoned at the time, have marginalized *Tel quel* with unpredictable consequences for both its audience and legitimacy in the intellectual field. In effect, the desire for continued commercial literary success kept this avant-garde's political adhesions lagging behind those of the rest of the intellectual field. The alliance with the PCF, on the other hand, gave *Tel quel* access to the PCF's still substantial press and was scandalous enough to generate considerable publicity for the review. Further, it gave *Tel quel* solid left-wing credentials, which it could and did use to denounce competitors on the literary scene. For these intellectuals short on structural legitimacy—that is, the proper curricula, degrees, and university positions—within the intellectual field, the alliance with the PCF was a shrewd maneuver, especially because it did not require that *Tel quel* change its literary practice. Borrowing from Derrida to define the text as "production," the telquelians established a link through the metaphor of production between their literary practice and Marxism that allowed them to continue unaltered their literary and theoretical work while defining it as revolutionary. According to Kristeva, the PCF served as a "loudspeaker" that allowed them to continue their work by making it public, which "seemed to us to be an imperative in the era of the mass media."[69]

Tel quel's hope that it would become the only literary avant-garde recognized by the PCF came to naught—but not for lack of trying. Although unwilling to alter its literary practice, *Tel quel* did not shrink—to the surprise of the PCF intellectuals who had initiated the dialogue with it—from adopting politically orthodox positions in order to ingratiate itself with the party. It issued Marxist-Leninist denunciations of the *gauchisme* of the student movement in 1968 and, although the invasion of Czechoslovakia was condemned by *Les Lettres françaises*, the Comité nationale des écrivains, and the Union des écrivains newly formed in May '68, *Tel quel* maintained a studied silence in the face of it. *Tel quel*'s bid for sanctification by the PCF failed because the PCF was not interested in choosing between the competing literary avant-gardes, but rather wanted to rally as many intellectuals to it as possible. This failure and the declining legitimacy of the PCF with *Tel quel*'s audience of university literature students led *Tel quel* to break off relations with the PCF and fully embrace Maoism in 1971.

Tel quel's Maoism was unlike that of other Maoists in France in the period from 1966 to 1976. Indeed, *Tel quel* never established links with French Maoist political organizations, and these Maoist political organizations never had a very high opinion of *Tel quel*. *Tel quel*'s Maoism was, like that of the GP, anti-authoritarian in nature. But *Tel quel*, unlike the GP, did not engage in puritanical militancy or mystical *ouvriérisme*. The telquelians never considered putting literature in the service of the people or going to the factories for reeducation. *Tel quel*'s target audience remained students and intellectuals, and its principle "Maoist" activity consisted of commentaries on Chinese texts. Maoism offered them hope for libertarian socialism and for a revolution that would be cultural (and textual), but it was above all else another way of promoting *Tel quel*'s literature through politics. *Tel quel*, for which the Chinese Cultural Revolution functioned as a utopian projection of May '68 onto China, was able to reconcile itself with May '68 through its Maoist turn. This brought it back into step with its student audience and gave it a new political platform from which it could judge its literary and political enemies. It made the journal more audacious, dangerous, and extravagant—qualities that it needed if it were to retain its fickle readership of university students, who mostly bought *Tel quel* by the issue. *Tel quel*'s Maoist turn, no less than its previous turn toward the PCF, paid off in increases in readership. The special numbers on China sold 20,000-25,000 copies, the ordinary circulation in the 1970s being between 5,000 and 6,000 per issue.[70]

The transition from Maoism to new philosophy was, by all appearances, very rapid at *Tel quel*. Sollers and the other telquelians held onto

Maoism as late as the summer of 1976, but the events following the death of Mao apparently convinced them that Maoism was actually Stalinist and that its Stalinism was a necessary consequence of Marxism.[71] Soon thereafter, on 9 December 1976, Sollers marked his political moderation by attending a lunch for intellectuals with President Valéry Giscard d'Estaing. By May 1977 Sollers was lending his complete support to Bernard-Henri Lévy's *La Barbarie à visage humain*, and Kristeva was singing the praises of dissidence as a model for French intellectuals. Although this shift from Maoism to dissidence and new philosophy was to some extent the product of disillusionment with the former in the autumn of 1976, other factors contributed to *Tel quel*'s political evolution, including: shifting strategies in the literary marketplace, *Tel quel*'s conception of the relationship between literature and politics, and *Tel quel*'s hostility to the parties of the Left (notably the PCF) and their politics. Upon closer examination, the transformation of *Tel quel*'s politics was less abrupt than the events of 1976 and 1977 at first indicate.

During *Tel quel*'s Maoist phase, its main political enemy was the PCF and its "dogmatic revisionism." Behind *Tel quel*'s animosity toward the PCF lay a desire to settle old scores as well as a commitment to an anti-authoritarian revolutionary politics that the telquelians had laid aside when allied with the PCF. Upon the formation of the Union of the Left in 1972, *Tel quel* attacked it for "revisionism" and called for the masses to take control of their own politics. Come the 1974 presidential elections *Tel quel* declared its refusal to "subordinate our work to the electoral horizons" of the Union of the Left that "only aim at the accession to power of rusty political schemers." *Tel quel*'s reception of Solzhenitsyn's *The Gulag Archipelago* and Glucksmann's *La Cuisinière et le mangeur d'hommes* is revealing in this regard. After an initial statement of March 1974 (before the French publication of *The Gulag Archipelago*) declaring that "protesting against his expulsion was self-evident" but rejecting Solzhenitsyn's politics in favor of "the *left-wing* critique [of Stalinism]… by Mao and the Chinese masses," *Tel quel* spoke in the autumn of 1974 of *The Gulag Archipelago* as the "monument of Solzhenitsyn." By December 1974 *Tel quel* was attacking the PCF for holding "the precise, documented critique of Stalinism in *The Gulag Archipelago*" to be "null and void."[72]

Hostility to the PCF and the Stalinist Marxism that *Tel quel* saw in its response to Solzhenitsyn made *Tel quel* receptive to Glucksmann's *La Cuisinière*, which it reviewed and discussed in its winter 1975 issue. Maria-Antonietta Macciocchi, for example, found Glucksmann's anger at the use of the authority of Marxist knowledge by communist parties to be appropriate, although she dismissed his global critique of Marxism. The responses to Glucksmann by Jean-Louis Houdebine and Philippe Sollers were more sympathetic and revealing of the political dynamic at *Tel quel*. Both were critical of Glucksmann's assertion that the pleb was the antidote to tyranny, believed that a Freudian addition to Marxism would help overcome the latter's shortcomings, were critical of the handling of the gulag question by the parties of the Left, and displayed more than a little political pessimism. In Sollers's analysis the response of the official Left was the big question: "That which must be explained without a doubt and increasingly is why the 'Left' distinguishes itself in its *lack of desire to know*. What hinders it from reading, from listening, from being *touched*." Glucksmann's book left Sollers the antilogocentric asking whether "*all philosophy*, in its very language, does not risk being hand in glove with a 'potential concentration camp'?" Houdebine considered the perspective opened up by Glucksmann on the real movement of communism in Russia and the response of Western intellectuals to it to be "fundamentally sound" and believed that Glucksmann was perfectly correct to critique Marxism for its role in domination in the USSR, but asserted that Marxism was not univocal. Houdebine wanted Glucksmann to recognize that the Chinese Cultural Revolution had made the critique of Soviet socialism possible, yet he quickly dismissed it as inapplicable to Europe. Attacking the PCF and the PS, "both clinging to their pathetic 'union'," for their hemming and hawing, Houdebine concluded that "communism and Marxism are, for us in Europe, to be reinvented." This reinvention could only be undertaken "beginning today, with the real movement of today, in 1975, and with all that it might contain of *new analytical capacity*" and might, Houdebine recognized, even turn against Marxism. *Tel quel*'s reaction to *La Cuisinière* was, as Glucksmann wrote in response to their questions, "friendly, indeed sympathizing." In fact, the telquelians had, as Houdebine's analysis of *La Cuisinière* suggests, already been somewhat disabused of their Maoist utopia by their trip to China in the spring of 1974—although there had been no mea culpa upon their return. As *Tel quel*'s Maoism faded, the conflict with the PCF became the central focus of the politics of the telquelians, who increasingly focused their energies on their critique of the Union of the Left. Sollers, who considered the Left's proposals "on the cultural and literary level as a pure and simple program of regression" found in the shift from Maoism to anticommunism new opportunities to champion cultural modernity. Likewise, in adopting a politics of dissidence *Tel quel* was able to prosperously reinvest its accumulated capital.[73]

The abandonment of Maoism made it possible for *Tel quel* to openly embrace the United States, where, it was becoming increasingly obvious, their fortunes were to be made. By the autumn of 1966 the telquelians Francis Ponge, Marcelin Pleynet, and Jean Thibaudeau had gone to the United States to teach. Enjoying compensation that they could not have dreamed of in France, they sent reports back to Sollers of a new El Dorado comprised of ignorant and gullible Americans buying into *Tel quel* and eager for more. In the 1970s, as more telquelians made the trip across the Atlantic, the United States became the cash cow and telquelian sphere of influence envisaged in 1966. By 1980 half of all copies of *Tel quel* were sold abroad, above all to American universities. In the case of Kristeva, whose work was considerably more successful in the United States than in France, self-interest and politics quickly converged. In the spring of 1974, after her first semester teaching at Columbia University in New York, Kristeva, the "Maoist," wrote that the American "'polytopia'" offered "the only manner that is non-depressive and enthusiastic without pathos of building an antitotalitarian space of real survival on the planet." With its triple issue on the United States in the autumn of 1977, *Tel quel* made its bid to become the intellectual merchants of America in France after becoming that of France in America. Although they appreciated the "polyvalency" of American society and American modernism, they were not uncritical of what they encountered across the Atlantic. What was important, Kristeva said, was "not to shout out 'the praises of New York' or 'down with New York', but to see what are the benefits, I would say the joy, of exchange, of the round-trip voyage."[74]

In turning toward dissidence and new philosophy in 1977 *Tel quel* adopted a radical individualism consonant with its American connection and also its long-standing valorization of literature vis-à-vis politics. Further, the turn toward dissidence allowed the telquelians to promote literature *against* politics. Kristeva, in theorizing the dissident intellectual for *Tel quel*, defined dissidence as a radical refusal of politics and of all social identities and groups. Against politics and society, which Kristeva held to always contain within them a "promise of totalitarianism," she argued that the intellectual should affirm the value of singularities and difference, something that literature was particularly well equipped to do. To do so was, she argued, dissidence, and it was a rejection of the "discourse of the Left." Kristeva's call for dissidence in the West hardly distinguished between the communist régimes and contemporary France. Like Glucksmann and Lévy, she and other telquelians drew a parallel between their relationship with the French Left and that of East European intellectuals with the régimes that ruled over them. Kristeva held, for example, that asking her about her electoral preferences in the upcoming 1978 legislative elections was "extremely revealing of a certain intolerance that does not stop gaining ground and that I fear a great deal."[75] Sollers's attachment to dissidence was buoyed by his conviction that it would be "two times worse" with the Left in power and that capitalism was ten times less repressive than socialism.[76]

The support of Sollers and *Tel quel* for Lévy and his *La Barbarie à visage humain* was important because Sollers was the only intellectual of importance to lend Lévy complete, unqualified, and sustained support. Sollers wrote an entirely laudatory review of *La Barbarie à visage humain* in *Le Monde* and opened up the pages of *Tel quel* to Lévy. Although Sollers also praised Glucksmann, calling him "one of the most brilliant of today's French philosophers," Lévy was his man. After Lévy won Sollers over to his book in the winter of 1976-77, he and Sollers together planned the campaign to promote it. The two apparently got along fabulously, no doubt because they had a great deal in common. Both were sons of industrialists and both had made their careers in French intellectual life as mass media, market-oriented intellectuals who had risen to positions of importance with the help of a bit of luck and a good dose of cheek. Their alliance was one of mass media intellectuals wagering against the Union of the Left.[77]

The Censors Censored: The Weakness and Isolation of New Philosophy's Opponents

There were, of course, some detractors, like Claude Mauriac and Jean Elle-instein, who repudiated new philosophy almost entirely, but what is most remarkable about them is their isolation. Few took stands as tough as those of Mauriac and Elleinstein. In fact, in the famous "Apostrophes" showdown the critics of new philosophy, François Aubral and Xavier Del-court, refused to criticize Glucksmann; Aubral even called his *La Cuisinière* a "beautiful book" and agreed with Glucksmann that Elleinstein's argu-ments were "absurd." The arguments of Mauriac and Elleinstein left most noncommunist intellectuals unconvinced. Indeed, as the inability of Althusser and the Althusserians to meet the challenge of new philosophy demonstrates, there was no significant hardcore opposition to new philos-ophy in French intellectual life.

Claude Mauriac's critique of new philosophy, entitled "Il ne faut pas tuer l'espérance" (one must not kill hope), focused on the use of the gulag in French politics. Mauriac—who had been de Gaulle's secretary (1944-49) and then the director of the Gaullist *Liberté de l'esprit* (1949-53) before grav-itating to *gauchisme* after May '68—confessed that he at first found new philosophy to be useful and agreed that it was necessary to denounce the gulag, but the extraordinary publicity surrounding them, such that a "col-lective hypnosis spread across all of France," made him suspicious.[78] The just crusade against the gulag was being used inappropriately against the hope that the French had placed in the Left by installing "that insidious and pernicious logic that abusively infers from the gulag Marxism, and from Marxism communism, from communism the Common Program, and from the Common Program the gulag." The new philosophers had taken the critique of the gulag beyond its legitimate bounds. Established intel-lectuals like Michel Foucault should, Mauriac added, take the new philosophers down a peg instead of showering them with accolades.[79]

Although Mauriac's article was taken seriously—*Le Nouvel Observateur*, for example, republished excerpts from it—few intellectuals agreed with it. In his response to Mauriac, Jean Daniel explicitly denied that one should fear the Right's exploitation of polemics within the Left and dismissed Mauriac's critique as an expression of "the general desire to find a scape-goat to explain the weakening of hope" placed in the Union of the Left. Jacques Julliard and Edgar Morin, although agreeing with Mauriac that the attention given to the new philosophers was a product of the 1978 elections, believed that it was justified and criticized efforts to silence the debate. Even some critics of the new philosophers rejected Mauriac's logic. Cornelius Castoriadis and Ilios Yannakakis, for example, both held—contrary to Mauriac—that new philosophy was actually a diversionary operation put on by the parties of the Left to discredit any and all challenges that the gulag question might pose to their politics by associating it with the impoverished ideas of Glucksmann and Lévy. For these and other intellectuals, hostility toward the Union of the Left ruled out Mauriac's rejection of new philosophy as a maneuver against it.[80]

Jean Elleinstein's intervention in the debate was less directly concerned with the politics of the French Left than with the interpretation of Stalinism and the gulag. Elleinstein, a communist since 1944 when he entered the party at the age of seventeen, was an *agrégé* in history (1960) and, beginning in 1970, *Directeur adjoint* of the PCF's Centre d'études et de recherches marxistes. Known to have Trotskyist sympathies as early as the 1960s, he published a Trotskyist-colored multi-volume *Histoire de l'U.R.S.S.* in the years 1971 to 1975, capped off by a *Histoire du phénomène stalinien* (1975) that challenged party orthodoxy on Soviet history. His history of Stalinism (as well as his *Le P.C.* of 1976), openness to dialogue with noncommunists, frank criticism of the Soviet Union, and position on the liberalizing wing of the PCF made him a prophet of liberal Eurocommunism and a highly visible and privileged interlocutor of the noncommunist intellectual Left in 1976 and 1977. In these years he could be found, for example, discussing his books on "Apostrophes," debating with Annie Kriegel in *Le Nouvel Observateur*, dialoguing with Jacques Julliard and Jean-Marie Domenach in *Esprit*, and presenting his opinions in *Le Monde*.[81]

Elleinstein's criticisms of the Soviet Union were not insignificant. He admitted, for example, that there was no freedom of expression in the Soviet Union and that if the USSR was socialist economically it was not so politically because it lacked political democracy. Reflecting on the failures of the Soviet Union, Elleinstein conceded that part of the responsibility for them lay with Marx and the Bolsheviks. Marx had been wrong to think that political democracy would follow directly from the installation of a socialist mode of production, and the Bolsheviks had not given sufficient thought to political democracy and the problem of the state. But Elleinstein insisted that Stalinism was the product of a history and not of the political theory of Bolshevism. Economic and cultural underdevelopment and the absence of a Russian democratic political tradition as well as the civil war, the white terror, and capitalist encirclement were all crucial to its emergence. Elleinstein also held that, although the gulag was "very very important," it was not as important as Solzhenitsyn claimed. Objecting that Solzhenitsyn's *The Gulag Archipelago* had been taken in France as the last word on Soviet history, he offered, in his discussion in *Esprit*, a debate on the Stalinist terror. Elleinstein argued, citing figures and sources in support of his case, that Solzhenitsyn had exaggerated the size of the gulag population and that the terror was, contrary to Solzhenitsyn, directed first and foremost against communists. Elleinstein concluded from his analysis of Soviet history that the situation was radically different in France because "for us socialism is the flowering of political democracy" and the PCF had founded its analyses on this French reality. Elleinstein considered the new philosophers' arguments to be discredited by their utterly ahistoric nature. The books of Lévy and Glucksmann were, he argued, "devoid of all historical references." There was not a word in *La Barbarie à visage humain* on the "historical conditions for the appearance of the Stalinist phenomenon." These books were simply not serious because "if one wants to seriously discuss things, one must not start with ideas to arrive at the historical realities."[82]

Elleinstein's perspective on the Soviet Union and French politics was rejected by almost all intellectuals on the noncommunist Left. Jean-Marie Domenach, for example, told Elleinstein that he considered the particulars of Russia and Soviet history to be irrelevant because he found the "principal characteristics of the Stalinist phenomenon ... in all countries in which Marxism has become a state ideology whatever the differences between their cultural tradition and that of Russia." It seemed to him more likely that there was "at the very heart of Marxism a phenomenon of ideological over-determination." Likewise, Pierre Rosanvallon, editor of *La CFDT aujourd'hui* (the CFDT's theoretical journal) and a major theorist of *autogestionnaire* politics in the perspective of the critique of totalitarianism, dismissed Elleinstein's analysis with the claim that "the possibility of Stalinism rests ... on two political and theoretical conditions: the contempt of theory for concrete history and the control of theory as a mode of the exercise of power." Jacques Julliard dismissed Elleinstein's effort to explain Stalinism by "particular historical circumstances" and thereby downplay its danger to France by arguing that "it was not Czarism that was responsible" when France had turned Algeria into a concentration camp twenty years earlier. When Elleinstein reiterated his arguments at the Biennale de Venise, Ilios Yannakakis responded, apparently to the approval of the rest of the participants, that because the Stalinist principle always yielded the same results when applied to different countries one must "dwell on the principle rather than on the history." Only a few isolated voices like that of Pierre Guidoni believed that French social and political history made fear of the gulag and totalitarianism unjustified— although some like Alain Touraine preferred to avoid rhetorical inflation and spoke in more moderate terms of the danger of left-wing authoritarianism. The discussion of the gulag and the new philosophers was not carried out on the terms offered by Elleinstein—terms that would have diminished the contemporary significance of Stalinism. The gulag, most noncommunist intellectuals agreed, had its origins in a certain political project and ideology and was therefore a danger in France.[83]

One might expect that new philosophy, given its hostility to Althusserianism, would have found intractable enemies in Althusser and his students. Indeed, to some degree the Althusserians resisted it. For example, Nicos Poulantzas condemned the new philosophers as insignificant right-wing irrationalists and affirmed that Marxism is "more alive than ever," and Jacques Rancière held that the new philosophers disguised the real roots of the gulag by concentrating on the texts of the "master thinkers." But many Althusserians were less than firm in their responses. Régis Debray, although he rejected new philosophy, was unwilling in 1977 to blame new philosophy on the media (as he later would in his *Le Pouvoir intellectuel en France*). He believed that "one has the anti-socialism that one deserves." Marxists had not done a very good job explaining "really existing socialism" and had therefore left the door open to the simplistic formulae of the new philosophers. Indeed, Debray would not rule out the possibility that Marxism was the ideology of socialism. Although publicly optimistic in 1977, Poulantzas was likewise troubled by the shortcomings of Marxism's understanding of the state and set out to remedy them in his anti-Leninist and markedly more pessimistic *L'État, le pouvoir, le socialisme* of 1978.[84]

The disarray of the Althusserians was most powerfully expressed by Althusser himself. After 1968, Althusser's Marxism had already taken a turn toward pessimism and incoherency as Althusser responded to his critics. In reaction to attacks on his theoreticism, he politicized philosophy, conceiving of it as "a political intervention in theory and a theoretical intervention in politics" (in the words of the scholar of Althusser Gregory Elliot) or as constituting "the class struggle in theory" (in the words of Althusser himself). While retaining his theoretical antihumanism, Althusser increasingly emphasized class struggle. The result, evident in his influential article on the ideological apparatuses of the state, was politically pessimistic. Defining subjects as existing "by and for their subjugation," Althusser offered no evident way out of the reproduction of the existing relations of production as there was little or no space within his argument for oppositional ideology. His recourse to the rhetoric of class struggle offered little comfort here. Althusser's pessimism only grew after he realized that the Chinese Cultural Revolution had failed to solve the problems posed by Stalinism and render possible a left-wing critique of Stalinism in the West. The Cultural Revolution had not, as Althusser had hoped, given China the socialist superstructure that corresponded to its socialist infrastructure. In 1976, in his preface to Dominique Lecourt's book on Lysenkoism, Althusser joined the chorus of those condemning present-day repression in the USSR and criticized the PCF's evasion of the issue. Further, he deplored the failure of communists "to account as Marxists for their own history" and asserted that it was time to "stop telling (ourselves) stories."[85]

In 1977 and 1978 Althusser did not speak up against the new philosophers, despite the fact that they assaulted his scientific Marxism as complicit in totalitarianism. Rather, Althusser reacted complacently to their challenges and actually came, Elliot writes, "to underwrite ... some of their pronouncements." His 1977 text "The Crisis of Marxism" bemoaned the lack of "any living reference for socialism" and, once again, the failure of Marxist efforts to explain Soviet history. Although Althusser rejected efforts to render Marxist theory responsible for the history made in its name, he submitted that one had to consider Marxist theory "involved in and compromised by" this history. Implicitly critiquing his own work, he argued that the crisis could not be solved by invoking a nonexistent original purity in Marxism. The theories and analysis of Marx and the great founding Marxists were *"mixed up with* difficulties, contradictions, and gaps" and had not escaped contamination by the dominant ideology. The theoretical unity of Marx's work was "in large part fictitious." Although Althusser claimed that the crisis opened up a "historical opportunity for liberation," the litany of shortcomings he identified in Marxism, including the lack of a Marxist theory of the state, belied his optimism. In the text "Le Marxism aujourd'hui" of late 1977 and early 1978, Althusser further repudiated his Marxism. Offering arguments that echoed those of the new philosophers, he asserted that the relationship between scientific theory and the workers' movement that one finds in Lenin and Kautsky "reproduces the bourgeois form of knowledge and power in their separation." Although Althusser maintained that Marx's theory remained revolutionary because it was rooted in the workers' struggle, he contended that the Kautskyist/Leninist misreading of Marx was facilitated by Marx himself. Marx had not sufficiently considered the problem of the organization of the class struggle, that the division between the apparatus and the militants "could reproduce the bourgeois separation of power and pose redoubtable problems, possibly ending in tragedy." Marxists had been unable to furnish the needed theory of the state, ideology, and the party, and as a consequence, the party ended up reproducing the structures of the bourgeois state in Stalinism. Beyond his critique of Marxism's shortcomings Althusser would have nothing to offer before his exit from French intellectual life in the autumn of 1980.[86]

Tacit Permission and Shared Assumptions: New Philosophy and the Larger Intellectual Community

Perhaps even more revealing of the nature of the moment of new philosophy is the reaction to it by the emerging "antitotalitarian front" comprised of the intellectuals associated with *Esprit*, *Faire*, *Libre*, and—for the most part—*Le Nouvel Observateur*, who increasingly understood as the 1978 elections approached that they were participating in a common political and intellectual endeavor.[87] Most of these intellectuals were neither unqualified supporters (like Foucault and Sollers) nor intransigent detractors (like

Mauriac and Elleinstein) of new philosophy. They criticized the simplifications and excessive pessimism of new philosophy, but most of them also
wanted it to be debated. Even those who considered new philosophy to be
unworthy of debate contended that, at the very least, it raised legitimate
questions that needed to be addressed. Finally, almost all of these intellectuals agreed that new philosophy was in one way or another symptomatic
of the bankruptcy of the parties of the Left. The reaction of these intellectuals to new philosophy clearly reveals the existence of an antitotalitarian
consensus defined by a common approach to the question of totalitarianism and the rejection of certain perspectives on it.

The debate over new philosophy in *Le Nouvel Observateur* was a debate
that Jean Daniel encouraged and considered important. Coming into 1977,
Daniel, although pleased by the evolution of the PCF since his dispute
with it over Portugal in the summer of 1975, maintained that *Le Nouvel
Observateur* had to remain vigilant because, he said, it "depends on us that
the soft logic of compromise with capitalism and the shameful fatality of
the gulag are avoided." Further, reflecting on the upcoming 1978 elections,
Daniel held that the Common Program had to be recast if the Left were to
emerge victorious. Above all, he and Michel Bosquet argued, the Left
should not grant Giscard the monopoly of liberalization. Contested by the
parties of the Left for their articles on the "good use of Giscardism," neither Daniel nor Bosquet backed down. Indeed, Bosquet warned that if
their prescriptions were ignored the socialist and communist parties
should expect "some people of the Left, including myself, [to contest]
already, in anticipation, your way of governing."[88]

After the March 1977 municipal elections, when both the campaign for
the 1978 legislatives and the negotiations over the reactualization of the
Common Program began, Daniel reiterated his demand that the Left's program be inflected in the direction of the Assises current of the Socialist
Party (PS). The Left, he argued, had to show that it merited to win, and to
this end it could "draw inspiration for regeneration" from the "enthralling
research" that is to be found "circulating around the journals *Faire, Esprit,
Libre*." Rather than distance *Le Nouvel Observateur* from new philosophy, he
organized a debate over it, which he inaugurated in March with an editorial note reminding his readers that new philosophy had been "welcomed
and defended" at *Le Nouvel Observateur* and asserting that "the Left has the
greatest interest in allowing itself to be questioned by a movement that is
rich, even in its excesses." A month later, Daniel again defended the debate
on new philosophy, maintaining that it had been "too quickly baptized
'Parisian.'" Professing surprise at the extent of anti-Stalinism and anti-
Marxism that it revealed among French intellectuals, Daniel argued that
the debate on new philosophy would be worth it if "there remained only
this unanimous profession of antitotalitarian faith" when it ended.[89]

When the negotiations over the reactualization of the Common Program stagnated and then failed in September, Daniel's pessimism over the

Left reached heights unequaled since the summer of 1975. Once again, he began to worry openly over the incomplete internal liberalization of the PCF and found new cause for concern over the "Marxist prophesies" of communist militants that could "bring about a totalitarian development despite the good will of the communist leaders." In June, Daniel revived the debate about the Portuguese Revolution, which he considered a "test case" for the Left, by attacking the denunciation of Soares's reformism by Jean-Pierre Chevènement (a leader of the PS's CERES current), which he considered to be based on ideas that fatally led to totalitarianism. Chevènement confirmed Daniel in his belief in "the absolute necessity of accepting the protest of the antitotalitarian intellectuals." In September, Daniel defined a forum on social experimentation put on by *Le Nouvel Observateur* and *Faire* as bringing together "those who do not intend to leave the responsibility for their future in the hands of a party general staff that prepares an oppressive state for them." Later that month, Daniel told a national television audience that the question of the gulag "obsesses" him and that he maintained a "worried vigilance" with regard to the Union of the Left. His embracing of the politics of dissidence at the Biennale in December capped off a year of radicalization of Daniel's critique of the Left.[90]

For *Esprit*, like *Le Nouvel Observateur*, the year preceding the 1978 legislative elections was a time to intensify, and not to soften, criticisms of the Union of the Left. For example, Jacques Julliard's influential article, "Un an avant," (One year before [the election]), published in *Esprit* in February 1977 and then republished in large part in *Le Nouvel Observateur*, sought, Julliard explained in a letter to Jean-François Revel, to "contribute to breaking the double language of official triumphalism and private anxieties that is in the process of ensconcing itself within and around the Left, notably the socialist Left."[91] "Un an avant" warned of the dangers of the PCF returning to Stalinism unless it undertook a self-criticism of its Stalinist past and "took measures of internal democracy." Further, Julliard, conscious that he had become more demanding than ever before of the PCF, asserted that it no longer sufficed that the communists said the same thing as enlightened noncommunists about the USSR: "it is further necessary that they feel it the same way we do." Julliard was also highly critical of intellectuals and their Marxism. Repeating the ambient condemnations of intellectuals' past support for totalitarian régimes, Julliard charged that *"Marxism is nothing more or less than the philosophy of intellectuals as a ruling class"* and that "socialism is the régime of intellectuals as capitalism is the régime of the propertied." Julliard called upon intellectuals to fight against their putative class interests and liberate civil society from political society rather than subordinate the former to the latter. Intellectuals that should serve as *"mediators between civil society and political society*—mediation should recall the place of an intellectual like Julliard in the media. Some intellectuals—identified as "a few men at *Le Nouvel Observateur*, *Libération*,

Le Quotidien de Paris and *Esprit* and a few unclassifiable intellectuals like Lefort and Glucksmann"—had resisted the PCF and forced its evolution. Their work had to continue as the elections approached.[92]

Paul Thibaud echoed Julliard's critique of intellectuals, and organized a meeting between *Esprit, Libre* and *Faire* on the question of whether intellectuals constitute a totalitarian class. After the Left's victory in the March 1977 municipal elections, Thibaud, like Jean Daniel, asserted that it was necessary to intensify the debate so that the Left could be liberated from its illusion, and as the Union of the Left fell apart, both Thibaud and Julliard called upon the PS to reassert its own identity and break with the Common Program. Although Thibaud and Julliard denied at times that the Common Program was leading to the gulag, they invoked the dangers of totalitarianism within the Left and emphasized the need to reflect on its causes at every opportunity. Julliard, for example, argued that if the Left came to power France would be menaced by "a global politicization of all of society and an increasingly developed state control over each of its sectors" that could only lead to a "catastrophe." Given that Julliard asserted that the illusion that "everything is political" leads to totalitarianism, his argument led to the conclusion that France was menaced by totalitarianism. Thibaud similarly identified a danger of totalitarianism in nationalizations and published an article by Blandine Barret-Kriegel entitled "Échapper à la dérive concentrationnaire" (Escape the drift to the concentration camp), which asserted that intellectuals needed to "reflect on and debate the means to escape it." Immediately before the 1978 elections, Thibaud spoke of the resolution of "the people of the Left" as revealing "a great self-confidence, a conviction that is perhaps naïve that the French will be spared the great calamities of economic regression and totalitarianism and that those things are for peoples less favored by fortune."[93]

Esprit's position toward the new philosophers was, not surprisingly, profoundly ambiguous. Certainly, intellectuals at *Esprit* generally preferred the analyses of totalitarianism by Castoriadis and Lefort over those by Glucksmann and Lévy. But Julliard, for example, saw the new philosophers as symptoms of a crisis between the Left and its intellectuals that went to three questions: the gulag, Marxism, and the method of social transformation. Julliard believed that the new philosophers had the merit of communicating the truth about totalitarianism on some level and popularizing it. Although he recognized that "that which one gains in popularization [with the new philosophers] one loses in depth," he argued that "truth is not worn out or exhausted by being shared by a greater number." Julliard found the argument that "all these campaigns come at the wrong time because they risk costing the Left votes" to be "quite simply abominable." Even though he himself could not subscribe to the critique of rationalism and the "provocative and overly complaisant paradoxes" of Lévy's *La Barbarie à visage humain*, he defended the book behind closed doors within the Left. Essentially in agreement with Glucksmann, he had his *La*

Cuisinière et le mangeur d'hommes republished in a "pocket" edition in the "Politique" collection, which he edited for the publisher Seuil. Thibaud, although also critical of the new philosophers' media campaign and simplifications, argued that they deserved credit for occupying "ground" and posing the question of whether "revolutionary politics is not a deception." The radical despair of the new philosophers was, Thibaud contended, the product of the crisis of the politics of the Left. The latter had to be addressed if, as Thibaud hoped, the former were to be overcome.[94]

Esprit was, as the comments of Thibaud and Julliard suggest, somewhat divided over the new philosophers. When, after some delay, the journal finally discussed the new philosophers at length, it published an elegy of them by Guy Coq and an article against them by Olivier Mongin. For Guy Coq the new philosophers were nothing less than "a new youthful thought in the old West" and the "visible portion of the iceberg" that testified to the upheaval of French thought since 1968. Mongin, who had presented the analyses of totalitarianism by Claude Lefort and Marcel Gauchet in the pages of *Esprit*, found that the new philosophers had liberated certain important questions that the Marxist vulgate had "muzzled," notably "the analysis of totalitarianism, the critique of the state and of the gulag, the fight for human rights, and the status of Western Reason," but, as a consequence of their marriage to the logic of the media, had simultaneously closed debate on them by imposing a globalizing, apolitical vulgate. The problem with the new philosophers was not that they offered a critique of totalitarianism, but, in the case of Glucksmann at least, that their reduction of differences between democratic and totalitarian states blocked the path to a true and effective antitotalitarianism. Like Castoriadis and Yannakakis before him, Mongin regretted that one could not discuss these questions "without being affiliated with new philosophy, the risk being that these questions might not be taken seriously if they are monopolized by it." The problem for Mongin was "how does one insist on the interest of *their* questions while identifying them with a pressure group spreading within the intelligentsia?" Mongin recognized that new philosophy was a "vast rumor that reached such a level only because of the political conjuncture," but was not this conjuncture in intellectual politics one for which *Esprit* bore some responsibility?[95]

The socialist journal *Faire*'s stated preference for "the opening of a true debate rather than the negotiation of artificial compromises" within the Left led it to discuss Glucksmann's *La Cuisinière et le mangeur d'hommes* in its third issue. The debate on Glucksmann's book, *Faire*'s editor Patrick Viveret explained, had been "botched" and needed to be reopened because of the danger that "Marxism can become an ideology contrary to its critical vocation." Although Alain Meyer's article—perhaps Viveret's concession to the Union of the Left—dismissed *La Cuisinière* as little more than a rehashing of the debates of the Cold War, that by Pierre Rosanvallon took it more seriously. The book had, Rosanvallon argued, the merit of asking "the essential question of the relationship between Marxist theory and Stalinist practice," but it "gave false responses to true questions." The problem with Marxism, as Rosanvallon saw it, was that it lacked a political philosophy, a lack that was itself the consequence of "the myth of absolute knowledge that is the global consciousness of society." Marxism offered a utopia "that promises liberation without having the concrete means to achieve it," something that "will always risk making the litter of totalitarianism." Against Glucksmann, Rosanvallon affirmed that "we do not accept that the critique of Marxism and/or Stalinism becomes the alibi of a political skepticism and a revolutionary resignation that plays into the hands of the dominant ideology and of bourgeois politics." What they needed to do was not to debate whether Marx was guilty for the gulag, but to "elaborate a realistic and operational political doctrine" that would navigate between the twin shoals of social-democratic reformism and Stalinism.[96]

Yet, beginning in late 1976, *Faire* became increasingly skeptical and critical of the parties of the Left without outlining much of a realistic political alternative of its own. In a November 1976 *Faire* article Pierre Rosanvallon announced the crisis of their politics. Although he was influenced less by *The Gulag Archipelago* than by Claude Lefort's reading of it,[97] Rosanvallon explained that the former had undermined their ideas of revolution, politics, and social domination, causing them to lose their sense that history has a direction and that the world is structured coherently. Consequently, Rosanvallon felt that "we can no longer think about our future as we have always expected it to be. And we do not yet know how to think about it otherwise." Although Rosanvallon rejected the "neo-romanticism" of Clavel, Lardreau, Jambet, and Benoist, which he considered a "flight into the irrational and … [a] reactionary drift of intellectuals finally relieved not to have to think about politics," he also found it to be symptomatic of the crisis of the Left's politics. Rosanvallon explicitly rejected the argument that they needed to subordinate these intellectual debates on politics to the fight for victory in 1978. "Rethink politics" was an imperative; it was not "a luxury of our practice, but the very condition of its existence." Beginning in January 1977, Patrick Viveret also radicalized his rhetoric. Viveret had, as late as June-July 1976, rejected the argument that the PS faced the danger of "crypto-communism," maintaining that "the electoral and political strength of the PS preserves it from it," but in January 1977 he began to argue that France faced a danger of totalitarianism because of the lack of democracy within the parties of the Left, the PS as well as the PCF. Increasingly in 1977 Rosanvallon and Viveret developed the distinction, drawn in Rocard's speech (written by Viveret) at the PS's April 1977 Nantes Party Congress, between the two political cultures of the Left: the *social-étatique* (social-statist), which threatened to end in bureaucracy or even totalitarianism, and the *autogestionnaire*, which offered a way out of the impasse of the politics of the Left.[98]

The most complete effort by *Faire* intellectuals to rethink their politics was Rosanvallon and Viveret's influential *Pour une nouvelle culture politique*, published at the end of 1977. Here the new philosophers were again presented as a new romantic response to "the crisis of the *social-étatique* political culture." Against their "culture of disenchantment and of *déclassement*," Rosanvallon and Viveret called for a new effort to "reflect both freely and positively, learn the politics of obstinate realism, and imaginatively confront necessity [*ruser avec la nécessité*]." Although the authors claimed at one point, like many others in the antitotalitarian front, that there was no risk that the French Left would "involve France in a totalitarian process comparable to the evolution of the USSR or of China," they found the threat of totalitarianism lurking everywhere in French politics. The specter of totalitarianism could be found in the French Revolution. Its Terror was totalitarian, and its casting of equality in terms of uniformity could lead to a "collective dependency of a totalitarian type." Totalitarianism is, according to Rosanvallon and Viveret, "as it were, the 'effect' of egalitarian individualism in a centralized and globalizing society," in other words, an effect of the French Revolution as they understood it. Both French communism and "social democracy" (that is, the SFIO and PS) exhibited totalitarian tendencies because they limited the "demand for democracy in time and in space." Their common *social-étatique* culture, firmly rooted in French traditions of Jacobinism and Republicanism, was the hegemonic political culture of the PCF and infected their projects with the germ of totalitarianism. Further, traditional parties focused on the conquest of power tend to confuse "political society" and government, a confusion that can "tend toward a totalitarian government." Finally, totalitarianism was favored by the revolutionary project common to the socialists and communists because of the role given to the state within it, its "project of the total reunification of society" and its "legitimization by force." Although Rosanvallon and Viveret claimed that the socialists' "democratic aspirations" were "too strong to authorize the use of force to bend reality to this project" and would therefore not allow a totalitarian outcome, their statements on the hegemony of the political culture of the PCF within the Left and on the limitation of "democratic demands" within the PS tended to undermine this conclusion.[99]

Rosanvallon and Viveret's new political culture, presented as an antidote to the totalitarian danger, was a radical alternative. Although they called upon the Left to replace its *social-étatique* political culture with an *autogestionnaire* one, *autogestion* itself did not suffice insofar as it could be the latest version of the desire for transparency and social harmony that favored totalitarianism.[100] What was needed was a disaggregation of sovereignty and of politics and a far more modest conception of political change. Politics could no longer be totalizing or seek to offer definitive solutions. The focus of politics on traditional political parties and their exercise of power had to be shifted to a politics of experimentation in which social movements would break out of their protest (*revendicatif*) role and move politics away from its identification with the pole of the state. Militants playing the role of political entrepreneurs would bring the political process to the grass roots. A reconceptualization of equality in terms of autonomy and recognition of the rights to difference and autonomy would involve "not only a right to pluralism, but a pluralist law." In brief, an *autogestionnaire* federalism would save France from totalitarianism and reinvigorate politics.[101] *Pour une nouvelle culture politique* offered an intoxicating perspective on French politics that hardly appears to offer the "realistic and operational political doctrine" that its authors hoped to elaborate, but if, as Viveret declared in an interview, their book had no "theoretical pretensions" and was "above all a book that intervenes in a strategic debate," its excesses become comprehensible within the context of the approaching 1978 elections.[102]

The last, but certainly not the least, of the journals participating in the antitotalitarian front is *Libre*. Through *Libre*, born in 1977 with an explicitly antitotalitarian agenda, Claude Lefort and Cornelius Castoriadis continued their parallel and sometimes conflicting reflections on and interventions in politics begun roughly thirty years earlier in *Socialisme ou barbarie*.[103] By 1977 both Lefort and Castoriadis had become living icons of French antitotalitarianism. Other antitotalitarian intellectuals reviewing the history of the French intellectual Left's relationship with communism during the Cold War concluded that they had been "right" in the 1950s against Sartre and other *progressistes* in their denunciations of the PCF and the Soviet Union.[104] Further, republished in the early 1970s, their writings of the late 1940s, 1950s, and 1960s, which culminated in critiques of Marxism and the revolutionary project, had a considerable impact on other intellectuals.[105] Their analyses of totalitarianism were preferred to those of the new philosophers by most antitotalitarian intellectuals, and as a consequence, an examination of their ideas and the contemporary reception of them offers a precious window onto the antitotalitarian moment.

Lefort and Castoriadis responded, like so many others, with some ambiguity to new philosophy. As mentioned earlier, Castoriadis criticized the new philosophers' work as doing a disservice to the struggle against the Union of the Left. More fundamentally, Castoriadis asserted that new philosophy offered a "*complementary ideology* of the dominant system" that prevented the real problems, notably finding political forms appropriate to the rupture opened up by May '68, from being discussed. Further, Castoriadis objected that the new philosophers had pillaged his work and deformed its meaning by turning his critique of Marx away from the revolutionary perspective. Lefort also evaluated new philosophy in relation to the status of the Union of the Left in 1977. He saw the great attention given to the new philosophers as a consequence of the public's justifiably growing fear that a "brutal acceleration of the process of bureaucratization" and possibly totalitarianism would result from a Left victory in 1978.

In 1979, he recognized certain merits in the new philosophers, notably, that they had "shaken a part of the Left out of its torpor," that "thanks to them, the accounts of the dissidents were spread widely," and that "they reduced plenty of Marxist-Leninist pedants to silence." They were useful in this negative role, but, Lefort recognized, constructed nothing new and, in fact, only opened up "paths that turn away from the demands of the political thought" that Lefort hoped to rehabilitate. For Lefort, unlike Castoriadis, it was not their dismissal of revolution that was problematic, but their simple identification of French society with totalitarianism.[106]

Lefort and Castoriadis did not, of course, entirely agree with each other in either their political projects or their analyses of totalitarianism.[107] Unlike Lefort, Castoriadis's critique of Marxism and revolutionary organization led him not to discard the revolutionary project or critique it as totalitarian, but rather to redefine it in light of direct-democratic exigencies and reassert its necessity.[108] Thus, for Castoriadis, the content of socialism became "the restoration, rather the institution for the first time in history of the domination of men over their activities," the content of the revolutionary project became the "aim of a society that has become capable of a perpetual recasting of its institutions," and the content of the postrevolutionary society would be "a society that explicitly institutes itself, not once for all time, but in a continuous manner." Such a project was justified not by a philosophy of History or a science of society or politics, which Castoriadis considered impossible in any case, but by the simple demand for autonomy and lucid self-mastery. Castoriadis's revolutionary project entailed the end to society's alienation of its power of *auto-institution* in a state separate from it. Castoriadis imagined that the principles that lay behind workers' factory councils would provide the basis for society's *auto-institution*, although the forms of postrevolutionary society could not, out of respect for the process of *auto-institution*, be prescribed before the revolution.[109]

Castoriadis's revolutionary project was, as a 1976 interview with Olivier Mongin, Paul Thibaud, and Pierre Rosanvallon reveals, difficult for other antitotalitarian intellectuals to accept. Thibaud doubted whether one could effectively rehabilitate the revolutionary project by repudiating the pretension to totalizing knowledge because it seemed to him that revolution itself "engenders a type of representation, a desire to place oneself in a bird's eye view and to be able to say at once what is the fate of humanity and of the world." It was an objection that was often made to his ideas, Castoriadis admitted. Further, Thibaud questioned whether the limits that Castoriadis placed on our knowledge should not also circumscribe our action. Castoriadis responded that he rejected the idea of the postrevolutionary society as "transparent to itself" and that there was no question of forcing people to be autonomous, but his responses evidently left his interlocutors unsatisfied. They all wanted to know, as Pierre Rosanvallon said, what "the concrete theoretical and practical conditions of a true *auto-institution* of society" were. But this Castoriadis would not answer because the forms of *auto-institution* could be "neither foretold, nor deduced from any theory." All that one could do to further the process was to "show people that that they themselves hold a possible response, that only they can invent it, that all the possibilities and capacities for organizing society are to be found within them." Castoriadis's radical direct-democratic exigencies made his revolutionary project both intangible and too ambitious for its intangibility—at least in the eyes of his interlocutors. Jacques Julliard, in his review of Castoriadis's *L'Institution imaginaire de la société*, could not refrain from asking whether Castoriadis had not brought an end "quite simply to the intellectual myth of Revolution." Even Castoriadis himself often struck a note of pessimism when he discussed the prospects for revolution, but he would not give up the fight because its necessity never ceased to impose itself upon him. Castoriadis was one of the last revolutionary intellectuals of his era. Most antitotalitarian intellectuals, critical of Castoriadis's claim that the undetermined forms of *auto-institution* would unproblematically abolish the division of society (notably as manifest in the state), evidently preferred the work of Castoriadis's colleague and rival Claude Lefort.[110]

If the main opposition in Castoriadis's political and social thought was that between bureaucratic capitalism and the permanent and explicit *auto-institution* of society, that in Lefort's thought was between democracy and totalitarianism. Lefort, who repeatedly emphasized in the late 1970s and early 1980s that one had to think of politics in relation to totalitarianism, argued that totalitarianism was both a prolongation and a reversal of the democratic revolution. The democratic revolution establishes the difference between the state and civil society and an irreducible "division within society" that makes social and political conflict inevitable. Further, the democratic revolution establishes power as an "empty place," that is, a place with which no group or individual can be identified. Totalitarianism is a prolongation of the democratic revolution because it feeds on the eternal contradiction within democracy between the irreducible internal division of society and the affirmation of the unity of the people. And totalitarianism is also a negation of the democratic revolution because it is an effort to eliminate the division of society and reconstitute its unity by occupying the "empty place" of power. Although Lefort did not dismiss revolution to the extent that it emerges spontaneously from society, he considered it to be more likely and viable in totalitarian states, where it takes the form of democratic revolution. On the other hand, revolutionary projects in democracies along the lines outlined by Castoriadis threatened to end in totalitarianism. Although he believed that "power" "will always be, in the best of cases, half bad" and that it was simply impossible for the people to conquer power, Lefort did not advocate political quietism in democracies. On the contrary, he believed that "absence of struggle" could itself lead to totalitarianism (since democracies are by definition conflictual). Lefort contended that "la démocratie sauvage," the fight for rights (established, usurped, and new rights), was central to democracy and that it was the struggle over rights initiated by it that kept democracy healthy and progressing. Lefort's politics was certainly more assertive than the new philosophers' in that he gave the struggle for human rights a progressive role, whereas they conceived of it as purely defensive. But because Lefort saw totalitarianism looming over every horizon and did not believe that there were any institutional guarantees against it, he maintained that politics had to remain modest. Totalitarianism was nothing less than the negation of the turbulence and conflict of democratic society, a project whose attraction would never vanish. The price of liberty was, as much as ever, eternal vigilance.[111]

Notes

1. Sylvie Bouscasse and Denis Bourgeois, *Faut-il brûler les nouveaux philosophes?: le dossier du "procès"* (Paris, 1978), 62. Lévy's *La Barbarie à visage humain* sold 37,000 copies in its first two weeks, and 30,000 copies of Glucksmann's *Les Maîtres penseurs* sold in less than a month, according to Danielle Marx-Scouras, *The Cultural Politics of Tel quel: Literature and the Left in the Wake of Engagement* (University Park, Pa., 1996), 192.
2. *Le Monde*, 27 May 1977, 24-25.
3. Régis Debray's insightful *Le Pouvoir intellectuel en France*, Collection Folio/essais ed. (Paris, 1979) strikes me as too reductionist in its explanation of the success of the new philosophers via the transformation of French intellectual life by the mass media. Indeed, it verges (on page 84) on an apology for the Left's failure to win the intellectual battle before the 1978 elections.
4. On the place of the media in the intellectual field since the 1950s see Niilo Kauppi, *French Intellectual Nobility: Institutional and Symbolic Transformations in the Post-Sartrian Era* (Albany, N.Y., 1996).
5. André Glucksmann, *Les Maîtres penseurs* (Paris, 1977), 131, 290, 310. "Apostrophes" episode broadcast on Antenne 2 on 27 May 1977 and "Questionnaire" episode broadcast on TF1 on 18 September 1977, both consulted at the archives of L'Institut national de l'audiovisuel (INA).
6. Ibid., 119, 128, 28 for the citations.
7. Ibid., 227 and 223 for the citations. Pages 220 to 223 reprint Glucksmann's review of Clavel's *Dieu est Dieu* and attack on the Union of the Left, "Les Ballots du ballottage," *Le Monde*, 9 April 1976, 18. Glucksmann attributes the invention of the expression "*mains sales tendues*" to Paul Thibaud.
8. André Glucksmann interviewed by Max Gallo, *L'Express* 1358 (18 July 1977): 62, 66-71; "Questionnaire," 18 Sept. 1977 and "Apostrophes," 27 May 1977. Glucksmann also explicitly discusses the significance of his book for the Left in *Libération*, 27 May 1977, 11.
9. Glucksmann, *Les Maîtres penseurs*, 289; *L'Express* 1358 (18 July 1977): 69; André Glucksmann, "En douce dans le XXIe siècle," *Le Nouvel Observateur* 658 (20 June 1977): 97. For examples of his positions of the 1980s see Lucien Bodard, "André Glucksmann," *Le Point* 495 (25 March 1982): 157-66 and Jürg Altwegg, "Von der Mai-Barrikade zur Atomstrategie. Der weiter Weg des Andrés Glucksmann – ein Gespräch," *Dokumente* 40, 1 (March 1984): 39-48.

10. Bernard-Henri Lévy, *La Barbarie à visage humain*, Livre de poche, biblio essais ed. (Paris, 1977), 9-10. "Apostrophes," 27 May 1977.

11. Ibid., 143, 131 for the citations.

12. Ibid., 151-52, 145, 207 for the citations.

13. André Glucksmann cited in Lucien Bodard, "André Glucksmann," 158.

14. André Glucksmann interview with Christian Descamps, *Le Monde Dimanche*, 30 March 1980, xvi.

15. *Le Monde*, 4 Nov. 1978, 11. Bernard-Henri Lévy, *L'Idéologie française* (Paris, 1981).

16. See chapter 3 above.

17. Cited in Edouard Brasey, *L'Effet Pivot* (Paris, 1987), 205.

18. Bernard-Henri Lévy, "Réponses aux maîtres censeurs," *Le Nouvel observateur* 659 (27 June 1977): 40-41; Bernard-Henri Lévy interviewed by Ludovic Bessozzi, *Tel quel* 77 (autumn 1978): 25. "Gilles Deleuze contre les 'nouveaux philosophes'," *Le Monde*, 19-20 June 1977, 16.

19. Glucksmann cited in Marx-Scouras, *The Cultural Politics of Tel quel*, 194. For Kristeva's talk see her "Un nouveau type d'intellectuel: le dissident," *Tel quel* (winter 1977): 3-8.

20. Thomas Ferenczi, "Jacques Attali dans la caravane," *Le Monde*, 26 April 1977, 27. Citation from André Glucksmann, "En douce dans le XXIe siècle," 97. See also André Glucksmann interviewed by Max Gallo, *L'Express* 1358 (18 July 1977): 70; Thierry Wolton, "Oublier Lénine," *Libération*, 21 November 1977, 15; and André Glucksmann, "Qui est le terroriste?" *Le Nouvel Observateur* 665 (8 Aug. 1977): 27.

21. Interview of Guy Lardreau and Christian Jambet by Gilles Hertzog, *Magazine littéraire* 112-113 (May 1976): 56; Christian Jambet and Guy Lardreau, "Le Goulag spirituel est déjà là," *Le Monde*, 27 May 1977, 24. Jean-Marie Benoit, "Dix mois pour en rire," *Le Monde*, 27 May 1977, 25.

22. Jean Daniel, "Le Matin des dissidents," in *L'Ère des ruptures* (Paris, 1979), 396; Jean Daniel, "Le Matin des dissidents," *Le Nouvel observateur* 680 (21 Nov. 1977): 45. *Tel quel* is discussed below. French participants and organizers of the Théâtre Récamier reception included Michel Foucault, Roland Barthes, Pierre Daix, André Glucksmann, François Jacob, Jean-Paul Sartre, Laurent Schwartz, Pierre Victor, Claude Mauriac, Simone de Beauvoir, Gilles Deleuze, Jean-Pierre Faye, and Eugène Ionesco. French participants in the Biennale de Venise included André Glucksmann, Cornelius Castoriadis, Jean Elleinstein, Alain Besançon, Emmanuel Le Roy Ladurie, Jean Daniel, Julia Kristeva, and Paul Thibaud. On the reception see David Macey, *The Lives of Michel Foucault* (New York, 1993), 379-81. On the Biennale see *Le Monde*, 23 Nov. 1977, 2 and Wolton, "Oublier Lénine." For an instance of dissent from the dominant perspective on dissidence see Robert Linhart, "Western 'Dissidence' Ideology and the Protection of Bourgeois Order," in *Power and Opposition in Post-Revolutionary Societies*, trans. from the French by Patrick Camiller and the Italian by Jon Rothschild (London, 1979), 249-60.

23. Bernard-Henri Lévy, *Bangla Desh, nationalisme dans la révolution* (Paris, 1973).

24. Information on Lévy's biography is drawn from *Génération perdue. Ceux qui avaient vingt ans en 1968? Ceux qui avaient vingt ans à la fin de la guerre d'Algérie? Ou ni les uns ni les autres?* (Paris, 1977), 165-68; François Dufay and Pierre-Bertrand Dufont, *Les Normaliens de Charles Péguy à Bernard-Henri Lévy, un siècle d'histoire* (Paris, 1993), 307-9; Jean-Louis Ezine, "B.-H. L., archange, comédien et martyr," *L'Express* 1721 (29 June 1984): 54-55.

25. Interview of Bernard-Henri Lévy and Michel Butel by Alain Chouffan, *Le Nouvel Observateur* 533 (27 Jan. 1975): 22; *Le Monde*, 21 Dec. 1974, 14; *Le Monde*, 25 Jan. 1975, 23; *Le Monde*, 7 Feb. 1975, 25. Monique Bel, *Maurice Clavel* (Paris, 1992), 310.

26. Philippe Nemo, Michel Guérin, Christian Jambet, and Guy Lardreau.

27. Rémy Rieffel, *La Tribu des clercs: les intellectuels sous la Ve République 1958-1990* (Paris, 1993), 495-502, 563-65. Hervé Hamon and Patrick Rotman, *Les Intellocrates: Expédition en haute intelligentsia* (Brussels, 1985), 82-89, 220-26.

28. On the new novel as a product of the cultural press and the publisher Minuit's marketing strategies see Kauppi, *French Intellectual Nobility*, 99-101.

29. The following analysis draws on the discussion of the promotion of new philosophy by François Aubral and Xavier Delcourt, *Contre la nouvelle philosophie* (Paris, 1977), 237-71.
30. Lévy published numerous book reviews and interviews with intellectuals (Lyotard, Barthes, Aron, Foucault) in *Le Nouvel Observateur* beginning in 1975.
31. Gérard Petitjean, "Les Nouveaux Gourous," *Le Nouvel Observateur* 609 (12 July 1976): 62-68. Lévy used his obituary of Heidegger to promote Dollé, Jambet, and Lardreau: "L'Héritage de Heidegger," *Le Nouvel Observateur* 603 (31 May 1976): 40. Sollers reviewed Françoise Lévy, *Karl Marx: histoire d'un bourgeois allemand* in *Le Nouvel Observateur* 630 (6 Dec. 1976): 90-91.
32. See his "L'Ange exterminateur" (review of *L'Ange* of Christian Jambet and Guy Lardreau), *Le Nouvel Observateur* 593 (22 March 1976): 60; "La Leçon de l'exode," *Le Nouvel Observateur* 594 (29 March 1976): 65, where he continues his discussion of *L'Ange*, and his "Un Lacanien chrétien" (review of *L'Homme structurel* by Philippe Nemo) *Le Nouvel Observateur* 547 (5 May 1975): 59.
33. "Inter-fluences de la philosophie contemporaine," *Magazine littéraire* 127-128 (Sept. 1977): 66-67.
34. See for example his "Les Lanciers de la métaphysique," *Le Monde*, 27 May 1977, 24 and his "Les 'Nouveaux philosophes' contre deux challengers," *Le Monde*, 29-30 May 1977, 16.
35. For a list of radio appearances see Aubral and Delcourt, *Contre la nouvelle philosophie*, 265-66. Texts of some of the November-December 1976 interviews with Jacques Paugam for the France Culture radio program "Parti pris" can be found in *Génération perdue*. On lectures in Paris see Bouscasse and Bourgeois, *Faut-il brûler les nouveaux philosophes?*, 53-55.
36. Petitjean, "Les Nouveaux Gourous," 65.
37. Again, the similarity to the "new novel" is striking.
38. Identified in the dossier as new philosophers were Michel Guérin, Christian Jambet, Guy Lardreau, Jean-Paul Dollé, Philippe Roger, Jean-Marie Benoist, Françoise Lévy, and Annie Leclerc. Only Leclerc was not published by Lévy.
39. See the advertisement on the inside cover of *Magazine littéraire* 127-128 (September 1977), which has as its headline "The 'New Philosophers' publish in the *FIGURES AND THEORICIENS* collections directed by Bernard-Henri Lévy."
40. Bernard-Henri Lévy, "Adresses," *Les Nouvelles littéraires* (10 June 1976): 15.
41. Bernard-Henri Lévy interviewed by Jacques Paugam, *Génération perdue*, 173. See also his "La Nouvelle Philosophie n'existe pas," *La Nef* 66 (Jan.-April 1978): 29-34 and his interview in *Tel quel* 77 (autumn 1978): 25-35.
42. Maurice Clavel interviewed by J.-J. Bronchier, *Magazine littéraire* 127-128 (September 1977): 60.
43. The preceding three paragraphs are based on Bel, *Maurice Clavel*.
44. Bel, *Maurice Clavel*, 276-77, 302-4; Maurice Clavel, "Mes repas avec René Andrieu," *Le Nouvel Observateur* 585 (26 Jan. 1976): 62; Daniel cited in Rieffel, *La Tribu des clercs*, 56. Clavel's article of 26 Jan. was preceded by the editorial comment: "We never asked Maurice Clavel anything other than to be himself—even if he is far from us. This is what he does today, more freely than ever…"
45. Maurice Clavel, *Ce que je crois* (Paris, 1975); Maurice Clavel, *Dieu est Dieu, nom de Dieu!* (Paris, 1976); Bel, *Maurice Clavel*, 318.
46. Clavel discusses Glucksmann's book throughout the summer of 1975 in *Le Nouvel Observateur* 553 (16 June 1975): 12 and his television reviews "Coups d'épingle sur Chirac," *Le Nouvel Observateur* 554 (23 June 1975): 65, "Une méditation atterrée," *Le Nouvel Observateur* 559 (28 July 1975): 60, and "Ne jamais croire au succès," *Le Nouvel Observateur* 560 (4 Aug. 1975): 60. As we have seen, Glucksmann returned the favor to Clavel in his review of Clavel's *Dieu est Dieu*.
47. Daniel, *L'Ère des ruptures*, 248.
48. Bernard-Henri Lévy, "Le Vrai 'Crime' de Soljenitsyne," *Le Nouvel Observateur* 555 (30 June 1975): 54-55 and François Furet, "Faut-il brûler Marx?" *Le Nouvel Observateur* 559 (28 July 1975): 52-53. Rieffel, *La Tribu des clercs*, 56.

49. Bel, *Maurice Clavel*, 324-34, citations on pages 325, 327, and 334; Maurice Clavel, "L'Ouragan Glucksmann," *Le Nouvel Observateur* 646 (28 March 1977): 17. See also the account of Clavel's "Cercle socratique" in Rieffel, *La Tribu des clercs*, 54-57.

50. See Alain Geismar, *L'Engrenage terroriste* (Paris, 1981); Michel Le Bris, *L'Homme aux semelles de vent* (Paris, 1977); Jean-Pierre Le Dantec, *Les Dangers du soleil* (Paris, 1978); and the Pierre Victor interview in *Le Nouvel Observateur* 671 (19 Sept. 1977): 47-48, as well as the discussion of Pierre Victor's (Benny Lévy's) adoption of Orthodox Judaism after leaving the GP in Judith Friedlander, *Vilna on the Seine: Jewish Intellectuals in France Since 1968* (New Haven, 1990), chap. 7.

51. See Rieffel, *La Tribu des clercs*, 143-45 for details.

52. By Pierre Viansson-Ponté, Bernard Pivot, and Gilles Deleuze respectively.

53. Bel, *Maurice Clavel*, 318; Maurice Clavel, "Pour la fracture," *Le Nouvel Observateur* 663 (25 July 1977): 62; *Magazine littéraire* 127-128 (Sept. 1977): 60. Glucksmann's letter in response to Lévy's *Le Nouvel Observateur* review of Clavel's *Dieu est Dieu, nom de Dieu!* in *Le Nouvel Observateur* (24 March 1976). *Libération*, 27 May 1977, 1, 10-11.

54. Audience figure from Marx-Scouras, *The Cultural Politics of Tel quel*, 192. On Glucksmann's television appearances: *Le Monde*, 26 April 1977, 27; *Le Monde*, 22 June 1977, 8; *Le Monde*, 6 July 1977, 25; *Le Monde*, 20 Sept. 1977, 33; the catalogue of the Institut national de l'audiovisuel. Thomas Ferenczi, "Bernard-Henri Lévy, intellectuel français," *Le Monde*, 29 Nov. 1977, 29. *Playboy* (June 1977) and *Marie-Claire* (Sept. 1977).

55. For contemporary impressions and their use of the media see Claude Sarraute, "Le Temps des roses," *Le Monde*, 6 July 1977, 25 and Brasey, *L'Effet Pivot*, 178 and 199. "Apostrophes" episode of 27 May 1977. Lévy's *La Barbarie à visage humain*, 8-9, explicitly made a generational appeal. On Giscard's lunch: Bouscasse and Bourgeois, *Faut-il brûler les nouveaux philosophes?* 126. Rieffel, *La Tribu des clercs*, 200-21. Clavel and Lévy accepted the invitation; Glucksmann refused it. For Glucksmann's reasons see his "Mon ami, votre injustice," *Le Monde*, 6 Sept. 1978, 8.

56. Barthes's "Lettre à Bernard-Henri Lévy," first published in *Les Nouvelles littéraires* of 26 May 1977 and republished in Bouscasse and Bourgeois, *Faut-il brûler les nouveaux philosophes?* 89-90.

57. Michel Foucault, "La Grande colère des faits" and "Pouvoirs et stratégies" in Michel Foucault, *1976-1979*, vol. 3 of *Dits et écrits*, ed. Daniel Defert and François Ewald (Paris, 1994), 277-81 and 418-28. Claude Mauriac, "Il ne faut pas tuer l'espérance," *Le Monde*, 7 July 1977, 1. "Gilles Deleuze contre les 'nouveaux philosophes'," *Le Monde*, 19-20 June 1977, 16. David Macey, *The Lives of Michel Foucault: A Biography* (New York, 1993), 387-89.

58. Peter Dews, "The *Nouvelle Philosophie* and Foucault," *Economy and Society* 8, 2 (May 1979): 127-71, citation on page 142.

59. Kauppi, *French Intellectual Nobility*, 134-36; Macey, *The Lives of Michel Foucault*, 172-73; Glucksmann, *Les Maîtres penseurs*, 237.

60. Contrary to Eribon, who argues that Foucault's support of Glucksmann's *Les Maîtres penseurs* was "dictated by considerations that were more political than philosophical." Didier Eribon, *Michel Foucault (1926-1984)* (Paris, 1991), 336.

61. Ibid., 168-69; Michel Foucault, "Le Monde est un grand asile," in *1970-1975*, vol. 2 of his *Dits et écrits*, 434.

62. Eribon, *Michel Foucault*, 194-95; Michel Foucault, "Crimes et châtiments en U.R.S.S. et ailleurs…," "Une mobilisation culturelle," and "La Grille politique traditionnelle," in *1976-1979*, 74, 330-31, and 506-7; Maurice Clavel, "'Vous direz trois rosaires'," *Le Nouvel Observateur* 633 (27 Dec. 1977): 55.

63. Michel Foucault, "Pouvoir et savoir," "Cours du 7 janvier 1976," and "Cours du 14 janvier 1976," in his *1976-1979*, 400-401; 160-74, citation page 167; 175-89, citation page 181.

64. Michel Foucault, "Non au sexe roi," "Cours du 14 janvier 1976," and "Enfermement, psychiatrie, prison," in his *1976-1979*, 266-67, 189, and 335 respectively. Michel Foucault, *Discipline and Punish: The Birth of the Prison*, trans. Alan Sheridan (New York, 1979), 297.

65. Michel Foucault, "Pouvoirs et stratégies" and "Cours du 7 janvier 1976," in *1976-1979*, 421-22, and 165 respectively. Note that Foucault speaks of the importance of the "non-proletarianized pleb" before Glucksmann as early as 1972 in his "Sur la justice populaire. Débat avec les maos," in *1970-1975*, 352 and passim.

66. Michel Foucault, "Cours du 7 janvier 1976," "Michel Foucault: crimes et châtiments en U.R.S.S. et ailleurs," "Pouvoirs et stratégies," and "Questions à Michel Foucault sur la géographie," all in *1976-1979*, 166-67, 69, 418-21, and 32 respectively.

67. By Pascal Ory and Jean-François Sirinelli, *Les Intellectuels en France, de l'Affaire Dreyfus à nos jours* (Paris, 1986), 225.

68. This and succeeding paragraphs draw heavily on Philippe Forest, *Histoire de Tel quel 1960-1982* (Paris, 1995), which, although apologetic, is by far the most informative of the histories of *Tel quel*. On *Tel quel*'s position in the literary marketplace see Niilo Kauppi, *The Making of an Avant-Garde: Tel quel*, Approaches to Semiotics, 113 (New York, 1994) and Niilo Kauppi, *French Intellectual Nobility*, chap. 8.

69. Julia Kristeva, "Mémoire," *L'Infini* 1 (winter 1983): 50.

70. Ibid., 51; Philippe Sollers, "Pourquoi j'ai été chinois," in his *Improvisation* (Paris, 1991), 75-113; Maurice Clavel and Philippe Sollers, *Délivrance: Entretiens recueillis par Jacques Paugam dans le cadre de son émission 'Parti pris' sur France-Culture* (Paris, 1977), 132-33. Ieme van der Poel, *Une Révolution de la pensée: maoïsme et féminisme à travers Tel quel*, Les Temps modernes, *et* Esprit, Faux Titre no. 65 (Amsterdam, 1992), chap. 4; Kauppi, *The Making of an Avant-Garde*, 103-12; Forest, *Histoire de Tel quel*, 378-491.

71. See Sollers' letter in *Le Monde*, 22 Oct. 1976, 3; Clavel and Sollers, *Délivrance*, 132-33; "A propos du 'Maoïsme'," *Tel quel* 68 (winter 1976): 104.

72. Kauppi, *The Making of an Avant-Garde*, 331; "Éditorial: nouvelles contradictions, nouvelles luttes," *Tel quel* 58 (summer 1974): 3 (dated March 1974); "A propos de 'la Chine sans utopie' (*Le Monde* 15-19 June 1974)," *Tel quel* 59 (autumn 1974): 7; Marc Devade, "Aller à contre courant," *Tel quel* 61 (spring 1975): 7 (dated 20 Dec. 1974);

73. Maria-Antonietta Macciocchi, "Marx, la cuisinière et le cannibale," *Tel quel* 64 (winter 1975): 61-66. Jean-Louis Houdebine, Philippe Sollers, Julia Kristeva, and André Glucksmann, "Réponses," *Tel quel* 64 (winter 1975): 67-73. Interview with Philippe Sollers, "Nous vivons une période de régression," *Les Nouvelles littéraires* 28 (Oct. 1976): 19. See Forest, *Histoire de Tel quel*, 478-86, on their return from China, but note that this apologetic reading fails to take into account the continued defense of the Chinese Cultural Revolution by telquelians until the autumn of 1976. See, for example, Sollers' intervention on the "Apostrophes" on "La Liberté en Chine" reported in J. H., *Le Monde*, 26-27 Jan. 1975, 5.

74. Forest, *Histoire de Tel quel*, 268-71 and 524-29; Kauppi, *The Making of an Avant-Garde*, 103; Julia Kristeva, Marcelin Pleynet, and Philippe Sollers, "Pourquoi les États-Unis?" *Tel quel* 71/73 (autumn 1977): 3-19, and 10 for the Kristeva citation.

75. Julia Kristeva, "Un nouveau type d'intellectuel: le dissident," *Tel quel* 74 (winter 1977): 3-8 (her Beaubourg presentation of May 1977); Julia Kristeva interviewed in *Le Nouvel Observateur* 658 (20 June 1977): 98-134, citations on pages 125 and 134; Julia Kristeva, "Le Discours de gauche en question," *Le Monde*, 27 Dec. 1977, 2 (the text of her intervention at the Biennale de Venise, published in a slightly different version in *Tel quel* 76 [summer 1978], a number devoted entirely to dissidence). Sollers echoed Kristeva's call that intellectuals be dissidents on FR3's "L'Homme en question" of 3 April, reported in Claude Sarraute, "Philippe Sollers tel quel…," *Le Monde*, 5 April 1977, 24, and in his review of Lévy's *La Barbarie à visage humain*, "La Révolution impossible," *Le Monde*, 13 May 1977, 19, 24.

76. Sarraute, "Philippe Sollers tel quel…," 24 and Philippe Sollers, "Les Intellectuels européens et la crise," *Le Monde*, 12 Nov. 1977, 2.

77. Philippe Sollers, "La Révolution impossible," 24. Forest, *Histoire de Tel quel*, 500-502. Sollers and *Tel quel* were not very receptive to the neospiritualism of Lardreau, Jambet,

and Clavel. See, for example, Antoine Compagnon and Philippe Roger, "Un Ange passe," *Tel quel* 67 (autumn 1976): 76-80.

78. Delphine Bouffartigue, "Mauriac (Claude)," in *Dictionnaire des intellectuels français: les personnes, les lieux, les moments*, ed. Jacques Julliard and Michel Winock (Paris, 1996), 771-72.

79. Mauriac, "Il ne faut pas tuer l'espérance."

80. Jean Daniel, "Précisions en forme de post-scriptum," *Le Nouvel Observateur* 662 (18 July 1977): 22; Jacques Julliard, "La Gauche et ses intellectuels," *Le Nouvel Observateur* 656 (6 June 1977): 49-51; Edgar Morin, "Le Bruit et le message," *Le Nouvel Observateur* 659 (27 June 1977): 38; Cornelius Castoriadis, "Les Divertisseurs," *Le Nouvel Observateur* 658 (20 June 1977): 50-51; Ilios Yannakakis, "De Prague 1947 à Paris 1977," *Le Nouvel Observateur* 662 (18 July 1977): 38-39. Jacques Julliard, *Contre la politique professionnelle* (Paris, 1977), 36.

81. Entry on Jean Elleinstein in Philippe Robrieux, *Biographies, Chronologie, Bibliographie*, vol. 4 of *Histoire intérieure du parti communiste* (Paris, 1984), 195-200; "Faut-il croire les communistes?" (debate between Jean Elleinstein and Annie Kriegel) *Le Nouvel Observateur* 660 (4 July 1977): 64-81; "Entretien avec Jean Elleinstein sur le phénomène stalinien, la démocratie et le socialisme," *Esprit* 454 (Feb. 1976): 241-62.

82. André Harris and Alain de Sédouy, *Voyage à l'intérieur du Parti communiste* (Paris, 1974), 282; "Entretien avec Jean Elleinstein," citations from pages 251 and 252; Jean Elleinstein, "Quelle barbarie à visage humain?" *Le Monde*, 27 May 1977, 25; interview of Jean Elleinstein by Pierre Viansson-Ponté, *Le Monde*, 23 Nov. 1977, 2.

83. Jean-Marie Domenach in "Entretien avec Jean Elleinstein," 256-57; Jacques Julliard, "La Gauche et ses intellectuels," 50; Pierre Rosanvallon, "Une Nouvelle culture politique," *Faire* 13 (Nov. 1976): 26; Pierre Rosanvallon, "Les Avatars de l'idéalisme," *Faire* 3 (Dec. 1975): 39; Pierre Guidoni, "Les Deux lignes et les deux cultures," *Le Nouvel Observateur* 662 (18 July 1977): 22; Yannakakis cited in Jean Daniel, "Le Matin des dissidents," 45. Daniel agreed with Yannakakis. Alain Touraine, *Mort d'une gauche* (Paris, 1979), 35, 123, where his journalistic analyses of 1977 are republished.

84. Nicos Poulantzas, "L'Intelligentsia et le pouvoir," *Le Nouvel Observateur* 655 (30 May 1977): 41; Jacques Rancière, "Portrait du vieil intellectuel en jeune dissident," *Le Nouvel Observateur* 663 (25 July 1977): 40-41; Régis Debray, "Les Pleureuses du printemps," *Le Nouvel Observateur* 657 (13 June 1977): 60-61; Nicos Poulantzas, *L'État, le pouvoir, le socialisme* (Paris, 1978).

85. Gregory Elliot, *Althusser: The Detour of Theory* (New York, 1987), passim and pages 198, 199, and 278 for the citations. Louis Althusser, "Idéologie et appareils idéologiques d'État," in *Positions* (Paris, 1976), 133-34. See also Louis Althusser, *Essays in Self-Criticism*, trans. by Grahame Lock (London, 1976). I follow Elliot in my reading of Althusser.

86. Elliot, *Althusser*, 282-323 and pages 283, 315, and 318 for the citations; Louis Althusser, "The Crisis of Marxism," trans. Grahame Lock, in *Power and Opposition in Post-Revolutionary Societies*, 225-37 and pages 226, 228, 232, and 237 for the citations.

87. The term "antitotalitarian front" is from Grémion, *Paris-Prague: la Gauche face au renouveau et à la régression tchécoslovaques (1968-1978)* (Paris, 1985), 306, although he identifies it as comprised of "the intellectuals formerly in *Socialisme ou barbarie*, the sphere of influence of *Esprit*, and the *Cercle aronien*." Contrary to Grémion, the rapprochement of the antitotalitarians of the Left with the Aronians largely occurred after 1977.

88. Citations from Jean Daniel, "La Gauche devant le dernier relais," *Le Nouvel Observateur* 619 (20 Sept. 1976): 23; Jean Daniel, "Le Pari de Giscard et le nôtre," *Le Nouvel Observateur* 616 (30 Aug. 1976): 23; and Michel Bosquet, "Lettre ouverte à quelques futurs ministres de gauche," *Le Nouvel Observateur* 618 (13 Sept. 1976): 33. See also Michel Bosquet, "Occupons le terrain," *Le Nouvel Observateur* 616 (30 Aug. 1976): 22-23 and the following *Le Nouvel Observateur* editorials by Jean Daniel: "Les Réponses de la gauche," 617 (6 Sept. 1976): 18; "Les Français n'aime plus leur avenir," 622 (18 Oct. 1976): 20-21; "Trois histoires pour espérer…," 632 (20 Dec. 1976): 20-21.

89. The following by Jean Daniel in *Le Nouvel Observateur*: "Ni émeutiers ni conserva-teurs...," 645 (22 March 1977): 20; "Les Grilles perdues," 650 (25 April 1977): 40-41; "Le Prince maudit," 651 (2 May 1977): 40; "L'Union est un combat...," 653 (16 May 1977): 40; editorial note, 655 (30 May 1977): 41; "Plaidoyer pour quelques mythes," 659 (27 June 1977): 20-21.

90. Jean Daniel's *Le Nouvel Observateur* articles: "Les Contestataires de François Mitter-rand," 656 (6 June 1977): 32-33; "Plaidoyer pour quelques mythes," 20-21; "Lettre à un socialiste en colère," 661 (11 July 1977): 16-19; "L'Avenir est votre affaire," 669 (5 Sept. 1977): 20. On Daniel's television appearance see Thomas Ferenczi, "Révolutions désen-chantées," *Le Monde*, 20 Sept. 1977, 33. For Chevènement's response to Daniel see his let-ter in *Le Nouvel Observateur* 660 (4 July 1977): 26-27.

91. Cited in Jean-François Revel, *La Nouvelle Censure: exemple de mise en place d'une mentalité totalitaire* (Paris, 1977), 253.

92. Jacques Julliard, "Un an avant," *Esprit* 2 (February 1977): 177-94, and 181, 188, 189, 192, and 194 for the citations.

93. Paul Thibaud, "A propos des revues, à propos des intellectuels, à propos de cette revue," *Esprit* 3 (March 1977): 519-28; T. P., "Trois revues s'interrogent: les intellectuels constituent-ils une classe totalitaire?" *Le Monde*, 29 April 1977, 5; Paul Thibaud, "La Gauche euphorique," *Esprit* 4-5 (April-May 1977): 247-50; Paul Thibaud, "Qualité de l'u-nion et qualité de la discussion," *Le Nouvel Observateur* 669 (5 Sept. 1977): 30; Jacques Jul-liard, "Le P.S. doit relever le défi," *Le Nouvel Observateur* 673 (3 Oct. 1977): 38-39; Paul Thibaud, "Introduction," *Esprit* 10 (Oct. 1977): 6; Jacques Julliard, *Contre la politique pro-fessionnelle* (Paris, 1977), 10, 66, 70, 77; Paul Thibaud, "Changer la politique," *Esprit* 9 (Sept. 1977): 4; Blandine Barret-Kriegel, "Échapper à la dérive concentrationnaire," *Esprit* 10 (Oct. 1977): 101; Paul Thibaud, "Mars et après," *Esprit* 14 (Feb. 1978): 137.

94. Jacques Julliard, "La Gauche et ses intellectuels," *Le Nouvel Observateur* 656 (6 June 1977): 49-51; Julliard, *Contre la politique professionnelle*, 36; Jacques Julliard, "Les n'importe quoi et presque rien," *Le Nouvel Observateur* 855 (30 March 1981): 60; Jacques Julliard, inter-view with the author, Paris, 21 June 1994; Thibaud, "Changer la politique," 7-9.

95. Olivier Mongin, "D'une vulgate à l'autre, à propos de la nouvelle philosophie," *Esprit* 12 (Dec. 1977): 64, 77; Guy Coq, "Le Témoignage d'un bouleversement," *Esprit* 12 (Dec. 1977): 80, 82. Jacques Julliard, interview with the author, Paris, 21 June 1994. In his inter-view Julliard confirmed the division within *Esprit* over the new philosophers, saying that he was more favorable to Coq's position.

96. *Faire* 1 (Oct. 1975): 2; Patrick Viveret, *Faire* 3 (Dec. 1975): 2; Alain Meyer, "Marx est-il coupable?" *Faire* 3 (Dec. 1975): 33, 35, 36; Pierre Rosanvallon, "Les Avatars de l'idéal-isme," 37, 40, 41.

97. See Rosanvallon's review of Lefort's *Un homme en trop*, *Faire* 12 (Oct. 1976): 41-42.

98. Pierre Rosanvallon, "Une nouvelle culture politique," *Faire* 13 (Nov. 1976): 25, 27; Patrick Viveret, "PS: l'exigence de la lucidité," *Faire* 9-10 (June-July 1976): 38; Patrick Viveret, *Faire* 15 (Jan. 1977): 2. See also Patrick Viveret, "Le PS et la difficulté démocratique," *Faire* 16 (Feb. 1977): 17-23; Patrick Viveret, "PS: les enjeux d'un congrès," 19 *Faire* (May 1977): 2-5; Pierre Rosanvallon, "La Gauche et le changement social," *Faire* 20 (June 1977): 17-18.

99. Pierre Rosanvallon and Patrick Viveret, *Pour une nouvelle culture politique* (Paris, 1977), notably pages 19, 23-25, 66-69, 83, 92-93, 96-97, 106-7, 138, and 152.

100. Pierre Rosanvallon had already developed a theory of *autogestion* influenced by liberal political theory and critical of direct democratic utopias in his *L'Âge de l'autogestion* (Paris, 1976).

101. Rosanvallon and Viveret, *Pour une nouvelle culture politique*, part two and pages 77 and 108-9 for the citations.

102. Patrick Viveret in "Débat avec Blandine Barret-Kriegel," *Faire* 27 (Jan. 1978): 51.

103. For *Libre*'s antitotalitarian agenda see the proclamation on the back cover of each edition of the journal. Previously, from 1971 to 1975, Lefort and Castoriadis had both published in the journal *Textures*.

104. Sartre did not accept this evaluation of *Socialisme ou barbarie*. In 1975 he said the following about it: "Today their ideas can perhaps appear to be more sound than those that I
formulated in 1952, but at the time they were not because their position was false."
"Autoportrait à soixante-dix ans," in Jean-Paul Sartre, *Situations, X: Politique et autobiographie* (Paris, 1976), 182.
105. Many of Claude Lefort's essays were collected in his *Éléments d'une critique de la bureaucratie* (Geneva, 1971), republished with some changes by Gallimard in 1979. Most of Castoriadis's essays were republished by the Union générale d'éditions beginning with his
Les Rapports de production en Russie, vol. 1 of *La Société bureaucratique* (Paris, 1973). His critique of Marxism and all forms of determination and his reformulation of the revolutionary project in terms of autonomy in *L'Institution imaginaire de la société* (Paris, 1975),
the first part of which was first published in 1965, were particularly influential.
106. Castoriodis, "Les Divertisseurs"; Claude Lefort, "L'Impensé de l'Union de la gauche,"
in his *L'Invention démocratique: les limites de la domination totalitaire* (Paris, 1981), 134-65
and especially pages 135-37; Claude Lefort, "Préface," in his *Éléments d'une critique de la
bureaucratie* (Paris, 1979), 21-23. Claude Lefort, "Maintenant," *Libre* 1 (1977): 22.
107. Their differences go a long way toward explaining why *Libre* did not last beyond its
eighth number. According to Lefort, Pierre Clastres played a crucial role in dedramatiz-
ing conflicts (essentially between himself and Castoriadis) within the *comité de rédaction*.
After Clastres's death in 1978, cooperation broke down, and when Castoriadis published a text in *Libre* 8 (1980) without having it read and discussed by everyone on the
comité de rédaction, Lefort decided that *Libre* had to end. The text argued that the Soviet
Union had become a *stratocratie* and was no longer totalitarian. It became the first chapter of Castoriadis's *Devant la guerre: tome I* (Paris, 1981). One suspects that Lefort's continued insistence on the totalitarian nature of the Soviet Union influenced his decision.
Interview of Claude Lefort with the author, 20 June 1994.
108. Indeed, Castoriadis explicitly rejected the thesis that revolutions produce totalitarianism
in his interview "L'Idée de révolution" (first published with the title "L'Idée de révolution a-t-elle encore un sens?" in *Le Débat* 57 [Nov.-Dec. 1989]), in *Le Monde morcelé: les carrefours du labyrinthe III* (Paris, 1990), 155-71.
109. Cornelius Castoriadis, "Introduction" (dated Oct.-Nov. 1972), in *Les Rapports de production en Russie*, 34-39, 53-55. This article offers an overview of the evolution of his thought
and his position in 1972.
110. "L'Exigence révolutionnaire," (interview of Cornelius Castoriadis with Olivier Mongin,
Paul Thibaud, and Pierre Rosanvallon originally published in *Esprit* 2 [Feb. 1977]) in
Cornelius Castoriadis, *Le Contenu du socialisme* (Paris, 1979), 323-66, citations on pages
328, 329, 333, 344, and 345. Jacques Julliard, "Castoriadis, Marx, et le Marxisme," *Faire* 9-
10 (June-July 1976): 51. For Castoriadis's relative pessimism see his "Introduction," 57-
61 and his "La Source hongroise," *Libre* 1 (1977): 79-80. Castoriadis appears as a lonely
defender of revolution in his interview "L'Idée de révolution."
111. For citations and clear enunciations of these positions see Lefort, "Maintenant," 22;
"Débat avec … Claude Lefort" (interview of Lefort with Pierre Rosanvallon and Patrick
Viveret), *Faire* 30 (April 1978): 56-58; "Entretien avec C. Lefort," *L'Antimythes* 14 (Nov.
1975): 15-18, 25, 29-30. Claude Lefort, "Avant-propos," "Droits de l'homme et politique,"
and "La Question de la révolution," all in *L'Invention démocratique*, 5-42, 45-86, 193-201;
Claude Lefort, "La Première révolution antitotalitaire," *Esprit* 1 (Jan. 1977): 13-19. See
also the influential article elaborating a Lefortian theory of totalitarianism by Lefort's
student Marcel Gauchet: "L'Expérience totalitaire et la pensée de la politique," *Esprit* 459
(July-Aug. 1976): 3-27. Castoriadis explicitly "responds" to Lefort's criticisms in "L'Exi-
gence révolutionnaire," 358-59. Helpful evaluations of Lefort's political thought include:
Hugues Poltier, "La Pensée du politique de Claude Lefort, une pensée de la liberté" and
Miguel Abensour, "Réflexions sur les deux interprétations du totalitarisme chez C.
Lefort," in Claude Habib and Claude Mouchard, eds., *La Démocratie à l'oeuvre: autour de
Claude Lefort* (Paris, 1993), 19-49 and 79-136 respectively.

Chapter 6

ANTITOTALITARIANISM AGAINST THE REVOLUTIONARY TRADITION

François Furet's Revisionist History of the French Revolution

By the end of 1977 antitotalitarianism clearly dominated the politics of the noncommunist intellectual Left. Intellectuals, fearing the worst from the parties of the Left in power, found threats of totalitarianism in all but the most impotent political projects. The political logic of their critique of the PCF and of the Union of the Left favored analyses that were focused on ideology and divorced from the concrete realities of contemporary France or Soviet history. While unconsciously drawing on resources within French republican political culture to combat the supposed totalitarian threat, they asserted that the apparent past blindness of French intellectuals to the gulag demonstrated that the political culture of the French Left was especially prone to totalitarianism. The Jacobin revolutionary tradition, they increasingly argued, was to blame.[1]

As it became hegemonic, the critique of totalitarianism induced a reevaluation of the past engagements of French intellectuals such that all past adhesions to or alliances with communism were seen as participating in a common intellectual blindness or naïveté with regard to their supposedly totalitarian consequences. For French intellectuals who had been deeply involved in revolutionary politics after the Liberation, a profound revision of their understanding and memory of their past politics accompanied the critique of totalitarianism. Jean-Marie Domenach, for example, honestly recognizing his resentment and need for self-justification, decided to turn over *Esprit*'s leadership to Paul Thibaud rather than allow his past to influence or hold back the journal's antitotalitarianism.[2] For François Furet and others who had been members of the PCF during its

---

most sectarian years (broadly, 1947 to 1956), the work of memory and understanding was even greater and posed troublesome questions. As accolades poured down on new heroes of intellectual politics—notably, Claude Lefort, Cornelius Castoriadis, and later Raymond Aron, praised for their intransigent opposition to the PCF and Stalinism in the late 1940s and early 1950s—it became imperative and, given the discrediting of any explanation by the political structures of the time, difficult for intellectuals like Furet to explain their involvement in "totalitarian" revolutionary politics. The flurry of memoirs by former communist intellectuals and the explosive growth in the number of polemical and scholarly historical works on intellectual engagement published in the late 1970s and 1980s attest to the sea change in the relationship between politics and intellectual legitimacy and the consequent urgency of efforts to comprehend or, in many cases, explain away discredited past political identities.[3]

Furet's 1978 revisionist history of the French Revolution, *Penser la Révolution française*, drew from and contributed to this critique of totalitarianism on three levels: those of rhetoric, interpretation, and the transformation of the political consciousness of French intellectuals.[4] As a rhetorician, Furet, already a master at integrating political with historical and interpretive criticism, skillfully used the opprobrium cast on Marxism, communism, and the revolutionary project to discredit his opponents and advance his theses. As an interpreter of the French Revolution, Furet directly applied to the Revolution the contemporary understanding that revolutionary politics necessarily ends in totalitarianism as a result of its inevitably Manichaean ideological dynamics. More generally, Furet interpreted the Revolution in a manner that resonated with the contemporary transformation of the political consciousness and memory of French intellectuals, himself included. While Furet's and other intellectuals' reworking of their memory of past intellectual politics (notably, communist engagement) fueled and made conceivable Furet's interpretation of the French Revolution along antitotalitarian lines, Furet's Revolution—cast as the founding moment of a proto-totalitarian political culture—became for both contemporaries and later historians the origin, foundation, and explanation of the postwar political adventures of intellectuals with communism and revolutionary politics.[5] By projecting totalitarianism onto the French Revolution, Furet was able to "explain" his generation's engagement in a manner consonant with the reductionism of antitotalitarian thought—the illiberalism of French political culture was to blame—and, to a certain extent, absolve his cohort of ex-communist intellectuals of responsibility for its actions. Having with his peers rejected the possibility that revolution could be a viable and reasonable alternative to a world gone wrong, Furet wrote a history of the French Revolution that was the history of the illusion of revolutionary politics. In projecting his present consciousness onto the past, Furet wrote not only the Revolution's history in the shadow of the gulag but also in light of the foundation myth of

French antitotalitarianism. By locating the origins of totalitarianism in the foundational event of modern French history and giving intellectual credibility to the attempt to link French revolutionary and Jacobin political culture with totalitarianism, Furet confirmed the belief of antitotalitarian intellectuals that a threat of totalitarianism existed within the French Left and provided them with historical ammunition in domestic political struggles. In this manner, Furet's *Penser la Révolution française* played a central role in the collapse of the postwar French intellectual Left.

This chapter illuminates the antitotalitarian moment in French intellectual politics by pursuing the links between the critique of totalitarianism, Furet's politics and memory of his past politics, and the evolution of his interpretation of the French Revolution. It seeks to explain why Furet was particularly well placed to marry the critique of totalitarianism and the history of the French Revolution and how the antitotalitarian tide made it possible for Furet, who considered himself to be on the Left, to produce a work that revived a reactionary historiography of the most fundamental event in modern French history. Further, this chapter endeavors to explain specifically what Furet's interpretation of the French Revolution owes to the antitotalitarian moment in French intellectual life and, conversely, what *Penser la Révolution française* contributed to the critique of totalitarianism. This chapter first explores Furet's biography and political trajectory, focusing on his relationship with communism and the significance of his recasting of his memory of his past communist politics while under the influence of antitotalitarianism. Next, the chapter analyzes the evolution of Furet as a historian of the French Revolution and in particular the place of the critique of totalitarianism in the making of his landmark text. Finally, the chapter concludes with a brief consideration of the antitotalitarian cast that *Penser la Révolution française* gave the history of the French Revolution in Furet's later work and the intellectual politics of the Revolution's bicentennial.

Furet's Antitotalitarian Ex-Communist Memory

Furet was born in 1927 into a *laïc* and republican Parisian *grand bourgeois* family.[6] In his words, his "tradition is the Third Republic, that of the bourgeois Left, hermetically separated from all religious culture."[7] His paternal grandfather was a highly cultured Dreyfusard doctor who practiced an integral anticlericalism, and his maternal grandfather was an opportunist republican senator from the Allier department in central France. His uncle Georges Monnet, first elected as a socialist deputy from the Aisne in 1932, became a minister in the Popular Front government of Léon Blum. Furet's father was the director of the Banque des Pays de L'Europe Centrale. Although his father's mother's branch of the family was Catholic from the Vendée, both Furet and his parents were alien to that milieu. Indeed, when Furet spent two years at the family home in Cholet (Vendée) during World

War II, it was out of the question for him to go to the Catholic *collège* where the local elite sent its children. Instead, he attended the local nonreligious *collège*, where he was the only bourgeois and, according to Furet, consequently gained an outsider's perspective on his social class.

When not in the Vendée, Furet grew up in bourgeois Paris, attending the prestigious Lycée Jeanson-de-Sailly in the sixteenth arrondissement and obtaining his *baccalauréat* in 1944. From Jeanson-de-Sailly, he traveled across Paris to the elite Lycée Henri IV in the Latin Quarter, where he took the *hypokhâgne* and *khâgne* courses in preparation for the entrance exam to the École normale supérieure (ENS). *Admissible* after the written exam, Furet failed the oral in 1946. Having decided not to retake the entrance exam, he entered a period of intellectual uncertainty, hesitating between pursuing studies in *lettres* or in law. He would complete a *licence de lettres* in 1949 and then a *licence de droit* in 1951 before settling on history, in which he finished a *diplôme d'études supérieures* in 1952 and passed the *agrégation* in 1954.

In addition to his disappointment at failing the ENS entrance exam, for Furet the years after the Liberation were "in all respects unhappy." His mother died of cancer in 1945; with her death, family life ended. Furet did not like his life as a student and was undecided about his future. He "was neither comfortable in his epoch nor in his existence."[8] Increasingly opposed—apparently on political grounds—to his father, who had withdrawn into himself after his wife's death, Furet joined the PCF in February 1949, in the depths of the Cold War.[9] Furet did not join the PCF earlier, despite an attraction to it that dated back to the Liberation, because, he said, he disliked its nationalism.[10]

Why did Furet join the party and what was the nature of his engagement? When asked this question since the mid 1970s, Furet characteristically responded that he joined the PCF out of conformism because "everybody" was in the party.[11] Although most young intellectuals refrained from joining the party after World War II, the PCF's postwar prestige among them was considerable. Furet, coming from a left-wing background, undoubtedly felt some pressure to become a communist. Once in the party, Furet recalled, he "found … a mythical link with the working class" and received "a global and exhaustive explanation of the society" in which he felt "rather ill at ease."[12] Furet obviously was swept up in the postwar cult of the Hegelian movement of history that the proletariat and, by proxy, the PCF were said to incarnate. For this very reason, his reading of Arthur Koestler's *Darkness at Noon* led him, like many other intellectuals, closer to joining the party.

Other evidence indicates that Furet also lived his party years as a rejection of his bourgeois upbringing. For example, when he learned of his success at the *agrégation* in history in 1954, Furet is said to have exclaimed as if he were a proletarian: "we [the communists] have left a few places for the bourgeois."[13] Furet's utter scorn for the bourgeoisie, as well as the extremely sectarian nature of his engagement, appear clearly in his 1950 review of *Les Communistes*, the socialist-realist novel of the party's prize writer, Louis Aragon. Here Furet fully adopts Zhdanovist ideas on culture, according to which the greatness of works of art and artists is measured solely by their contribution to the communist cause. Presented as a response to the "bourgeois" critique of *Les Communistes*, the review dubbed the book "one of the most authentic masterpieces of the French novel."[14] The article is worth quoting at length to give an idea of the era's intellectual climate and the extremes to which Furet went in his communist engagement:

> The richness and truth of its characters [those of Aragon's novel] do not exist *in spite of* the political and social analysis in which he indulges; on the contrary, they are the direct effect of it. Consciously and lucidly, he strives to show us how the class struggle transforms individuals from the interior right into the most secret folds of their conscience and their private life; even more, how the rise and the action of the working class create a type of new man, qualitatively superior to the old, far richer, stronger, and more complex than the most "distinguished" specimens of bourgeois humanity in decomposition.[15]

In concluding the article, Furet contends that it is by adhering to the project of the Communist Party that one succeeds in making great works of art:

> The human enrichment described by Aragon … , far from being autonomous, independent of the class struggle and of history, would not in fact be comprehensible without them; the content of this enrichment is of a new type, proletarian, and history is ever-present within it. And of this the particular case of Aragon is startling evidence because his rallying to the ideological positions of the working class, in permitting a full flowering of his genius, has made him the greatest of our contemporary poets and novelists.[16]

If Furet was able to be so sectarian, it was only partly due to his belief that the party incarnated the movement of history.[17] Furet also developed an affective link with the party, the importance of which was intensified by the fact that his family had become less central to his life after the death of his mother in 1945. In effect, the party dominated all aspects of Furet's life, from the public to the most private, those related to sexuality and sickness. Furet married within the party, and when he was committed to student sanitariums while sick with tuberculosis from 1950 to 1954, the party, he said, "created for us a kind of family. We, the invalids, drew from it the feeling of participating in the life of the world. In this sense, my passage through the Communist Party helped me greatly to heal myself because it gave me a point of attachment in life."[18] Having repudiated his bourgeois upbringing and forged his identity as a young adult in the crucible of the party, Furet's later effort to distance himself from the PCF was probably difficult and painful. A bulwark against the return of his repressed bourgeois past, Furet's adhesion to the Communist Party lasted, according to his friend and fellow historian and former communist Emmanuel Le Roy Ladurie, as late as 1958 or 1959, when "he still held onto the party by a thread and kept his card, 'not wanting, he said, to lay himself open to the ironic or hostile regards of the bourgeois adversary.'"[19]

Although conformism, a Hegelian view of history, and all of the previously mentioned factors culled from Furet's statements after 1978 (that is, after the critique of totalitarianism) were undoubtedly important reasons for Furet's initial adherence to the PCF and his continued engagement within it, one vital factor is largely absent from Furet's retrospective presentation of his communist engagement: the concrete political issues that impassioned and mobilized him. An analysis of his writings in *France observateur* in the late 1950s and early 1960s indicates, contrary to Furet's own later memory, that he was engaged in more than "revolutionary gesticulation."[20] For example, decolonization—a topic on which his journalism focused—was evidently very important to Furet, and since the PCF was the only political force that firmly supported it during the Indochinese War, Furet undoubtedly found some justification for his adherence to the party in its position.[21] Antifascism was also central to Furet's politics. Although the importance Furet accorded to antifascism may have reflected the Cold War's Manichaean politics, it was nonetheless rooted in a real history and struggle, ten years of veritable civil war in France (1934 to 1944), at the conclusion of which the PCF claimed with some justification to be the premier antifascist force.[22] Furet, who had fought in a maquis in the Cher in the summer of 1944, would, despite his horror of the excesses of the Resistance, continue for some time to see politics as a battle between revolution and fascism or between communism and Gaullism—the only political choices he considered realistic at the Liberation.

Furet's discussion of when he left the PCF and of the immediate aftermath of his withdrawal from the party elicits important and troublesome questions about the nature of ex-communist memory in the wake of the critique of totalitarianism. Furet implies in one interview that he left the party in 1954, but elsewhere he says that he left in 1956.[23] Yet, as previously mentioned, Le Roy Ladurie claims that Furet remained in the party as late as 1958 or 1959, and recent comments by Gilles Martinet and Mona Ozouf confirm that he left the party in 1958.[24] Further, Furet's politics in the late 1950s and early 1960s can be traced, and they belie his memories of them that date to the second half of the 1970s and later years. According to Furet, the party's spell over him was broken even before the June 1953 uprising in East Berlin. While claiming to have left the party "discreetly" in 1956, Furet related,

> I became fundamentally anticommunist since that time [i.e., 1953]. In other words, I understood that I had made a complete error, and I have not tried any makeshift solutions [*essayé de ravauder*]. For me, it was like a vaccination. From then on I have been absolutely vaccinated against communism and all that resembles it, notably communist revisionism, which is at the core from the same family and springs in my opinion from the same error. So well, moreover, that I have not been involved in politics since that time, except with regard to the Algerian War.[25]

Furthermore, Furet claims that upon leaving the party, his thought turned immediately to the problem of the relationship between democracy and totalitarianism.[26]

In fact, in the late 1950s, Furet was a member of the dissident communist group Tribune du communisme.[27] Using the humorous pseudonym François Lelièvre, Furet served on the editorial committee of the group's journal.[28] When Tribune du communisme merged with other left-wing splinter groups on 3 April 1960 to form the PSU, Furet became a member of the new party's *Comité directeur*. Founded on 2 July 1958 by oppositional currents within the PCF, Tribune du communisme was formed in reaction to the failure of the PCF to offer effective resistance either to the Algerian War or to General de Gaulle's coup of May 1958. Its members had decided that the PCF's failure to de-Stalinize and face the political and economic realities of France in 1958 made it necessary to work outside the party to rejuvenate the working-class movement.[29] This would be accomplished by its reunification in a democratic, socialist party that would forge the path to a humane French socialism. Tribune du communisme would be the first step in that direction. In short, the group set out on a revisionist communist path.[30]

Furet's articles in *France observateur*, in which he began to publish under the pseudonym Jean Delcroix in February 1958, reveal that Furet was deeply involved in the politics of the Marxist left in the late 1950s and early 1960s.[31] To be sure, Furet was critical of the parties of the Left. He believed that de Gaulle's arrival in power and the revival of the specter of fascism in May 1958 was due to the weakness of the Left (the PCF, but also the SFIO), itself a product of its inability to adapt to changing conditions (it was still stuck in the 1930s) and its demobilization of the masses.[32] Yet, he remained hopeful that the PCF could reform itself and maintained the correctness of Marxist analyses into the mid 1960s. Likewise, although Furet was critical of the *tiers-mondisme* of some intellectuals, this did not mean that he had abandoned the struggle for socialism or revolutionary politics. Rather, he believed that the *tiers-mondiste* identification with the Algerian FLN was profoundly unrealistic and distracted the Left from its goals: "the liquidation of Gaullism and a socialist France."[33]

Furet's considerable interest in the history of the 1936 to 1944 period in his journalistic output from 1958 through 1961 demonstrates the importance of the experience of these crisis years to his worldview. For Furet this history was dominated by two themes: the triumph of fascism, in which the French Right is entirely complicit, and the weakness of the Left, which had demobilized the masses and thereby made possible the victory of fascism.[34] This analysis of the past mirrors Furet's contemporary analysis of May 1958, demonstrating the continued centrality of the battle of his youth between fascism and socialism to his political thought in the late 1950s and early 1960s. In these articles, as well as in many of his other historical pieces in *France observateur*, Furet wrote with the aim of illuminating current politics. In the 1950s, as in the 1970s, contemporary and historical battles were inseparable in Furet's mind.

The inconsistencies in Furet's statements about when he entered and left the PCF and the discrepancy between his memories and the reality of his politics after leaving the PCF may be read as a conscious or unconscious effort on his part to place himself strategically in the ideological structures of the critique of totalitarianism, according to which remaining in the party after 1956 or engaging in revisionism signified a certain lack of wisdom. To maintain that the "magic" of the party had been broken and that one had been "vaccinated" against communism at an early date (the earlier the better) became a source of political legitimacy in a French intellectual community haunted by totalitarianism. In particular, those who had been in the party and had come out of it "vaccinated" against totalitarianism could maintain that they were more objective observers of communism and contemporary politics. The claim by former communists that they were vaccinated against communism and extremist politics was widespread.[35] Furet himself did not tire of repeating it.[36] He would later claim that if he was able to understand communism, "it is because I went through the interior experience of communism, even if only on a minuscule level."[37]

Furet's discourse on his past also indicates that his global repudiation of his communist engagement was such that his memory of it was distorted and his responsibility for it was denied. The coherence and the content of his politics in the party was lost to his memory, and adhesion to communism became a sign of immaturity and maladjustment. Furet spoke of his period in the party as a "late adolescence" and claimed that, because he was afraid of autonomy and liberty, his becoming a communist was "a search for security before the anguish of life."[38] In this discourse, communism was a disease of youth, a virus against which one is eventually vaccinated, not the informed, rational political choice of a mature adult. In short, Furet's memory of his communist and revisionist politics became reductive and communism became nearly inexplicable as a historical phenomenon.

The type of relationship that Furet had to his communist past was not uncommon for others of his generation in the France of the 1970s and 1980s. Indeed, this attitude was so widespread that Furet's friend, historical collaborator, and fellow former communist Denis Richet,[39] by contrast, found himself at the end of 1978 protesting the fashion "among some of my former comrades to renounce their past, to vainly try to exorcise the ghost of it, to have left communism only to enter an anticommunism forgetful of its origins." Richet saw no reason to "renounce that which was the essential, the participation in the fight for decolonization, the insertion in a milieu of militants that opened me up to treasures of human qualities, practical knowledge of political action."[40] Although ex-communist memory has presented pitfalls for others in different places and times,[41] the period of the critique of totalitarianism was hardly a propitious moment for a balanced recollection of past political engagements.

The gulf between their experience in the 1940s and 1950s and their situation in the 1970s made it difficult for Furet and his colleagues to fully reconstruct or understand their youth in the party. While the discredit into which communism had fallen discouraged their identification with their communist past, the contrast between the relative placidity of the politics of the 1970s—the debate over the Union of the Left notwithstanding—and the intense Manichaean politics of the early Cold War made the latter opaque and mysterious, difficult for them to fathom. Furthermore, their ascension to the ranks of the intellectual elite favored their repudiation of a past in which, at least in retrospect, they had willingly subordinated their intelligence to that of the party leadership and of which they now had "guilty memories."[42]

This reductive ex-communist memory of communism became in the years of the critique of totalitarianism the dominant memory of communism as a consequence of the mutually reinforcing relationship of this memory with the critique of totalitarianism and the disproportionate influence of former communists in French intellectual politics as a result of their turn to political and cultural journalism after leaving the party in the 1950s. Former communists established with remarkable success that their political judgment was (because tempered by their experience of communism) particularly acute. Having been through the experience of communism, ex-communists were supposedly no longer susceptible to the "illusions" of extremist politics. As a consequence, when Furet was asked in an interview regarding his work *Penser la Révolution française* whether he was immune to the reproaches he had made to Marxist historians of the French Revolution for investing the Revolution with their present-day concerns, he not only admitted that he too was "rooted in a present," but also claimed that his rootedness, contrary to that of the Marxists, "leads to a disinvestment of this past rather than to its superposition onto current situations."[43] Furet had no pretense that his history was objective, but he apparently believed that his subjectivity was more objective than that of others. In the climate of the critique of totalitarianism, Furet's position was easily accepted.

The Making of a Historian of the French Revolution

Furet's interest in the French Revolution dates back to the early 1950s. Indeed, if Le Roy Ladurie is to be believed, Furet and his friend Jean Poperen were at the time already engaged in a polemic with Albert Soboul, attacking him on his left with the writings of the Trotskyist historian Daniel Guérin.[44] After writing in 1952 a *diplôme d'études supérieures* directed by Ernest Labrousse on the night of 4 August 1789, Furet began his first serious historical research in the mid 1950s when Fernand Braudel offered him a position at the Centre national de la recherche scientifique (CNRS).[45]

At the CNRS, Furet worked on a doctoral thesis inspired and directed by Labrousse on the eighteenth-century Parisian bourgeoisie. Labrousse, conscious of the lack of significant research on the bourgeoisie that was supposedly the key actor in the "bourgeois" French Revolution, had "launched a campaign to track the bourgeoisie to his hiding place in the archives," and Furet responded to the call.[46] Doing his research within the framework of Labrousse's working group at the sixth section of the École pratique des hautes études, Furet used notarial records to study the social structure of eighteenth-century Paris, hoping, he would later say, to find the Revolution's origins within it. Apparently disappointed by the decreasingly interesting results of his research and apparently convinced that he would not be able to explain the origins of the Revolution through an analysis of social stratification, Furet wrote a small book with Adeline Daumard on the social structure of Old Régime Paris and abandoned his thesis.[47] This decision was very important for Furet. In France the state doctorate was the most significant sign of intellectual legitimacy. By failing to complete it, Furet condemned himself to a certain marginality within French academia.[48] According to Furet, the decision not to finish his thesis was in part political: "it is true that my political history was not perhaps without import on the conversion of problems and orientations that was going on with me at this moment."[49]

Marginality relative to the republican university could be advantageous in some respects. The *Annales* school of historians to which Furet belonged was, as a consequence of its relative marginality in the 1950s and 1960s, open to foreign influences. The critique of the prevailing "social interpretation" of the French Revolution by Anglo-American scholars such as George Taylor and Alfred Cobban certainly greatly influenced Furet's attack on the dominant historiography, although his innovative reinterpretation of the dynamic of revolutionary politics owes relatively little to foreign sources.[50] Furthermore, the marginality of the *Annales* school encouraged its members to invest their energies in the mass media as an alternative circuit of legitimization. Here too Furet was representative of his generation of *Annales* historians. He was very much engaged in journalism, writing on the French Revolution and other historical and political issues first in *France observateur* and then in its successor *Le Nouvel Observateur*, an experience that would help Furet elaborate and sell an interpretation of the Revolution wedded to contemporary politics.[51]

Furet's first important intervention in the interpretation of the French Revolution as a whole came in 1965 when he and Richet published *La Révolution française*. The impetus for the book came from the publisher, Hachette, which wanted to publish an illustrated history of the Revolution and undoubtedly hoped that the journalistic notoriety of Furet and Richet would boost sales.[52] Furet and Richet took advantage of the opportunity, however, to write a book that challenged the prevailing orthodox view of the Revolution upheld by the communist historian Soboul, who was soon (in 1967) appointed to the top position in the field, the chair of history of the French Revolution at the Sorbonne.[53]

The book was key to Furet's professional and political development. While working on the manuscript, he discovered the nineteenth-century liberal historiography of the French Revolution, which led him to reconsider the diversity of the Revolution's political forms and, in particular, the relationship between 1789 and the Jacobin dictatorship. The book also marked a shift in Furet's professional orientation from the eighteenth century to the revolutionary period—two eras kept separate in French historical periodization and academic structures. This shift was, in turn, closely related to the success of Furet's and Richet's effort to inaugurate a polemical debate—the dimensions of which they may not have anticipated—with their attack on the established *marxisant* interpretation of the Revolution.[54] The responses to *La Révolution française* provoked Furet to "better define" the questions that interested him.[55] Indeed, Furet, who had lost direction as a historian for lack of a research subject that engaged his interests and invested his energies into journalism after abandoning his thesis, found a focus for his historical research as a result of the controversy surrounding the book. Further, the book allowed Furet to convert his journalistic celebrity into academic merit, a move that enabled him to move his historical career forward despite the fact that he had not finished his doctorate. The publication of *La Révolution française* inaugurated Furet's career as a revisionist historian of the French Revolution.

The mid to late 1960s was a period of transition for Furet. In addition to finding his historical subject, Furet moved away from Marxism, the Marxist Left, and political activism and turned to the Left Center. He soon entered the anticommunist liberal circles that had welcomed his *La Révolution française* and published a few articles in their journal, *Preuves*, in the late 1960s.[56] Furet also curtailed his journalistic activity in *France observateur* and its successor *Le Nouvel Observateur*, although he continued to play an important role in the latter, being at the center of the negotiations surrounding its creation in 1964, occasionally contributing to the weekly, and decisively influencing it to support the "new history."[57] Finally, on a personal level, Furet ended his long rebellion against his bourgeois upbringing by marrying the sister of the *grand bourgeois* intellectual Pierre Nora.[58] Furet was now everything that his youth—except, of course, his experience in the PCF—had shaped him to be: a left-leaning reformist, bourgeois intellectual.[59]

In *La Révolution française*, Furet and Richet's interpretive innovations were essentially two.[60] First, they questioned the interpretation most coherently developed by Georges Lefebvre, according to which the three revolutions of 1789 (those of the bourgeois Third Estate representatives, of the urban populace, and of the peasants) were, despite their different aims, a bloc in that the 1789 bourgeois revolution was made possible and affected in its content by the popular revolutions. They argued that "there is not one revolution of the summer of 1789, nor even successive revolutions. There is a telescoping of three autonomous and simultaneous revolutions that upset the calendar of enlightened reformism."[61] For them the "true" content of the Revolution was defined by the philosophy of Enlightenment: tolerance, liberty, equality, the rights of man, and the critiques of despotism and of the Church. The popular intervention in 1789 "transforms the rhythms of revolution; it does not yet touch its content."[62]

Because the popular revolutions are seen as almost totally independent of the 1789 bourgeois revolution and the content of the bourgeois revolution is defined exclusively by Enlightenment philosophy, the radicalization of politics after a "happy year" (the title of chapter 4) is considered accidental, a *dérapage* (skidding off course) of the Revolution. The "accidents" that led to the *dérapage* of the bourgeoisie's "liberal revolution to which the eighteenth century gave birth" are the use of the *assignat* as money and the recourse to inflation, the division of the revolutionary elite, the flight of the king, and the war. Here, as in Furet's later writings, the counterrevolution was not to blame. It was in fact powerless, although it could produce—presumably, accidentally—"the collective psychosis of a perpetual plot and thereby give rise to disorders."[63]

Although Furet and Richet maintained that the Revolution was bourgeois, in the course of their exposition, they offered some challenges to the social interpretation of the Revolution. In addition to attacking unnamed historians for abusively reading 1793 as a precursor to 1871 or to 1917, they held that the Montagnards and Girondins did not differ in their social origins and that the Enlightenment was far from being uniquely bourgeois. They also tended to minimize the importance of the popular movement of 1793 and 1794, proclaiming that it was an accident that announced nothing for the future. The *sans-culottes* militants were portrayed as a minority that imposed its will on the sections, and the motives of the revolutionary crowds were relegated to the irrational by gratuitous psychologizing.[64] For example, Furet and Richet asked whether the fear of an aristocratic plot was not due to the "resurgence of the old terrors that periodically seize the unconsciousness of the humble" or whether "the adoration of the 'holy pike' [by the *sans-culottes*] does not mask a very old symbolism of sexual origin." Furthermore, they contended that the forms taken by punitive action during the September massacres were "incontestably of sexual origin."[65]

The most important immediate response to Furet and Richet by the defenders of orthodoxy was that of Claude Mazauric, who gave their *Révolution française* an extended analysis in 1967 in the journal of the then dominant historiography, the *Annales historiques de la Révolution française*.[66] Ever since Furet's devastating critique of the "revolutionary catechism" of the communist historians of the French Revolution, it has been easy to dismiss Mazauric's review as nothing more than a call to political orthodoxy written in a "commissarial tone."[67] In fact, Mazauric offered an intelligent and not always irrelevant response to Furet and Richet, despite the political garb in which it was clothed. Indeed, by adding bibliographical references to and deleting psychoanalytical references from the second edition (1973) of *La Révolution française*, Furet and Richet implicitly recognized the validity of two of Mazauric's more minor criticism: that it is irresponsible not to include a scholarly apparatus in a book challenging existing interpretations and that their gratuitous psychoanalytical references were inappropriate.[68]

Mazauric's principal criticism of the work was that its refusal to see the Revolution as a bloc and the corollary of this refusal, the thesis of *dérapage*, were simply wrong. The bourgeois revolution of 1789 was possible only because the bourgeoisie accepted the support and demands of the popular classes. As for the *dérapage* thesis, it relied on wishful thinking: the supposition that the bourgeois revolution had to be liberal. In fact, during the period of the so-called *dérapage*, the bourgeoisie realized its major, illiberal goal: the extermination of the counterrevolution.[69]

Curiously, by virtue of its challenges to the connection that Furet and Richet made between the French Revolution and liberalism and its insistence on the Revolution's inevitable radicalism, Mazauric's interpretation of the Revolution has more in common with Furet's analysis in *Penser la Révolution française* and his later works than does *La Révolution française* of 1965. For example, Mazauric's contention that the Feuillants' failure was a consequence of their "lack of audacity"[70] runs contrary to *La Révolution française*, which holds Louis XVI's inability to compromise responsible for the Feuillants' fate, but it is strikingly similar to the analysis offered in the 1988 *Dictionnaire critique de la Révolution française* edited by Furet and Mona Ozouf.[71] And while *La Révolution française* considers the war to have been an accident that led to a *dérapage* of the Revolution, Mazauric insists that it was not fortuitous. He asks, "Can one affirm that the war is at the origin of the so-called *dérapage* of the Revolution if it is almost a *natural* component of it?"[72] Although Furet would ridicule Mazauric's analysis of the war in his 1971 article "Le Catéchisme revolutionnaire,"[73] by 1978 the war would become for Furet too a necessary consequence of the revolutionary dynamic established in 1789. If on these points Mazauric seems to anticipate the later Furet, it is not because Furet ever admitted that Mazauric was right—far from it; rather, it is because the later Furet, like Mazauric, came to see the Revolution as a bloc governed by a logic, ideological in Furet's case, that largely determined its development from 1789 to 1794.

The polemic launched by *La Révolution française* and Mazauric's response to it became increasingly acrimonious. Soboul added fuel to the fire with his 1970 preface to a collection of Mazauric's articles in which he lambasted "certain, in this case more publicists than historians, ungrateful sons or renegades of 'our common mother'" who had brought the advances of a half a century of historiography into question.[74] The exchange reached a vitriolic anticlimax when Richet publicly accused Soboul of plagiarizing his work in *Crise de l'Ancien Régime*, volume 1 of *La Civilization de la Révolution française*, and used the occasion to ironically comment on Soboul's use of authors on whom he cast anathemas. While Soboul humbly apologized for his oversights and vowed to correct them in the second edition of his book, he found Richet's attack to be confirmation of the correctness of his prefatory remarks in Mazauric's book.[75]

As the content of this exchange hints, intellectual and ideological differences were only part of what separated Soboul from Furet; issues of temperament, personality, and identity were key. Soboul had been a war orphan, a ward of the state, and as a *Pupille de la Nation*, he had been ensured a free education. Owing his opportunities to the republic (and, by extension, the French Revolution), Soboul had worked hard and, although he had failed to gain admittance to ENS (like Furet), he rose to the top of the academic hierarchy by virtue of his excellent state thesis on the *sans-culottes*. A man with a strong sense of loyalty, Soboul defended the meritocratic but hierarchical values of the French state and educational system just as he defended the Revolution. Consequently, Soboul was openly and bitterly hostile to the sixth section of the École pratique des hautes études because, he believed, it competed "unfairly" with the university and allowed individuals to advance in the academic hierarchy without submitting to the difficult tests—notably, the state doctorate—that he had successfully endured. Soboul's commitment to the PCF was also rooted in loyalty, in this case to his communist aunt who had raised him from age eight. At least according to Richard Cobb, Soboul was a far-from-orthodox communist who easily forgave the heresy of others, but he could not forgive those who failed to stick with the party.[76] Similarly, Mazauric, who had known Furet from when they were both tubercular communist students in the early 1950s, received Furet's abandonment of the party as an "unbearable break that was moreover more affective than political."[77]

Furet, whom Soboul wrote off as an "ambitious young arriviste,"[78] was everything that Soboul despised. He had abandoned his state doctorate and was making his way up the academic hierarchy through the back staircase, the "chapelle braudélienne," with the help of his journalistic career. He had also abandoned the PCF. When Furet began to attack the *marxisant* historiography of the French Revolution from the Right, Soboul undoubtedly found plenty of reason to hold Furet in contempt. In turn, Furet—exposed to Soboul's disdain and indignant over the laxness and doctrinaire nature of Soboul's more recent histories of the Revolution—was decidedly angry when he sat down to write his withering attack on Soboul's "revolutionary catechism."[79]

The rhetorical strategy of Furet's 1971 article, "Le Catéchisme révolutionnaire," reflected this anger. Rather than directly address the criticisms made of *La Révolution française*, Furet went on the offensive. Indeed, he only half-heartedly defended his 1965 book, which he implicitly abandoned by admitting that he would not rewrite it the same way.[80] Rather, Furet masterfully turned Mazauric's political rhetoric against him in order to accuse him and Soboul of having produced a vulgate that, because it identified completely with the revolutionaries, commemorated and relived the Revolution rather than interpreted or analyzed it. Furet argued that although the French Revolution has been read ever since the histories of Albert Mathiez as a bourgeois revolution and the precursor to the proletarian revolution to come, its historians have been more neo-Jacobin than Marxist. Consequently, Soboul's analysis of the eighteenth century was little more than a rehashing of Emmanuel Sieyès's pamphlet *Qu'est-ce que le Tiers État?* and the so-called Marxist interpretation of the Terror as a phase in the bourgeois revolution contradicted Marx's own analysis of the Terror as a consequence of the state becoming its own end.

Furet's critique was merciless, effective, and written with tremendous rhetorical force. His analysis of Mazauric's and Soboul's writings made them look ridiculous. They were "Marxists" who did not even know Marx and armchair revolutionaries who relived the Revolution rather than wrote its history. On two historiographical points Furet's critique was decisive. First, the French Revolution's origins were much more complicated than Soboul would have it. Second, the concept of "bourgeois revolution" had been abusively used to unite all elements of the Revolution into one total explanation. It was deemed to explain the Revolution's economic, social, and politico-ideological course and outcome "as if the heart of the event, its most fundamental character, was of a social nature."[81] If the concept of bourgeois revolution were to be used, it would have to be controlled and limited.

In his article "Le Catéchisme révolutionnaire," Furet offered a cogent synthesis of recent research that had been slowly bringing into question parts of the prevailing "social" or "Marxist" interpretation of the Revolution and drew out some of the conclusions implicit in this new research. The most difficult work remained to be done: the construction of an alternative interpretation of the revolutionary dynamic. To be sure, Furet concluded his essay with some suggestive comments on the importance of Jacobin ideology in fueling this dynamic, but a fully developed analysis emerged only with his *Penser la Révolution française* of 1978, when French intellectuals were in the midst of their antitotalitarian moment.

The Making of an Antitotalitarian History of the Revolution

Between the publication of *La Révolution française* and that of *Penser la Révolution française*, French politics and intellectual life changed a great deal. The events of 1968 and post-1968 *gauchisme* came and went, de Gaulle departed from the scene, the PCF and the PS advanced closer to political power, and, of course, the critique of totalitarianism began to occupy the center stage in French intellectual politics. How did Furet negotiate his way through this decade of change? On the one hand, he placed himself within the camp of the Aronians in the late 1960s, seemingly regretting that the political disillusionment of *progressisme* had led intellectuals to structuralism rather than the liberal and empirical critique of Marxism offered by Raymond Aron.[82] Yet, on the other hand, in 1968 Furet did not follow Aron, who, enraged by the student movement, launched an appeal for the creation of a Comité d'action contre la conjuration de la lâcheté et du terrorisme (Action committee against the conspiracy of cowardice and terrorism) in early June 1968.[83] In 1970 when Aron, Alain Besançon, and others founded the journal *Contrepoint*, which took a right-wing liberal position frankly hostile to the movements that emerged out of 1968, Furet refused to join them. According to Furet, "As opposed to someone like Raymond Aron, with whom I discussed it at the time, I did not live the event [May '68] either in fear or in a state of tension." Furet did not believe that the French university system deserved to be defended. He also never feared that extremists would take over, because "a certain wisdom told me that when the banks and the Communist Party are against something, it cannot work."[84]

Furet's reformist attitude and previous contacts with Edgar Faure, whom he had met in the late 1950s and had assisted with the research for Faure's 1961 book *La Disgrâce de Turgot, 12 mai 1776*, which Furet subsequently reviewed in *France observateur*,[85] opened the door for him to become one of Faure's counselors for his *Loi d'orientation de l'enseignement supérieur* of October 1968. This reorganized the French university system in response to the May '68 crisis. Although Furet believed that a modernization and democratization of the educational system was important, he did not see the crisis as having its origin in the university. Rather, the principal problem was the permanent adolescence to which French society condemned its youth because it was unwilling to allow for advancement by means other than seniority and diplomas. Although Furet saw the maintenance of an extended adolescence as the product of the actions of society as a whole, he had little patience with the post-1968 Gaullist state, which, instead of attacking the root cause of the problem, retreated into "the sterile cycle of police repression and moralizing homily."[86] Furet believed that he had experienced the trial of a "late adolescence" and the tyranny of the diploma, and he did not wish them on the younger generation.

When the decline of post-1968 radicalism came, Furet was well placed to take advantage of the conjuncture. He remained on the Left, albeit in its reformist wing, and as a keen observer of intellectual and party politics, about which he occasionally wrote in *Le Nouvel Observateur*, he knew where the intellectual Left was going. Furet could address its concerns from within its political problematic. Not blinded by fear of student radicalism, he clearly saw that the surge in Marxism and revolutionary politics after 1968 was not as deep a current as some believed. Furet believed that student Marxism was more a sign of the rupture of youth with traditional channels of integration than a serious commitment. If the student revolutionary is most often Marxist, he wrote, it is "in order to better break with what he considers to be 'established' Marxism." If the revolutionary venerates Mao, Guevara, or Castro, "it is in the exact measure that it is a matter not of real historic leaders, but of myths created by him for his exclusive use." The student is less interested in third-world revolution than in "discrediting official communism, Soviet bureaucratism, and the conservatism of the communist parties." In France, references to third-world revolutionaries are more signs of "student revolutionary amnesia" than "symbols of a true loyalty."[87]

Whereas others saw a danger in the post-1968 revolutionary movements, Furet understood how weak they were—just as he understood how hyperbolic communist historians' political rhetoric was regarding the French Revolution. The same year that Furet exposed the ambiguous nature of student Marxism, he commented in his response to Mazauric's political interrogations that "this debate in its politico-theatrical aspect is in reality a farce or a shadow battle. On the political level, neither anything nor anyone in today's France threatens the achievements of the French Revolution. ... all historical debate regarding it no longer has a real political stake."[88] As early as 1971, Furet saw the possibility of moving intellectual politics to the center.

After 1974, when the intellectual Left's critique of totalitarianism emerged, Furet, although not among the critique's originators and largely outside the direct-democratic politics that initially inspired it, was attentive to its development. In 1975 he wrote a hagiographic review of Solzhenitsyn's *Oak and the Calf* and an article on the influence of Solzhenitsyn that discussed Elleinstein's *Phénomène stalinien* and Glucksmann's *Cuisinière et le mangeur d'hommes*.[89] Furet believed that Solzhenitsyn had succeeded in making the link between Marxism and the Soviet Union "the unthinkable [*impensable*] of the Western Left" and that there would be "a before and an after Solzhenitsyn." He clearly understood that Elleinstein, his back to the wall, had failed politically. Furet concluded that Elleinstein's attempt to save Marxism from Stalinism by blaming Stalinism's horrific features on the legacy of the Russian past was uninteresting because, even if one accepts that Elleinstein salvaged a "Marxism with clean hands," it was still a "Marxism without hands." But Furet was not, at least at this point, convinced by Glucksmann's book, which he qualified as "a Parisian soapbox declamation in a rather empty season." Nor did he believe that one should "put Marx on trial before the Russell tribunal ... on the pretext that the Bolsheviks deified the most extraordinary mind of the nineteenth century." For Furet, Glucksmann, the late *gauchiste*, had, through an abusive use of Foucault, done little more than "return to his camp after losing it: that which he detests in Soviet socialism is Western capitalism!"[90]

But Furet did not maintain his distance from the emerging critique of totalitarianism for long. By 1977 he too was willing to accept the gulag's discrediting of Marxism. Discussing Louis Dumont's *Homo aequalis* and Glucksmann's *Maitres penseurs*, Furet wrote: "Today, Marx no longer escapes his heritage, and the boomerang effect is that much stronger for having been so long delayed."[91] Whatever reservations he may have had about Glucksmann's *Cuisinière*, Furet had come to the conclusion that the gulag undermined the legitimacy of Marxism and revolution.[92] Furthermore, the critique of totalitarianism also made inroads into Furet's ideas on politics such that for him, as for antitotalitarians like the new philosophers, politics itself became a dubious undertaking; only moral battles remained worthy causes. Asked in an interview occasioned by the publication of his *Penser la Révolution française* if there were any Bastilles left to take, Furet responded, "No, and for some time now: I want to say that there are no more battles in the twentieth century that are not *dubious*. And this explains why Sartre is far from being Voltaire!" Questioned about totalitarianism, torture, and racism, Furet continued: "Of course, those are decisive battles that are totally unambiguous. The novelty of this last quarter century is that they are not political but rather moral concerns."[93] This is a telling statement from someone who rejected and criticized revolutionary ideology for its reduction of politics to morality and a Manichaean battle between good and evil. Apparently, antitotalitarianism escaped from a similar critique because "totalitarianism" was evil.

In *Penser la Révolution française*, Furet—commenting on the conditions that make his reinterpretation of the French Revolution possible—recycled the boomerang image that he had previously used against Marxism to extend the "gulag effect" to the French Revolution:

> Solzhenitsyn's work has become the basic historical reference for the Soviet experience, ineluctably locating the issue of the gulag at the very core of the revolutionary endeavor. Once that happened, the Russian example was bound to turn around, like a boomerang, to strike its French "origin." In 1920, Mathiez justified Bolshevik violence by the French precedent, in the name of comparable circumstances. Today the gulag is leading to a rethinking of the Terror by virtue of an identity in their projects. The two revolutions remain connected; but while fifty years ago they were systematically absolved on the basis of excuses related to "circumstances," that is, external phenomena that had nothing to do with the nature of the two revolutions, they are today, by contrast, accused of being, consubstantially, systems of meticulous constraint over men's bodies and minds.[94]

Furet clearly saw that that the critique of totalitarianism was leading the intellectual Left "to criticize its own ideology, interpretations, hopes, and rationalizations. It is in left-wing culture that the sense of distance between history and the Revolution is taking root, precisely because it was the Left that believed that all history was contained in the promises of the Revolution."[95] The critique of totalitarianism made possible Furet's new interpretation of the Revolution and gave it a significance that extended far beyond revolutionary historiography. Centering, as he would say in 1982, his own work around the problem "of the relations between democracy and totalitarianism, a problem that appears to me to be characteristic of the communist experience" and finding the French Revolution to be "the moment in which the continued ambiguities of the democratic phenomenon appear," Furet was "led to propose a critical analysis of the French Revolution without which the entire experience of the twentieth century is unintelligible."[96]

Furet's political and interpretive maneuver was bold, a defining moment in his career. Much more than a marker of the circumstances in which his book was written, Furet's reference to the gulag entailed a declaration of interpretive intent. Following Glucksmann's example, Furet would use the discredit into which the Soviet Union had fallen to reverse the significance of the connection Mathiez made between Jacobinism and Bolshevism, discredit Jacobinism, and taint it with totalitarianism.[97] Furet vertiginously substituted historiography for history and the politics of interpretation for interpretation itself, thereby lodging—as much as any historian before him—contemporary politics at the heart of the Revolution's history. Furthermore, Furet's rethinking of the French Revolution in light of contemporary condemnations of Marxism, revolution, and Jacobinism as totalitarian did not deviate from the terms of analysis offered by contemporary antitotalitarianism. Rather, in asserting that the dynamic of revolutionary ideology, most fully developed in Jacobinism, necessarily led to and was the sole cause of the Terror, Furet stuck to the path blazed by recent analyses of totalitarianism and marked by the failure of Elleinstein's history of Stalinism. The result was politically explosive but intellectually suspect, a contravention of professional historians' most basic admonitions against anachronism. With *Penser la Révolution française*, Furet wagered on politics and historiography, a bet that he would continue to make for the rest of his career.

What was new in this book, and what places it squarely within the critique of totalitarianism, is its emphasis on revolutionary ideology as the key to understanding the Revolution's development from 1789 to 1794. Furet had not developed this argument before 1976. To be sure, he had already taken a tentative first step in this direction in the last pages of his article "Le Catéchisme révolutionnaire." There he argued, contrary to the interpretation of *La Révolution française*, that it was necessary to explain why the radicalization of the Revolution began as early as summer 1789. Furet suggested that Jacobin ideology could explain this radicalization in that it functions largely independently of political and military circumstances as a "source of escalation [*surenchère*] all the more indefinite since politics is disguised as morality and the principle of reality has disappeared." But Furet did not offer any further explanation and was unwilling to push his argument very far. He contended that the war and the invasion were not circumstances totally independent of the Revolution, as the Revolution had wanted the war, but suggested that only the Great Terror of 1794 could be understood independent of circumstances. "The first two terrorist eruptions, those of August 1792 and of the summer of 1793" were, he wrote, "evidently linked to the conjuncture of national emergency."[98] Furet went no further than this until 1976, when, under the influence of the critique of totalitarianism, he developed his ideas on revolutionary consciousness.[99]

Furet's September 1976 *Esprit* article outlining the characteristics of revolutionary consciousness was directly a product of the critique of totalitarianism. Furet first presented his ideas in an *Esprit*-sponsored discussion on revolution in early 1976 and then developed them into publishable form in response to a request by Thibaud, who organized the critique of totalitarianism at the journal *Esprit*.[100] Published in an issue titled "Revolution and Totalitarianism," Furet's article did not belie the rubric.

In his article, Furet argued that the French Revolution inaugurated the idea of Revolution—still "at the center of our political representations"—which radically divides the world into a before and after such that everything before the Revolution is evil and condemned to die while that which comes after is good. The revolutionary consciousness makes a tremendous psychological and ideological investment in politics; all problems come to have political solutions. In dividing the world into good and bad, the revolutionary ideology shows its "essential intolerance." It invests the objective universe with subjective wills "of leaders and scapegoats. ... the action of the good and the plots of the bad. ... In brief, for the revolutionary consciousness, action does not have objective limits; it only has adversaries." These aspects of revolutionary consciousness are "at work in French revolutionary discourse *right away*, as if there had been a hole to cover or a vacuum to fill." Not only is this revolutionary consciousness present in the discourse, but "society naturally lodges in it and immediately marries its logic."[101]

Significantly, here and in all his later texts, Furet's interpretation of the revolutionary dynamic is no less dependent on the revolutionary actors' consciousness of their actions than the historiography Furet reviles. When he argues that the revolutionaries' Manichaean ideology effectively guided their actions, Furet accepts that there was a total transparency between their discourse on the Revolution and their actions as revolutionaries. Even more, for Furet the history of the French Revolution is its discourse: "Read the speeches of Robespierre and Marat, and you will see that the revolutionary dynamic assumes and maintains with an incredible constancy the theme of the plot."[102]

In his contemporary discussion of Furet's 1976 article, the antitotalitarian and libertarian political philosopher Lefort cautioned Furet that his explanation oversimplified the experience of revolution and accepted the idea of Revolution at face value: "One cannot problematize revolution in holding to its *idea*—or, more specifically, to the self-representation of actors who behave like missionaries of universal History and claim that the Revolution speaks from their mouths. [This idea of Revolution] ... would not have been formed or would have remained deprived of efficacy if a mass uprising had been lacking."[103] Although Furet might not have disagreed with this point, Lefort carried the argument into areas that challenged the premises of Furet's analysis. Lefort argued that revolutions begin without those who revolt having a clear notion of the new order. With the collapse of the old order's legitimacy, a vast space is opened up in which diverse collectivities reorganize society and politics. The revolutionary upheaval owes nothing to the idea of Revolution; indeed, the diversity of forms that the Revolution takes makes it hard to speak of Revolution in the singular. The idea of Revolution is the product of this revolutionary upheaval and consequently is neither the first nor the only force shaping the course of revolutions. Perhaps because he lacked Lefort's libertarian perspective, Furet could find neither virtue nor agency in the revolutionary masses and remained convinced that they could only be their leaders' tools. Heedless of Lefort's warnings, Furet's *Penser la Revolution française* reads like an extended discussion of the singular importance of revolutionary consciousness in determining the course of the French Revolution.

Penser la Révolution française is a curious book; it is neither a history of the French Revolution nor a book on the historiography of the Revolution, although it contains elements of both. A collection of essays united by a single problem, it is a programmatic statement and a provocation from beginning to end. Its title conveys both an implicit interpretation of the historiography and an imperative: although recent historians have supposedly only relived the French Revolution, Furet commands the reader to think about it and interpret it.

The book consists of two parts. The first, titled "La Révolution française est terminée," presents a synthesis of Furet's position in 1978. The second, "Trois histoires possibles de la Révolution française," consists of three historiographical essays—the first two of which ("Le Catéchisme révolutionnaire" and an essay on Tocqueville) had previously been published—that trace the evolution of Furet's historiographical musings. The book effectively starts where Furet had left his question in 1971 when, in "Le Catéchisme révolutionnaire," he had argued that the critique of the Soboulian interpretation of the Revolution opened up the question of the revolutionary dynamic. As for Tocqueville, Furet found him provocative and useful insofar as Tocqueville broke from the consciousness of the revolutionaries to develop an explanation of the Revolution. Tocqueville's fundamental contribution was his observation that in revolutionary periods an ideological veil hides "the profound meaning of the events from the actors," which in the case of the French Revolution was a continuation and acceleration of the processes of democratization and centralization.[104] Although Tocqueville had momentary insights into the dynamic character of revolutionary ideology, he remained a prisoner of his thesis of continuity and failed to develop these insights. Where Tocqueville fell short, Furet found an explanation of the revolutionary dynamic in the work of Augustin Cochin.

Cochin, whose reputation Furet sought to rehabilitate, was the histori-ographical linchpin of Furet's new interpretation. Furet saw in Cochin someone who, like Tocqueville, eschewed explanation by narrative in favor of conceptual or critical history. It is essentially for this reason, argued Furet, and not because of his counterrevolutionary stance or the quality of his scholarship, that Mathiez and Alphonse Aulard—the domi-nant historians of the French Revolution of the first quarter of the twenti-eth century—rejected and failed to understand Cochin's work. As historians who could only imagine explanation in the narrative mode and who were intent on reliving rather than analyzing the Revolution, Mathiez and Aulard could not comprehend Cochin. As a result of their rejection of Cochin and an essential continuity in the presuppositions of the leading historians of the Revolution, Cochin had never been taken seriously.[105]

Contrary to Furet's picture of a Cochin who had been ignored and poorly understood, Cochin's work had been given a fair hearing. Histori-ans carefully evaluated his work and rejected it because Cochin failed to provide the evidence that would have been needed to support his conclu-sions. For example, Jean Egret, the premier expert of his generation on the prerevolution, analyzed Cochin's most significant empirical study, *Les Sociétés de pensée et la Révolution en Bretagne (1788–1789)*, and concluded that "Augustin Cochin has constructed a seductive thesis that does not stand up to a close examination of the facts." And if Mathiez rejected Cochin's thesis and use of sociology in his review of the same book, it was not, as Furet implied, because Mathiez necessarily rejected sociology in general. Rather, Mathiez argued that Cochin had no evidence to support his argument and that his "sociological law" was consequently nothing more than a replacement for the role that providence had played in older counterrevolutionary histories.[106]

The implications of Furet's contention that there had been a conspiracy of silence about Cochin's work are important. It allowed Furet to treat Cochin's theses as essentially correct because they were unrefuted. Cochin, Furet implied, could be trusted because even though he had a "philosophical mind," as a graduate of the École des chartes, he had also "learned the rules of erudition."[107] That the evidence needed to seriously establish Cochin's thesis—the archives of the Masonic and philosophical societies—had become available only after World War II did not bother Furet, who made no visible effort to consult them.[108] Having established Cochin's scholarly cre-dentials and politically and epistemologically (because their epistemology was said to follow from their commemorative politics) discredited Cochin's critics, Furet ignored the questions of evidence that were at the center of ear-lier objections to Cochin's work and thereby cleared the way for his elabo-ration of an explanation of the revolutionary dynamic based on Cochin.

While the legitimacy of Furet's use of Cochin was ensured by the ambi-ent suspicion of communist intellectuals during the critique of totalitari-anism, the vogue for oligarchic theories of democracy in the late 1970s in the wake of disappointment with hopes placed on direct democracy also contributed to it. Pierre Rosanvallon, a leading theorist of *autogestion* become antitotalitarian, revived the works of Moisei Ostrogorski and Robert Michels to criticize the functioning of political parties and elucidate the difficulties of *autogestionnaire* socialism. Likewise, the socialist intellectual Gilles Martinet, reflecting on the Portuguese Revolution, concluded that in Portugal direct democracy had proven to be dangerous because, as in the sections during the French Revolution, "spontaneous expression gave way to manipulation." Other intellectuals, notably Furet's friends and fellow former communists Alain Besançon and Annie Kriegel, were also drawn to Cochin in this period. Cochin's work figured prominently in Besançon's *Origines intellectuelles du Léninisme* and was well received by Kriegel, who, like Besançon, believed that Cochin "illuminated the modes of action and organization of the Bolshevik party." In 1979, Cochin's *Sociétés de pensée et la démocratie* was republished with a laudatory preface by the sociologist Jean Baechler.[109]

Although his work was useful in 1978, Cochin proved to be less attractive over time. When in subsequent years Furet sought to consolidate the scholarly legitimacy of his new interpretation of the revolution, he dropped direct references to Cochin. For example, the section of his 1988 *Dictionnaire critique de la Révolution française* on historians of the Revolution did not include an entry on Cochin. And, in their dictionary article "Clubs et sociétés populaires," Furet's students Patrice Gueniffey and Ran Halévi, although hanging onto Cochin's "intuition," admitted that Cochin's historical practice was "occasionally rash and his erudition faltering."[110]

Furet's use of Cochin is also important for the politics that it entailed. Cochin's work had been a staple of the twentieth-century right-wing historiography of the French Revolution because it was well adapted to the Right's needs in an era of mass democracy. Instead of blaming the Revolution on the passionate masses as Hippolyte Taine had done in part, Cochin tried to demonstrate that popular sovereignty deceives the people. With Cochin, the Right could mobilize the masses and be against the Revolution in good faith. Indeed, Cochin proved to be a key influence on Pierre Gaxotte's right-wing history of the Revolution. During Vichy, while Lefebvre's *Coming of the French Revolution* was burned by the régime, Cochin's thesis became through Gaxotte the quasi-official history of the Revolution.[111] That Furet could adopt Cochin without even openly considering his politics and the politics of those who had used him was possible only because Furet had established an enormous distance between himself and the antifascism that had been the staple of his politics of the 1940s and 1950s. In arguing as he did that "the Revolution is over," Furet contended that the battles of his youth were, if not without significance, then at least no longer relevant to the world of the 1970s. It mattered little to Furet if he drew from the counterrevolutionary tradition, as long as he brought an end to revolution as a model for political change.

According to Furet, Cochin's thesis was that Jacobinism was a developed form of the philosophical society of the second half of the eighteenth century.[112] The members of these societies divested themselves of all social distinctions and interests. Comprised of abstractly equal individuals, these societies became machines to manufacture a democratic consensus. As precursors to the institution of a Rousseauian general will in society, they become the matrix upon which the political culture of the Revolution would be built. They become "a model for pure, not representative, democracy, in which the collective will always lays down the law."[113] But the sovereignty of the collective will is a fiction; pure democracy necessarily entails a machine or inner circle that manufactures and controls consensus. This machine is an objective force, the consequence of a sociological law of democracy. Because of this, those within the inner circle were as much manipulated as manipulators, and the transfer of the model of the philosophical societies to society as a whole was not—despite the key role of militant minorities—the product of a plot. The position of the leaders, sociologically necessary but illegitimate within the ideology of direct democracy, was precarious. As a consequence, there was a cascade of purges and usurpations of power. Jacobinism was merely the full development of this model. In 1793 it ruled in the name of *le peuple* on the basis of a fictitious consensus over a society imagined to be one with the state. Resistances to this fictitious consensus were crushed by a murderous application of the revolutionary ideology. Furet's conclusion is provocative: "Through the general will, the people-king now corresponds mythically with power; this belief is the matrix of totalitarianism." According to Furet, Cochin discovered a central feature of the French Revolution and revolutions that followed. Indeed, he described "in advance many of the features of Leninist Bolshevism."[114] Furet believed that he had found in Cochin's work the explanation of the mechanism by which societies take up and follow the logic of revolutionary consciousness.

In accepting the bulk of Cochin's analysis as if it were proven, Furet avoided the very questions that should have been addressed. Furet's contention that Cochin had discovered a sociological law, or rather a sociological law relevant to the history of the French Revolution, is exactly what had to be demonstrated. Otherwise, Cochin's thin empirical work was nothing more than a paranoid effort to prove that the philosophical societies were behind every corner manipulating French public opinion—against its better judgment—into revolution. Indeed, before he discovered the virtues of "sociology," Cochin was quite willing to argue that the Revolution of 1789 was the product of a conspiracy.[115]

Despite his willingness to accept Cochin's primary thesis at face value, Furet was not entirely uncritical of Cochin. He found troublesome Cochin's failure to explain the origin of the ideology of direct democracy. More important, he criticized Cochin for presupposing that direct democracy was the only model of politics available during the revolutionary years. Furet was not sure that Cochin's analysis "does justice to the efforts made in 1790 to establish a representative democracy, and that it does not overemphasize a retrospective historical 'necessity.'"[116]

Whatever reservations Furet had about Cochin's analysis were abandoned in the first part of *Penser la Révolution française*, which presented Furet's position in 1978. In this essay, "La Révolution française est terminée," Furet elaborated on the interpretive shortcomings of the Jacobin-Marxist school, which, according to Furet, almost all derive from its identification with the consciousness of the actors in the Revolution. In addition, Furet developed his analysis of the revolutionary dynamic. As in his 1976 article, Furet contended that 1789 created revolutionary consciousness that is nothing other than the illusion of politics. Everything has a political solution, and if these political solutions fail, the revolutionary consciousness sees it to be not a result of objective obstacles but of the opposition of subjective wills or the enemy. Furet argued that the French Revolution invented democracy, but he defined the Revolution's democratic politics as a system of beliefs and a new legitimacy according to which "the 'people,' to install liberty and equality, which are the finalities of collective action, must break the resistance of its enemies." The Revolution also opened up society to "all its possibilities," but these possibilities were hardly probable, as the Revolution from 1789 to 1794 was a "rapid drift from a compromise with the representative principle toward the absolute triumph of this rule of opinion: a logical evolution because from its origins the Revolution constituted power with opinion." As with Cochin, for Furet "circumstances" explain nothing about the radicalization of the Revolution; "ideological one-upmanship [*surenchère*] is the rule of the new system's game."[117] The model of political sociability that had emerged in the philosophical societies of the eighteenth century became the model of political sociability for all of France. The Terror was a product of 1789, the delirious consequence of the application of the ideas of equality and direct democracy.

Contemporary French reviews of *Penser la Révolution française* demonstrate that Furet's work was read in the context of the critique of totalitarianism. Jean Chesneaux, writing in *Le Monde diplomatique*, found Furet's book to be no less politically motivated than those that Furet himself critiqued. Furet's intervention (*demarche*) is, Chesneaux said, the same as that of the New Philosophers, the New History, and the Trilateral Commission. His book is a "rallying to the established order" that "hides behind an apparently unattackable approach—the rejection of the gulag and of totalitarianism." Other critics also saw the affiliation of Furet's work with anti-totalitarianism but viewed it more favorably. Le Roy Ladurie believed that the great merit of Furet's book was precisely that it had found in eighteenth-century philosophical societies "prodromes" of the communist parties of the twentieth century. Roger Chartier noted in his favorable review that Cochin's model of the logic of functioning of democratic societies can, if used with care, "have a heuristic value for revolutionary situations other than the French and root in reason the comparisons that the reader of F. Furet cannot avoid making between the functioning of Jacobin pure democracy and that of more recent revolutionary and militant experiments." Many reviewers of Furet's book saw the connection it made between 1789 and totalitarianism, and two of the most prestigious of these critics found it plausible if not correct.[118]

The two most sophisticated French reviews of Furet, those by Lefort and Jean-Pierre Hirsch, also noticed the antitotalitarian thrust of the book, although Lefort argued that Furet did not mean to "find totalitarianism in the Jacobin ideal" or to "confuse the system of the gulag with that of the Terror."[119] In his 1980 review, as in his 1976 critique of Furet's ideas on revolutionary consciousness, Lefort tried to save Furet from himself and the innovations of the Revolution from Furet's critique of its political illusions. Lefort regretted—although at the same time finding the omission understandable—that Furet had only mentioned that the French Revolution saw the invention of democratic politics and culture without indicating what this was or how it differed from "the phantasmagoria of popular power." For essentially the same reason, Lefort questioned the wisdom of following Cochin.[120] Finally, Lefort suggested that both the difficulty that representative democracy had in establishing itself and the "excesses" of the Revolution may have less to do with ideology than the fact that the Revolution opened up a vast space for the development of society and an infinite debate on the foundations of legitimacy.[121] While generously giving Furet the benefit of the doubt, Lefort argued for an interpretation of the French Revolution that focused more on the birth of democratic politics than its negation in totalitarianism.

Legacies of Antitotalitarian Historical Revisionism

Furet's work on the French Revolution in the 1980s closely followed the choices of *Penser la Révolution française* in favor of historiography and an interpretation of the Revolution, inscribed in contemporary politics, in terms of the dynamic of revolutionary ideology. *Penser la Révolution française*'s passing references to poststructuralist approaches to language and politics—which, as Mark Poster has shown, do not add up to a poststructuralist or postmodern interpretation of the Revolution—were not developed in Furet's later work.[122] Rather than explicitly engaging poststructuralist thought, developing a clear and unambiguous position on the relationship between language and politics, or returning to the archives, Furet devoted his energies to studying nineteenth-century historiography and its politics, believing that it held the key to a reconceptualization of the history of the French Revolution. Nineteenth-century historiography was the focus of Furet's 1986 books on the interpretations of the Revolution by

Edgar Quinet and Marx. Especially in Furet's contributions, this historiography pervades the *Dictionnaire critique*, eclipsing the twentieth-century "academic history" of the Revolution, which Furet criticized as comparatively less profound because it had abandoned earlier, nineteenth-century questions of philosophical inspiration about the politics and course of the Revolution.[123] In his 1988 narrative *La Révolution*, Furet—uninterested in most recent scholarly research, dismissive of social history (the decline of which he connected to that of the PCF),[124] and focused on reconceptualizing the Revolution in light of early "philosophical" commentaries on it (especially those of Burke, Tocqueville, Quinet, and Cochin)—offers what is in many regards an old-fashioned history of disincarnated ideas.[125]

In the 1980s, and especially as the bicentennial of the French Revolution approached, such conservatives as the historian Pierre Chaunu used *Penser la Révolution française*'s interpretation of the Revolution to better stigmatize the entire Revolution with its supposed totalitarian descendants. This appropriation of Furet's work, as well as the historian Maurice Agulhon's spirited defense of Jacobinism and critique of Furet's use of comparisons between the French and Russian revolutions, eventually led Furet to defend 1789 from conservative attacks and state that he did not believe that 1789 or 1793 should be read in terms of 1917.[126] But the distance that Furet took from his 1978 gulag analogy was primarily rhetorical; it did not entail a shift from the antitotalitarian interpretive framework of *Penser la Révolution française*. Although, for example, the preface to the *Dictionnaire critique* denounced the parallel between 1789 and 1917 as anachronistic, it still euphemistically justified interpreting the French Revolution in light of an antitotalitarian agenda, that is, "certain old questions" that "the late twentieth century has rediscovered, by force of circumstance."[127] Although nuanced and sometimes qualified, the logic of revolutionary ideology remains in both the *Dictionnaire critique* and Furet's narrative history the motor that drives the Revolution from 1789 to the Terror and explains its most notorious deeds (the repression in the Vendée) and radical legislation (the Maximum).[128] If Furet's work offered a "liberal" history of the French Revolution, its liberalism was one informed by an antitotalitarianism that viewed the Revolution as a distinctly illiberal event.[129]

Furet's project in the 1980s was as much political and institutional as intellectual, aimed at solidifying his politico-intellectual credentials and securing a hegemonic position for his interpretation of the French Revolution. Institutionally, Furet's project was one of building a power base in the École des hautes études en sciences sociales (EHESS), intimately linked to the mass media and illuminated by the aura of the great antitotalitarian intellectual heroes who had been "right" about communism from an early date. Already enjoying friends and allies within the EHESS (Le Roy Ladurie, Richet, Besançon, Nora, Lefort), Furet secured the election of others to positions as *directeurs d'études* within it (Castoriadis, Julliard, Marcel Gauchet, Rosanvallon) after becoming EHESS's president in 1977, a position Furet held until 1985. Furet's difficult but successful campaigns to elect Julliard in 1979 and, after a long struggle, Gauchet in 1990 reinforced his relations with *Le Nouvel Observateur*, in which Julliard played an increasingly important role, and the influential journal *Le Débat*, directed by Nora and edited by Gauchet.[130] The election in 1980 of Castoriadis, who joined Lefort, elected in 1976, and then Furet's founding of the Institut Raymond Aron in 1985 consolidated Furet's association with the political legitimacy of venerable antitotalitarian icons.

In the 1980s, Furet, ever attentive to contemporary intellectual and civic debates, fixed his attention on the bicentennial of the French Revolution, determined to ensure that he and his interpretation would prevail. Indeed, in 1982 and 1983, Furet and his collaborator Mona Ozouf fired the first shots in the debate on the bicentennial by questioning whether and, if so, how the Revolution should be commemorated. Worried that the communists and their sympathizers might gain control of the official celebrations, Furet asserted that "the bicentenary of the Revolution will have to take into account the twentieth century. Reflecting on 1789 or 1793 from the perspective of this end of the twentieth century should lead to celebrations that are intellectually less simplistic than those held a hundred years ago."[131] To ensure that he and his interpretation would be at the forefront of the debate in 1989, Furet quit his position as president of EHESS in 1985 so that he could dedicate his energies to preparing his bicentennial works from the relative comfort of his position as director of the Institut Raymond Aron.[132] Given his own extraordinary preparations for 1989, Furet considered it "unthinkable" that his principal rival, the communist historian of the Revolution Michel Vovelle, did not put out a bicentennial book aimed at a general intellectual audience.[133]

In 1989, Furet's efforts as a historian and political animal were rewarded. *Le Nouvel Observateur* crowned him "king" of the bicentennial; his interpretation of the French Revolution and the connection between the Revolution and totalitarianism lay at the center of French debates. As Furet could have expected, *Le Nouvel Observateur* and *Esprit*, the vectors of antitotalitarianism in the 1970s, greatly contributed to the diffusion and triumph of his interpretation. Domenach and Julliard, for example, presented the French Revolution as affiliated with totalitarianism. They and others, like Jean-François Revel, who asserted that the Vendée was an example of genocide, opened the door to respectability for counterrevolutionaries like Chaunu, who, harking back to the debates of the 1970s, asked whether his fellow citizens would side with Stalin or Solzhenitsyn in the bicentennial debate. Thanks, no doubt, to Furet's media presence and the widespread diffusion of antitotalitarianism, his interpretation of the Revolution made considerable inroads among the intellectual masses; a July 1989 poll by *L'Express* found that 42 percent of all secondary school history professors agreed that between the Terror and Stalinist totalitarianism "there are differences, but they are phenomena of the same order."[134]

*   *   *

When one follows Furet's career as a historian of the French Revolution from its beginnings until the 1980s, one conclusion clearly emerges: Furet always closely intertwined his historical work with contemporary politics. This was especially true after 1965, when the souring of his relations with communist historians led Furet to orient his work toward a confrontation with them. This confrontation resulted in a historiographical landmark essay, "Le Catéchisme révolutionnaire," after which Furet took the positive reception of his attack on their politicization of the history of the Revolution as an authorization of his repoliticization of it in an antitotalitarian key.

An antitotalitarian logic pervades Furet's *Penser la Révolution française*. Furet reasoned that if the French Revolution was so attractive to communists as a precursor and justification of the Bolshevik Revolution, it must be because the French Revolution was totalitarian or prototototalitarian. And if the "commemorative" historians had rejected Cochin, it could not have been because he was wrong, but rather because their politics blinded them to his nonidentificatory and "sociological" approach to the Revolution's history. Obsessed by the politics of interpretation and the weight of the Revolution in contemporary French civic culture, Furet confused historiography with history and the discrediting of his enemies with an accreditation of an interpretation inverting the "revolutionary catechism" according to the principle that "the gulag leads to a rethinking of the Terror by virtue of an identity in the projects."[135] As a consequence of this inversion, it is hardly surprising to find that Furet's 1978 interpretation of the Revolution has less in common with his 1965 interpretation than it does with Mazauric's 1967 critique of Furet's earlier work.

In the making of *Penser la Révolution française* and the success that it received, historical revisionism and the revision of the memory of communism are closely linked. The reduction of past communist *engagement* to a pathology of a late adolescence of which the principal symptom is a Manichaean politics without foundation in reality made it—for lack of any cause other than the maladjustment of individuals—nearly inexplicable. By projecting selected characteristics of French communist life during the Cold War (inflexible and unreal ideological discourse and party cells where decisions were made unanimously in a manipulated direct democracy) onto the French Revolution, Furet completed the circuit connecting his historical and memorial revisionisms, explaining the Revolution as the moment in which this Manichaean ideology emerged and explaining his communist *engagement* as the product of the continued influence of the Revolution's political culture. The French Revolution had, Furet said, legitimized in the eyes of the communist militants the "most horrible episodes" of the Russian Revolution, including the Stalinist terror.[136] Certainly it is not a coincidence that the one great continuity in Furet's work since 1965 is his effort to delegitimize 1793, first by making it a historical accident and later, while under the influence of antitotalitarianism, by making the Terror an inevitable consequence of revolutionary ideology. Fittingly, Furet's last major work was, to cite its subtitle, an "essay on the communist idea in the twentieth century" that, as Diana Pinto observed in her penetrating review, explains "gullibility towards the communist 'illusion'" as a consequence of "the European culture of revolutionary democracy" that finds its origins in the French Revolution.[137]

Furet's interpretation of the French Revolution was successful because, like Furet's memory, it tapped into powerful currents in French intellectual life. An acute observer of and a participant in contemporary political and ideological debates, Furet capitalized on the discrediting of communism and modulated his interpretation into a resonant key. And if Furet had ever faltered in this task, Nora, with whom Furet had worked closely in drafting the first part of *Penser la Révolution française* and who was ever attentive to intellectual politics, would have undoubtedly nudged Furet in the right direction.[138] If Furet's "boomerang" was accepted, it was because many other intellectuals had already come to the conclusion that the "excesses" of the Bolshevik Revolution were a consequence of the revolutionary project and its ideology and in no way attributable to "circumstances." Because French intellectuals had begun to suspect revolution in general, Furet found it easy to gain acceptance of an extension of the supposed lessons of the gulag to the French Revolution. By interpreting the Revolution in accordance with the critique of totalitarianism that was then current, Furet grounded the critique in the heart of French political culture. For those seeking an antitotalitarian worldview or searching in the connection between French political tradition and totalitarianism for the key to the postwar follies of French intellectuals and the apparently dangerous politics of the Union of the Left, Furet presented a powerful and exciting argument.

Furthermore, one might argue that Furet's reductionist memory of his communist experience, his insistence that "everyone" in his generation had been communist, and his suggestion that the reasons for young intellectuals' postwar enthusiasm for communism should be sought in the depths of the political culture of the French Revolution, demonstrate Furet's inability to confront his own communist past in terms other than those of complete rejection that had been established by the critique of totalitarianism. As a consequence, the history of Furet's history writing reads like a long effort to remove the weight of "guilty memories" from his shoulders. While Furet may have found in history writing a measure of catharsis for himself and his contemporaries, he followed a path that made *Penser la Révolution française* a book in conformity with the hegemonic ideology of its time.

Notes

1. Glucksmann, *La Cuisinière et le mangeur d'hommes: essai sur les rapports entre l'État, le marxisme et les camps de concentration* (Paris, 1975), 212–13; Edgar Morin, "La Liberté révolutionnaire," *Le Nouvel Observateur* 555 (30 June 1975): 22–23; Bernard-Henri Lévy, *La Barbarie à visage humain* (Paris, 1977), 150; Jacques Julliard, *Contre la politique professionnelle* (Paris, 1978); Pierre Rosanvallon and Patrick Viveret, *Pour une nouvelle culture politique* (Paris, 1977).
2. See chapter 3 above.
3. The emergence of a significant historiography of French intellectual politics dates to this period. Examples of these memoirs include Dominique Desanti, *Les Staliniens: Une expérience politique, 1944–1956* (Paris, 1975); Pierre Daix, *J'ai cru au matin* (Paris, 1976); Emmanuel Le Roy Ladurie, *Paris-Montpellier, PC-PSU, 1945–1963* (Paris, 1982); and Alain Besançon, *Une génération* (Paris, 1987).
4. François Furet, *Penser la Révolution française*, Collection Folio/Histoire (Paris, 1978), published in English as *Interpreting the French Revolution*, trans. Elborg Forster (New York, 1981). Forster's 1981 text was consulted and some of its wording was used in my translations of *Penser la Révolution française*.
5. Implicit in Furet's work, this interpretation of postwar French intellectual politics is explicitly developed by Tony Judt, *Past Imperfect: French Intellectuals, 1944–1956* (Berkeley, 1992) and Khilnani, *Arguing Revolution: The Intellectual Left in Postwar France* (New Haven, 1993).
6. According to Kaplan, Furet viewed himself as belonging to the *moyenne bourgeoisie* (Steven Laurence Kaplan, *Farewell, Revolution: The Historians' Feud: France, 1789/1989* [Ithaca, N.Y., 1995], 50). Information on Furet's trajectory is drawn primarily from the following sources: Steven L. Kaplan, *Adieu 89*, trans. André Charpentier and Rémy Labrechts (Paris, 1993), 673–75; François Furet, "La Révolution et ses fantômes," in Nicole Muchnik and Carol Kehringer, eds., *De Sartre à Foucault: Vingt Ans de grands entretiens dans Le Nouvel Observateur* (Paris, 1984), 231-45, first published in *Le Nouvel Observateur* 732 (20 Nov. 1978); Furet interviewed by François Ewald, "Penser la Révolution," *Le Magazine littéraire* 228 (Mar. 1986): 92–97; Jean-Maurice de Montrémy, "La Révolution couronne François Furet," *L'Histoire* 120 (Mar. 1989): 74–77; Emmanuel Le Roy Ladurie, *Paris-Montpellier*; Rémy Rieffel, *La Tribu des clercs: les intellectuels sous la Ve République 1958-1990* (Paris, 1993); Furet interviewed by Mona Ozouf, Jacques Revel, and Pierre Rosanvallon, *Histoire de la Révolution et la révolution dans l'histoire*, Savoir et mémoire, 5 (Abbeville, France, 1994).
7. Furet cited in Montrémy, "La Révolution couronne François Furet," 75.
8. Ibid.
9. In "La Révolution et ses fantômes," 239, Furet asserts that he entered the PCF in 1947, yet in all other interviews he says 1949. The significance of his contradictory statements on the dates on which he entered and left the party is discussed below.
10. François Furet, interview with author, Paris, 10 Feb. 1994. Kaplan reports that "the postwar nationalist climate and the '*surenchères*' of the Resistance cooled Furet's militant ardor" after the war (*Historians' Feud*, 52). While always present, the nationalism of the PCF—at its height after the Liberation—was a less important part of its political rhetoric during the Cold War.
11. Furet, interview with author, Paris, 10 Feb. 1994; Kaplan, *Adieu 89*, 674.
12. Furet, "La Révolution et ses fantômes," 239.
13. Kaplan, *Adieu 89*, 674.
14. François Furet, Alex Matheron, and Michel Verret, "Psychologie et lutte de classes: Sur 'Les Communistes' d'Aragon," *La Nouvelle Critique* 13 (Feb. 1950): 108.
15. Ibid., 109.
16. Ibid., 118.

17. For further confirmation of the sectarian nature of Furet's *engagement* in the party, see Le Roy Ladurie's memoirs, where he speaks of Furet as being in a "full Stalinist transformation" in 1949 or 1950, undertaken with "an energy comparable to mine, but with an attractive and brilliant appearance" (*Paris-Montpellier*, 235).

18. Furet cited in Montrémy, "La Révolution couronne François Furet," 75. According to Annie Kriegel, Furet was at one point the spokesman of the *postcures* (students who had left the sanitariums and took classes in Paris but were still given medical treatment for tuberculosis) within the Union nationale des étudiants de France (*Ce que j'ai cru comprendre* [Paris, 1991], 419).

19. Le Roy Ladurie, *Paris-Montpellier*, 198.

20. Furet, *Histoire de la Révolution et la révolution dans l'histoire*, 4. For a detailed analysis of his journalism see Michael Scott Christofferson, "François Furet Between History and Journalism, 1958-65," *French History* 15, 4 (Dec. 2001): 421-47.

21. According to Le Roy Ladurie, Furet hid a Vietnamese activist and partisan of Ho Chi Minh in the late 1950s (*Paris-Montpellier*, 233).

22. Furet mentions antifascism as a factor in his adherence to communism in an early 1982 interview, but he immediately qualifies his antifascist engagement as masochistic (Furet interviewed by Emile Malet, "L'Élection du 10 mai: Un cas de figure exceptionnel dans notre histoire," in Malet, *Socrate et la rose: Les Intellectuels face au pouvoir socialiste* [Mayenne, 1983], 189).

23. Furet, "La Révolution et ses fantômes," 239.

24. Gilles Martinet, review of *Un Itinéraire intellectuel*, ed. Mona Ozouf in *Le Monde*, 26 Feb. 1999, Le Monde des livres section, xi. Mona Ozouf, "Préface," *Un Itinéraire intellectuel: l'historien journaliste du France observateur au Nouvel Observateur* (Paris, 1999), 8.

25. Furet, *Histoire de la Révolution et la révolution dans l'histoire*, 7.

26. Furet interviewed by Malet, "L'Election du 10 mai," 190.

27. Tribune du communisme was first known as the Comité provisoire de liaison pour la réunification du mouvement ouvrier.

28. *Lièvre* translates as hare and *furet* as ferret.

29. Although, according to Guy Nania, Tribune du communisme also continued to work within the PCF for some time (*Le PSU avant Rocard* [Paris, 1973], 66).

30. Nania, *Le PSU avant Rocard*, 64–66; Michel Dreyfus, *PCF: Crises et dissidences: De 1920 à nos jours* (Brussels, 1990), 123–26; Jean-François Kesler, *De la gauche dissidente au nouveau Parti socialiste: Les Minorités qui ont rénové le PS* (Toulouse, 1990), 265–66; Rieffel, *La Tribu des clercs*, 134. Also see its declaration at its founding, "Un Appel de l'opposition communiste," *France observateur* 429 (24 July 1958): 4.

31. Furet claims that he began writing in *France observateur* in 1956, but I have found no trace of writings by him before 8 Feb. 1958. Furet switched to the pseudonym André Delcroix on 8 May 1958 and then François Delcroix on 26 November 1964. He began using his real name on 1 December 1965.

32. In his article "Pourquoi la deuxième vague a presque tout submergé," Furet made the connection between Gaullism and fascism (*France observateur* 448 [4 Dec. 1958]: 3); and in "La France 'gaulliste' de 1944," he blamed de Gaulle's success in 1958 on the demobilization of the masses (*France observateur* 477 [25 June 1959]: 19). In "Le Congrès de Maurice Thorez," Furet reveals the hope that he still had in 1958 for PCF leadership of the working class when he writes of the "verdict of the spring of 1958" on the PCF: "We all remember with sadness that Monday in May on which only a small minority of the Parisian working class stopped working" (*France observateur* 478 [2 July 1959]: 3). In "Qui a repondu non," Furet explains communist electoral losses as a reflection of the "maladjustment of the French workers' movement to the problem of the modern wage-earning class" (*France observateur* 439 [2 Oct. 1958]: 13). All of Furet's *France observateur* articles cited in this and other footnotes are signed A. Delcroix, André Delcroix, or A. D.

33. "La Gauche française et le FLN," *France observateur* 524 (19 May 1960): 7. Christofferson, "François Furet Between History and Journalism," 427-32.

34. For example, in his article on Léon Blum, "L'Homme que la bourgeoisie française a la plus haï," Furet speaks of the Right as "openly complicit" with foreign fascism (*France observateur* 464 [26 May 1959]: 14), and in "Il y a vingt ans: Munich," the acceptance of Munich is portrayed as the consequence of a demobilization of the masses due mainly to the abandonment of the Popular Front and the policy of nonintervention in Spain (*France observateur* 438 [25 Sept. 1958]: 16). Other lengthy articles written by Furet on this period of French history are "La Fin de la IIIe République," *France observateur* 532 (14 July 1960): 14–15; "Défaite militaire et victoire de 'l'ordre,'" *France observateur* 528 (16 June 1960): 14–15; "Hitler, l'Allemagne et la presse," *France observateur* 511 (18 Feb. 1960): 18; "Le Mémorial de Colombey," *France observateur* 497(12 Nov. 1959), 7–8; and A. Delcroix and Roger Paret, "L'Été 39: Le Pacte germano-soviètique," *France observateur* 485 (20 Aug. 1959): 10–12 ; and A. Delcroix and Michèle Christophe, "L'Été 39," *France observateur* 484 (13 Aug. 1959): 9–11.
35. See, for example, Emmanuel Le Roy Ladurie cited in Michel Labro and Jacques Roure, "Les 'Ex' du PC," *L'Express* 1493 (16 Feb. 1980): 14; and Maurice Agulhon, "Vu des coulisses," in *Essais d'ego-histoire*, ed. Pierre Nora (Paris, 1987), 59.
36. In addition to Furet, *Histoire de la Révolution et la révolution dans l'histoire*, 7, see François Furet, *L'Atelier de l'histoire* (Paris, 1982), 7, and *Le Passé d'une illusion: Essai sur l'idée communiste au XXe siècle* (Paris, 1995), 16. In an interview with the author, Furet stated that "leaving communism, I was vaccinated against the totalitarian experience" (Paris, 10 Feb. 1994). Kaplan writes of Furet saying about his exit from the PCF that he "'got out in good shape,' … in contrast to others who either remained because of a 'weakness of character' or who left, sooner or later, but 'understood nothing'" (*Historians' Feud*, 53).
37. Furet interviewed by Jean Daniel, "L'Irruption totalitaire" *Le Nouvel Observateur* 1582 (2 Mar. 1995): 57. Alain Besançon, a historian of the Russian Revolution and friend of Furet, made the same claim for himself in Labro and Roure, "Les 'Ex' du PC," 75.
38. Furet, *L'Atelier de l'histoire*, 7; Furet interviewed by Daniel, "L'Irruption totalitaire," 58.
39. They wrote François Furet and Denis Richet, *La Révolution française*, 2 vols. (Paris, 1965 and 1966), analyzed later in this chapter.
40. Denis Richet, "Pourquoi j'aime l'histoire? Essai d'autobiographie intellectuelle," in his *De la Réforme à la Révolution: Etudes sur la France moderne* (Paris, 1991), 547–48.
41. Koestler wrote the following of ex-communist memory of communism: "As a rule, our memories romanticize the past. But when one has renounced a creed or been betrayed by a friend, the opposite mechanism sets to work. In the light of that later knowledge, the original experience loses its innocence, becomes tainted and rancid in recollection. … Irony, anger, and shame kept intruding; the passions of that time seem transformed into perversions, its inner certitude into the closed universe of the drug addict; the shadow of barbed wire lies across the condemned playground of memory" (Koestler, "Arthur Koestler," in *The God That Failed*, ed. Richard Crossman [New York, 1949], 55).
42. See Furet, *L'Atelier de l'histoire*, 7, for Furet's reference to "guilty memories" that he shares with his former communist colleagues.
43. Furet, "La Révolution et ses fantômes," 233.
44. Le Roy Ladurie, *Paris-Montpellier*, 48; Emmanuel Le Roy Ladurie, "Éclaireur de la Révolution," *Libération*, 17 July 1997, 4. The following article indicates that at least Jean Poperen attacked Soboul in the early 1950s: Poperen, "Albert Soboul: La Révolution française (1789–1799)," *Cahiers du communisme* 29, 2 (1952): 203–10. Whatever Furet's position in the early 1950s, in 1959, in a review of Soboul's thesis on the *sans-culottes*, he found Soboul's analysis more convincing than that of Daniel Guérin ("Du pain et des têtes," *France observateur* 456 [29 Jan. 1959]: 19).
45. Braudel's support proved to be an important asset for Furet. He held his position at the CNRS until 1960 or 1961, when Braudel again pushed Furet's career forward, this time by having him appointed to the position of *chef de travaux* at the sixth section of the École pratique des hautes études.

46. Robert Darnton, *The Great Cat Massacre and Other Episodes in French Cultural History* (New York, 1985), 111.

47. Adeline Daumard and François Furet, *Structures et relations sociales à Paris au milieu du XVIIIe siècle*, Cahiers des Annales, 18 (Paris, 1961).

48. According to R. Emmet Kennedy, Furet said in 1978 that because he had not completed his state doctorate, "they used to take me as a little boy, hardly seriously" ("François Furet: Post-Patriot Historian of the French Revolution," in *Proceedings of the Eleventh Annual Meeting of the Western Society for French History, 3–5 November 1983, Riverside, California*, ed. John F. Sweets [Lawrence, Kans., 1984], 197).

49. Furet interviewed by François Ewald, "Penser la Révolution," 93.

50. In his address before an audience of American historians, Furet acknowledged his debt to Alfred Cobban, George Taylor, and Robert Palmer in the following terms: "The first showed before I did the inconsistencies of the Jacobin history of the French Revolution, the second has decisively demonstrated the noncapitalist character of the French bourgeoisie of the Old Régime, and the third has rediscovered the value of the concept of democracy in his comparative history" (Furet, "A Commentary," *French Historical Studies* 16, 4 [fall 1990]: 792). As this citation indicates, *Penser la Révolution française* drew on Taylor and especially Cobban in its critique of the Jacobin "social interpretation." Whatever its later impact on Furet, Palmer's work appears to have had little influence on Furet through the 1970s. Although Taylor and Cobban both pointed toward a political interpretation of the Revolution, they did not develop it, nor did they abandon a social perspective on the Revolution. Consequently, Furet's political and ideological interpretation of the revolutionary dynamic necessarily found its inspiration in other sources. For the work of Cobban and Taylor, see, above all, Alfred Cobban, *The Social Interpretation of the French Revolution* (New York, 1964) and *Aspects of the French Revolution* (New York, 1968); and George V. Taylor, "Noncapitalist Wealth and the Origins of the French Revolution," *American Historical Review* 72, 2 (Jan. 1967): 469–96 and "The Bourgeoisie at the Beginning of and during the Revolution," in *Die Französische Revolution—zufälliges oder notwendiges Ereignis? Akten des internationalen Symposions an der Universtät Bamberg, vom 4.–7. Juni 1979*, ed. Eberhard Schmitt and Rolf Reichardt (Munich, 1983), 1: 41–61.

51. Christofferson, "François Furet Between History and Journalism."

52. Richet had also written—although less than Furet—in *France observateur* under the pseudonym Augustin Picot.

53. Richet claims that he was the one who led the fight against the orthodoxy at the time. See Kaplan, *Adieu 89*, 681. This is essentially confirmed by Furet in *Histoire de la Révolution et la révolution dans l'histoire*, 9. Richet was also a *fils de famille* of the Parisian bourgeoisie who, having rejected his family and bourgeois life, joined the party in 1949 (after long conversations with Furet) only to leave it after 1956. He was also Furet's brother-in-law ("Pourquoi j'aime l'histoire? Essai d'autobiographie intellectuelle," 543–51).

54. Furet, *Histoire de la Révolution et la révolution dans l'histoire*, 23. *Libération*, 20 Oct. 1988, 2.

55. Furet interviewed by Ewald, "Penser la Révolution," 93.

56. Excerpts from the book were published in *Preuves* 188 (Oct. 1966): 11–21.

57. Rieffel, *La Tribu des clercs*, 519, 579.

58. Furet divorced his first wife in the late 1950s. On Pierre Nora's background, see Rieffel, *La Tribu des clercs*, 476.

59. For more on the importance of *La Révolution française* in Furet's career see Christofferson, "François Furet Between Marxism and Journalism," 432-37.

60. Although Furet and Richet accepted collective responsibility for the book, it should be noted regarding the authorship of part one (covering the Revolution until Thermidor) that Furet wrote the sections on the Old Régime, the pre-Revolution, and the Revolution through summer 1789, and that Richet wrote the most controversial parts, those on the history of the Revolution from summer 1789 to the fall of Robespierre.

61. For Lefebvre's interpretation, see his *Coming of the French Revolution*, trans. R. R. Palmer (Princeton, 1947), 212–13, first published in French in 1939. François Furet and Denis Richet, *La Révolution française*, 2d ed. (Paris, 1973), 101.

62. Furet and Richet, *La Révolution française* (1973), 102.

63. Ibid., 127. See pages 125–29 for the "thesis of accidents."

64. Ibid., 203–4; 65, 163; 207.

65. François Furet and Denis Richet, *La Révolution: Des États généraux au 9 thermidor*, vol. 1 of *La Révolution française* (Paris, 1965), 240, 249, 300. To be fair, psychoanalytical references are not reserved for the popular classes; the importance of Marie-Antoinette's conjugal frustrations are pondered on page 46 of volume 1. All of these references were removed in the 1973 edition.

66. Claude Mazauric, "Sur une nouvelle conception de la Révolution," republished with some additions in his *Sur la Révolution française: Contributions à l'histoire de la révolution bourgeoise* (Paris, 1970), 21–61. A few years later, Michel Vovelle offered a point-by-point refutation of Richet and Furet (*La Chute de la monarchie, 1787–1792* [Paris, 1972]).

67. Furet, "Le Catéchisme révolutionnaire," in *Penser la Révolution française*, 133–207. For Mazauric as a political commissar, see Khilnani, *Arguing Revolution*, 164.

68. However, in their preface to the second edition they did not reject their psychoanalytical references in principle; rather, they noted that "they would require an immense amount of work that is beyond our ambitions" (Furet and Richet, *La Révolution française* [1973]: 10).

69. Mazauric, "Sur une nouvelle conception de la Révolution," 28–29.

70. Ibid., 31–32.

71. Ran Halévi, "Feuillants," in François Furet, Mona Ozouf, and collaborators, *Dictionnaire critique de la Révolution française: Acteurs* (Paris, 1992), 341–53.

72. Mazauric, "Sur une nouvelle conception de la Révolution," 57.

73. Furet, *Penser la Révolution française*, 198.

74. Albert Soboul, "Avant-propos," in Mazauric, *Sur la Révolution française*, 5.

75. The entire exchange is in "Correspondance," *Annales ESC* 25, 5 (Sept.-Oct. 1970): 1494–96. Although the dispute was nominally between Richet and Soboul, Furet was obviously implicated in it as indicated by the header given to the section, "F. Furet, D. Richet et A. Soboul."

76. Richard Cobb, "Albert-Marius Soboul: A Tribute," in his *People and Places* (New York, 1985), 46–92; James Friguglietti, "The French Revolution Seen from the Left: Albert Soboul as a Historian," in *Proceedings of the Twelfth Annual Meeting of the Western Society for French History, 24–27 October 1984, Albuquerque, New Mexico*, ed. John F. Sweets (Lawrence, Kans., 1985), 100–107; Antoine de Baecque, "Soboul (Albert)," in *Dictionnaire des intellectuels français: Les Personnes, les lieux, les moments*, ed. Jacques Julliard and Michel Winock (Paris, 1996), 1066–67. At least from the perspective of his 1951 articles in praise of Maurice Thorez, Soboul appears considerably more orthodox than Cobb would have us believe ("Chronique historique," *La Pensée* 37 [July–Aug. 1951]: 119–22, and "L'Histoire du Parti communiste et du peuple français à travers les œuvres de Maurice Thorez (juin 1931–février 1932)," *La Pensée* 35 [Mar.–Apr. 1951]: 127–30).

77. Claude Mazauric, "Penser l'œuvre de François Furet," *L'Humanité*, 16 July 1997, 7.

78. Cobb, "Albert-Marius Soboul," 68. Although Cobb names no one, this citation of Soboul obviously refers to Furet.

79. For Furet's anger, see Furet, *Histoire de la Révolution et la révolution dans l'histoire*, 27.

80. Furet, *Penser la Révolution française*, 185.

81. Ibid., 187.

82. François Furet, "Les Intellectuels français et le structuralisme," in *L'Atelier de l'histoire*, 37–52, originally published in *Preuves* 92 (Feb. 1967).

83. Raymond Aron, *Le Spectateur engagé: Entretiens avec Jean-Louis Missika et Dominique Wolton* (Paris, 1981), 263.

84. Furet interviewed by Ewald, "Penser la Révolution," 93. In a 13 June 1968 letter to Aron, Furet criticized right-wing demagogy and argued against Aron that there was, given the PCF's position, no immediate danger of subversion and that the student movement should be seen as more than its manipulation by revolutionary groups (Nicolas Baverez, *Raymond Aron: Un Moraliste au temps des idéologies* [Paris, 1993], 397).

85. Furet, "Turgot sous l'œil d'Edgar Faure," *France observateur* 594 (21 Sept. 1961): 15-16.

86. François Furet, "L'Adolescence permanente," *La Nef* 43 (July–Sept. 1971): 39.

87. Ibid., 24.

88. Furet, "Le Catéchisme révolutionnaire," 134–35.

89. François Furet, "Le Moteur inusable de Soljénitsyne," *Le Nouvel Observateur* 545 (21 Apr. 1975): 76–77; François Furet, "Faut-il brûler Marx?" *Le Nouvel Observateur* 559 (28 July 1975): 52–53.

90. Furet, "Faut-il brûler Marx?" 52–53. As for Glucksmann's response to the question of whether one should burn Marx: "At the price of domestic fuel, clever, my dear!" ("Réponses," *Tel quel* 64 [winter 1975]: 71).

91. François Furet, "L'Enfance de l'individu," *Le Nouvel Observateur* 660 (4 July 1977): 55.

92. In 1994, Furet said that he was divided in his opinion of Glucksmann at the time. He did not find Glucksmann's work very good, but he believed that Glucksmann was performing a useful task (interview with author, Paris, 10 Feb. 1994).

93. Furet, "La Révolution et ses fantômes," 245.

94. Furet, *Interpreting the French Revolution*, 12, translation modified.

95. Ibid., 11, translation modified.

96. Furet interviewed by Malet, "L'Élection du 10 mai," 190.

97. Glucksmann wrote that the West "now hesitates to recognize its own history in the Russian mirror. The open-minded who visited the Bolsheviks in the 1920s identified in them the inheritors of an old Europe—of its Platonism (Russell), of its Jacobinism (Mathiez), of its industrialization (Lenin who openly borrowed from the models of Rathenau and Taylor). Today when the uncovered face of Bolshevism proves to be terrifying, we fear reading our own features in it." Glucksmann, *La Cuisinière et le mangeur d'hommes*, 212-13.

98. Furet, *Penser la Révolution française*, 202.

99. See, for example, Furet's "Tocqueville et le problème de la Révolution française," originally published in 1971, in *Penser la Révolution française*, 209–56; "Ancien Régime et Révolution: Réinterprétations," *Annales ESC* 29, 1 (Jan.-Feb. 1974): 3–5; "Les États généraux de 1789: Deux baillages élisent leurs députés," in *Conjoncture économique structures sociales: Hommage à Ernest Labrousse*, Civilisations et sociétés, 47 (Paris, 1974), 433–48; "Les Élections de 1789 à Paris: Le Tiers État et la naissance d'une classe dirigeante," in *Vom Ancien Régime zur Französischen Revolution: Forschungen und Perspektiven*, ed. Ernst Hinrichs, Eberhard Schmitt, and Rudolf Vierhaus, Veröffentlichungen des Max-Plank-Institut für Geschichte, 55 (Göttingen, 1978), 188–206 (a paper given in a May 1975 colloquium); and "Mentalité des révolutions," dialogue by E. Le Roy Ladurie and François Furet, Dialogues de France-Culture, Paris, Radio France, 10 Apr. 1973, sound recording.

100. In a letter of 6 Feb. 1976, Thibaud asked Furet if it would be possible for him "to put on paper the essence of what you said in the rue Cabanis debate the other evening on the idea of revolution? It seems to me that, without lingering on the details, this debate went directly to the essential questions and that it was for this reason particularly stimulating." In his response of 9 Feb. 1976, Furet agreed to Thibaud's request and notified Thibaud that he would need "a little time to flesh out this talk" (IMEC ESP2.S16-08.01).

101. François Furet, "Au centre de nos représentations politiques," *Esprit* 460 (Sept. 1976): 172–78.

102. Furet, "La Révolution et ses fantômes," 241.

103. Claude Lefort, "La Question de la révolution," in his *L'Invention démocratique: Les Limites de la domination totalitaire* (Paris, 1981), 196. First published in *Esprit* 460 (Sept. 1976).

104. Furet, *Penser la Révolution française*, 250.

105. Ibid., 262–63, 302–3.
106. Jean Egret, "Les Origines de la Révolution en Bretagne," *Revue historique* 213 (Apr.–June 1955): 212, cited in Charles Porset, "Les Francs-Maçons et la Révolution (autour de la "Machine" de Cochin)," *Annales historiques de la Révolution française* 279 (Jan.–Mar. 1990): 23; Albert Mathiez, review of *Les Sociétés de pensée et la Révolution en Bretagne (1788–1789)*, by Augustin Cochin, *Annales historiques de la Révolution française* 4, 19 (1927): 80–82, reproduced in Porset, "Les Francs-Maçons," 26–28. Furet mentions neither Egret's article nor Mathiez's review in his essay on Cochin.
107. Furet, *Penser la Révolution française*, 258.
108. The author thanks Margaret Jacob for bringing this to his attention. Jacob's recent book on Freemasonry vigorously contests Furet's reading of the relationship between Enlightenment sociability and the Terror. According to her, the Freemasons never practiced direct democracy and never sought to impose ideological purity within their lodges. Furthermore, Furet's link of Freemasonry and Jacobinism is brought into question by the failure of Jacobinism to appear in such cities as Amsterdam, Brussels, and Philadelphia, despite the similarity of Freemasonry in these areas to that in France (Margaret C. Jacob, *Living the Enlightenment: Freemasonry and Politics in Eighteenth-Century Europe* [New York, 1991], 14–18).
109. Moisei Ostrogorski, *La Démocratie et les partis politiques: Textes choisis et présentés par Pierre Rosanvallon* (Paris, 1979); Pierre Rosanvallon, "Avancer avec Michels," *Faire* 17 (Mar. 1977): 31–34 (Michels's *Political Parties* was the focal point of interest in his work); Alain Besançon, *Les Origines intellectuelles du léninisme* (Paris, 1977); Gilles Martinet, "En France que ferions nous?" *Faire* 2 (Nov. 1975): 35; Kriegel, *Ce que j'ai cru comprendre*, 615, which suggests that Kriegel was the one who introduced Furet to Cochin's writings; Augustin Cochin, *L'Esprit du jacobinisme: Une intépretation sociologique de la Révolution* (Paris, 1979).
110. Patrice Gueniffey and Ran Halévi, "Clubs et sociétés populaires," in François Furet, Mona Ozouf, and collaborators, *Dictionnaire critique de la Révolution française: Institutions et créations* (Paris, 1992), 109. In his 1988 narrative history Furet still follows Cochin in his analysis of the elections to the Estates General in 1789 (*1770–1814*, vol. 1 of *La Révolution* [Paris, 1988], 109).
111. On these issues see Alice Gérard, *La Révolution française, mythes et interprétations (1789–1970)* (Paris, 1970) and Paul Farmer, *France Reviews Its Revolutionary Origins: Social Politics and Historical Opinion in the Third Republic* (New York, 1944; reprint, New York, 1963), esp. 83 and 111.
112. The correctness of Furet's presentation of Cochin's work may be questioned. In particular, it is not clear that Cochin ever distinguished between representative and pure democracy, saving the former from his critiques of the latter (Olivier Bétourné and Aglaia I. Hartig, *Penser l'histoire de la Révolution: Deux Siècles de passion française* [Paris, 1989], 20–26).
113. Furet, *Interpreting the French Revolution*, 176.
114. Furet, *Penser la Révolution française*, 281–82, 314.
115. Augustin Cochin, "La Campagne électorale de 1789 en Bourgogne," in *L'Esprit du jacobinisme*, 50. This piece was originally published as a book in 1904.
116. Furet, *Interpreting the French Revolution*, 202.
117. Ibid., 51, 80, 84, 94.
118. Jean Chesneaux, "'Penser la Révolution française' à l'âge de la Commission trilatérale," *Le Monde diplomatique* 300 (Mar. 1979): 2; Le Roy Ladurie, *Paris-Montpellier*, 48; Roger Chartier, "Une Relecture politique de la Révolution française," *Critique* 382 (Mar. 1979): 270. Le Roy Ladurie wrote essentially the same thing in his *Le Monde* review of 1 Jan. 1979 but added that Jim Jones, the leader of the Guyana mass suicide, should be included among the imitators of Robespierre and Saint-Just. Chartier later distanced himself from Furet's interpretation of the Revolution, notably in Chartier, *The Cultural Origins of the French Revolution*, trans. Lydia G. Cochrane (Durham, N.C., 1991).

119. Claude Lefort, "Penser la révolution dans la Révolution française," in *Essais sur le politique (XIXe–XXe siècles)* (Paris, 1986), 117. Originally published in *Annales ESC* 35 (Mar.–Apr. 1980). Jean-Pierre Hirsch, "Pensons la Révolution française," *Annales ESC* 35 (Mar.-Apr. 1980): 331.

120. Lefort, "Penser la révolution dans la Révolution française," 129. Lynn Hunt developed an interpretation along these lines suggested by Lefort. Indeed, her interpretation is influenced by Lefort's critique of Furet (*Politics, Culture, and Class in the French Revolution* [Berkeley, 1984], 49, n. 86).

121. Lefort, "Penser la révolution dans la Révolution française," 138–39.

122. Lynn Hunt, review of *Interpreting the French Revolution* by François Furet, *History and Theory* 20, 3 (Oct. 1981): 313; Khilnani, *Arguing Revolution*, 170–73; Mark Poster, *Cultural History and Postmodernity: Disciplinary Readings and Challenges* (New York, 1997), 72–107, esp. 88–90. Furet denied any connection between his work and that of Derrida. Of Derrida, Furet said: "I detest what he does" (interview with author, Paris, 10 Feb. 1994).

123. François Furet, *Marx et la Révolution française* (Paris, 1986); François Furet, *La Gauche et la Révolution française au milieu du XIXe siècle: Edgar Quinet et la question du jacobinisme (1865–1870)* (Paris, 1986); Furet and Ozouf, *Dictionnaire critique de la Révolution française*.

124. Kaplan, *Adieu 89*, 736.

125. Furet, *1770–1814*.

126. Maurice Agulhon, "Plaidoyer pour les Jacobins. La Gauche, l'État et la région dans la tradition historique française," *Le Débat* 13 (June 1981): 55–65; Maurice Agulhon, "Faut-il avoir peur de 1989?" *Le Débat* 30 (May 1984): 27–37; François Furet, "Réponse à Maurice Agulhon," *Le Débat* 30 (May 1984): 38–43; François Furet, "1789–1917: Aller et retour," *Le Débat* 57 (Nov.–Dec. 1989): 4–16.

127. These questions are identified as "the tension in revolutionary politics between the will of the majority and the general will; . . . the anonymity of sovereign power, all the more constraining for being more neutral; . . . the permanent possibility that sovereignty will be usurped by a faction; and . . . the lack of any recourse for the opposition in a system in which the representation of the sovereign people is conceived as being indivisible and omnipotent" (François Furet and Mona Ozouf, preface to *A Critical Dictionary of the French Revolution*, trans. Arthur Goldhammer [Cambridge, Mass., 1989], xix).

128. For details see Kaplan, *Adieu 89*, esp. 691–97 and 742–44.

129. Isser Woloch, "On the Latent Illiberalism of the French Revolution," *American Historical Review* 95, 5 (Oct. 1990): 1452–70. Alternatively, a liberal might view the French Revolution, as Anne Sa'adah does, as the moment in which liberal politics was born in France (Sa'adah, *The Shaping of Liberal Politics in Revolutionary France: A Comparative Perspective* [Princeton, 1990]).

130. Hervé Hamon and Patrick Rotman, *Les Intellocrates: Expédition en haute intelligentsia* (Brussels, 1985), 45–46; Kaplan, *Adieu 89*, 679, 804.

131. Furet interviewed by Malet, "L'Élection du 10 mai," 192; Furet's comments are from winter 1982. See also François Furet, "Faut-il célébrer le bicentenaire de la Révolution?" *Histoire* 52 (Jan. 1983): 71–77; and Mona Ozouf, "Peut-on commémorer la Révolution française?" in her *L'École de la France: Essais sur la Révolution, l'utopie et l'enseignement* (Paris, 1984), 142–57, first published in *Le Débat* 26 (Sept. 1983).

132. Furet, interview with author, Paris, 10 Feb. 1994.

133. Kaplan, *Adieu 89*, 844.

134. Ibid., 38, 80–81, 217, 662, 682.

135. Furet, *Penser la Révolution française*, 29.

136. Furet, "La Révolution et ses fantômes," 240.

137. Furet, *Le Passé d'une illusion*; Diana Pinto, "Light at Midnight?" *French Politics and Society* 13 (spring 1995): 85.

138. Furet mentioned his close collaboration with Nora, his editor, in the writing of *Penser la Révolution française*, in Furet, interview with author, Paris, 10 Feb. 1994.

Epilogue and Conclusion

Between 1977, the year of the new philosophers, and the Left's coming to power in 1981 the critique of totalitarianism made further progress in French intellectual life, recasting intellectual politics and the lines of demarcation between the different currents within it. For one, the critique of *tiers-mondisme*, which had emerged in 1976 and 1977, took off in 1978 and 1979. Critiques of revolutionary *tiers-mondisme*, such as Gérard Chaliand's *Mythes révolutionnaires du tiers monde* (1976) and the *Deuxième retour de Chine* (1977) of Claudie Broyelle, Jacques Broyelle, and Evelyne Tschirhart, were followed by the mea culpas of Jean Lacouture (*Survive le peuple cambodgien!*) and Jean-Claude Guillebaud (*Les Années orphelines: 1968-1978*), both of which were published in 1978 in Jacques Julliard's *Interventions* series at Éditions du Seuil.[1] *Tiers-mondisme* came under further fire in *Le Nouvel Observateur*'s summer 1978 public debate on it, launched by Julliard. As the 1977-80 French debate over Noam Chomsky's criticism of Western press coverage of Khmer Rouge atrocities in Cambodia as an effort to rehabilitate American imperialism revealed, not only *tiers-mondisme*, but also anti-imperialism had few adherents among French intellectuals—focused on the threat posed by "totalitarian" communism—by the end of the 1970s.[2]

The critique of *tiers-mondisme* became a matter of intellectual engagement with the November 1978 founding of the committee Un bateau pour le Vietnam, which had the explicitly humanitarian and implicitly anticommunist mission of sending a boat to Southeast Asia to save the Vietnamese boat people and highlight the alleged totalitarianism of the Vietnamese régime. Bringing together former *gauchistes* (like Jacques Broyelle, André Glucksmann, and Alain Geismar), other left-wing intellectuals (like Michel Foucault, Jean-Paul Sartre, Jean Lacouture, Olivier Todd, and Yves Montand), liberal anticommunists (like Raymond Aron and Jean-François Revel), and East European dissidents in exile, it—and especially the apparent reconciliation of Sartre and Aron within it—came

Notes for this section begin on page 275.

to symbolize the near consensus of noncommunist French intellectuals behind an antitotalitarian humanitarianism in the late 1970s.[3]

Although *Un bateau pour le Vietnam* was largely the work of former *gauchistes*, the liberal anticommunists of *Preuves* and *Contrepoint* pedigree also did their best to take advantage of the reconfiguration of intellectual politics in the late 1970s. In early 1978, in anticipation of the likely victory of the Left in the legislative elections, they reasserted themselves, founding the antitotalitarian Comité des intellectuels pour l'Europe des libertés (CIEL) in January 1978 and launching their new journal *Commentaire* in March 1978. *Commentaire*, declaring itself opposed to both "the unarticulated cry and pure revolt on the one hand and absolute knowledge and totalizing ideology on the other hand," explicitly sought to rally left-wing antitotalitarian intellectuals to its liberalism, citing with approval the work of the journal *Libre* and the *autogestionnaire* current's discovery of civil society and its critique of "fatal socialist-statist equation."[4] Although *Commentaire*'s success at rallying left-wing intellectuals to its liberal program was rather limited in the late 1970s and early 1980s, CIEL proved to be somewhat more successful in this respect. Claude Mauriac, Jean-Marie Domenach, Jean Lacouture, Julia Kristeva, and Philippe Sollers, for example, signed on to its founding manifesto, "La Culture contre le totalitarisme: la liberté ne se négocie pas" (which called for the defense of individual liberties and gratuitous cultural expression throughout Europe and especially against totalitarianism), despite—or perhaps because of—its implicit identification of the Left with totalitarianism and option for the status quo.[5]

Notwithstanding these convergences between anticommunist liberals and left-wing antitotalitarians in the late 1970s and early 1980s, there was no conversion of the latter to the politics of the former in this period. The cult of Raymond Aron initiated by antitotalitarians in the early 1980s did not, for example, represent an embrace of his politics, which, unlike that of the antitotalitarian intellectual Left, was elaborated from the perspective of a "responsible" (and liberal anticommunist) exercise of political power. At most, this interest in Aron was an expression of the conviction that Aron had been "right" during the Cold War to take positions against Sartre and others when evaluating communism and Marxism. Further, although Aron did not speak out against the new philosophers in 1977 (having, like many others, "no reason to start a polemic with them"), he found them entirely superficial and was angered by their condemnation of reason and modern civilization.[6] As Aron, André Glucksmann, and Bernard-Henri Lévy all recognized, new philosophy was not Aronian in either its origins or later development.[7] Nor was, for example, Claude Lefort's "*démocratie sauvage*" or other efforts to reinvent the Left in light of the critique of totalitarianism fundamentally Aronian in temperament.

Having noted the continued relevancy of old political divisions, there is no doubt that, although tensions between the antitotalitarian intellectual Left and the parties of the Left remained high in the late 1970s and early 1980s, those between left-wing and right-wing intellectuals (excepting the extreme Left and Right) declined considerably in the same period. Although, for example, left-wing intellectuals did not sign up with *Commentaire*'s program, they generally respected the journal—unlike its predecessor *Contrepoint*, which, it should be recalled, was a reactionary enterprise vis-à-vis May '68. The journal *Le Débat*, created by Pierre Nora and Marcel Gauchet in 1980, was the primary beneficiary of this reconfiguration of allegiances and divisions within intellectual politics. Promising to be "open to everyone" "with the exception of all forms of intellectual terrorism" in the interests of promoting democratic intellectual debate, *Le Débat* became the principle forum for centrist reformist intellectuals in the 1980s.[8]

When the Left came to power in 1981 the antitotalitarian intellectuals' suspicion of it was, as could have been expected from the debates of the 1970s, immediate and substantial. There was no "silence of the intellectuals" in 1981, as the summer 1983 debate by that name would seem to indicate; rather, intellectuals spoke loudly and clearly of their fears of the new government.[9] As during the debate on the Union of the Left in the 1970s, the problem was the PCF and the PS's relation to it. Briefly put, many French intellectuals feared that liberty was threatened in France by the communist ministers in the second Mauroy government, socialists whom they considered to be ideologically subordinate to the communists, and Soviet expansionism (greatly feared after the USSR's 1979 invasion of Afghanistan), which, they believed, would benefit from the new French government. At the extreme, CIEL launched an appeal in July 1981 against the presence of communists in the government, calling the PCF's principles, practices, and solidarity with communist régimes to be "diametrically opposed to the essential values" defended by CIEL and arguing that communist participation in the government was "morally unacceptable" and demanded "a great deal of vigilance."[10] The intellectuals at *Esprit*, although not opposed to communist ministers in principle, objected that the socialists conceded too much to them. Paul Thibaud, who held that "the electoral victory of Mitterrand has not made the earlier debates on the political culture of the French Left outdated," argued that Mitterrand and the socialists had as a consequence of their retrograde political culture proven to be incapable of understanding the "radical and determinant importance of totalitarianism" and, as a consequence, were incapable of reining in the communists.[11] Similar concerns could also, to cite one more example, be found in the pages of *Les Temps modernes*, which, unlike *Esprit*, had hardly been at the vanguard of the critique of totalitarianism in the 1970s.[12]

It was precisely this suspicion and fear of the new French government that lay behind the intellectuals' campaign against the December 1981 declaration of martial law in Poland. Again, as in the protests against repres-

sion under communism in the 1970s and earlier, the domestic political significance of events in Poland was the key factor motivating intellectuals'
protests. Indeed, it was less events in Poland than the French government's response to them that sparked the intellectual mobilization. When,
the day after martial law was declared, French Minister of Foreign Relations Claude Cheysson declared that the Polish situation was an "internal
Polish affair" and that "we will do nothing," intellectuals interpreted these
words as confirming their worst fears and suspicions of the new French
government and raised their voices against them.[13] The collective statement of protest launched by Cornelius Castoriadis, entitled "Illusions ne
pas garder" (Illusions to be discarded), indignantly denounced Cheysson's
failure to see the hand of Moscow in events in Poland and demanded that
"the French government ... speak with the same clarity about the so-called
'socialist' totalitarian régimes as about the dictatorships of Latin America."[14] Another protest written by Michel Foucault and Pierre Bourdieu,
entitled "Les Rendez-vous manqués" (Missed appointments) and subsequently signed by hundreds of artists and intellectuals, likewise denounced
Cheysson's statement as "an immoral and deceitful assertion" and asked
whether "the French socialist leaders do not give more importance to their
internal allies than to the assistance due to a nation in danger?"[15] The manifesto of CIEL, entitled "Parler clairement; agir" (Speak clearly; act), not
only condemned the socialist government's reaction, but demanded that
the communists leave the French government because "one must exclude
the presence of the leaders of a sister party of the Soviet totalitarian party
in the French government" now that "resistance to Soviet totalitarianism
has become the primordial political question of our time."[16]

Indicative of the narrow anticommunist focus of antitotalitarian intellectuals' engagement against repression in these years is the fact that some
intellectuals considered it necessary in the face of the socialist government's criticisms of military dictatorships in Latin America to make it clear
that they considered the communist régimes of Eastern Europe to be qual-
itatively more repressive. CIEL's "Parler clairement; agir," signed by the
same Jean-Marie Domenach and François Fejtö who had launched the
Comité Tibor Déry in support of Hungarian intellectuals a quarter century
earlier, declared that while "all infringements on human rights are odious"
and "all dictatorships are bad in themselves," "it is all the same necessary
for us all to recognize that the oppression that is the most menacing in its
extent, everyday nature, utter cynicism, will and capacity for expansion is
that of Soviet totalitarianism."[17] Paul Thibaud similarly argued in early
1982 that totalitarian régimes are far more insidious than the military dictatorships of Latin American and that "one does not place all those who
attack liberty on the same level."[18] Although not all antitotalitarian intellectuals would make this argument, none of them would challenge it. Consequently, it was Poland under martial law and not repression by Latin
American dictatorships that preoccupied them in the early 1980s.

In the protests prompted by the Polish situation and the French government's response to it one finds almost no references to the dream of reconciling socialism with liberty that had motivated intellectuals' mobilizations in the two decades after 1956. Socialism retained little of its past attractiveness. Even the editorial committee of *Les Temps modernes* could not unite behind a declaration that, while very critical of the French socialist government's response to the Polish affair, held out a modest hope for a renewal of socialism once liberty was secure. Two of the editorial committee's members, Dominique Pigon and Pierre Rigoulot, dissented from the majority's statement, declaring that support for Solidarity must be informed by the realization that "democratic socialism does not exist and [that] the Marxist-Leninist doctrine that nourishes to a greater or lesser extent the entire Left leads inevitably to oppression and dictatorship."[19]

The critique of totalitarianism's discrediting of socialism, revolution, and globalizing transformative political projects, combined with the concrete failure of French socialism in power, made the 1980s a period of flux and uncertainty in French intellectual politics. The disorientation of French intellectuals can be seen in the contemporary assertions that the French tradition of the prophetic intellectual was dead. For some—notably those inclined to the 1980s revival of liberalism—prophetic intellectuals were to be replaced by experts who would limit their political interventions to issues that touched on their expertise. For others—notably postmodernists—the death of the prophetic intellectual was quite simply the death of the intellectual. According to Jean-François Lyotard, the notion of the intellectual, inseparable from that of the universal subject, could not survive the death of the latter following the collapse of Marxism.[20]

As this discussion of the prophetic intellectual's death indicates, liberalism and postmodernism were the immediate beneficiaries of the critique of totalitarianism. Indeed, both currents emerged out of the critique of totalitarianism to some extent. The leading figures in the rediscovery of the French liberal tradition in the 1980s (François Furet, Marcel Gauchet, and Pierre Rosanvallon) had been in the forefront of the antitotalitarian currents of the 1970s, and French postmodernists like Jean Baudrillard and Lyotard, while not antitotalitarians as such, clearly sympathized with them and capitalized on the antitotalitarian critique of the Left to legitimize their postmodern reading of the contemporary world.[21] Yet the success of these currents in the early and mid 1980s was largely a product of the disarray of the period. Like contemporary humanitarianism, both thrived on a fear of radical politics and dearth of political projects following the collapse of the socialist ideal. Both would lose ground in the 1990s to the medium-term winner in French intellectual politics: republicanism.

Antitotalitarianism lost momentum in the 1980s as the political issues that had given birth to it became less pressing. Mitterrand's 20 January 1983 Bundestag speech, in which he vigorously supported the positions of the American and German governments on Euromissiles, did much to diminish the fear that the French government would capitulate to the USSR. Likewise, the French socialists' abandonment of any attempt to break with capitalism and the departure of the communists from the French government in July 1984 brought an effective end to concerns about the threat that the Left appeared to pose to freedom. The collapse of East European communism at the end of the decade further reduced the relevancy of antitotalitarianism. To be sure, French intellectuals continued to use the concept, but they increasingly discovered its limits. Paul Thibaud would criticize the "antitotalitarian vulgate" in 1988 for impoverishing democracy and hindering efforts to understand Nazism by focusing on ideology and "assimilating totalitarianism to the dictatorship of utopia." Antitotalitarianism failed to provide a clear and unambiguous roadmap for French intellectuals confronting the war in Yugoslavia. As a consequence, antitotalitarian intellectuals were deeply divided in their analyses and commitments regarding it.[22]

At the same time that antitotalitarianism was losing its relevancy, new domestic political problems were emerging—notably the rise of the National Front and the politics of immigration in the 1980s, and then the socio-economic issues related to globalization in the 1990s—that recast intellectual politics and sociabilities along new lines. In the debates on these issues it has been republicanism and not liberalism or postmodernism that has been dominant. Especially after the *affaire du foulard* (headscarf affair) of 1989, the Jacobin republican tradition, previously denounced as totalitarian, has enjoyed a revival—in a form that finds its inspiration in the early Third Republic—as an integrative and solidaristic force promoted by some intellectuals as a solution to the problems that come under the rubrics of "immigration" and "globalization." This recourse to the Republic and republican solidarity has also entailed a revival of universalism, which—although more defensive and less ambitious than earlier, revolutionary universalisms—offers an alternative to the dominant model of American civilization that promises to humanize social relations. Not surprisingly, republican universalism has offered ample ground for the revival of the prophetic intellectual, most clearly visible in Pierre Bourdieu's interventions in the 1995 strikes.[23]

*   *   *

In conclusion, the French critique of totalitarianism of the 1970s was, this book argues, more political than intellectual. Motivated by and focused on French domestic politics, French antitotalitarianism was insular. Indeed, the French debate on totalitarianism functioned almost without reference to the substantial Anglo-American and German literature on the subject, which began to interest French intellectuals only in the 1980s. It was a strange—albeit predictable—fate for a concept with such an international pedigree. The instrumental political use of 1970s French antitotalitarianism also made its focus highly selective. Developed to criticize the PCF and the PS's alliance with it, the critique of totalitarianism focused almost exclusively on left-wing totalitarianism, finding the origins of totalitarianism in Marxism, utopian ideology, revolutionary politics, and the French revolutionary tradition. The concrete analysis of Soviet history was given short shrift, and Nazism hardly entered into 1970s analyses of totalitarianism. Nor was the concept applied to Vichy in the obsessive discussion of it during those same years. The most important effort to make the connection between the reevaluation of Vichy and antitotalitarianism, Bernard-Henri Lévy's *L'Idéologie française* of 1981, was—unlike Lévy's earlier *La Barbarie à visage humain*—generally condemned by French intellectuals.[24]

The insular and selective focus of the French critique of totalitarianism can, of course, be attributed to the self-centeredness of French intellectuals, apparently convinced that French politics and history is universal history. Yet, beyond the specific characteristics of French intellectual life, the history of the concept of totalitarianism was throughout the Cold War one of its instrumentalization. If the French use of the concept appears insular and self-centered compared to that in West Germany or the United States, this reflects, in part, the fact that in the German and American cases uses of the concept of totalitarianism were much more closely aligned with the international politics of the Cold War. There domestic communism was insignificant and détente and *Ostpolitik* were key to the concept's fortune in the 1970s.

The problem for historians of French intellectual politics is that this instrumental use of the concept of totalitarianism has been disguised. Seeking to universalize their critique of French communism and the politics of the Union of the Left, French intellectuals claimed that their critique of totalitarianism was not motivated by specific domestic political concerns, but was rather a result of their being awakened to communist repression by Solzhenitsyn's *The Gulag Archipelago*'s. Historians' acceptance of this reading of the critique of totalitarianism's origins has made it impossible to understand either the critique of totalitarianism or the evolution of French intellectual politics between the Liberation and the 1970s. This book's examination of the critique of totalitarianism's long-term origins in left-wing intellectuals' criticisms of "really existing socialism," divorce from the parties of the Left, and direct-democratic reformulation of the revolutionary project in the 1950s and 1960s should help us rethink postwar French intellectual history. Likewise, this book's analysis of the 1970s critique of totalitarianism hopes to cast new light on the antitotalitarian moment by focusing on its intimate relationship with the debate of the Union of the Left and thereby show what can be gained from a close and profoundly contextualized reading of French intellectual politics.

To close this book, a few words on the intellectual, political, and moral balance sheet of the antitotalitarian moment are in order. The critique of totalitarianism has been represented as an event in which left-wing intellectuals tore off their blinders to see the world in a more accurate light, revised their politics accordingly, and saved their tarnished moral reputation by vigorously campaigning against repression by communist régimes. Yet, upon closer examination French antitotalitarianism appears intellectually, politically, and morally problematic. Originating less in profound reflection on supposedly totalitarian régimes than in domestic political disputes, the critique of totalitarianism proceeded along lines that were largely determined by domestic politics and for that reason did little or nothing to advance understanding of régimes or politics considered to be "totalitarian." Further, it did much to confuse the issues by identifying French revolutionary political culture with totalitarianism and by failing to consider that "totalitarianism" might have roots outside of revolutionary ideology and the revolutionary project. The price of this confusion would become evident by the late 1980s when, for example, Furet, confronted with reactionary appropriations of his work, would be forced to admit that his formulations of the 1970s were too strong and Thibaud would find himself criticizing the "antitotalitarian vulgate" of the 1970s.

Intellectually inadequate because of its political vocation, the critique of totalitarianism was no less politically misguided. The critique of totalitarianism largely misjudged the politics of the party-political Left in the 1970s. It failed or refused to recognize either the weaknesses of the PCF or the legitimacy and success of the Mitterrandist strategy for coming to power, choosing instead—despite mounting evidence to the contrary—to insist that the PCF and its ideology effectively dominated the Left. Beyond the Rocardian option, these intellectuals had little or nothing constructive to offer as an alternative and, as a consequence, often found themselves during the second Mauroy government playing a purely negative, oppositional role. To the extent that it focused on the danger of totalitarianism in France, their politics was one of irresponsibility and self-induced illusions.

Finally, the moral balance sheet of antitotalitarianism is hardly as inspirational as some would have it. Although it focused more attention on East European dissidents than ever before, left-wing intellectuals' defense of them against repression was not entirely new. Furthermore, the specifically antitotalitarian cast of protests against repression in the late 1970s and early 1980s purposefully focused intellectuals' attention on repression under communism at the expense of that by noncommunist régimes. Given the murderous brutality of the Latin American military dictatorships of the period, the moral balance sheet of antitotalitarianism is at the very least ambiguous. In the final analysis, French antitotalitarianism thrived on and suffered from both the openness of the concept of totalitarianism to political instrumentalization and the propensity of French intellectuals to universalize and ideologize domestic political debates.

Notes

1. Gérard Chaliand, *Mythes révolutionnaires du tiers monde* (Paris, 1976); Claudie Broyelle, Jacques Broyelle, and Evelyne Tschirhart, *Deuxième retour de Chine* (Paris, 1977); Jean Lacouture, *Survive le peuple cambodgien!* (Paris, 1978); and Jean-Claude Guillebaud, *Les Années orphelines: 1968-1978* (Paris, 1978).

2. On the debate over Chomsky's position on Cambodia see François Hourmant, *Le Désenchantement des clercs: Figures de l'intellectuel dans l'après-Mai 68* (Rennes, 1997), 177-92 and Noam Chomsky, *Réponses inédites à mes détracteurs parisiens*, Spartacus Cahiers mensuels, Séries B, no. 128 (Paris, 1984).

3. Louis-Winoc Christiaens, "La Défense des droits de l'homme en France à travers les comités politiques (1969-1979). Un cas pratique: le comité 'Un bateau pour le Vietnam,' 1979" (DEA Thesis, Université Charles de Gaulle, Lille III, 1990). Jacques Broyelle, in an interview with Christiaens reproduced in his thesis, reveals that he and some of the founders of the initiative (Glucksmann and Todd, for example) wanted to give it a very explicit anticommunist orientation but were out-maneuvered by Bernard Kouchner, who used the effort to launch his humanitarian organization Médecins du monde.

4. "Commentaire," *Commentaire* 1, 1 (spring 1978): 3-6. See also Rémy Rieffel, *La Tribu des clercs: les intellectuels sous la Ve République* (Paris, 1993), 252-57.

5. In the context of the impending legislative elections, its statement that "the present crisis, even its worsening, remains preferable to the outcome the temptation of which appears at each moment of doubt: totalitarian certainty" implicitly identified the Left with totalitarianism and opted for the status quo. *Le Monde*, 27 January 1978, 13. This critique of CIEL was enunciated at the time by an "Appel contre le manifeste du comité des intellectuels pour l'Europe des libertés," *Le Monde*, 12-13 March 1978, 3. Among the founders of CIEL were Abel Gance, Raymond Aron, Arrabal, Alexandre Astruc, Jean-Marie Benoist, Etienne Borne, Raymond Bourdon, Michel Bouquet, Robert Bresson, Jean-Claude Casanova, Claude Chabrol, Pierre Clostermann, Michel Crozier, Gérard Depardieu, Jean-Marie Domenach, Jacques Ellul, François Fejtö, Jean Fourastié, Paul Goma, Pierre Hassner, Eugène Ionesco, Julia Kristeva, Emmanuel Le Roy Ladurie, Jean Lacouture, Claude Mauriac, Pierre Nora, Jean d'Ormesson, Kostas Papaioannou, Louis Pauwels, Krzystof Pomian, Alain Ravennes, Jean-François Revel, Pierre Schaeffer, Alexander Smolar, Philippe Sollers, Pavel Tigrid, and Ilios Yannakakis.

6. Raymond Aron, *Mémoires* (Paris, 1983), 985 for the citation. Raymond Aron, "Pour le progrès après la chute des idoles," *Commentaire* 1, 3 (autumn 1978): 223-43.

7. In addition to the sources cited above see Raymond Aron, interviewed by Bernard-Henri Lévy, *Le Nouvel Observateur* 592 (15 March 1976): 85, where Aron insists that Glucksmann "belongs to an intellectual current that is fundamentally different from mine"; Raymond Aron, *Le Spectateur engagé: entretiens avec Jean-Louis Missika et Dominique Wolton* (Paris, 1981): 300, where Aron asserts that the mobilization for the boat people did not signify a conversion of intellectuals to his position; Bernard-Henri Lévy, *Le Quotidien de Paris*, 13 Sept. 1983, where Lévy denies any influence of Aron on his or on Glucksmann's books of the 1970s; and André Glucksmann, *Le Matin*, 9 Sept. 1983, where Glucksmann explains that "the events of May '68 brought an end to our relations" (between himself and Aron) until the Boat for Vietnam campaign.

8. Inside cover blurb, *Le Débat* 1 (May 1980). See also Pierre Nora, "Que peuvent les intellectuels?" *Le Débat* 1 (May 1980): 3-19. According to Pierre Nora, *Le Débat* sold 8,000 to 15,000 copies per number in the 1980s. Rieffel, *La Tribu des clercs*, 392, fn. 3. See also Hourmant, *Le Désenchantement des clercs*, 213-22.

9. On the 1983 debate see Martyn Cornick, "The Silence of the Left Intellectuals in Mitterrand's France," in *The Mitterrand Years: Legacy and Evaluation*, ed. Mairi Maclean (New York, 1998), 300-13.

10. *Le Monde*, 5-6 July 1981, 5.

11. Paul Thibaud, "Mouvement social ou réforme politique?" *Esprit* 55-56 (July-Aug. 1981): 37-47; 42 and 46 for the citations. See also Philippe Reynaud, "L'Accord PC-PS," *Esprit* 55-56 (July-Aug. 1981): 89-92.

12. Pierre Rigoulot, "Épicerie, morale et scepticisme," *Les Temps modernes* 419 (June 1981): 2076-81. Rigoulot's position was not shared by the majority of editorial board members of the journal. On divisions within *Les Temps modernes* see Hourmant, *Le Désenchantement des clercs*, 230-36. Much more measured in its judgments and appreciative of the extent of the PCF's subordination to the PS within the Left is Le Débat, "Le Sens de la victoire socialiste," *Le Débat* 15 (Sept.-Oct. 1981): 3-12. For an overview of French intellectuals' reactions to the second Mauroy government see Rieffel, *La Tribu des clercs*, 152-56.

13. Cheysson cited in Jean-François Sirinelli, *Intellectuels et passions françaises: Manifestes et pétitions au xxe siècle* (Paris, 1990), 298.

14. For the full text and the list of signatures see Cornelius Castoriadis, "Illusions ne pas garder," in his *Domaines de l'homme: les carrefours du labyrinthe II* (Paris, 1986), 51.

15. "Les Rendez-vous manqués," *Libération*, 17 Dec. 1981. See also Didier Eribon, *Michel Foucault (1926-1984)* (Paris, 1991), 383-85.

16. *Le Monde*, 6 Feb. 1982, 7, which includes a list of the first 100 signatures.

17. Ibid. This was fairly common rhetoric within CIEL in the 1980s. See for example: Alain Besançon, "La Liberté comme légitimité," *CIEL* 4 (spring 1980): 5; Jean-Marie Domenach, "L'Amour de la liberté," *La Lettre du CIEL* (2nd trimester, 1984): 5; Raymond Aron, "La Politique des droits de l'homme," *Commentaire* 64 (winter 1993-1994): 705-17, an article written shortly before Aron's death in 1983 and first published in English in 1985.

18. Paul Thibaud, "Et le Salvador?" *Esprit* 63 (March 1982): 98. *Esprit* sponsored the committee "Liberté pour la Pologne et l'Europe de l'Est," founded in early 1982. See "Liberté pour la Pologne et l'Europe de l'Est," *Esprit* 62 (February 1982): 1-4 for its founding manifesto, which echoes the concerns of the protests against the French socialist government's conduct in the face of martial law in Poland.

19. Simone de Beauvoir, Jacques-Laurent Bost, Claire Etcherelli, Elisabeth de Fontenay, André Gorz, Claude Lanzmann, and Jean Pouillon, "La Normalisation en sous-traitance," *Les Temps modernes* 426 (Jan. 1982): 1137-38 (dated 19 Dec. 1981) and Dominique Pigon and Pierre Rigoulot, "La Gauche schizophrène et la Pologne," *Les Temps modernes* 426 (Jan. 1982): 1138 (dated 20 Dec. 1981). Rigoulot resigned from the editorial committee at this point.

20. Eric Fassin, "Play it Again, Sartre? New Drefusards in Search of a New Dreyfus," *French Politics & Society* 16, 1 (winter 1998): 26-27. Jean-François Lyotard, "Tomb of the Intellectual," in his *Political Writings*, trans. Bill Readings and Kevin Paul Geiman (Minneapolis, 1993), 3-7.

21. See Interview of Jean-François Lyotard with Bernard-Henri Lévy, *Le Nouvel Observateur* 585 (19 Jan. 1976): 52-53; Lyotard, *Political Writings*; and Jean Baudrillard, *La Gauche divine* (Paris, 1985).

22. Paul Thibaud, "Du Goulag à Auschwitz: glissement de la réflexion antitotalitaire," *Esprit* 136-137 (March-April 1988): 138-39. Daniel Lindenberg, "D'une guerre à l'autre: la Yougoslavie des intellectuels," *Matériaux pour l'histoire de notre temps* 48 (Oct.-Dec. 1997): 52-54.

23. On these issues see the essays of Jean-Philippe Mathy ("Repli sur la République: la nouvelle donne des intellectuels français," *L'Esprit Créateur* 37, 2 [summer 1997]: 41-55 and "L'Exigence prophétique: Zola, Bourdieu et la mémoire du Dreyfusisme," *Contemporary French Civilization* 24, 2 [summer/fall 2000]: 321-40), Michael F. Leruth ("The Neorepublican Discourse on French National Identity," *French Politics & Society* 16, 4 [fall 1998]: 46-61 and "French Intellectuals Come to Terms with Globalization," *Contemporary French Civilization* 25, 1 [winter/spring 2001]: 42-83), and Eric Fassin ("Play it Again, Sartre?" and "Two Cultures? French Intellectuals and the Politics of Culture in the 1980s," *French Politics and Society* 14, 2 [spring 1996]: 9-16).

24. Bernard-Henri Lévy, *L'Idéologie française* (Paris, 1981).

SELECTED BIBLIOGRAPHY OF
SECONDARY SOURCES

Becker, Jean-Jacques, with the collaboration of Catherine Simon and Jean Loignon. "Le Modèle soviétique et l'opinion française." In *La France en voie de modernisation, 1944-1956. FNSP colloque des 4 et 5 décembre 1981.* Vol. 2, no pagination.

Bel, Monique. *Maurice Clavel.* Paris, 1992.

Bell, D. S., and Byron Criddle. *The French Socialist Party: The Emergence of a Party of Government.* 2nd ed. Oxford, 1988.

Birchall, Ian H. "Sartre and Gauchisme." *Journal of European Studies* 19, 1 (Mar. 1989): 21-53.

Bosworth, R. J. B. *The Italian Dictatorship: Problems and Perspectives in the Interpretation of Mussolini and Fascism.* New York, 1998.

Brown, Bernard E., ed. *Eurocommunism and Eurosocialism: The Left Confronts Modernity.* New York, 1979.

Burnier, Michel-Antoine. *Choice of Action: The French Existentialists on the Political Front Line.* Translated by Bernard Murchland. New York, 1968.

Burrowes, Robert. "'Totalitarianism' The Revised Standard Version." *World Politics* 21, 2 (Jan. 1969): 272-94.

Caute, David. *Communism and French Intellectuals 1914-1960.* London, 1964.

Charle, Christophe. "Academics or Intellectuals? The Professors of the University of Paris and Political Debate in France from the Dreyfus Affair to the Algerian War." In *Intellectuals in Twentieth-Century France: Mandarins and Samurais,* edited by Jeremy Jennings, 94-116. New York, 1993.

Chebel d'Appollonia, Ariane. *Des lendemains qui déchantent.* Vol. 1 of *Histoire politique des intellectuels en France, 1944-1954.* Brussels, 1991.

_____. *Le Temps de l'engagement.* Vol. 2 of *Histoire politique des intellectuels en France, 1944-1954.* Brussels, 1991.

Christiaens, Louis-Winoc. "La Défense des droits de l'homme en France à travers les comités politiques (1969-1979). Un cas pratique: le comité 'Un bateau pour le Vietnam,' 1979." DEA Thesis, Université Charles de Gaulle, Lille III, 1990.

Christofferson, Michael Scott. "The Antitotalitarian Moment in French Intellectual Politics, 1975-1984." Ph.D. Diss., Columbia University, 1998.

_____. "An Antitotalitarian History of the French Revolution: François Furet's *Penser la Révolution française* in the Intellectual Politics of the Late 1970s." *French Historical Studies* 22, 4 (fall 1999): 557-611.

_____. "François Furet Between History and Journalism, 1958-65." *French History* 15, 4 (Dec. 2001): 421-47.

_____. "French Intellectuals and the Repression of the Hungarian Revolution of 1956: The Politics of a Protest Reconsidered." In *After the Deluge: New Perspectives on French Intellectual and Cultural History,* edited by Julian Bourg. (forthcoming)

Christofferson, Thomas R. *The French Socialists in Power, 1981-1986: From Autogestion to Cohabitation.* Toronto, 1991.

Cohen, Paul M. *Freedom's Moment: An Essay on the French Idea of Liberty from Rousseau to Foucault.* Chicago, 1997.

Cohen, Stephen F. *Rethinking the Soviet Experience: Politics and History Since 1917.* New York, 1985.

Cohen-Solal, Annie. *Sartre 1905-1980.* Paris, 1985.

Contat, Michel, and Michel Rybalka. *A Bibliographical Life.* Vol. 1 of *The Writings of Jean-Paul Sartre.* Translated by Richard C. McCleary. Evanston, Ill., 1974.

Davies, Howard. *Sartre and 'Les Temps Modernes.'* New York, 1987.

Le Débat. *Les Idées en France 1945-1988: une chronologie.* Paris, 1989.

Debray, Régis. *Le Pouvoir intellectuel en France.* Paris, 1979.

Deli, Peter. *De Budapest à Prague: les sursauts de la gauche française.* Paris, 1981.

Descombes, Vincent. *Le Même et l'autre: quarante-cinq ans de philosophie française (1933-1978).* Paris, 1986.

Desjardins, Robert. *The Soviet Union Through French Eyes, 1945-85.* London, 1988.

Dews, Peter. "The *Nouvelle Philosophie* and Foucault." *Economy and Society* 8, 2 (May 1979): 127-71.

Dioujeva, Natacha, and François George, eds. *Staline à Paris.* Paris, 1982.

Dosse, François. *L'Histoire en miettes: des "Annales" à la "nouvelle histoire."* Paris, 1987.

_____. *The Sign Sets, 1967-Present.* Vol. 2 of *History of Structuralism.* Translated by Deborah Glassman. Minneapolis, 1997.

Drake, David. "*On a raison de se révolter*: The Response of *la Gauche prolétarienne* to the Events of May-June 1968." In *Violence and Conflict in the Politics and Society of Modern France*, edited by Jan Windebank and Renate Günter, 61-72. Vol. 5 of *Studies in French Civilization.* Lewiston, N.Y., 1995.

_____. *Intellectuals and Politics in Post-War France.* New York, 2002.

Dreyfus, Michel. "1956: l'année terrible." *Communisme* 29-31 (1st-3rd semester 1991): 237-47.

Dreyfus, Michel, Bruno Groppo, Claudio Sergio Ingerflom, Roland Lew, Claude Pennetier, Bernard Pudal, and Serge Wolikow, eds. *Le Siècle des communismes.* Paris, 2000.

Dunlop, John B., Richard S. Haugh, and Michael Nichelson, eds. *Solzhenitsyn in Exile: Critical Essays and Documentary Materials.* Hoover Press Publication, no. 305. Stanford, Calif., 1985.

Elliot, Gregory. *Althusser: The Detour of Theory.* New York, 1987.

Eribon, Didier. *Michel Foucault (1926-1984).* Paris, 1991.

Evans, Martin. *The Memory of Resistance: French Opposition to the Algerian War (1954-1962).* New York, 1997.

Farmer, Paul. *France Reviews Its Revolutionary Origins: Social Politics and Historical Opinion in the Third Republic.* New York, 1944. Reprint, New York, 1963.

Fassin, Eric. "Two Cultures? French Intellectuals and the Politics of Culture in the 1980s." *French Politics & Society* 14, 2 (spring 1996): 9-16.

_____. "Play it Again, Sartre? New *Drefusards* in Search of a New Dreyfus." *French Politics & Society* 16, 1 (winter 1998): 23-37.

Feré, Vincent. "Le Comité national des écrivains et les compagnons de route du parti communiste français (février 1946-avril 1953)." DEA Thesis, Paris IEP, 1998.

Forest, Philippe. *Histoire de Tel quel, 1960-1982.* Paris, 1995.

Fields, A. Belden. *Trotskyism and Maoism: Theory and Practice in France and the United States.* New York, 1988.

Francis, Claude, and Fernande Gontier. *Simone De Beauvoir: A Life ... A Love Story.* Translated by Lisa Nesselson. New York, 1987.

Gérard, Alice. *La Révolution française, mythes et interprétations (1789-1970).* Paris, 1970.

Gleason, Abbott. *Totalitarianism: The Inner History of the Cold War.* New York, 1995.

Gombin, Richard. *Le Projet révolutionnaire.* The Hague, 1969.

_____. *The Origins of Modern Leftism.* Translated by Michael K. Perl. Baltimore, 1975.

Grandmaison, Olivier Le Cour. "Le Mouvement de la paix pendant la guerre froide: le cas français (1948-1952)." *Communisme* 18-19 (1988): 120-38.

Grémion, Pierre. *Paris-Prague: la gauche face au renouveau et à la régression tchécoslovaques (1968-1978).* Paris, 1985.

_____. *Intelligence de l'anticommunisme: le Congrès pour la liberté de la culture à Paris.* Paris, 1995.

Groppo, Bruno, and Gianni Riccamboni. "Le Parti communiste italien face aux crises du 'socialisme réel.'" *Communisme* 3 (1983): 65-83.

Gundle, Stephen. *Between Hollywood and Moscow: The Italian Communists and the Challenge of Mass Culture, 1943-1991.* Durham, N.C., 2000.

Hamon, Hervé, and Patrick Rotman. *Les Intellocrates: expédition en haute intelligentsia.* Brussels, 1985.

_____. *Les Années de rêve.* Vol. 1 of *Génération.* Paris, 1987.

_____. *Les Années de poudre.* Vol. 2 of *Génération.* Paris, 1988.

Harris, André, and Alain de Sédouy. *Voyage à l'intérieur du Parti communiste.* Paris, 1974.

Hazareesingh, Sudhir. *Intellectuals and the French Communist Party: Disillusion and Decline.* Oxford, 1991.

_____. *Political Traditions in Modern France.* New York, 1994.

Herf, Jeffrey. *War by Other Means: Soviet Power, West German Resistance, and the Battle of Euromissiles.* New York, 1991.

_____. *Divided Memory: The Nazi Past in the Two Germanys.* Cambridge, Mass., 1997.

Hermet, Guy, ed. *Totalitarismes.* Paris, 1984.

Hirsh, Arthur. *The French New Left: An Intellectual History From Sartre to Gorz.* Boston, 1981.

Hourmant, François. *Le Désenchantement des clercs: Figures de l'intellectuel dans l'après-mai 68.* Rennes, 1997.

Joffrin, Laurent. *Mai 68: histoire des événements.* Paris, 1988.

Judt, Tony. *Past Imperfect: French Intellectuals, 1944-1956.* Berkeley, 1992.

Julliard, Jacques, and Michel Winock, eds. *Dictionnaire des intellectuels français: les personnes, les lieux, les moments.* Paris, 1996.

Kaplan, Steven Laurence. *Adieu 89.* Translated by André Charpentier and Rémy Labrechts. Paris, 1993.

_____. *Farewell, Revolution: The Historians' Feud: France, 1789/1989.* Ithaca, N.Y., 1995.

Kauppi, Niilo. *The Making of an Avant-Garde: Tel quel.* Approaches to Semiotics, no. 113. New York, 1994.

_____. *French Intellectual Nobility: Institutional and Symbolic Transformations in the Post-Sartrian Era.* Albany, N.Y., 1996.

Kershaw, Ian. "Totalitarianism Revisited: Nazism and Stalinism in Comparative Perspective." *Tel Aviver Jahrbuch für deutsche Geschichte* 23 (1994): 23-40.

Khilnani, Sunil. *Arguing Revolution: The Intellectual Left in Postwar France.* New Haven, 1993.

Kusin, Vladimir K. *From Dubček to Charter 77: A Study of 'Normalization' in Czechoslovakia, 1968-1978.* New York, 1978.

Lazar, Marc. *Maisons rouges: les Partis communistes français et italien de la Libération à nos jours.* Paris, 1992.

Le Goff, Jean-Pierre. *Mai 68: l'héritage impossible.* Paris, 1998.

Le Sueur, James D. *Uncivil War: Intellectuals and Identity Politics During the Decolonization of Algeria.* Philadelphia, 2001.

Legendre, Bernard. *Le Stalinisme français: qui a dit quoi? (1944-1956).* Paris, 1980.

Leruth, Michael F. "The Neorepublican Discourse on French National Identity." *French Politics & Society* 16, 4 (fall 1998): 46-61.

_____. "French Intellectuals Come to Terms with Globalization." *Contemporary French Civilization* 25, 1 (winter/spring 2001): 42-83

Liauzu, Claude. "Les Intellectuels français au miroir algérien." In *Les Intellectuels français au miroir algérien: mouvements sociaux maghrebins,* by Claude Liauzu, Nora Benallegue, and Salah Hamzaudi, 1-180. Cahiers de la Méditerranée, no. 3. Nice, 1984.

_____. "Le Tiersmondisme des intellectuels en accusation: le sens d'un trajectoire."
   Vingtième siècle 12 (Oct.-Dec. 1986): 73-80.
Lichtheim, George. *Marxism in Modern France*. New York, 1966.
Lindenberg, Daniel. "D'une guerre à l'autre: la Yougoslavie des intellectuels." *Matériaux
   pour l'histoire de notre temps* 48 (Oct.-Dec. 1997): 52-54.
Loignon, Jean. "Un mouvement maoïste en France, la Gauche prolétarienne, 1968-1973."
   DEA Thesis: Paris IEP, 1982.
Macey, David. *The Lives of Michel Foucault: A Biography*. New York, 1993.
Macleod, Alex. *La Révolution inopportune: les partis communistes français et italien face à la
   Révolution portugaise (1973-1975)*. Montreal, 1984.
Malaurie Guillaume, in collaboration with Emmanuel Terrée. *L'Affaire Kravchenko*. Paris,
   1982.
Maran, Rita. *Torture: The Role of Ideology in the French-Algerian War*. New York, 1989.
Markovits, Andrei S. "The West German Left in a Changing Europe: Between Intellectual
   Stagnation and Redefining Identity." In *The Crisis of Socialism in Europe*, edited by
   Christiane Lemke and Gary Marks, 171-90. Durham, N.C., 1992.
Jean-Philippe Mathy, "Repli sur la République: la nouvelle donne des intellectuels
   français." *L'Esprit Créateur* 37, 2 (summer 1997): 41-55.
_____. "L'Exigence Prophétique: Zola, Bourdieu et la mémoire du Dreyfusisme."
   Contemporary French Civilization 24, 2 (summer/fall 2000): 321-40.
Maxwell, Kenneth. *The Making of Portuguese Democracy*. New York, 1995.
Miller, James. *The Passion of Michel Foucault*. New York, 1993.
Monchablon, Alain. *Histoire de l'UNEF de 1956 à 1968*. Paris, 1983.
Ory, Pascal, and Jean-François Sirinelli. *Les Intellectuels en France, de l'Affaire Dreyfus à nos
   jours*. Paris, 1986.
Painter, Jr., Borden W. "Renzo De Felice and the Historiography of Italian Fascism."
   American Historical Review 95, 2 (April 1990): 391-405.
Pas, Nicolas. "Sortir de l'ombre du Parti communiste français: Histoire de l'engagement de
   l'extrême gauche française sur la guerre du Vietnam, 1965-1968." DEA Thesis, Paris IEP,
   1998.
_____. "'Six heures sur le Vietnam': Histoire des comités Vietnam français 1965-1968." *Revue
   historique* 613 (Jan.-March 2000): 157-85.
Pinto, Diana Orieta. "Sociology as a Cultural Phenomenon in France and Italy: 1950-1972."
   Ph.D. Thesis, Harvard University, 1977.
Pinto, Louis. *L'Intelligence en action: Le Nouvel Observateur*. Paris, 1984.
Poperen, Jean. *La Gauche française: le nouvel âge 1958-1965*. Paris, 1972.
Porset, Charles. "Les Francs-Maçons et la Révolution (autour de la "Machine" de Cochin)."
   Annales historiques de la Révolution française 279 (Jan.–Mar. 1990): 14-31.
Portelli, Hughes. *Le Socialisme français tel qu'il est*. Paris, 1980.
Poster, Mark. *Existential Marxism in Postwar France: From Sartre to Althusser*. Princeton, 1975.
_____. *Cultural History and Postmodernity: Disciplinary Readings and Challenges*. New York,
   1997.
Reynolds, David, ed. *The Origins of the Cold War in Europe: International Perspectives*. New
   Haven, 1994.
Rieffel, Rémy. *La Tribu des clercs: les intellectuels sous la Ve République*. Paris, 1993.
Rigoulot, Pierre. *Les Paupières lourdes: les français face au goulag: aveuglements et indignations*.
   Paris, 1991.
Rioux, Jean-Pierre, and Jean-François Sirinelli, eds. *La Guerre d'Algérie et les intellectuels
   français*. Brussels, 1991.
Rivenc, Jean-Pierre. "Le Mouvement maoïste français." Troisième Cycle Thesis, University
   of Toulouse, 1982.
Robrieux, Philippe. *(1972-1982)*. Vol. 3 of *Histoire intérieure du Parti communiste*. Paris, 1982.
_____. *Biographies, Chronologie, Bibliographie*. Vol. 4 of *Histoire intérieure du Parti communiste*.
   Paris, 1984.

Rollet, Jacques. "Histoire politique de la revue 'Esprit' 1950-1956." DEA Thesis, Paris IEP, 1981.

_____. "Le PS et l'autogestion." Thesis, Paris IEP, 1982.

Roth, Michael. *Knowing and History: Appropriations of Hegel in Twentieth-Century France.* Ithaca, 1988.

Rousso, Henry. *The Vichy Syndrome: History and Memory in France Since 1944.* Translated by Arthur Goldhammer. Cambridge, Mass., 1991.

Roy, Albert du, and Robert Schneider. *Le Roman de la rose: d'Épinay à l'Élysée, l'aventure des socialistes.* Paris, 1982.

Samuelson, François-Marie. *Il était une fois Libération: reportage historique.* Paris, 1979.

Sapiro, Gisèle. "La Politique culturelle d'Elsa Triolet au CNE (1949-1951)." In *Elsa Triolet un écrivain dans le siècle: Actes du colloque international 15-17 novembre 1996 Maison Elsa Triolet-Aragon Saint-Arnoult-en-Yvelines,* edited by Marianne Gaudric-Delfranc, 205-21. Paris, 2000.

Scammell, Michael. *Solzhenitsyn: A Biography.* New York, 1984.

Shatz, Marshall S. *Soviet Dissent in Historical Perspective.* New York, 1980.

Schalk, David L. *The Spectrum of Political Engagement: Mounier, Benda, Nizan, Brasillach, Sartre.* Princeton, 1979.

_____. *War and the Ivory Tower: Algeria and Vietnam.* New York, 1991.

Schissler, Hanna. *The Miracle Years: A Cultural History of West Germany, 1949-1968.* Princeton, 2001.

Schnapp Alain, and Pierre Vidal-Naquet. *The French Student Uprising.* Translated by Maria Jolas. Boston, 1971.

Sirinelli, Jean-François. "The Ecole Normale Supérieure and Elite Formation and Selection During the Third Republic." In *Elites in France: Origins, Reproduction, and Power,* edited by Jolyon Howorth and Philp G. Cerny, 66-77. London, 1981.

_____. "Les Normaliens de la rue d'Ulm après 1945: une génération communiste?" *Revue d'histoire moderne et contemporaine* 32 (Oct.-Dec. 1986): 569-88.

_____. "Guerre d'Algérie, guerre de pétitions? Quelques jalons." *Revue historique* 565 (Jan.-March 1988): 73-100.

_____. *Intellectuels et passions françaises: manifestes et pétitions au xxe siècle.* Paris, 1990.

Spiro, Herbert J., and Benjamin R. Barber. "Counter-Ideological Uses of 'Totalitarianism.'" *Politics and Society* 1, 1 (Nov. 1970): 3-21.

Skilling, H. Gordon. *Charter 77 and Human Rights in Czechoslovakia.* London, 1981.

Smith, Robert J. *The Ecole Normale Supérieure and the Third Republic.* Albany, N.Y., 1982.

Sorum, Paul Clay. *Intellectuals and Decolonization in France.* Chapel Hill, N.C., 1977.

Stora, Benjamin. *La Gangrène et l'oubli: la mémoire de la guerre d'Algérie.* Paris, 1991.

Sullivan, Marianna P. *France's Vietnam Policy: A Study in French-American Relations.* Contributions in Political Science, no. 12. Westport, Conn., 1978.

Tétart, Philippe. "*France Observateur* 1950-1964: histoire d'un courant de pensée intellectuel." 6 vols. Ph.D. Thesis, Paris IEP, 1995.

Tismaneaunu, Vladimir. *The Crisis of Marxist Ideology in Eastern Europe: The Poverty of Utopia.* New York, 1988.

Traverso, Enzo, ed. *Le Totalitarisme: le XXe siècle en débat.* Paris, 2001.

Treiner, Sandrine. "La Revue Arguments: 1956-1962. Un lieu de rencontre d'itinéraires intellectuels et politiques." DEA Thesis, Paris IEP, 1987.

van der Poel, Ieme. *Une Révolution de la pensée: maoïsme et féminisme à travers Tel quel, Les Temps modernes, et Esprit.* Faux titre, no. 65. Amsterdam, 1992.

Verdès-Leroux, Jeannine. *Au service du parti: le parti communiste, les intellectuels et la culture (1944-1956).* Paris, 1983.

_____. *Le Réveil des somnambules: le parti communiste, les intellectuels et la culture (1956-1985).* Paris, 1987.

Verdier, Robert. *P.S./P.C.F.: une lutte pour l'entente.* Paris, 1976.

Vernaudon, Dominique. "'Esprit' de la mort d'Emmanuel Mounier à la fin de la guerre d'Algérie: enquête socio thématique." Masters Thesis, Paris VII, 1978.

Vidal-Naquet, Pierre. "Une fidélité têtue: la résistance française à la guerre d'Algérie." *Vingtième siècle* 10 (1986): 3-18.

Wall, Irwin M. *French Communism in the Era of Stalin: The Quest for Unity and Integration, 1945-1962.* Contributions in political science, no. 97. Westport, Conn., 1983.

_____. *The United States and the Making of Postwar France, 1945-1954.* New York, 1991.

Werth, Nicolas. "Le Stalinisme au pouvoir: Mise en perspective historiographique." *Vingtième siècle* 69 (Feb.-March 2001): 125-35.

Whiteside, Kerry H. *Merleau-Ponty and the Foundation of Existential Politics.* Princeton, 1988.

Whitfield, Stephen J. *The Culture of the Cold War.* 2nd ed. Baltimore, 1996.

Wilkinson, James D. *The Intellectual Resistance in Europe.* Cambridge, Mass., 1981.

Willener, Alfred. *The Action-Image of Society: On Cultural Politicization.* Translated by A. M. Sheridan Smith. New York, 1970.

Winock, Michel. *Histoire politique de la revue "Esprit": 1930-1950.* Paris, 1975.

INDEX

and the GIP, 69, 71, 87n. 201
and May '68, 54, 56
resignation from direction of *Esprit*,
140-41
and the Union of the Left, 94, 123-25,
126, 136, 137, 148n. 33, 149n. 46,
150n. 61
Dostoyevsky, Fyodor, 91, 99
Dreyfus affair, 106, 157
Dreyfus, Alfred, 91, 99
Droit, Roger-Pol, 192
Dubček, Alexander, 163, 166, 181n. 40
Duclos, Jacques, 31
Duhamel, René, 175, 176
Dumont, Louis, 245
Durand, Claude, 99, 102, 182n. 71
Duvignaud, Jean, 46, 82n. 107, 154n. 128

E

École des chartes, 250
École des hautes études en sciences sociales
(EHESS), 43, 105, 255, 256. *See also*
Annales school
École nationale d'administration (ENA), 43
École normale supérieure (ENS), 30, 43, 57,
191, 232, 242
École pratique des hautes études, 43, 238,
242, 261n. 45. *See also* Annales school
Economist, The (weekly), 156
Éditions S.E.L.F., 33
Egret, Jean, 250
elections. *See also* referedums
cantonal, 110n. 69, 118,
in the German Federal Republic, 12
legislative, 20, 30, 31, 39, 84n. 130, 90,
106n. 7, 115, 118, 119, 120, 121, 124,
135, 142, 146, 158, 173, 184, 185,
190, 196, 201, 206, 208, 211, 212,
213-14, 218, 221n. 3, 268, 275n. 5
municipal, 30, 31, 146, 184, 212, 214
in Portugal, 130, 131
presidential, 94, 108n. 33, 115, 118,
119, 120, 121, 122, 126, 128, 129,
150n. 61, 194, 204
Elleinstein, Jean, 20, 207-9, 212, 222n. 22, 245,
247
Elliot, Gregory, 210, 211
Enlightenment, 5, 10, 11, 188, 240, 265n. 108
Enriquez, Edgardo, 174, 182n. 72
Épinay Congress (PS), 115, 119
Escarpit, Robert, 108n. 37
Esprit (journal), 20, 34, 35-36, 37, 41, 42, 48-49,
54, 55-56, 71, 74, 77n. 40, 79-80n. 68, 80n.
73, 94, 98, 99, 142, 144, 145, 154n. 136, 165,
173, 208, 211, 212, 229, 248, 256, 269
and the birth of antitotalitarianism,
136-141

and the new philsophers, 213-15
and the Union of the Left, 122-25, 127,
150n. 49
Estier, Claude, 132, 135, 144
établis, 58, 60, 62, 85n. 146
Étincelle, L', 40
Euromissiles, 187, 271
European Defense Community, 35, 142
Ewald, François, 195
Express, L' (weekly), 37, 40, 41, 44, 49, 125,
142, 144, 155n. 139, 256

F

Faire (journal), 136, 175, 211, 212, 213, 214,
215-17
Fanon, Franz, 41, 43
fascism, 4, 5, 13, 14, 15, 17, 27, 31, 38, 41, 51,
84n. 130, 88n. 218, 92, 101, 136, 176, 234,
235, 251, 260n. 32, 261n. 34
anti-fascism, 15, 17, 92, 234, 251, 260n. 22
Fasquelle, Jean-Claude, 192
Fassbinder, Reiner Werner, 13
Fast, Howard, 36
Faure, Edgar, 244
Fauvet, Jacques, 144
Faye, Jean-Pierre, 109n. 49, 165, 202, 222n. 22
Fédération de la gauche démocrate et
socialiste, 142
Fédération de l'éducation nationale, 162, 171
Fejtö, François, 37, 77n. 41, 159, 270, 275n. 5
Feuillants, 241
Fichte, Johann Gottlieb, 186
Fifth Republic, 18, 39, 40, 43, 78n. 52, 114-15
Figaro, Le (newspaper), 99, 133, 142
Figaro littéraire, Le (weekly), 142
Fitzpatrick, Shiela, 8
Flaubert, Gustave, 50, 68
Fleron, Frederick, 8
Flins, 58, 85n. 149
Force ouvrière, 30
Foucault, Michel, 19, 20, 30, 49, 50, 59, 66, 68,
110n. 66, 151n. 78, 165, 192, 195, 197, 202,
207, 211, 222n. 22, 267, 270
and the *Gauche prolétarienne*, 68-73,
88n. 217
and Glucksmann, 102, 103, 198-201, 245
Fouchet, Max-Pol, 32, 93, 95-96, 109n. 49, 135
Fourth Republic, 114
Fraisse, Paul, 31
France observateur (weekly), 37, 41, 44, 49,
142, 234, 235, 238, 239, 244, 260n. 31,
262n. 52
French Communist Party (PCF), 16-17, 30-31,
33-34, 43, 45, 50, 52, 57,58, 78n. 52, 90-91,
108nn. 36 and 37, 113, 157, 158, 161, 164,
180nn. 18 and 29, 182n. 65, 243, 260n 29
compared to PCI, 14, 92, 131-32